D0984507

DATE DUE

FEB 1 6 1984

NATIONS OF THE MODERN WORLD

HUNGARY	Paul Ignotus *Formerly Hungarian Press Counsellor, London, 1947–49, and Member, Presidential Board, Hungarian Writers' Association*
MODERN INDIA	Sir Percival Griffiths *President India, Pakistan and Burma Association*
MEXICO	Peter Calvert *Senior Lecturer in Politics, University of Southampton*
NORWAY	Ronald G. Popperwell *Fellow of Clare Hall, and Lecturer in Norwegian, Cambridge*
PERU	Sir Robert Marett *H.M. Ambassador in Lima, 1963–67*
THE PHILIPPINES	Keith Lightfoot *Naval, Military, and Air Attaché, British Embassy, Manila, 1964–67*
POLAND	Václav L. Beneš *Late Professor of Political Science, Indiana University* Norman J. G. Pounds *Professor of History and Geography, Indiana University*
SUDAN REPUBLIC	K. D. D. Henderson *Formerly of the Sudan Political Service and Governor of Darfur Province, 1949–53*
SWEDEN	Irene Scobbie *Senior Lecturer in Swedish, University of Aberdeen*
SYRIA	Tabitha Petran
MODERN TURKEY	Geoffrey Lewis *Senior Lecturer in Islamic Studies, Oxford*

NATIONS OF THE MODERN WORLD

SWITZERLAND

SWITZERLAND

By CHRISTOPHER HUGHES

PRAEGER PUBLISHERS
NEW YORK

Published in the United States of America in 1975
by Praeger Publishers, Inc.
111 Fourth Avenue, New York, N.Y. 10003

Library of Congress Cataloging in Publication Data

Hughes, Christopher
Switzerland

(Nations of the modern world)
Includes index
Bibliography:
1. Switzerland.   I. Title.   II. Series
DQ17.H8   914.94'03'7   73-15169

ISBN 0-275-33320-5

Printed in Great Britain

Preface

LIKE OTHER BOOKS in this series, this one is intended for a special
class of traveller, of reader, and of student. It is meant for the
traveller who wishes to understand with his mind what he sees with
his eyes; for the reader who is lured (as the writer has been challenged) by the single word 'Switzerland' of the title. It is meant for
the student who already has an interest in one aspect, in history or
government or in economic structure, or language or religion, for
example, but who wishes a brief guide to the aspects of the country
with which he is not primarily concerned. Switzerland, in any case,
is so near and so welcoming that the categories of student and intelligent visitor coincide.

For the sake of the traveller, I have mentioned many names of
places, but have endeavoured also to keep some sort of balance, so
that the more important places are more frequently mentioned than
the less significant. There has been a problem of how much discussion to give to the scenery, the railways, the old towns, the banks,
the industries, the fields, and the mountains, the places the tourist
regularly visits and the places he avoids. I have had in mind the
sort of visitor who is interested in the language, even the dialect, in
the religion, even the political colour and the social manner, of the
place he visits, and who has perhaps previously read something about
Switzerland. To him, and to the student, I have tried to offer something which is, in English, quite new, a fresh look at all the topics I
have touched, based on many years happy reading of the secondary
material stacked in Swiss libraries and on as many years of personal
impressions of places, people, landscape, and buildings. To the
general reader, English-speaking or Swiss, I offer an attempt to see
the country as a whole, and to see its problems as interrelated, as
necessary rather than accidental.

Because I wrote this book during the early stages of an acute social
and political crisis in Britain, my mind has been full of questionings
on how the example of Switzerland can assist my own people. This is
why I have been so much interested in the relationship of the ethos
of the Swiss system to its practice, in the part played by resolute

leadership, and in Swiss social peace and the operation of trade unions, as well as in the constructive role of traditional values. But before we ask how Swiss experience can help us deal, say, with the problems of Ulster, it is necessary to examine what the reality of Switzerland is. If it is of a democracy, then is democracy the cause of her success? And if it is of an oligarchic and status-ridden country, as I have been sometimes inclined to think, is that not the cause of her felicity? This preoccupation has affected the balance of my chapters: I have given due weight to what is beautiful and old (for this is where my heart lies), but have tried also to give weight to the industrial and financial factors and to problems arising out of prosperity and immigration, for these also have effects visible to the eye and which need to be understood.

The work in hand was prepared in 1973. The long-drawn business of correction has enabled me to modify some statements down to January 1974. This brings me to the subject of mistakes, which particularly abound in books concerning Switzerland. They will be of three sorts: simple mistakes, caused by ignorance; mistakes due to the small devil who stands at one's elbow and writes 1921 instead 1291; and mistakes due to a slip of memory of the sort which one could easily correct if one lived in Switzerland with a good library available, but which one cannot so easily rectify from a house in the countryside of the English midlands.

In this book I follow the older English usage of preferring words in their French form, and more convenient plurals. I also prefer the French spelling of place-names not fully domesticated in English. But it is not possible to be quite consistent without pedantry, and I have taken account of the modern tendency to favour the spelling of the local inhabitants – Schaffhausen, Aargau, St Gallen, Solothurn, etc.

Saddington,   C. J. HUGHES
Leicestershire,
April 1974

Contents

List of Illustrations

(All are inserted between pages 144 and 145)

13

List of Maps

Acknowledgements

MY WIFE I thank for her help and her forbearance, my friends for timely mockery and encouragement. My colleagues at work and on committees have borne my absence as stoics, or as epicureans. Very many scholars in Switzerland have afforded me pleasure and interest by their writings, and unnumbered people casually met have been considerate or generous to me.

Especially I must record my gratitude to my personal friends, notably Dr Hans Hubschmid, Dr Hans Lang, and Professor Erich Gruner, all of Berne, and their families and friends.

The debt I owe to institutions is easier to reckon. In Britain, the University of Leicester has been my generous patron, assisting me with study leave, encouraging my research, and allowing me during a semester to hold the post of Visiting Professor of History at the Federal Institute of Technology (ETH) at Zurich. Successive cultural attachés at the Swiss embassy in London, also, have been most helpful (and especially Dr Paul Stauffer).

In Switzerland, I must thank the staff, and the delightful students, of the ETH, and especially Professor Bergier. I must also thank the other Swiss universities, which in turn in one way or another have all helped me. Among libraries, I owe a special debt to the National Library in Berne, and the Central Library (and Staatsarchiv) in Zurich, but I have also read in other libraries (including the excellent collection of the Peasants' Secretariat in Brugg), where the librarians have invariably been helpful.

The Swiss Office for Commercial Expansion (OSEC) in Lausanne most generously assisted me in a visit to various Swiss industrial sites and financial institutions, to which individually I am also most grateful.

In the Note on Books, or in footnotes, I have tried to record those literary debts which are most considerable and identifiable. This is not always an easy matter over a period of thirty years. I have, to help the reader, especially cited the most modern literature. But this literature is necessarily itself based in large part on the same sources that I have myself resorted to, and my views were sometimes formed before these books were available.

C.J.H.

ACKNOWLEDGEMENT for kind permission to reproduce illustrations is made to the following, to whom the copyright of the illustrations belongs:

Aerofilms, Limited: 7, 8, 22, 27
Kunsthaus, Zurich: 13
Musée d'art et d'histoire, Geneva: 20
Photopress, Zurich: 14, 15
Paul Popper Limited: 16, 17
Swiss National Tourist Office, London: 1, 2, 3, 4, 5, 6, 9, 11, 18, 19, 21, 23, 24, 25, 26, 28, 29
Universität Zürich, Kunstgeschichtliches Seminar: 10

CHAPTER I

Land, Homes, People

I. The Land

IN THE DESOLATE VALLEY of Urseren, at Hospenthal, on the wall of the wayside chapel, a German verse is written:

Here the way parts: where go you, friend?
North to Cologne, or south to everlasting Rome?
East is the German Rhine, west the Frankish land you find.

The modern traffic signs, to Germany, Italy, Austria, and France, are not less emotive. Here is a great crossroad, and here is a centre for the destiny of Switzerland, guardian of the roads and of the pass.

The river of this valley, the Reuss, escapes to the north through a gorge, and runs into the Lake of Lucerne. It carries the waters of the forest cantons, the nucleus of Switzerland, through the walled city of Lucerne and the Aargau. In this territory it ultimately joins the Aare just below the ancient bridge from which Brugg obtains its name, and the Limmat joins with them almost at the same place. The conjoint streams soon flow into the Rhine – the Swiss Koblenz derives its name from this great confluence, and the Rhine is actually at this point the less mighty of the two rivers (since it receives few and short tributaries on its right bank after entering Lake Constance, and the Danube clips it fairly close).

Here, near Brugg, is therefore another nodal point for Switzerland, where streams meet again which separated within a few leagues of Hospenthal. It is also a focus of Swiss history. The Roman military capital, Vindonissa, is nearby, and so is the castle of the Hapsburgs and their burial place at Königsfelden. Baden, frequently the seat of the confederal Diet, is close. The propinquity of these sites inspired Gibbon, and is the theme of a famous, but inaccurate, passage in *The Decline and Fall*. North of Lucerne, indeed, the lines of communication fan out variously, and at each place where the north–south roads intersect the routes between Constance and Geneva there is a town of some significance, historical or economic. Olten, dominated militarily by the Bernese Aarburg (where the Basle–Gotthard line crosses the south-west to north-east diagonal), is the modern intersecting point for motorway and for rail communication, and it has been at

most times of importance as a crossroads. The economic and governmental pre-eminence of Zurich and Berne, on the other hand, is
conditioned by politics more than geography, for both lie slightly off
the directest routes.

To the south of Urseren and our chapel is the granite mass of the
Gotthard, which to the Swiss patriot is as evocative as the white
cliffs of Dover are to the Englishman, the symbol of Switzerland's will
to defend herself against all invaders. The chapel on the summit of
the pass, dedicated to a German bishop canonized in 1131, stands at
the frontier of Latin and German civilization and of the mediterranean and northern climates. Beyond is the Italian-speaking canton
of Ticino.

To the west, beyond the pass of the Furka, is the shrunken glacier
which is the source of the Rhône, whose valley soon broadens into the
Valais, *Vallis*, *the* valley, a giant sport of nature, an axe-cleft of huge
dimensions through the highest mountains, meeting a right-angle
cleft at Martigny in order to flow north into the Lake of Geneva.
Above this Rhône glacier is the dizzy ridge, named after the traitor
Naegeli,[1] that leads to the summit of the Grimsel pass and the source
of the Aare.

To the east is a much less satisfactory route, leading over the
Oberalp pass into the upper Rhine valley, which is dominated by the
abbey of Disentis. Below this high valley, Romansch-speaking and
largely catholic, are the savage gorges of the Rhine: the road is of
local, not international, importance.

Until the middle of the last century, the difficult section of a pass
was not the dramatic saddle at the highest point, but the gorge
through which the stream runs when it has grown into a torrent,
perhaps half-way up the pass. The Via Mala, of which the name
speaks for itself, was not, for example, the summit of the Splügen pass,
but a part of the approach road where a wide detour has to be made
or a canyon penetrated. This was the case with the Gotthard. The
pass itself had long been used, the Roman coins have been found at
the top, but the gorge of the Reuss as it leaves the Urseren valley had
been judged impenetrable. The approach road through it, the
Schöllenen, is a work of human engineering constructed at a particular – but unknown – date around the year 1200. The key of the
system was the Devil's Bridge, where the Devil himself exacted the
first bridge-toll, together with the half-bridge cantilevered into the
cliff face and, later, bypassed by the road tunnel, the 'Hole of Uri'.

This artificial road was the queen of the passes, linking the Lakes
of Lucerne and Maggiore, and going straight from south to north by
a single stiff ascent – more or less, for the old roads follow the hillsides
and not the valley bottom (and survive as by-roads linking villages).

Until it reaches Lake Lucerne, the road descends from the summit through the canton of Uri, from where all the traffic went by boat until an astonishingly recent date (1865). For this reason William Tell in the saga was transferred by boat from Altdorf, the scene of his archery: there was no other way.

Until, therefore, the Schöllenen road was made, Uri had been uniquely isolated. When the road had been made, Uri became above all a pass-state. As the matter is the starting-point of Swiss history, one would like to be certain whether the pass was opened before the year (1231) in which Uri finally obtained imperial immediacy, *Reichsunmittelbarkeit*, the status of a fief held *in capite* of the emperor, which was the nearest to independent sovereignty that the law of the Holy Roman Empire recognized. The door to Italy had been unlocked: the emperor, it is evident, needed it in his hands, but was it already so, or did the emperor make it so as an act of policy? The detail would be useful for the interpretation of Swiss history, for we should like to know if Switzerland is the product of the will of her own people who thus obtained for themselves this first foothold on the ladder to freedom, or the story of the mistakes and negligent generosity of others.[2]

The greater part of the narrative of this book concerns, not the mountains, but the fertile crescent, with Brugg at its centre, which fringes to the north the great chain of the Alps, linking the Lakes of Geneva and of Constance. But it is important to start with the mountains for three reasons. First, for military reasons: Switzerland, one may say, exists for military-political reasons – partly in that she can defend herself in her hills, and partly in that she stands at the intersection of other great-power interests, who preserve her neutrality as an act of policy. The centre of Swiss military defence is still this redoubt formed by the Urseren valley defending the Gotthard. Secondly, because it is arguable that Switzerland is primarily a land of transit, a channel, and a meeting-place of cultures belonging to others, but flowing up the passes and through the mountains. Thirdly, because we see Switzerland, and Switzerland tends to see herself, as a mountain state with the mountain virtues, however much economic realities belie this image. So in this chapter, first come the mountains, the cradle of Swiss federal history and of the romanticism concerning Switzerland. Then the agricultural life of the foothills, the fertile rolling country between the Alps and the Juras; then the towns, the other pole of Swiss life, dominating the history of the greater part of the area of Switzerland, and the seat of actual power and the achievement of Switzerland; thereafter come pages on the settlement of Switzerland as indicated by place-names. This will leave space for the story of the population of Switzerland

and, in later chapters, for incidents from Swiss history and discussion of Swiss political, economic, and cultural life.

THE MOUNTAINS

The mountains, we assure ourselves, are the cradle of liberty and the bastions of its defence, and it has just been mentioned that again in 1940 the Gotthard approaches (and certain mountains at the knee of the Rhône near St-Maurice and Martigny, around the Landquart in Grisons, and elsewhere) were the great Redoubt which the Swiss people in arms were to defend. A famous speech at the Rütli by General Guisan proclaimed this new military policy, and the Rütli meadow above the Lake of Lucerne is considered (by a happy fusion between a legend referring to the years 1306–08 and a document bearing the date of 1291) to be the actual, literal, birthplace of Swiss liberty. Having said this, one must confess that the matter was not put to the test in the second World War, and that the actual battles of liberation in Switzerland have not been in the mountains: they were nearly all in woods by lakes, and seem often to have relied on a simple strategy of an undefended palisade to disrupt cavalry, together with a sudden attack before the cavalry had reformed. The only time when the mountains have been put to the test militarily, during the Napoleonic Wars, they proved singularly penetrable: Russian infantry, and French and Austrian, roamed freely over the highest passes, and the Devil's Bridge was stormed under fire, blown up, and the torrent crossed, with complete success. The problem of Swiss medieval invulnerability remains. It may have been derived from the agricultural organization, but when the curtain of history rises, the future Swiss are serfs and free peasants in the same mixture as elsewhere. It may have been due to the pastoral life, but the documents suggest that this was a secondary phenomenon, following and not preceding liberty. It may have been due to poverty, and an excess of young males eager to fight, or to the economic prosperity derived from the stream of merchants through the passes. At any rate, when we come to look into the detail of why this mountain people became free, the reason proves hard to formulate.

The romanticism of the Alps, too, is not very old, and has only recently been felt by those actually dwelling within them. It seems to have risen spontaneously around 1760, when suddenly it was felt by sensitive souls of a romantic turn of mind. Rousseau felt it, but one does not know how much this did not arise from a desire to be perverse, and his observation is somewhat vague and a little abstract. Albrecht Haller had pioneered an alpine romanticism, and within a few years after 1760 it was difficult to remember that people had hitherto failed to perceive mountains as beautiful. The geological structure of mountains rapidly became better understood, and they were no longer depicted and remembered as structures of arbitrary shape and loose construction which might at any moment fall, the haunt of various, probably three, species of dragons (mentioned in the early guidebook, *Les Délices de la Suisse*). That the mountains held a political message was indeed felt, and the taste for mountains has followed the fortunes of the liberal ethic: at first they were appreciated by reformers, then after 1789 the sublime was claimed also by young tories as their birthright and, after a period of political ambiguity, the mountains were adopted by the open-air middle class as one of its spiritual values. The mountains are a symbol of liberty and nature, but these words change meaning and are connected in different ways.

On the heels of the aesthetic and moral appreciation of the mountains, and closely connected with it, came tourism, for beauty dwells in the eyes of those who have fed well, and for whom a comfortable bed is not too far distant. Tourism is discussed later, for it can be accounted as one of the industries of Switzerland, and tourism also is culturally and politically conditioned. One generation follows the steps of Rousseau and sees the mountains from afar, the next ventures into their valleys, the third climbs them, the fourth takes a railway up them. One generation sends its sick limping to the waters of Schinznach or Ragaz, and the milk cure draws royalty to Appenzell. A subsequent generation goes, consumptive, to Davos and returns with rosy cheeks. Today (it is well said) they go in robust health to the same place and return on crutches.

As for winter sports, it is strange to remember that skis were only introduced to the western Alps in 1891, as a result of Nansen's description of his means of crossing Greenland. At first they provided a graceful and rather slow means of progression, the turns being made by leaning backwards and advancing one ski before the other, using a single stick and primitive bindings. The bindings improved, new and more violent techniques were introduced and used for warfare in the Dolomites. Between the wars ski-ing took on recognizably modern forms, and spread its catchment area slowly. But the second World War revealed again its military potential, and in Switzerland it became a universal and fairly inexpensive sport, subsidized for the poorer lads at school. During winter the young people, healthy and beautiful, sunburnt and with flashing smiles exceeding those on the advertisement, jump and twist and shout on the hills, and it seems for the elder generation that this is much more desirable than gangs and motor-cycles, and even than political outlets for juvenile aggression. These new winter sports have exerted a profound influence on the physique and outlook of a whole generation, so that one comes to look upon health and eagerness also as the inalienable gift of a mountain environment. Unhistorically, for Switzerland receives rather than sets fashions, with a time lag, and when the fashion changes one may expect that the open air too will become outmoded, or survive for a minority and as a spectacle: there are suggestions that this is already happening.

The story of the passes of the Alps, too, has a large socio-political content. Commodities change, roads fall into disrepair or their guardians charge high fees. The very deities to whom pilgrimage is made may cease to perform their miracles. A tunnel may replace the road, then the road replace the tunnel or claim another tunnel for itself; a pipeline or a cable or an aeroplane may replace a pass. Something always remains which is dictated by nature, but changes may reach far, and they have been frequent throughout history. The varied fortunes of the mineral resources of the Alps and Juras, and the advent of electrical power generated by electricity, are also discussed later.

THE ALPINE ECONOMY

In what we may broadly (but infelicitously) call the agriculture of the Alps, cattle pasture and forest predominate. About one-quarter of the whole area of Switzerland is reckoned as unproductive (but not useless) rock, ice, water. A further quarter, by no means all situated in the Alps, is woodland, and one-half of the area is used as pasture or for agriculture in the narrower sense. The Alps themselves may be considered to cover some 60 per cent of the area of the country, and the Juras a further 10 per cent. Their economy displays elements which seem timeless and a part of the universal European (to go no further) management of mountains, so that one is tempted to find an origin for some practices in Celtic or earlier times, and the spread of certain pre-German technical terms and word-uses supports this, at least at first look. It shows other elements, however, indubitably modern and a great deal that looks very old but probably is not, and could be allotted a precise date in particular places, perhaps between 1500 and 1850, when the old regime of the Alps may be judged to have ended. Of this economy much survives and more is remembered to have survived until, say, 1950.

The word 'alp' itself is claimed (by some) to be celtic, connected with our latinate word 'alimentation', and to mean just that. Caesar already used the word for the whole mountain chain, as the modern tourist does, but there seems to be no continuity behind this modern usage: it is a learned revival. The alps in the traditional sense, in the sense mountain farmers use the word, the high pastures, are variously owned – occasionally privately, but more often by some semi-public body such as the civil-parish. Alps also can belong to a *Genossenschaft* or Corporation, alp-communities of formidable antiquity from which the state (or canton) may originally have sprung, and which seem likely to survive it.

We may construct a sort of pure model of alpine economy – the variations are numerous, and the key to the reason for variation is often lost, for in detail neither climatic-geographical necessity nor any detectable cultural reasons quite account for these variations.

The high alps, the summer pastures, reach up to the rock and snow, and are but temporarily inhabited, perhaps one or two men and a boy sharing a rough, but permanent, shelter with the cattle. They may have a pig to consume the cheese-whey, perhaps some hens. On a level below this may sometimes run a fence, with a path along its upper edge, below which are the privately-owned hay-plots of the may-settlements (*Maiensäss, mayens, maggiense,* or some other term locally). Here is a rough village occupied in May and again briefly in autumn, at first by the men with the cattle and later by (perhaps) the whole family for a part of the summer. Here hay is made, after the beasts have cropped the land and dunged it. The hay may be stored in stalls for the cattle to eat there, or carried down, now or in winter. Below this again may be the forests, interspersed with wild-hay plots, the woods once again being perhaps communal in some form, or perhaps cantonal. Below again, on the valley floor and clustered round a church on an avalanche-free site, is the village proper. Around it are hay-plots and cultivated ground, potatoes and some cereals, rye perhaps, and near the house lettuces and so on. Nearby are the stalls for the beasts in winter, perhaps grouped together or perhaps near each house, and barns of various sorts according to the custom of the locality, with subsidiary specialized buildings nucleated or scattered – for it is often easier to take the animals to the fodder than vice-versa. Thus there are three types of settlement, the alps, the may-village, and the permanent church-village, with a regulated interchange between them. Beyond this, the alpages are usually more extensive than is needed for the number of cattle that can be fed on home-grown hay, so cattle will be sold to communities lower down, and cattle may be summer-pastured from far afield.

An expectation of an isolated community, perched on a remote crag like a swallow's nest and scarcely in contact with the world, is disappointed. The economic area was formerly often very large, including a whole long valley, at the least, and extending in old times far into northern Italy or other neighbouring countries. Two types of annual movement may be distinguished. The older form may be that traditional in the Valais (and some valleys on the Italian slope of the Alps). Here the whole community migrated, taking school and clergyman and post office with it, leaving the temporary village quite empty at certain seasons. This form, which has nearly disappeared in very recent years, is coupled with an absence of family specialization, so that a family may be vineyard-owners and wine-makers in the Rhône valley, plough and sow higher up, scythe hay at all levels, and make cheese and herd cows in the Alps up to the snow level, ranging from a climate resembling Africa to one like the Arctic. Such a family may provide its specialists, carpenter or smith, from its own ranks. The other form of organization is of limited migration, with specialized herdsmen and dairymen, an organization which seems more modern and rational: the actual priority is hard to determine, and perhaps communities have changed from one to the other and what looks like a tribal pastoralism may be a secondary pastoralism rather than the primitive one: records of legal transactions, which often go back to the thirteenth century, shake *a priori* expectations, and the matter is full of puzzles. As we shall see, much settlement is not really very old, and ancient documents[3] may tell the whole story together with the evidence of place-names, from the first clearance of the forest, or rather, one feels, tell nearly the whole story. And in many districts, in the Valais and Grisons and in the lowlands, and in places with Rhaeto-Romansch names or those names one hopefully attributes to 'the Ligurians', one seems to be among peoples with links to the late bronze age, though without any conclusive evidence.

To the traveller who can read a landscape, nothing is more delightful for the eye or the mind than this 'immemorial' life. Yet it is in full decay. Plots which have been struggled over for centuries, the objects of lawsuits or assassinations and antique feuds, are now left uncultivated. Often there is an orderly degradation. The high alps are unpastured, the may-settlements treated as alps, the fat haylands, once dunged, become thin pastures or wild hay, even wood. The whole harsh process of land settlement that started ten centuries ago is being reversed. Sometimes factory methods or a sort of capitalist's kolkhoz are tried, successfully in their own, plastic-age, terms. One has less the feeling of an inexorable economic change than that of a moral change, a change in ethical values, a spiritual degradation. In situations such as this, the old regime has one unfair advantage: all its products are desperately beautiful, from the tiniest details of tool or joinery to the whole landscape it created and which now barely survives. The degradation has taken less than a single lifetime. The girl who span wool while watching her family's three sheep and two cows,[4] proud of their wealth and hoping to add a share in a third cow as wages of a lifetime's work, still clutches a black shawl and scratches for potatoes, prematurely aged, like her mother, while her sons work in the factory that stands where their fruit-trees were, own a car, travel to Spain, and forget – forget not everything, but much.

THE LOWLANDS

The term 'lowlands' is entirely relative, for the Swiss lowlands are as hilly as the highlands of Scotland, and in a sense higher. The word plateau is used by geographers and the military, while the term 'Mittelland' would, for a Swiss, cover the greater part of it. Seen from the air, it is rich agricultural-pastoral country, interspersed with woodland, the dark spruce mixing with beech and yielding to it as the level lowers.

Wind, hills, and rain set the pattern of this countryside, the rain brought by the wind which the hills cool: the map of cultivation is largely the rainfall map. The west winds blow across the flat lands and low hills of France and meet the wall of the Juras, discharging showers on that green landscape. At the base of the inner range is a rain shadow, along which are the vineyards of the Lakes of Neuchâtel and Bienne, and then the rainfall increases to the east as the hilly country between Juras and Alps erupts into the fore-alps, and then rises into the snow-clad rocks of holiday Switzerland. If one imagines a relief model of Switzerland flooded by a source of light set low in the north-west, one roughly visualizes the rainfall map.

The west wind nourishes the thin soil of the Juras, the fat lands of intermediate Switzerland, the pastures of the Alps. It provides also water-power, the possibility of electrical energy, to the high valleys, and it feeds the scattered woods in each parish. There are deep rain shadows, notably in the Valais and Engadine: when these occur in lowlands or overlooking a lake, the slopes are often terraced for vines, baking in the sun – in former days vineyards were more widespread than today. In the Valais and Ticino there must be irrigation, but given this, southern fruits can be grown on the valley floor.

The quantity of rain brought by the west wind is considerable. The Briton who lives and works in the south of England is accustomed to about 2 feet of rain in the year, or a little more. But the Juras receive 4 or 4½ feet, the Mittelland nearly 4 feet, and the high mountains terrifying quantities, mostly as snow, 6, 9, even 12 feet of water. The rain, of course, is heavier when it falls, and the hours of sunshine may be much longer even where the rainfall is greater, and the sun, of course, has more strength. The fields of Valais, receiving even less rain than Essex, would shrivel without irrigation, for its climate is Spanish in its harshness.

The other great wind of Switzerland is less expected: the Föhn (Favonius). This strikes from the south, not typically a balmy southern breeze, but a hot draught that feels as if breathed from the

Sahara. Except for the gashes of the uppermost valleys of Rhine and Rhône, the lines of the great valleys of the Alps run like cracks from south to north, and the hot breath of the Föhn brings a southern climate to those parts where it blows often and strongly, and it sweeps the pastures clear of snow some weeks earlier than the sun could do. The Föhn shrinks the glaciers, ripens maize and grapes, adds gold to the silver of the western winds, and gives to Switzerland her happy patchwork of Mediterranean, Western, and central European micro-landscapes. The average annual number of days on which it blows varies much from place to place: in Altdorf, 48 days, but 79 days in the Haslital. Its effects are not all happy: it scorches buds, it causes devastating village fires, it exasperates the native Swiss, gives them headaches, and raises their suicide rate – the northern visitor finds it rather agreeable. Its cause is popularly explained by the interaction of two natural principles. One is the principle on which an electrical refrigerator works: a gas, released, gets cold, and when compressed heats. The other is the principle of latent heat: it absorbs cold to turn steam to water at the same temperature. What happens is that a wind from the south strikes the wall of the main Alps, cools quickly, and sheds rain. Then the wind, very dry, intrudes down the northern slope of the Alps, and reaches valley bottom very hot. Be that as it may, the wind is not the ordinary south wind to be expected, and it gives to Switzerland a more southern climate than one would expect from her latitude.

The third godmother is the Bise, about which the less remembered the better. This blows from the north-east, and the Jura hills, by an unkindly caprice of nature, lie in straight lines along just that axis. The Bise gives a touch of cruelty to the climate. To it Geneva is uncompromisingly exposed. The old farmhouses of west Switzerland turn a windowless wall to this wind, a killer, which bites the early blossom and shrivels the backbone.

The woodlands of Switzerland are carefully supervised, and their area may not, under a Federal Law of 1902, be diminished: they are to be seen as complementary to agriculture, not as a derogation from it. Woods affect the climate, but above all they consolidate the soil, and they moderate erosion both by wind and water: the environmental punishment for excessive felling is dramatic and irrevocable. At lower levels, the forests are of beech, then mixed beech and conifer (the red and the white *Tanne*, of slightly different visual effect), then conifer alone: these are the usual tree crops, but Switzerland is a country of variety. One-third of the wood is used as fuel, the remainder for construction: one-third of constructional wood needs still to be imported from abroad. The woods are rarely clear-felled and they regenerate naturally, and are thus of great beauty, especially the woods of mixed sorts of tree. Game is (in most cantons) well preserved and plentiful. Entering Switzerland from France, one is delighted to see deer, shy, grazing the pasture edges in the early morning and on fine evenings. Chamois have been reintroduced to several parts from where they had disappeared: carefully protected, they are sometimes so little timid as to destroy the natural illusion. Game laws differ between cantons, but hunting rights are regarded as separate from the ordinary rights of landownership: some cantons retain the 'aristocratic' *Revier* system, where shooting rights over an area are conceded; others have the licence system, where the hunter buys a permit (*Patent*) to shoot a number of certain game during a certain period, a system which produces a more democratic social atmosphere. Seventy per cent of forests are in some sort of public ownership.

THE FARMS

In the early middle ages, Switzerland was set to become a country of the big landowner, a countryside of nobles and ecclesiastical corporations feeling their way towards sovereignty. The holders of the superior fees, however, chose to give out their lands to tenants on payment of a perpetual rent-charge and subject to tithes, and to a fine when one tenant was substituted for another: subject to these dues, the fee was hereditary in many cases, or nearly became so in practice. A new republican sovereign almost everywhere evicted the secular lords during the later middle ages and, often, the surviving ecclesiastical ones at the Reformation, retaining their legal rights in its own land. The fines and tithes became the financial basis of cantonal government – though some remained in private hands, most usually of patricians. Then in the years between the Helvetic Republic and 1848 the 'feudal burdens' were redeemed or abolished, leaving the peasant with the fee simple of his land.[5]

Swiss farms now are small, and therefore numerous (in 1955, 200,000; the number is decreasing rapidly), a fact which assists the political power of the land. It is not easy to find a meaningful figure for the average size of holding: some of the smallest may be sizeable vineyards, in whole or part, and there survive in certain districts a good many part-time cultivators. Further, in those places where land is subdivided on inheritance,[6] one son may work in the city and lease his land to his brother, and so on. What is certain is that large farms over 120 acres are rare, and most of these are held by public bodies. The real average size, however, is certainly increasing fast.

Only half the farms are entirely owner-occupied, but of those who are tenants of land only 25,000 work entirely on the farms of others: there is most rented land in Neuchâtel and rural Geneva, least in German Switzerland and Valais. Indeed the problem is that there is sometimes too little leasehold available to provide a ladder up which the labourer can climb to the bliss and dignity of peasanthood, but the quantity is increasing.

What strikes the eye of the traveller is the subdivision of holdings, the patchwork of oblong cultivations (especially in Aargau and Schaffhausen in the lowlands, and in Valais, Grisons, and Ticino among the hills). The eye further observes (in places, for the pattern is changing) that around the nucleated villages the holdings are most fragmented: where the farms themselves are scattered, as with the stately peasantry of the Emmenthal, cultivations are larger. Statistically, Valais and Ticino are the classic lands of *parcellement* (subdivision): the situation which looks so absurd on a map may be less distressing in reality, for even a small potato patch or vineyard may occupy a whole morning, and after returning home for midday the peasant sets out for another, perhaps by motor-cycle. The results of consolidation of holdings, imposed from above, are not always felicitous. One holding, consolidated and sold for development, can turn that particular peasant into a rich townsman living on his shares in industry, and condemn his less lucky neighbour to the plough for eternity.

There is much complaint of agricultural indebtedness.[7] A sound currency means a low rate of interest, but it also means that the burden of debt is not lightened by rapid inflation. The problem is linked to another, that of mechanization. Swiss farms, which into the 1950s relied on horses, are rapidly increasing their reliance on machines wherever the terrain allows one to be used, and electrical power is normally available. Mechanization accompanies a decline in the labour force, a decline of 50 per cent from 1920 to 1962, and of this labour force some are foreigners – villagers from Italy or Spain or from farther afield. Previously, the number of labourers was one-half that of independent farmers; it is now less than one-third. The native Swiss agricultural labourer has become scarce: he is often advancing in years and, sadly, unmarried, for the lot of a labourer's wife is hard. This change, already destructive of rural society, is accompanied by a sharp drop in the amount of help that can be expected from a modern country wife out of doors, and even a certain drop in the assistance of the children of the farm.

Before losing ourselves in a peasant nostalgia, it is also fit to be reminded that much of what looks like immemorial agriculture is really decentralized industry. Appenzell, to take an extreme example, appears to be a country of miniature farms, but is in reality an industrial landscape, of which the material basis used once to be textile-weaving and, later, embroidery. Small industry, and part-time farming, is widespread, almost universal, in former times more so than now, and there are many intermediate forms, as where the young people work in the towns. Switzerland industralized very early and in a manner so easy on the eye that one often does not recognize industry for what it is.

The future of the peasantry, of the peasant way of life and the peasant ethos, remains in doubt. Rural society has faced successive crises in the last two centuries, and displayed its resilience and adaptability while giving the misleading impression of following immemorial patterns.

The national government is well aware of the ethical and environmental importance of a healthy peasantry[8] (*ein gesunder Bauernstand*) even if its maintenance is no longer an aim of governmental policy, which prefers a 'rational agriculture', or, rather, 'a rational management of land' (*eine rationelle Landwirtschaft*).

All too often, however, the government's endeavours to assist the countryside have side-effects which result in speeding its dereliction, even though an agrarian political party has, as we shall see, the express aim of representing the free peasantry and rural society, and there is a special place for small landownership in the social doctrines of Roman catholicism. Of all industrial countries, Switzerland cares most about her yeomen, and perhaps she possesses the yeomanry most worth caring about.

ON THE HISTORY OF SWISS AGRICULTURE

The broad belt of the Swiss Mittelland, from Constance to Geneva, was cultivated under the open-field system, following a pattern that was the common heritage of much of western Europe, and which varied little from that which prevailed, for example, in my own village in the midlands of England (the modern fields of which were, as it happens, laid out by a Swiss surveyor in the 1770s). The system came to an end at various dates during the eighteenth century. The system was characterized by a customary law (the *Flurzwang*) which compelled the landholders of the village to plant the crops agreed upon, and which controlled also the use of the common wasteland (*Allmend*), and the grazing over the open fields. The third characteristic was the scattering of holdings in parcels throughout the component fields of the (usually) three-field rotation.

In England, the process of 'enclosure', which latterly employed a private Act of Parliament, in one operation swept away the old customary law, enclosed the waste, and consolidated the holdings into compact areas. Farms were built among these new holdings, and villages ceased to be strictly nucleated. Thus in a single year an English village lost its ancient plan, its ancient legal and economic system, its older order, and its appearance. In Switzerland these operations were separate, and might be spread over two centuries. If we take as an example the old canton of Berne (including then the Vaud and much of Aargau), the first step was to abolish the *Flurzwang*. The initiative, the original impulse, of this step came from a group of patricians, of whom the most intellectually notable was J. R. Tschiffeli. With an eye on England and her country-gentleman ethos, these landowners pioneered a new crop-rotation. To the ideas of this society, the *Ökonomische Gesellschaft*, the state was within limits sympathetic, and took the necessary steps to permit villages to abolish the *Flurzwang*: the state also attempted, without complete success, to see that the poorer cultivators were not disadvantaged, but there can be little doubt that the very poorest and the landless did in fact suffer. The historian of Berne, Richard Feller, holds that between 1760 and 1780 the legal *Flurzwang* there disappeared. Contemporaneously, but by a separate process, a decision of the Great Council of that republic in 1765 gave the village communities general power to enclose the *Allmend* (common waste) into private properties. The final stage, the physical consolidation of holdings into compact areas, is still not completed today, though much has been done by legal compulsion in the last three decades. If certain parts of Switzerland and, in greater degree, parts of France and Germany, appear to the traveller to look like England before the enclosures, this impression is entirely justified: in Schaffhausen and the lower Aargau the façade of the old system has survived longest.

In practice, the three-field system often long outlasted the legal necessity for it. In Aargau, Zurich, and Schaffhausen it was only generally superseded in the last half of the nineteenth century, and examples survived in all three cantons well into the twentieth. One reason for its survival was the difficulty in providing the field paths needed by modern holdings under the free disposition of their owners. Only in Merishausen (Canton Schaffhausen) does it (allegedly) now survive in its lowland form:[9] there may be survivals in Valais of a still older two-field system. A dozen years ago there were many instances of survival in Germany not far from the Swiss border.

The results of these processes of enclosure in Switzerland were already very great in the eighteenth century, and the new agricultural order was universalized during the years following the Helvetic Constitution, when Switzerland was a puppet-state of revolutionary France. Full private property in land was achieved, whereas it had originally been held in fee from (usually) the state for various terms and under various conditions. Specialization increased, so that, for example, the vineyard disappeared from the ordinary village. Milk, originally regarded as a thrifty by-product of the wastelands and stubble, became a prime object of production, and clover was grown so that cattle could be fed in the stall in winter (the old farmhouses, one notices, had small stalls, but many rooms for farm-servants). The cultivation of potatoes increased, and other root crops were introduced. In north and north-east Switzerland the agricultural pattern resulted which is known as *assolement triennal amelioré* (improved three-field system), while in the reduced canton of modern Berne a further modification[10] increased the areas of grass and clover.

II. The Towns

The Federal Statistical Office calls communes with more than 10,000 inhabitants 'towns', and modern Swiss administrative law has no more to add: the commune, parish or township one might call it in English, has a secure legal status, and although legislation in the cantons may well differentiate between large and small communes, concepts of privilege, antiquity, characters, and a different sort of legal personality do not come into the question. The old regime had a very different use for the term, equivalent to the English borough, with a precise legal status at its kernel. However large a community such as Herisau or Zurzach[11] might grow, it would no more easily hap (after about 1200) unperceived into the status of town than a rich man would imperceptibly become a noble. Everyone knew which was a town and which was not, even though it is difficult today to recapture this precision.

At the census of 1798, the first to cover most of Switzerland, there were ten communities with over 5,000 inhabitants: Geneva (24,000), Basle (15,000), Berne (12,000), Zurich (10,500), and Lausanne, St Gallen, Herisau, Altstätten, Schaffhausen, and Fribourg: La Chaux-de-Fonds must nearly have come within this class. Of these ten, only Herisau was not an ancient town with *Stadtrecht* (as we would say, with charters). La Chaux-de-Fonds smilingly still claims to be a village, while the smaller Le Locle was a 'town' by the end of the old regime. Since then the list of the largest towns has remained rather constant. In 1850 there were eight with over 10,000 inhabitants: Geneva (31,000), Berne and Basle (27,000), Lausanne and Zurich (17,000), and La Chaux-de-Fonds, St Gallen, and Lucerne (10,000 to 12,000). It was through an expansion of its boundaries in 1893 that Zurich stepped into the first place. The largest towns of today still form the same list of 1850, in a different order, but Zurich has passed a sort of size-frontier and become 'a great-town', different in kind to the other considerable towns of Switzerland, with half a million inhabitants, still small in comparison with the historic capitals of Europe. It is really only in Zurich that one has the feeling of unmanageable self-generating growth, though Basle and Geneva may come to share this quality. One has the uneasy feeling of being in sight of the day when there is a continuous town along both banks of the Lake of Zurich, thin on the south bank, thick on the north, extending westwards through Baden to Olten, and northwards towards Winterthur, barely divided from Basle by the line of the Juras. This would be paralleled by a greater Lausanne, continuous along the whole north bank of Lake Geneva and extending inland. These urban monsters already exist on the working maps of planners. But when Switzerland reaches the 10 million-mark, a linguistic balance will be preserved by the greater Lugano, Italian at least in theory and governmental intentions.

This question of balance is important. If one reckons that one Briton in five lives in the London complex, then only one in nine resides in the Zurich complex. The victim of this expansion in relative influence is not French Switzerland, but east Switzerland, and this has proved less politically dangerous. The balance is not only one of numbers. The power of Zurich lies in the combination of financial power, insurances and banks, with a certain industrial power: the words 'a certain' are intruded because a good deal of Swiss industrial power has been transmuted into financial power – the plant physically abroad, but a subsidiary of a Swiss company. Swiss political conditions bring this type of double power into the corridors of government, but these corridors are physically situated in Berne, although the economic pressure-groups themselves have their offices in Zurich. 'Berne is the seat of government' is a partial truth which detracts from the centrality of Zurich. Basle and Geneva are also financial, especially banking, centres, and both are industrial and transit centres in their own right: of these two, the former may be adjudged to take the lead, as having nearly the monopoly of the rapidly expanding chemical industry, but Geneva has its important centre of international bureaucracies, engaged in their own concerns at once dark and illustrious, detached from the local soil but attracting their own type of pressure-group to act upon them. Nor is Zurich at the nodal point of Swiss or European communications, though it sits astride the north–south Gotthard route as firmly as in the past: it is slightly to the east of the centre of economic gravity. Philosophers, poets, artists, and scientists have followed the rich men to Zurich: this goes without saying.

The big towns are getting bigger, but in very recent years one has seen medium-sized towns getting bigger too; socially and politically this is a healthy sign, though there is a price to pay in beauty. Many of these are historic towns – Winterthur and Zug, for example, were free imperial cities, but a few, such as Oensingen, are relative newcomers. Dorigny, a satellite of Lausanne, is not to be found even on the motoring maps of a few years ago, while it would date this book too rapidly even to name the urbanizations planned or perpetrated in the Valais.

One might fancy that this urban domination was entirely new in Switzerland, but a longer perspective leads to certain distinctions. The post-Roman period of minimal dominance by towns started to end around 1250. The next period of minimal urban-dominance may (perhaps artificially) be said to have been the nineteenth century, and especially the years 1848–74, during which a peasantry armed and in possession of political rights could actually have secured political power and perpetuated itself. Apart from the middle and later period of the last century, the history of the Swiss Confederation is the history of this urban dominance, with the very important exception of the 'democratic' cantons of Inner Switzerland, Uri, Schwyz, Unterwalden, and, in a sense, Glarus, to which one may add Appenzell and certain small areas at certain times. Whereas in Germany the princes found themselves the normal successors of the power of the empire on the one hand and of the nobility on the other, though with a minor role allocated to the free cities and the ecclesiastical dominions, in Switzerland the cities were in possession as the chief heirs of feudalism by the outset of the sixteenth century.

The long domination of the cities was more than a merely political privilege, for the cities assured themselves legal monopolies of certain trades through their guild organization, typically allowing the countryside only smiths, tailors, and carpenters (though some new industries such as cotton- and linen-weaving and straw-plaiting were often able to locate themselves in the countryside). Much modern location of industry is still only explicable in the light of situations created under the old regime. The sovereign cities permitted the towns of lesser and least rank to continue and let them enjoy certain old, limited, economic privileges, frozen as at the date of acquisition from their feudal suzerains.

Historically, one may distinguish two layers in the foundation of the towns of what is now Switzerland. The oldest layer is Roman, that is to say, a Roman town founded near a celtic centre and bearing a celtic, or older, name. Typically the celtic 'town' was in a defensible position, on a rock or hilltop, while the Roman town was on a site convenient for traders, nearby and on level ground, so we can think of the celtic town migrating to the plain. When Rome fell, the old necessities made themselves felt, and the town moved to its old defensible site once more. In very modern times, the centre tends to shift once more to the plain.

The heir to the traditions of Rome was the church. In Geneva, at Basle, Coire, Sion (and Constance), a bishopric rose on, or reasonably near, the Roman site, while Lausanne – the neatest illustration of all these changes – took over the mantle of Aventicum, sacked by the barbarians in A.D. 260. In other places, such as Zurich, important abbeys preserved a continuity or re-created a tradition. The modern history of the communities, as opposed to the sites, goes back to these ecclesiastical foundations and the settlement that grew around them. The history of legitimate sovereignty on Swiss soil usually shows lawful power passing from a *Gau-graf*, the holder of one of Charlemagne's countships, to a modern community, directly or through the hands of an intermediary abbey or noble, very often the former, for church rule would seem to have been if not kindly at least ineffective.

The later layer of sovereign cities and of towns is the series of deliberate foundations, mostly between 1150 and 1350, by feudal lords. The two greatest, Berne and Fribourg, were founded as acts of policy amid the sparsely populated boundary forest between the Burgundians and Alemannians,[12] the boundary between bishoprics and also (along a differing line) between French and German tongues. These did not grow into towns, but were towns from the start (though a site might show continuous settlement into celtic times, since good sites are re-used). Some lords (especially Peter of Savoy) quite peppered their dominions with towns. Throughout the fertile belt, but especially in west Switzerland, towns are ridiculously common – towns in the old legal sense. We might be tempted to call them fortified villages, but from villages they are rather sharply distinguishable in organization and structure and, usually, in appearance and history. It is much more difficult to distinguish them from castles: indeed the word that signifies castle in German (*Burg*) signifies town, borough, in French (*bourg*), for a castle welcomed a community for its manning and provisionment and to provide its economic basis.[13] Very often these towns are tiny, some have disappeared, and a few sunk into villages. In Vaud there are more than thirty ancient 'towns', a dozen in Fribourg and as many in the modern Aargau, a dozen and a half in modern Canton Berne. At the peak of their medieval prosperity (around 1400) one hearth in three was within a town in broad areas of west Switzerland, one in four farther east. But very large areas were, significantly, townless: in the Alps there are no towns outside the broad intruding valleys (such as the Rhône valley), and it was an act of policy on behalf of the rulers of the peasant cantons of the centre to allow no 'towns' to arise, no city walls or immunities or powerful guilds: in the protestant 'democratic' part-cantons of Glarus-Evangelical and Appenzell-Outer Rhodes the exclusion of effective guilds for the new trades was important during the industrialization of the eighteenth century.

The political history of the former sovereign cities, those that have given their name to their canton, for example, is the history of

Switzerland itself. The history of the dwarf boroughs is a legal and social investigation of considerable antiquarian interest. Between the two is a class of middle-sized towns which deserves a word for itself. Some of them attained the dignity of free imperial city, which would seem to have predestined them for an independent life as city states in their own right. It is not always quite easy to say which town preserved this status and, if it were lost, quite when this happened. It was the usual practice of a dominant town to guarantee the existing rights of a chartered borough to which its protection was extended, so that rights became frozen as at a date in the fourteenth or fifteenth century until the very end of the old Confederacy. By and large it was more advantageous to a city-state to have two protectors than one, and best of all to have a permanent alliance with all the cantons or at least with all the cantons of one confession. St Gallen, Rapperswil, Biel, are examples of towns that preserved the show of sovereignty in different degrees down to the end of the old regime. Usually the time of the Reformation was decisive, as it was for Lausanne, Burgdorf, Winterthur, and many others: it revealed which were just below a certain line and destined to sink decisively into the category of subject towns with a political and economic grievance.

The Helvetic Republic of 1798 liberated these towns: it was its greatest achievement. The sovereign cities sulked over the loss of their old pre-eminence, but the municipal patriciates of the minor towns flowered in the sun of individualism and displayed a dynamic economic enterprise and a passion for liberal, and later, radical, ideas. They dominate Swiss political and economic life from 1830 until 1919. Vaud took its style from the lawyers and teachers of Lausanne, Berne from families of Burgdorf and Biel and other minor centres, Zurich from Winterthur (which provided four of its Federal Councillors), and from some important industrial villages such as Stäfa and Uster, during all the years when the Radical party was predominant. A certain political style, characteristically Swiss but not entirely agreeable, derives from these second-rank towns, and it was they, not the peasantry, who gave the tone to the Swiss nineteenth century.

III. Villages and the Evidence of Place-names

It is not possible to be as confident in speaking of the origins of the smaller settlements as it is of the towns – villages, paradoxically, are less old than the oldest towns – and the question of continuity of rural settlements beyond the sixth century in German Switzerland and a rather earlier period in French and Romansch Switzerland is an open one. Archaeological evidence does not often suggest such continuity, and we are left with the evidence of names for the early history beyond Carolingian times or so (unless there is a very early church; these are significantly often on the foundations of a Roman villa). Words, it sometimes seems, are the most durable part of an inheritance, and the place-names of Switzerland provide a book, the only book, on the history of settlement of much of the country. This book all can spell, but as yet few or none can understand, though it may be expected to contain information about the language spoken, the laws, the economy, the political structure, and the approach to life of early settlers. Scholars have an advantage over the traveller in that they know the earlier forms of the name: sometimes this may go back to the ninth century and (in the case of cities) earlier, but sometimes even village names are only known from the middle ages, and field names from much later: there may be names two thousand years old which have not yet been written.

Switzerland has special advantages for such a study, particularly in the interaction of French, German, and Rhaeto-Romansch tongues (see below, pp. 47–52): this means that layers of names can be distinguished, with romance and earlier names underlying German names, but also with germanic names penetrating deep into romance territory, so that almost everywhere there exists a scattering of names taken over from a language no longer spoken in the district. Secondly, there are wide border districts where places have two names: here the German-French language frontier is particularly interesting. The aesthetic of the two tongues is different: the French names more beautiful, but the German more interesting because more conservative. Thus we have the delightful name Arconciel (German, Ergenzach), where no rainbow ends, and Macolin (Magglingen), Vully (Wistenlach), Soleure (Solothurn), Montsevelier (Mutzwiler), Cressier (Grisach), and sometimes identical names difficult to recognize as such, as Courroux (Lüttelsdorf). Such double names tell us much, the name of the original lord, for example, and how we should interpret the French names for which we have no German doublet. They also allow us to guess at the date of the contact of the two races and even whether they lived side by side or whether the conquered were expelled. Even then, caution must be exercised, for some apparent survivals in speech may be learned revivals from the time of the Bernese conquest in the sixteenth century, or coined then to suit the conqueror's idiom. The French names too may not be in their present form particularly old: the first one cited here is said only to date in that spelling from the eighteenth century.

The German form of Romansch names does not typically preserve an earlier form, nor is it a thorough adaptation to the germanic style of names – Flums, Flims, Mols, Mels, Truns, Trins, and their like are neither German nor Romansch in feeling. They are most

interesting when found in the wide belt, stretching into the Vorarlberg, where Romansch was spoken into Carolingian times. As part of
linguistic policy, the maps are now restoring the Romansch form into
districts which speak one of the languages or dialects of this ancient
tongue, to the confusion of the traveller and the native (e.g., Pignieu
for Panix, Sigl for Sils).

'Around the year 500' – it seems ridiculous to be so vague about
an event so significant and so relatively recent, but which cannot be
undiscussably placed within a period of two centuries – Alemannic
tribes had come to occupy what is now German-speaking Switzerland, a country in which for the most part an originally 'celtic'
population had come to speak a latinate tongue, but of which much
was still uncleared forest. The names of important towns, Avenches,
Winterthur, or Zürich, for example, survived the onrush. We should
be able to trace the progress of settlement by noting the phenomenon
known as mutation of consonants (*t* to *z*, *p* to *pf*, *k* to *ch*, and later
d to *t*), but the light shed is fitful and dark. It should also be possible
to distinguish Frankish, Alemannic, and Burgundian personal names,
for these are the commonest component (in modern interpretations)
of village names. The earliest germanic settlers (but also later ones)
used the tribal termination -*ingen*, and others, doubtless later, also
used -*hofen* and -*dorf*. In dialect, -*ingen* is often pronounced -*igen*, and
some of these names have got on to the map in this form, e.g.,
Diemtigen. In Zurich, where speech is fast, terminations such as
-*inghofen* have become -*ikon* (Rumikon, Rusikon, Kefikon, sounding
like modern Greek villages), but Bernese names are typically less
contracted. The personal name plus -*heim*, common in Alsace, hardly
extends south of Basle, and one notices that the ending -*hausen* is also
not much to be found in Switzerland appended to a personal name.

The ending in -*wil*, often prefixed by a personal name in the
genitive, is very common in the Mittelland and in zones where
settlement was on new land cleared from the forest (as in Appenzell
or the Emmenthal). It seems to indicate securely a secondary settlement and often a small and a relatively modern one. The word
Weiler is in current use today for an isolated farmstead. Both word and
termination come from the Latin *villa*, but there seems to be no name
whatever with this termination which is actually in origin Roman.

The underlying dialect of most of French Switzerland is not true
French, but a sort of Franco-Provençal – only in the Ajoie (Elsgau)
round Porrentruy is a true French patois the basis. Some differences
in place-names that stem from this variation of French leap to the eye.
One is that the germanic *w* becomes *v* (instead of a hard *g* in French):
thus Vufflens is the place-name from Wifflingen. Another is that
many Franco-Provençal nouns end in a vowel, particularly *a*: thus

pré (from *pratum*) becomes *pra*. This, like other words, is often now written *praz* to comply with French orthographic style. Such a final *z* or *x* or *s* is in Vaud (but not in Fribourg) silent (Rivaz, Combaz, Vufflens, pronounced Riva, Comba, Vufflen) since it is only added for appearance. The termination *-ens* (and *-enges*, *-anges*) is usually the germanic *-ingen*, but *-inges*, paradoxically, is something else, more likely to be celtic.

Many French-Swiss village names are 'of celtic origin' in a Latin rubbed down by time nearly beyond recognition. The typical termination is derived from the ending *-iacus*, considered to be the possessive formed from the personal name of the lord of the villa who founded the estate and its settlement, the name of a romanized 'Celt' (perhaps in reality a north Italian). Thus there is Savigny, from Sabiniacus, Cugy from Cupidiacum, or, more extreme, Agy from Abidiacum (German Ebsach, for such names are usually terminated in *-ach* in their germanic form, though the converse does not hold; *-ach* names may derive, for example, from a stream-name in *-a*).

The names of small places among mountains often denote the process of clearing – *schwend* or *schwendi* (from *schwinden*, to disappear), Rüti (from *roden*, to clear), as with Ronco in Italian Switzerland. A peculiarity of the Juras is the frequency of appellative names, names which are words still in use, such as Les Verrières (glassworks), La Chaux-de-Fonds (the lower chalk-pit), intermixed with *-wiler* names (e.g., Glovelier, I presume) and *Cour-* or *-court* names from an older settlement. This latter translates the German *-hofen* (but is also used in place of *-dorf* and other elements). It has been surmised that when the *Court-* element comes first, as in Corban (German, Battendorf) or Courgenay (Jensdorf), the inhabitants were French-speakers under a Burgundian lord bearing a germanic name, but that where, less commonly, the names end in *-court*, the German-speakers were a major factor. *Cour-* names are also common in Canton Fribourg near the language frontier.

As regards the names of streams, these seem often to be pregermanic, but are mainly rather dull: *Aa* is presumed to be equivalent to Aqua in some celtic idiom, as widespread as Avon is in Britain. Rhine may just mean 'stream', Lütschine and its cognates, and Sense-Saane-Sarine, may, for all one knows, be water-goddess names. The names of other great rivers, Rhône (Rotten), Reuss, Limmat, Ticino, are probably from some remote tongue inaccessible to us and unidentifiable, formerly happily called Ligurian or Etruscan. Ticinese village names in *-asco* are romantically ascribed the same origin (as is Urnäsch in Appenzell).

The names of mountains, so often ancient in Britain, render little profit. Of the famous trio, Eiger, Mönch, and Jungfrau, the first is exceedingly ancient and quite unintelligible, the second seems to be an anti-clerical joke of the nineteenth century, and the third may be a reference to the medieval nunnery which owned it, if it be so old. Some are the product of romanticism, and there seems to have been some cultural factor inhibiting the naming of certain formidable peaks.[14] The majority are all too easily intelligible, Dent Blanche, Weisshorn, Rotstock, and their kindred.

Speculation on names enlivens travel, but is replete with traps and traps within traps. Modern forms, to take an example, may be no older than the Dufour maps, planned by the victor of the Sonderbund War. Experts are confident and censorious, but do not agree. Often there seems to be a lesson that has political implications lurking within the study – such as the underlying roman-ness or german-ness of the population, or the original dominance of the lord or of the people, but on closer examination this too recedes, to our disappointment and to our relief.

IV. The People of Switzerland

The concept of 'Switzerland' for the centuries before 1815, when the country received nearly precisely its modern boundaries and international status, is not easy to use or define. The term was used, by the Austrians first of all, from the fifteenth century onwards, and there are isolated examples of its use in the century before. It spread from the Canton Schwyz (as its name is now spelt, for the dialect word for the country and the canton is identical except for the definite article, and the present clear distinction only dates from the late eighteenth century) to the league of the four cantons and thence to the widened league of the Thirteen Cantons, the *Eidgenossenschaft*, the Ancient League of High Germany. Like other proud appellations, the name was first applied with contempt (the word Swiss is close to 'sweat' in German), but victories and long stability changed this attitude. By the mid-seventeenth century the word 'Swiss' and then the word 'Switzerland' had taken on for most people their modern meanings, foreshadowing the boundaries of 1815. That is to say, they had come to include the whole area of the system of Swiss neutrality or neutralities (for the protestant and catholic neutralities might not always coincide). This usage became universal, except in official texts, in the eighteenth century. Thus when the Reverend William Coxe visited 'Switzerland' in the 1770s and 1780s, and wrote an excellent book about it, he included in the term the outlying areas, Geneva, Porrentruy, the Grisons, the Valais, and the various subject territories such as the Ticino. In the same century the Swiss themselves, especially those of an enlightened outlook, came to see this Switzerland as the object of their patriotism, though the term still had no legal currency within the Confederacy. Indeed, the concept held a little more than today, for it included the Valtellina, lost to Austria in 1799 (and, later, to Italy), and might be held to include even Mulhouse, and also a little less, for Geneva has received accretions from Savoy, Aargau has received the Fricktal from Austria, and there have been other small changes. But, by and large, the concept Switzerland had been on the mental map of western Europe for two centuries and more before it received the status of a juridical appellation as 'the Swiss Confederation' in 1803.

The point needs to be laboured here, for we are concerned with the population, and the history and culture, of 'Switzerland' long before there was a place so named. For a fuller discussion, it would be necessary also to delimit the concept 'Germany', and when it came to exclude 'Swiss'. As a compromise between three national languages the word 'Helvetia' has been found useful: it is coined from a genuinely classical name for a tribe or union of tribes, the Helvetii of west Switzerland, but unhappily inapplicable to east Switzerland (Rhaetia). The English word 'swiss' is now used as acceptable to the three language communities, as in *Swissair*, for English is the unofficial technical tongue today, having an air of the progressive, the lively, and the interesting.[15]

POPULATION HISTORY

For the history of 'Switzerland's' population we are favoured and vexed with many sources. The first census for (more or less) the whole of Switzerland is of 1798–1803, the next of 1836–38, and then of 1850. Thereafter, in principle, they are decennial. The fifteenth and sixteenth centuries, however, provide numerous documentary sources for military purposes and taxation, which can be used today for statistical purposes. From the second quarter of the seventeenth century onwards, indeed, there are censuses from various cantons, but not simultaneous nor at regular intervals. Further, the reformed churches early started registers of baptisms and marriages and, in the next century, of deaths. The Council of Trent ordained the same for the Roman church. From the early seventeenth century onwards, foreign diplomats and foreign and Swiss scholars concerned themselves with statistics and estimates, Their guesses were usually too high. One such investigator, Johann Heinrich Waser of Zurich (not the burgomaster of that name), was even executed in 1780 for prying too closely into state secrets, and deserves therefore to be commemorated as a martyr to statistical research. Of the modern works, Dr Wilhelm Bickel's *Bevölkerungsgeschichte und Bevölkerungspolitik der Schweiz*[16] deserves to be especially recollected; it is perhaps the most informative single volume on Switzerland to be obtained.

The history of our area opens with a confident set of statistics, in Caesar's *Gallic War*: modern students are not convinced by them, for the figures appear too large. The population must have increased under Roman occupation, then fallen with the barbarian invasions, being at its lowest around the year A.D. 500. Bickel's earliest estimate of a figure is 600,000 for the year 1300.[17] For the year 1400 an estimate can be based on evidence for certain districts which can serve as samples, and is '600,000 to 650,000 inhabitants' (the 1300 estimate depends on this). If we go on to the year 1700, of which we can speak with a hesitant confidence, and assert the population was 1,200,000, then we can project a steady growth between 1400 and 1700 of 2.1 to 2.3 per thousand, that is to say: 1500, 800,000; 1600, one million. There were factors making for increase and for decrease. The natural increase, though it varies with the age-structure of a population, contains no surprises over the long period, even though there may be times (as after an attack of plague or during a period of opening new country to settlement) where it was locally very heavy. More interesting are the checks to increase which kept Swiss population within bounds and permitted riches to accumulate.

From the time of the Reformation until the end of the old regime, social and economic factors worked in harmony to check population. Until the agricultural revolution of the mid-eighteenth century, and the introduction of potato culture about the same time, there must have been a steady, but small, increase in productiveness. The number of the landowning peasantry would seem to have increased little during this period, and the privileged classes in general would not have increased notably in numbers. (The citizens of full right actually decreased in number.) Local studies show that the large augmentation was of the nearly-landless and the quite landless workers of the Mittelland, one of the preconditions of the industrialization of this part of Switzerland. The alpine districts, once carrying relatively large populations, did not increase in proportion, and this decisive shift in the centre of gravity of old Switzerland is behind the domination of the protestant cantons after the early eighteenth century.

The propertied classes, including the substantial peasantry, would seem to have secured this stability by a combination of legal and social pressures. The law of citizenship (of each village) restricted, sometimes severely, the choice of wife. The law of inheritance counselled prudence, and a delayed marriage. A son might renounce marriage so that the farm should continue undiminished in the family, a daughter because a dowry was not available for all. Governments, torn between a desire for a large population for defence, and the expense of maintaining paupers, might insist on the possession of some property before sanctioning marriage. Parents of illegitimate children might be harshly punished, the children would join the ranks of the dispossessed, with no rights of citizenship. All these sanctions touched the propertied, the very poor could not be restrained so effectively, there was starvation and disease, certain prudential customs, and some suggestion of quiet infanticide: about the mass of the population one knows little.

One institution about which posterity is well informed is foreign mercenary service. A very large number of boys and young men were in military service abroad during the part of their life they might be expected to be most prolific. Some estimates suggest that during the period of the old regime, say from 1400 to 1800, one million Swiss may have been, in total, in military service under foreign sovereigns: the loss of population resulting has been put higher. The early industrialization of Zurich has some connection with the long religious opposition in that canton to foreign mercenary service and the consequent increase in population. As against this, the increase of population in Appenzell after joining the Confederacy as full member (in 1513) is ascribed to the prosperity derived from a share in the capitulation monies from abroad – these payments were more widely distributed in a democratic canton. Among the social effects of this absence abroad must be reckoned a heavy imbalance of the sexes, an excess of women within Switzerland.

There remain the topics of emigration and immigration, of which the latter merits a special chapter as an urgent problem of modern Switzerland. Throughout the centuries Switzerland was a land whose people emigrated: the tide first turned in 1890.

Before 1500, movement in west-central Europe was rather free, and new settlers were granted citizenship on easy conditions – proverbially in a town after residence of a year and a day, though matters were probably at no time quite so simple. The time of restriction was not the gothic age, but the Enlightenment. In general it is not a gross exaggeration to say that as many were granted citizenship of the leading Swiss cities during a normal year in the fifteenth century as were granted in the whole hundred years ending in 1798. The lists of families admitted to citizenship close in the mid-seventeenth century nearly completely, in country as well as town, and the price of naturalization rises very fast. This does not mean that immigration quite stopped. A fair number of Huguenots, for example, were received in Geneva, Vaud, and Neuchâtel as tolerated denizens, and everywhere a thin trickle of foreigners obtained residence in some form or other.

Emigration on an individual basis has a long history, and had left its trace in family names, the Schweitzers in Alsace for example. There were customs of temporary emigration too, in various trades, stonemasons from Italian-speaking valleys, sugar-bakers from Grisons, dairymen from central Switzerland, which might result in permanent migration. In the early middle ages there were planned migrations of German-speaking Valaisans which have left traces in north Italy, in Austria, and elsewhere. After the Reformation there was persecution of sectarians, especially of 'Anabaptists', and after the Thirty Years War colonies were invited to the Palatinate and elsewhere. Such colonies of Swiss settlers were invited by enlightened despots of the mid-eighteenth century, to Prussia, the Baltic, and to the north of Jaén in Spain. The most considerable of these migrations were to the Americas, North and South, but especially to Carolina and Pennsylvania; these continued into the nineteenth century, sometimes attaining proportions of an epidemic. Cantonal governments were uncertain whether to encourage or discourage such movements, adopting now one policy, now another. These large settlements long retained their Swiss character, unless the venture proved totally unsuccessful, and provided contacts for export trades. Individual Swiss are to be found all over Europe during the eighteenth century. The various religious confessions (for especially dissidents migrated) and the three languages assisted this spread.

After 1800, cantonal governments, and (later) private societies and commercial agencies, encouraged emigration, chiefly to the United States (New Glarus, for example), but also to Russia and Brazil. The hunger years after 1815, when crops failed three years running, accelerated the movement, but the years of greatest emigration were the 1880s, exceeding 12,000 in the peak year as a result of agricultural depression. Often these emigrations were of whole families, grandfathers, babies, and all, travelling with their household goods, a picturesque but depressing feature of the landscape before the railway age. Until 1930, apart from the war years, emigration continued at a high level and reached a second but lower peak in the early 1920s. As late as 1922, Federal Councillor Schulthess suggested to Giuseppe Motta, the Foreign Secretary, that massive emigration was the only solution to unemployment and poverty. It is necessary to remember this pessimism, because it determined the plans of the federal administration after 1945, and led them to expect economic and population history to repeat itself, the war to be followed by the slump.

There were also unplanned checks. In Switzerland, as elsewhere, three or four times in every century the plague took monstrously heavy toll, the death figures being almost unbelievable in some cases, and often one-third or more of particular local populations. But this ceased after the great plague of the late 1660s, conquered by effective government action and the isolation of outbreaks and not by medical means, an early example of the blessings of the state and its police. Epidemics occurred, but never again reached disastrous proportions. From war the territory of Switzerland was nearly entirely preserved. The average age can be calculated for some cities, and this increased notably (e.g., from 21 to 35) throughout the period of record from the end of the 1500s to the fall of the old regime.

NOTES

[1] An impoverished peasant who in mid-winter 1799 led French troops this path to outflank the Austrians who then held the Grimsel. He stipulated for the ownership of the mountain as his reward. The Austrian soldiers died: Naegeli remained poor.

[2] Over a matter so important as the opening of the Gotthard the scholarly dispute is frustrating. Older historians assumed that the pass was of immemorial antiquity, probably Roman, certainly Carolingian, and that the St Gotthard itself was the highest of mountains. Johannes von Müller, the Gibbon of Switzerland, first observed the silence of early documents. J. E. Kopp in the 1840s drew the modern conclusion from this, that the way down the Reuss was unused until the first mentions of it in the thirteenth century – merchants of Lucerne are known to have used the Septimer in Grisons until around then. Only in the 1870s was the doctrine expounded that the opening of the pass was the start of Swiss history, that the Devil, as it were, was the founder of the Confederacy rather than William Tell. The Tell saga itself ignores the economic basis of history and attaches no importance to an event one might have thought to be of shattering moment. As to the relationship of the Devil's Bridge to 'the seething bridge', the received interpretation is as I give it, but it neither quite fits the place nor the contemporary descriptions: travellers of the acutest sensibility shuddered over the Devil's Bridge (a structure which was rebuilt, but finally collapsed in 1887) and paid no attention to the rounding of the smooth rock later avoided by the Hole of Uri: only when this tunnel was completed (1708) do we have descriptions of what it used to be like and of a former bridge suspended by chains. The Reuss is here as dangerously smooth as a millpond, before it roars over the edge and breaks into spray around the roots of the older bridge: an electricity-works makes the phenomenon intermittent today. The seething bridge is mentioned early, 1303, 1370, but as a frontier mark only, and the two bridges are not mentioned separately in the same document or description (I think) before the tunnel was pierced. Finally, too much significance should not be attached to the Rhaeto-Romance topographical name Schöllenen (from *Scalinae* – stairs) until the painfully obvious derivation from 'schellend', noisy (ordinary German), is disposed of: it is noisy, but the resemblance to a staircase does not strike an age accustomed to this device as a close one.

[3] In Appenzell, Emmenthal, and Jura.

[4] Roman catholic newspapers in mountain districts have working-class obituaries, which amply support this sad romance.

[5] A wooden house was a moveable, belonging to the tenant, while a stone house would be a part of the realty, belonging to the lord: only the houses of the lords of manors or of the clergy are usually of stone – thus the earlier land law has left visible traces on the cultural landscape.

[6] The custom of the Emmenthal, as readers of Gotthelf know, is that the land itself passes entire to the youngest son on the death of his parents, or upon their retirement, for which purpose a dower house (*Stöckli*) of modest dimensions is provided as part of the complex of farm buildings. The portions of the elder children are transformed into a charge on the land, and there used to be an elaborate system of settlements and notional sales. To keep the farm together, an elder brother might serve his younger on the farm and remain unmarried. In other parts the land is physically divided, and so are the barns and even the houses, so that in Valais an inheritance might include a sixteenth of a hayloft and a portion of a chalet

and little bits of stall and barn and cheese larder in the summer and winter villages as well as land and animals: the Valaisans used, moreover, to be much given to minor litigation. Cantonal land law is still applied within the limits of the Swiss civil code.

[7] On the head of indebtedness, one may question whether a holding mortgaged to the hilt belongs to the nominal owner or to the lender: the distinction between rental and mortgage interest may seem fictive until the land comes to be sold for building.

[8] See Oscar Howald's contribution to the *Festschrift für Fritz Marbach zum 70 Geburtstag*, Berne, 1972. In writing this chapter, I have used the word 'peasant' to translate *Bauer*. A Swiss *Bauer* looks down upon a mere *Pachter*, farmer, of another's land and occupies the highest position and standing in his rural society. The archaic word 'yeomanry' best represents the overtones of the word in English. Chaucer's Franklin, who had often been Knight of the Shire (i.e., in Parliament as a county member), was a *Bauer*. There is, one might add, no real concept of a landed gentry in Switzerland, though in some places there is something rather like it. The equivalent estate of the realm to the non-noble gentry of the countryside is the peasant-yeomanry.

[9] See Max Bronhofer, *Die ausgehende Dreizelgenwirtschaft in der Nord-Ost Schweiz. Mitteilung der Naturgesellschaft Schaffhausen*, XXVI, 1956 (etc.). Having given as impressive reference as this, it is disappointing to add that in 1972 I could not perceive on the ground the survival of this system in Merishausen. I have in recent years seen articles in newspapers stating vaguely that it does so survive, implying a blameworthy backwardness. My belief is that no attempt having been made to preserve the system for its scientific and antiquarian interest, it has disappeared in the lowland form. The supposed alpine form in the Valais may be a confusion of the three-field system with the three-year rotation of individual holdings' crops.

[10] The two rotations are (1) improved three field: grain, roots, grain, roots, grain with undersown clover, and then for three or more years, clover and grass. (2) Berne: grain, grain, roots, grain with clover undersown, then a lengthy period of clover and grass. In French Switzerland and Lucerne there are variations, such as the inclusion of permanent grass in Lucerne, with scattered fruit-trees, as opposed to fruit-trees nucleated around the farmhouses, producing a slightly different landscape. The story of variation could be multiplied. As the altitude increases so does the proportion of old grass, and there is a wide band of transition between these semi-pastoral economies and the alpine economy proper, which is conditioned by the difficulty of overwintering cattle and is therefore a mixed stock-raising and milk product system, complementary to that of the Mittelland.

[11] Zurzach, just above the Rhine–Aare confluence, is a conspicuous anomaly. As a Roman bridging-point and the owner of the relics of an important saint, it should have become a bishopric and a free imperial city, independent before the Reformation, protestant after it, perhaps a cantonal capital. Instead, it remained a market 'Flecken', a town in size but not in law, and partly catholic – its bridge was the lifeline of catholic Switzerland. But its fairs were the most important of the old Confederacy, and its saint, Verena, gives a typical name to girls in protestant Berne and, thence, to the figure on the gold coin of Switzerland, Vreneli, and to the coin itself.

There are a few other examples of ancient urbanizations which never became towns, from ecclesiastical influence, as Beromünster, as well as from democratical inhibitions in the *Landsgemeinde* cantons. If they had not achieved the status by 1450, they had to wait until 1850. There are English parallels to this. For success, a community needs decisive action at the right moment as well as geographical factors: in order to take this decisive action it may need oligarchic governance.

[12] Alemannic, Alemannian (there are other spellings) are words with a spurious precision, but which are not quite meaningless, and the same can be said with a different degree of confidence for 'celtic' and 'Burgundian'. In its original use, 'Alemannic' was applied to a confederacy of tribes, which included the Suevi (Swabians) located in the south-west corner of the modern Germany which includes the Black Forest. These were the peoples who invaded the north of what is now Switzerland. Later usages refer sometimes to the language or dialect they

spoke, sometimes to the area they occupied, sometimes to the race, and sometimes to the political allegiance to the tribal dukes of Swabia at one time or another. In Switzerland today the term 'Alemannic' is used to describe that which German Switzerland (except perhaps Basle and Samnaun, at the extremities) has racially or linguistically in common with south-west Germany – including also social structures, patterns of settlement, or styles of building – while Swabian is used when it is required to stress the differences between the Swiss and the German proper. The Vorarlberg (including Liechtenstein) calls itself Alemannian, while the rest of Austria sometimes calls itself *bajuwarisch*, Bavarian. These usages, whatever the historical status of the myth they imply, are of some political importance.

[13] Some wild, and later deserted, castles seem to have had a pastoral economy as their basis, and this starts some interesting speculations: see H. G. Wackernagel, *Altes Volkstum der Schweiz*, Basle, 1959.

[14] 'Mountains do not have names', the goatherd tells Heidi. But Alm-uncle, an educated man, names them all.

[15] A go-ahead tunnelling firm thus names itself 'Swissboring'.

[16] Zurich, 1947. I have made much use of it in this chapter. K. B. Mayer's *The Population of Switzerland*, New York, 1952, is also based on it. My own interests being slightly different, I have not used this latter work here.

[17] Bickel, op. cit., 48.

CHAPTER 2

Language and Religion

I. Language

THE LANGUAGE FRONTIER today is, on first impression, one of the most ancient of frontiers. On the west, the boundary between French and German had its origin in the tribal frontier-forest which separated the Burgundian tribes from the Alemannic confederacy, and it still bears this imprint. The line of crests that divides northern Europe from Italy provides approximately (but not in detail) the northern frontier for the Italian language, and the heartland of Romansch, most sadly shrunken, is still in the Rhaetian Alps. This constancy loses its hard outline when examined, and when looked at in the light of the intervening history, but it is the first lesson Swiss experience teaches.

The second lesson is the primacy of the political factor: the opposite lesson to the apparent primacy of the cultural factor. The reason for the flows and ebbs is political, language is subservient to military power and to social prestige, but above all to a ruling idea. If it is true that our thoughts are couched in language, a change in the language is the most intimate victory power can achieve, more insinuating than the control of religion. It must be added that language is very resistant to the deliberate assaults of power: it is the absent-minded erosion that endures – the appointment of a new schoolmaster or clergyman at the time when the prestige conferred by one language is greater than another. The matter is further complicated by the changing value attached to dialect as opposed to the literary language, itself determined by political opportunities. A prime fact in Swiss political life is that the language frontier is rather independent of the religious frontiers.

The third lesson is a prudential one. Those who rule Switzerland are conscious of the explosive quality which romanticism has conferred upon language disputes. It is of the stuff of the sentiment of nationality that the community of language is the primal community, the one that most grips the emotions and the personality, and therefore sits in judgement on the state. The trail of gunpowder runs throughout Switzerland, though it is an additional difficulty that the burden of policing it falls upon rather few cantons – Berne, Fribourg, Valais, and Grisons, of which only the last-named has shown a consistent sensitivity to the issue. The prudence of the Confederation has been to renounce any attempt to alter the frontier, and indeed to lean majestically towards a policy of not letting it be altered by one tittle. Underlying the facts of political federalism are the facts of a religious federalism and the facts of a linguistic federalism, and supporting all these is a *policy* of federalism, an active belief that the manner of life implied by federalism is of itself morally right, and that therefore the relative strength of the partners to the bargain must be preserved intact. From the weaknesses of Switzerland, by a bold paradox, can be created her strength, her moral and intellectual flagpost.

HISTORY

The boundaries of the dark ages were not thought, it seems, as lines, but as areas, bands of wasteland, marches. Small communities had small wastelands, woodland often, surrounding them while the great tribes had huge forests, which often survive as such, to keep them apart. The greatest march of all, of course, was the shifting march between German and Slav, the East Mark. These greater marches, owned by kings, were colonized by a different type of settlement, sometimes the deliberate implantation of artificial boroughs – germs of later republican ambitions – sometimes monasteries bringing capital and factory labour into the waste, sometimes a free and soldierly peasantry, sometimes a warlike nobility acting under a different feudal law. Much of the dynamic of European history comes from these marcher barons, founders of great dynasties. But the frontier lands also gave rise to an opposing tendency: the frontier between the French and German languages is the great belt of tiny states and separatist traditions, of free cities, ecclesiastical principalities, sovereign lordships, and of political liberty: this is one of the keys to Swiss history.

The most natural boundary between Burgundians and Alemannians, and therefore between French and German speech, might have been the Aare, and on occasions it seems to have been there (though in the early middle ages it retreated to the Sarine). Even in modern wars, as in 1914, the Aare has seemed to the French their natural military frontier against the Germans, and it is a line of demarcation for popular traditions. Significantly, in the present context, the boundary of the ancient episcopal jurisdiction of Lausanne and that of Constance ran along the Aare.

However, when the dukes of Zaehringen founded Fribourg in 1170,[1] it was already on the language frontier – the town spans the Sarine river – and the traditional language boundary runs through the town itself, the lower town German, the upper French. This ancient and long-maintained division has lasted into modern times, and is distinguishable to the antiquarianizing eye at the present day. Berne, on the Aare, founded in 1191, has always been incontestably a German city. Dominance over the countryside surrounding the two cities was long contested between German- and French-speaking princely dynasties, the counts of Kyburg and the dukes of Savoy, and in the background lurked the two mightier dynasties of Hapsburg and Burgundy, and, from central Switzerland, came the seditious example of the free peasant republics of the Confederacy.

In Fribourg itself it must have seemed at first that the romance element was destined to predominate under the influence of a Savoyard nobility and a French-speaking patriciate, but the increasing success of the military power of Berne, usually a friend, and of the nearby Confederacy, led the town to decide to throw in its lot permanently with the Swiss in the 1470s. Thenceforth a policy of deliberate germanization of the city was followed. This seems to have been consciously done for ideological reasons, namely to make manifest that Fribourg was a sovereign member of the Confederacy, of the 'Ancient League of High Germany'. The State Clerk was appointed 'of German tongue', a German-speaking preacher installed in the principal church, the town school was germanized, and in 1495 all French private schools closed. In 1572 there was an edict that 'children should speak German in the house, and not the coarse Welsh [i.e. French, or French dialect] speech'.[2] The repeated fulminations against the use of French betray their own inefficacy. In the seventeenth century the tide turned. The formal state language remained German, but the French and catholic connection was openly valued and the speech reasserted itself. Gonzague de Reynold in his evocation of the Fribourgeois patriciate of the old regime tells how the leading families at first germanized their names, and then gave them a French aristocratic tinge (Reynaud, Reynold, de Reynold, for example), laying an affectation of being Germanic on a French substructure, and superimposing on this again a French and aristocratic tincture.

Fribourg was one of several bilingual states astride the language frontier. To the north was the paradoxical language predicament of the prince-bishopric of Basle. Originally both the prince-bishops and their titular city spoke German. But when the ambition of the kings of France succeeded in obtaining the election of French-speaking bishops (from 1306 to 1418), they lost effective political control over the city of Basle. But the last links of their sovereignty were only snapped by the Reformation. They were left with their French-speaking territories (and Arlesheim and Laufen), yet from this time until the end of the ecclesiastical state in 1792–97, bishops were always chosen from the German catholic nobility. The main part of their territory, Porrentruy, Delémont, St-Ursanne, was French in culture, and is now the part of Canton Berne that desires separation. During recent centuries, the language frontier has shifted slightly according to political influences, but it is only in the last century that Biel (Bienne), where the bishop held certain relics of his former suzerainty, has become a town where the French language dominates. The German dialect there threatened is now Bernese: originally it had been a Baslois German.

To the south-east of Fribourg there had been another bilingual princedom, the county of Gruyère. This survived until 1555, when the count's mortgaged territories were divided between Berne and Fribourg. Here German had encroached during the great years of the Confederacy, because of the fellow-feeling of the free peasantry with the rebel republics of Inner Switzerland, but this was followed by a reassertion of French in most of the territory.

The Valais showed after the Renaissance a pattern similar to Fribourg's. It was originally, that is to say when the curtain rises at the end of the dark ages, French-speaking – employing a Franco-Provençal dialect which has only in the last years receded into folklore. But germanic settlers intruded into its upper valleys, hitherto perhaps scarcely populated. The race possessed astonishing vigour, and spread down the valley as far as the Pfynwald. The skill of the German Valaisans, the *Walser*, in clearing the forests and in irrigation became widely known, and medieval lords in the Grisons,[3] Austria, north Italy, and elsewhere imported them as settlers, and they usually retained their language, indeed their dialect, into modern times. At first the Valais formed part of a bilingual principality under the bishops of Sion, but when this was conquered by Savoy and reconquered by the peasant communities of the Upper Valais, political supremacy passed to the Walsers, and the German language advanced to include Sion itself. The bishop, selected locally and from a local patrician family, presided over a republic allied with the peasant communities of Inner Switzerland and Berne. The cause of German, which had been the cause of a free peasantry, insensibly became the cause of the Counter-Reformation and of the old regime, and ultimately (as in Fribourg) a symbol of the closed oligarchy who spoke the French of Paris at the courts of the continental monarchs – as mercenaries of the Swiss Guard – and affected to govern their patois-speaking subjects in German.

In their language policy, Valais and Fribourg stand a little apart from the other two-language states of Switzerland. In both, as Latin fell away, German was used as a language of government for (saving the anachronism) ideological reasons. In both it became the symbol of an oligarchy, in both the French-speaking subjects were substantially a majority, and in both they avenged themselves with the advent of the French Revolution and again in the years following 1830. Even today one can detect an un-Swiss arrogance and desire to predominate within the French majority, in whose favour the language frontier has (here and there) shifted. One would not guess that one-third of the inhabitants of Canton Fribourg spoke German, so completely does it seem a French canton, and French has advanced to its old frontier in the level valley of the Rhône. The Freiburgers protest little. Of the two German-speaking groups, one is content so long as the government is conservative and catholic, and the other is protestant, a relic of a condominium with Berne of territories bordering the Lake of Morat (Murten). Yet their grievances are real, seemingly due to a francophone policy rather than to mere oversight. The fiercer Upper Valaisans have formed a defence-of-the-language society, *Der Rottenbund*, which might (in a country less politically sophisticated) have been a sign of danger.

The republic of Berne, on the other hand, traditionally displayed an aristocratic indifference to linguistic evangelism. Its patricians were pleased to ally themselves with the surviving nobility of the Vaud when they conquered that rich land in 1536, and they were ready to speak to whom they encountered in their interlocutor's tongue. When German did spread, it was, at least in form, on the initiative of the inhabitants. Thus the Bernese exclave of München-wiler (Villars-les-Moines), which had always been French-speaking, and where the fields and the older burger families have French names, declared itself in favour of a German-speaking village schoolmaster in 1738: the commune, and some neighbours, now speak German. (But the district in which Münchenwiler lies is unusual: it is in the spatter of sovereignties, tongues, and religions south of the Lake of Morat.) In spite of this tolerance, some feeling of linguistic hostility was felt in those former territories of Berne, and some feeling of linguistic pride in the German territories, and some awareness of the advantage to the Bernese republic of a spread of German language.

Vaudois discontent on national grounds, as in other nationality-movements, entangles with social and religious factors. There was the romanticizing old nobility, and there was also the realistic old nobility intermarried with the conquerors. There was the peasant who realized the advantages which the yeoman-friendly policy of Berne offered, as against the tallaged peasantry of France, and there was also the peasant who saw that a rebellion would free him of state tithes and feudal dues. There was the protestant who saw Berne as shielding him from the dragonnades of France, and the protestant sectarian who desired a freed sectarian church. There was the old middle class whose burger rights were frozen as at the instant when Berne took over from Savoy, content to maintain privileges, and there was also the new middle class suffocated by the paternal blanket of Bernese supervision, longing for the liberty to live as Voltaire could live in France or Rousseau in Neuchâtel. Yet, in all, the French Revolution was welcomed in Vaud, but received sullenly in the old German-speaking lands of Berne: in the marginal case, the French-speaking territories that were administered among the old German bailiwicks of Berne (they had come by an earlier conquest at the time of the Burgundian wars), the people threw in their lot with their language-brothers and did not pause to historicize.

ITALIAN SWITZERLAND

Uri was the kernel of the first Confederacy, as Berne was of its westward later extension. In 1317 Urseren, the upland valley where the Gotthard and the east–west roads cross, became autonomous, subject only to the empire. This independence it exchanged for an unequal alliance with Uri: *Landsgemeinde* democracy is not only limited by the reach of the human voice, by the difficulty of deciding where the majority lies, and the limitations on debate forced by large numbers, but it is also limited by transport, or rather by the distance that can be covered in a morning on foot, and these considerations force federalism, or imperialism, on republics governed by such assemblies. With this alliance Uri extended to the summit of the Gotthard pass, and soon stretched over it by an alliance with the community of the Val Leventina on the Italian side. It was probably from the Leventina that the idea of communal liberty had crossed the Alps into the infant Confederacy, and in the early fifteenth century it seemed that the Leventina might be the nucleus of an Italian-speaking canton, but in 1422 it fell temporarily to a Visconti of Milan and when re-united to Uri in 1441 it found itself in a subordinate position, though retaining an extensive liberty within Uri until 1755 when, following a revolt, it was reduced into subjection. So Uri was for some centuries a two-language state, but with the usual pattern of a political superiority for the German partner: this did not mean a shift of the language frontier in favour of German, and for long it seemed more likely that Urseren (in which German had replaced the original Romansch) would become Italian-speaking or bilingual.

The present frontier of Switzerland to the south, the wedge of land extending deep into Italy, like a spearhead pointing at Milan, seems at first sight irrational, but, like other boundaries, it is in fact intelligible. The apparent anomalies of the Swiss frontier are frequently bridgeheads (Geneva, Basle, Schaffhausen, Constance), but in the case of Ticino it is, as it were, the head of a pass road extending far enough towards the plains for roads to converge upon it – the largest of several examples of a process geographically and historically entirely rational. Its conspicuousness, too, is modern. The old Italy, until a century ago, had for centuries been divided into spheres of influence of France, Austria, and Spain, and these were again sub-divided into numerous shifting sovereignties. Switzerland owes her shape, as well as her being, to the tendency for a small sovereignty to arise where large, jealous powers meet, and, as a relatively strong power in Renaissance Italy, was able to intrude, like lava flowing into a crevasse, between French and Hapsburg spheres of influence.

This may be a suitable place to narrate how this conquest came about. The topic is important, since it is the possession of the Italian valleys, and especially the Mesocco and Ticino, which gives Switzerland her interest and her federal mission.

After the extension of Uri into the Leventina (the upper valley of the Ticino river) the next permanent extension was the occupation of the area dependent on Bellinzona (a nodal point and fortress on the Gotthard approaches) by the three oldest cantons in Inner Switzerland – as a result of the incautious invitation of the citizens of Bellinzona in 1500. Beyond this the Swiss area was extended to the present international frontier, between 1512 and 1516. The new territories thenceforth were ruled by the Twelve Cantons (for Appenzell had not yet received full membership), the bailiwicks[4] being governed in rotation, two years at a time, by regents (*Landvögte*) from the ancient cantons. It is a form of government that evokes no nostalgia. The ploy of sharing rule among so many was just, for all had contributed to the annexation, and prudent, for it gave all an interest in defending the new frontier. Ill-governed as they often were, the 'bailiwicks beyond the mountains' were covered by Swiss neutrality and therefore exempt from invasions. They had no cause to envy other Italians, and they retained not only their language but their religion – for the Counter-Reformation was permitted to extirpate protestantism.

To the history of these conquests there is a larger background. Since the Burgundian marriage of Maximilian (in 1477, with Mary of Burgundy, heiress of Charles the Bold: the betrothal was in Lausanne cathedral), France and the empire were locked in a cosmic battle. Of this fight, the cantons were spectators and (when the contestants were not looking) beneficiaries. The great middle kingdom broke up and disappeared. From the Swiss perspective, indeed, it looks different. This is the 'heroic period' of Swiss history: valorous and united, Switzerland took on and routed all enemies – Charles the Bold at Grandson and Morat (1476–77), the empire in the Swabian war (1499), and the multifarious contestants in

Renaissance Italy when the confrontation spread into Lombardy.

The heroic period had an unheroic end. There were two destinies available for Switzerland. The first was to be the nucleus of a great confederal republic, stretching beyond Nuremberg, and including the Austrian Alps, Venice, Lombardy, the Franche-Comté, and Burgundy, based on a free peasantry and free republican cities. For this truly heroic mission, her virtues were insufficient. The second option, the one actually attained, is the stump or ruins of the first, but of interest nevertheless. The crux, the crossroads, came at the time of the Italian acquisitions. The units of the Confederacy were under continual temptation to fight for their own hand, but beyond this, inside the cantons themselves, the society that could have carried the greater Swiss mission was disintegrating. The disintegration came in the form of individual mercenary service under foreign princes, and through this mercenary service the military power of Switzerland neutralized itself: the cantons did not, in fact, disintegrate, and retained a great deal of control over their citizens, but sold themselves corporately for a sound price. Nor did the Confederacy in fact disintegrate, and it even managed to sell its mercenaries collectively to the king of France for long periods. This second option has its own lesser greatness, and the state that emerged from the Italian wars has its inner logic. The individual mercenary and cantonal capitulations[5] were not a derogation from neutrality – they were the condition of neutrality and its rationale, a self-neutralization. The stability of the borders of Switzerland (after 1535 – when Berne occupied Vaud – for by 1512 the Valtellina had been taken by Grisons, and Valais reached its present frontiers in 1536) is another condition of this neutrality, as, it long seemed, was the inner weakness of Switzerland, and her lack of artillery or a national army. The cantons adopted a new internal social structure: political power took on the objective of obtaining bailiwicks or a share in the mercenary monies, and was monopolized by a new (or largely new) oligarchy with a new political style.

Various dates, around 1512, can be set for this crucial point. Internal disintegration was sealed by the failure of the *Pensionenbrief* of 1502, the Federal Charter that never was. 1513 saw the last admission of a new canton to the old Confederacy. The battle of Marignano in 1515 awoke the confederates to the realization that the age of easy or miraculous victories was over (though the idea that courage, a good cause, and a just polity can lead cavalry to prevail over tanks still persists, to the despair of professional soldiers, today). Within seven years the Reformation, taking advantage of this restored disunity and with the controversy about mercenary service as one of its elements, split Switzerland permanently into two camps, just as

Appenzell was to split in 1597. The governance of the Ticino was itself a subject of contention and civil war (as well as a slender bond of unity).

Problems of Ticino

The difficulties of Ticino are not strictly difficulties of language, but are inseparable from language. The federal bargain has been well kept on the governmental side: Ticino has its autonomy, its religion, and its speech constitutionally protected, and the law has been filled out with a generous and sympathetic practice. Even before 1939, the economic strength of Switzerland made union with Italy unattractive, and now provides an overwhelming argument against secession: the matter is nowadays never proposed. The Ticinese, as in 1798, wish to remain 'free and Swiss', and prosperous. In the past, there have been moments of temptation, but so long as Italy remains politically and economically unattractive there is no reason why the cultural and social links should pull the Ticino into its mother country: from Italy's point of view, the possession of the Mezzogiorno and Sicily can be regarded as an alternative choice to reunion with the Ticino.

Nevertheless, there are difficulties. There is the historic burden of the *Vögte*, which robs the Ticino (unlike the Italian valleys of the Grisons) of any history the Ticinese can look back upon with satisfaction and regard as their own. This burden just about balances the positive historical links with Switzerland before 1800.

In the era since 1800, the link with Switzerland has become interwoven with the political divisions of Ticino. In a country split between liberals and catholic conservatives, the liberals may look with satisfaction upon the long years of liberal dominance in the Confederation, the conservatives with nostalgia on the Restoration of 1815–30, and with pride on the long tenure of power of Federal Councillor Motta between 1912 and 1940. The connection is with a particular Switzerland, radical or conservative, rather than with Switzerland herself. Connected inextricably with this internal war of ideas was another heritage of the old regime, the subdivision of the area. For a long time it seemed the canton would separate into two parts, above and below Monte Ceneri, one catholic-conservative and the other liberal – these party labels represent patronage groups in the Italian style as much as ideologies. The choice of a capital, Lugano, Locarno, or Bellinzona, was contentious, and it was the compromise candidate who won. Political life in Ticino long had a rare intensity, and retained the assassination and putsch style into the 1890s – for the canton was so evenly balanced that a small adjustment of the electoral laws could keep power for a faction indefinitely – with federal help.

Then there are the problems connected with immigration and emigration. Sunny, accessible, beautiful, and not too expensive, Ticino attracts German-speaking Swiss and Germans in large numbers as holidaymakers, week-enders, and pensioners. Against ordinary tourists it can incapsulate itself in the manner of Geneva and other Swiss honey-pots, but the German settlers have brought with them their own infrastructure of tradesmen and prejudices and permeated the surface of the autochthonous community, so that Italian is threatened with becoming the minority tongue of a depressed class. At the same time, for other reasons, valleys are depopulated or ravaged by hydro-electric schemes, industrial and residential development destroys the beauty of the lowland towns, villages, and countryside, while the lakes are unable to digest the crude sewage about which, formerly, one asked no questions. The immigration of foreign workers adds a further social grievance. There are half a million Italians in Switzerland as immigrant workers, despised and rightless, the Swiss form of the colour problem. The Ticinese would gladly join in this attitude of contempt, but are themselves in danger of being assimilated to this class. In early days of immigration a Ticinese thought himself a little superior to the northern Italian with the same social culture and a kindred dialect: he now fears to be confused (by German-speakers) with the dispossessed of Sicily and Naples.

There is also a cultural problem. German Switzerland can consider itself a province or perhaps an élite of German culture, or even a cultural entity for itself. French Switzerland could conceivably do so, at a pinch, and there is a small group that wishes to do so. Italian Switzerland (about one-twentieth of Switzerland) cannot and does not entertain such an idea. For example, there is no university in Italian Switzerland, and resistance to such a proposal would come from within the Ticino itself. This makes Ticino in a way the only truly federal problem of the Confederation apart from Bernese Jura. The Italian-speaking valleys of the Grisons have their own, rather different, problems.

The wireless and television demonstrate all too clearly that it is difficult to find programmes worth transmitting (as opposed to laughably provincial) which are distinctively Ticinese and not generically Italian. Localism is a cultural value in German Switzerland, but not in Italy, so it is hard to steer a course which, on the one hand, asserts the difference between Ticino and Italy, and, on the other hand, preserves the difference between German-Swiss values and those held by educated Ticinese.

There used to be Walser, that is to say German-speaking, settlements in the Ticino as in other high valleys of northern Italy. One of these – Gurin (Bosco) – has survived on to the language maps of the present day as a curiosity. The only one of these settlements south of the Alps which seems destined to endure is Simplon (Simpeln) in Canton Valais, on the Italian side of that pass.

THE GRISONS

It was left to the Grisons (Graubünden) to pioneer the modern Swiss solution to the language problem, at least in one respect: the rule of total tolerance of native language and of maximum give-and-take in matters of collaboration. Originally, the whole country of Grisons, and far beyond it to the north, west, and east, spoke that decayed and bitten-off Latin which we call Ladin or Romansch (Romanche, Rumantsch). Less melodious than Tuscan, having hived off from vulgar Latin at a slightly earlier date (in all probability) and therefore a shade more primitive than the north Italian dialects, it claims without contradiction[6] to be a language in its own right. Outside Switzerland, I have heard it spoken in certain parts of the Dolomites, and it is said to survive in a remote pocket on the confines of Yugoslavia. The place-names of the Vorarlberg and of parts of eastern Switzerland (around the Walensee, for example) betray its wider extent in the early middle ages.

The language suffered a grave blow when the prince-bishops of Coire (or Chur: the word possibly derives from a celtic name transliterated into the Roman-sounding Curia) separated their imperial from their episcopal lands and settled a germanic nobility on the former around A.D. 806. Some of these interloper settlements were, indeed, romanized in subsequent centuries and then gradually teutonized again at the close of the middle ages, but the nobility retained its German alliances, and there was no medieval Romansch literature. In 843 (or perhaps 887) Coire was detached from the archbishopric of Milan and aggregated to Mayence. A further blow was the introduction of pioneers from the Valais, who (mostly) retained their language and their privileges and planted large splashes of German speech in the valleys, as in the Prätigau around Davos for example. Thereafter Romansch ceased to prevail in a coherent territory, and the country's labyrinthine configuration encouraged three, or five, dialects of the language to consolidate themselves, a fissiparous tendency encouraged by the Reformation and which seriously decreases the languages' viability. On the other hand, the same Reformation encouraged preachers, translators, and pamphleteers to use the tongue of the people, and they raised Romansch thereby to the rank of a written language with a classical literature of its own, somewhat slender, which formed a basis for literary elaboration in the age of romanticism.

A deciding factor in survival as a family language, as well as a legal, literary, and religious vehicle, has been the peculiar political structure of the Grisons, 'the Grey Leagues of Rhaetia', which is further discussed below (pp. 264–8). At the end of the middle ages each of the four dozen jurisdictions obtained a degree of autonomy approaching sovereignty[7] and considered themselves as banding voluntarily into three leagues named respectively the Grey League, the League of God's House, and the League of the Ten Jurisdictions, and these three leagues as forming together a doubly confederal republic, allies of the Swiss Confederacy. The collectivity happed into possession of sovereign rights over the Valtellina, with Chiavenna and Bormio, entirely Italian-speaking, and destined to remain catholic and to be lost at the time of the French Revolution.

Each of the three leagues had within its confines both Romansch- and German-speaking sovereign communities, and two of them also had Italian member-communities, not as subjects but as equals: these remain in Grisons as small intrusions of Swiss territory south of the Alps, Poschiavo, Val Bregaglia, and, largest of them, the Mesocco and Calanca valleys thrusting into Ticino. Italian and Romansch survived, secure in parochial autonomy and in the equality of the confederal union. Only in modern times has this same communal autonomy proved a danger to the survival of Romansch rather than its safeguard, for it remains open to a commune to change its school-language: several have in fact done so within rather recent years, preferring the utility of German to the more secret satisfaction of preserving an ancient, but unmarketable, inheritance.

The Romansch spoken 'above the forest', above the gorges of the (Vorder-) Rhine, is called Surselvisch. This is (principally) catholic country under the ancient influence of the abbey of Disentis ('in the deserts'), with its own bi-weekly Romansch newspaper and almost, until recent urbanization, its own tiny world. Ladin is the language of the Engadine, the upper valley of the Inn, and spreads into the Münstertal: there are two (or perhaps three) dialects. Between the two areas, and precariously bridging them, are Sotselvisch and Sur-meierisch in so far as German is not spoken. Each of the three main groups of the language has its Bible, its vehicle of news, its legal language, and its poetry and songs. The peculiarity of these survivals contributes to the strangeness that still haunts this land and gives it an air.

THE LEGAL FRAMEWORK OF LANGUAGE

Article 116 of the Federal Constitution states that German, French, Italian, and Romansch are 'the national languages of Switzerland and German, French, and Italian are office-languages,

Amtssprachen, of the Confederation'. The federal administration has clothed this cold language in a garb of interpretation, and it remains in the popular memory not as a bureaucratic afterthought tucked away under the heading 'Miscellaneous Provisions', but as a Freedom Right, the Freedom of Languages. There is much in the constitution of the Confederation which is not in the Federal Constitution, and the best way to understand the Freedom of Languages is to regard it as an extra-constitutional practice having all the moral force of law and anchored, as it were, by the tail in the Constitutional Document. We may note that the article was revised in 1938 so as to include Romansch as 'a national language' – the phrase does not really mean anything – largely as a political gesture against the claims of Italian irredentism, which pocketed Romansch as an Italian speech, and saw in the Grisons the next bite after Ticino in the pan-Italian banquet of the future. A firmer status for Romansch than this gesture of confederal sympathy is provided by the cantonal constitution of Grisons itself, the only canton in which the tongue is spoken.

Two principles are involved, wise but contradictory. One is the Territorial Principle. This regards the map of the country as divided into French, German, Italian areas, the boundaries of which are unalterable. The other is the Personal Principle, whereby everyone can speak 'his' language in communicating with emanations of the state. The territorial principle takes precedence over the personal one in most cases of conflict.

The crisis of the territorial system comes over the question of the school: it is here that official recognition has to be made when the actual boundary of the spoken tongue has shifted, as it sometimes has – in Bienne (Biel), for example. The burden of practical decisions usually falls upon the canton, and in particular the all-important decision as to which is the official language of the lowest unit of local government. The power to determine this last point is called the *Sprachenhoheit*, language-sovereignty, of the canton, and federal authorities acknowledge the cantonal decision here. In Grisons, following the tradition of the former parochial autonomy, this vital power is left to the commune: it is a power of death over Romansch.

The personal system also reaches far. A careful eye is kept on language-balance proportions within the public service, both in the Confederation and in bilingual cantons, particularly within the collegiate executives and the courts, but also within the officialdom proper: there is a Federal Directive of 1950 to this effect. Educated German Swiss are certainly able to work in French, as are educated Italian Swiss. The compliment is less frequently reciprocated, and one discerns traces of a recognition that English is in practice the third language of most Swiss. Higher federal officials are expected to have two federal working languages. In a humbler sphere, the officials of 'the decentralized federal administration' – postal and railway-workers in particular – have a positive obligation under the territorial system to speak the language of the area, rather than the language of their interlocutor. The ticket-collector walks down the train calling for tickets in French until the unseen frontier is passed and continues through the carriage in German. The politically wise territorial system, in fact, prevails over the convenient personal system, so the freedom of languages is only really to be exercised in one's own language area: like other personal freedom rights it can be reduced to a tautology. Dialect, the native speech of two-thirds of the citizens, is not recognized as enjoying rights.

The difficulties of the Ticino, menaced by German, and of the Bernese Jura, infected by the symptoms of nationalism, and of the federal capital, which is also the capital of the canton which feels itself most nearly a state in its own right, persist. The problem that remains is whether the Swiss language-system is right for Switzerland, and beyond that, whether it is right for all countries. Few states have not this problem.

The Language Mission of Switzerland

Switzerland is a state different in kind to any other European state, and this gives its existence a legitimacy. The world civilization is a civilization of western Europe, and the mission of Switzerland, if there be one, is as a part of the western European mission to mankind. Other great European moral powers, Italy, for example, or Greece or Spain, are the homeland and the essence of an eponymous civiliza-tion, language, art, literature. The swissness of Switzerland com-prises some elements of a specifically Swiss total-approach to the world. But it is also a part of swissness that, on inspection, many of its triumphs disintegrate into contributions to German, French, Italian civilization, and are only intelligible as standing within those civiliza-tions, derived from them, and flowing into them. 'The Swiss Nation', as the constitution calls it, derives much of its swissness from its status as an anti-nation. Neutrality, extreme decentralization, are other aspects of the state that refuses to be a state, that seeks its unity in diversity, its cohesion in liberty. There are three aspects of this, the religious settlement, the cantonal and communal settlement, and the language settlement, and of all the components of the Swiss miracle, the language miracle is the most surprising in this era of suppressed nationalism. Does the secret of this felicity lie in the political balance, the Council of States, for example, or does it lie in the happy non-coincidence of language, religious and regional boundaries, or does it lie in the peculiarly wise language laws, or more nebulously, in the quality of Swiss democraticness? The reply is that all contribute, but none explain. In the first place, benefits of language laws are aspects of the benefits of constitutionalism in general. The rule against arbitrariness in governmental action (which has attached itself to Article 4 of the Federal Constitution) or the freedom to live where one likes in one's own country, an obvious right today, would alone afford sufficient guarantee of such language rights of self-defence of whole communities. Secondly, it is usually politically quite impossible to oppress the French minorities, next door to their own linguistic heartland, vocal, indeed armed. The majority, of course, needs no protection against democracy. Italian? This is a different matter, and there are minorities here and there whose situation invites a little repression, but the biggest minority, French, is politically un-conquerable.

Finally, there is the possible reply that Switzerland flourishes, in language and in other matters, not on account of these sufficient causes, but because of her social structures, unimitated elsewhere. A country whose fate is firmly guided by an interlocking set of compact ruling classes, informed by traditional values, might operate within worse laws than Switzerland's. The secret of 'cultural co-existence' may lie in the wisdom of an Establishment, and the secret of much else also. Such themes, brushed here, recur.

DIALECT

Dialect, perhaps to a greater degree than language, is the product of social and political ideals held continuously over a period. To speak a dialect is to claim to belong to a community, and from observing the use of dialect much can be learned about the society and state. In the whole German-speaking area, three trends can be observed in different parts. In the north of Germany, dialect is in various degrees an expression of a traditional urban working class, or of a remote peasant culture. Among the professional middle classes it is never used as the language of the home, and only in exceptional cir-cumstances as an optional colouring of speech when addressing inferiors – a rural landlord among his own villagers, a native-born citizen of a Hanseatic town wishing to maintain a comradely or jocu-lar atmosphere. A revival, or a resurrection, could only occur as a deliberate policy of local segregation – as the last king of Saxony affected the local drunken-wheedling speech, romantically playing tribal leader of an autochthonous spiritual secession from Prussia. Platt-Deutsch, or even Frisian, will only survive where state-feeling rescues it. In Holland, of course, what might have remained a dialect has become a language. The Dutch solution must be remembered when reflecting on the problems of Swiss German: it lies at the other extreme to the north German solution.

In the big area of Swabia, Bavaria, and Austria, a rich and living dialect is heard on all sides, an accomplishment of the upper classes, the friendly and intimate communication of the others, but its use between educated people may be confined to the maudlin or the bawdy anecdote, the song and the folklore play. The imperial tradition, a fresh memory, made necessary the *Hochsprache*, or correct German tinged with various degrees of slovenly homeliness as one descended the scale of living. To facilitate intercommunication between dialect and *Schriftsprache* a halfwayhouse speech is sandwiched, a sort of compromise language to which the unlettered may with effort ascend, and the high well-born effortlessly lower themselves, and which is common to the whole German-speaking area in question, the *Umgangssprache*.

In the Alemannic area, however, in which Switzerland can be included, everyone native-born now again speaks a homely dialect in the family, and those who require it can speak the *Hochsprache* as a learnt language, softened indeed with an unconscious local film. A whole attitude of man-to-man democracy is implied in this solution.

In German Switzerland proper, there is an endless gradation of local shades of dialect, so that no town or valley speaks totally the same as another. Within this localism, we can distinguish the speech of Berne, *Bärndütsch*, the speech of Zurich, *Züritüütsch*. This Zuricois speech, modified, can for our purposes be taken to extend to the Arlberg pass, for the Austrian province of the Vorarlberg is within the Swiss language-area, though we may wish to distinguish an eastern Swiss group and not to lump it all under Zurich. *Baseldytsch*, the speech of Basle, actually belongs to a different, but neighbouring, dialect family, and only national patriotism includes it as Swiss German, while excluding the Vorarlberg. If we call the German of Basle a part of Low Alemannic, the remainder of the Swiss middle country High Alemannic, the dialects of the mountains, with very archaic features, can be bundled together as Highest Alemannic, however great their possible incomprehension of each other. Some of the distinguishing marks of each dialect can be gathered from the dialect name here given.[8]

It is said that there is no Swiss *Umgangssprache*, for a Swiss everywhere speaks his own, native, tongue. If a Bernese, he speaks Bernese in Zurich. In principle, this is so, but does one not notice some attempt to modify robustness of provincialism according to the situation? There is certainly a hybrid language available, called often *Grossratsdeutsch*, 'the German of county councillors', but this is the written High German language spoken according to the rules of dialect. Strictly speaking, therefore, there is no Swiss German, but all too many inflections of a language family, a family belonging to several generations, grandparents in the hills, a wife in Basle, and a daughter living abroad, and something crooning in the pram. A Swiss German language, this is a possible solution to certain difficulties: it does not yet exist.

For the dialect situation is not easy. It is said that when the Swiss Dialect Dictionary was projected in the 1860s, the object of the learned venture was to pickle the surviving oddities for the delectation of future generations of philologists, a recording of a dying linguistic culture. The future, it was thought, clearly lay with High German. The scholarly forebodings were misplaced: more speak a Swiss German than ever before, and dialect is annually making new empires. It has conquered the army, interfered with the radio, proclaimed itself on solemn occasions, practised in the courts of law, stood for election to assemblies, crept unwillingly into schools, salted the sermon. There are more dialect-speakers: absolutely, because there are more Swiss; relatively, because now all Swiss speak it; qualitatively, because it is spoken on *rather* more occasions – one must not exaggerate here: the real life of the country could continue without change in High German, but would seize up if dialect were compelled on all occasions.

On the debit side, consider the question of increased geographical mobility. Parents may speak Bernese in Winterthur, but woe to the child open to the vengeance of the playground! What then speaks that child at home? Furthermore, just as to the German-German, or English, traveller dialect seems a little ridiculous, so there are few things more subtly diverting and more worthy of caricature, if one has the good fortune to live in Lucerne, than the Swiss German of a relative from Appenzell. Dialect is clownish to dialect. All stand in involuntary awe of the crisp German of the visitor from the Federal Republic, which the Swiss in part despise, in part half shrink from out of atavistic memories, and in part absorb. For there is a splendour in good High German, the German of the stage, the German that commands: in comparison, dialect sounds like a mixed farmyard, many hens and a few geese, unwomanly, unlearned, inurbane.

Furthermore, though Swiss German can be read and written, it only contains a small, if delightful, literature. There are the gentle lyrics of Hebel – not a Swiss, but from the borders of Baden, 'the Margrave's land', yet speaking direct to Swiss ears – and there are historical novels, such as those of Rudolf von Tavel in Bernese. The great Gotthelf breaks into Bernese, and his style is suffused by it. There are chronicles of antiquity also, for in the old regime it was long the language of state, and songs have clad themselves in it – it seems (curiously) that no words-and-music in popular tradition are born of the Swiss soil, however localized some of the present words seem. The language is, also, impossibly difficult to write *consistently*, and what is written is either a phonetician's exercise or good High German spiced with local phonetic spellings and words and turns of speech.

These matters are of great importance for nation and society. The usage of dialect marks off Switzerland from her most dangerous neighbour, Germany. The defeat of Germany in 1918, the dishonour of Germany in 1933, the threat of Germany in 1940, are responsible for the present high tide of Swiss German. The international standing of Switzerland, even the metallic hardness of the franc, the collaring of Nobel prizes, and a hundred little irrelevant things have given the nation a self-confidence that has expressed itself in the germanic part by a love of dialect. Dialect is also an expression of, even a substitute for, democracy: it has a slight class tinge, but this element greatly understates actual class differences, so it seems to be classless. It is homely, local, traditional, egalitarian – all these are Swiss values – and it is national as well as being, as it were, federal. Even within Switzerland, the self-confidence element is noticeable. Bernese is spreading its area; the massive self-confidence of that canton is imposing itself, for example, on Basle.

But just here, in matters of state, is a difficulty that halts the movement dead, the difficulty of French. French Switzerland has a different convention: there dialect was long lower-class, is now folk-lore. There is a Swiss coloration of the French of Paris, and the admirable numerals *septante, huitante, nonante* are used, so that 'ninety-nine' can be spoken in two words instead of four, yet one can live long and hear no French-Swiss dialect. French Switzerland has no sympathy for dialect as such, and furthermore finds no sympathy for Swiss dialect: one can learn German at a pinch, but to learn a barbarous peasant patois is asking too much. In federal company therefore, one must speak High German. This is particularly bitter for Berne, with its important native French minority in the Juras, and its influential French incomers in the capital city, for it is an unbroken tradition in Berne to speak Swiss German in the cantonal and city parliaments: this is a grievance for the French which strikes at the root of the viability of the pan-Bernese state.

English in German Switzerland. Loan words

Words for new concepts (such as Hell's Angels, Jeans, Bars, Happening, City-Center) are usually taken from English, often in the transatlantic spelling. Advertisements for smart new bars for young businessmen offer an extraordinary catenation of English nouns linked by German verbs and prepositions, and so do those for (to use the German word) Sexfilms. 'Eine Callgirl macht Carrière in Londons Highsociety': English is the language also of pornography. Business and technology employ English words in profusion – Know-how, Management, die Hardwarequalität des Computers, Job-Kontrolle-Sprache. Sport also uses loan-words, often far beyond necessity. The Swiss usage is frequently different from the native English one: thus one cannot park one's car in the place marked 'Parking reserviert für Cars'.

English is the language of upward social mobility, hence its appeal to the young. Until recently, Swiss German was conspicuous for its borrowings from French – 'Merci vielmals, pardon', and so on, and the written and spoken languages have many more words of French origin than the German of the Federal Republic – though not quite in the style of the old-fashioned German aristocratic jargon of pre-war days, even in Berne.

French Switzerland, in this and other matters, follows the usages of France as regards English, but German words and formations also creep in, sometimes with their spelling modified.

The Course of the Language Frontier

In general one can say that the language frontier is a single line, while the religious areas are a patchwork. But this only holds good on large-scale maps, and excludes the Romansch areas of the Grisons, a tattered rag, for this language's area has been hollowed out by Valai-san settlements and the march of time. Along the French–German language border there is, in fact, a discontinuous band of communes which are legally bilingual (i.e., the territorial principle operates in these communes so as to recognize within their boundaries the personal principle for both languages), and no fewer than sixteen communes are enclaves of bilinguality surrounded by single-language areas. These are either in the Juras (where the frontier is confused by Baptist settlements, sectarians expelled from Berne in the sixteenth century, and is complicated also in other respects) or along the border of Fribourg with Berne.

Ticino's German-speaking village, Bosco (Gurin), has been mentioned. It is not strictly a language island, but a portion of a larger language area south of the Alps, nearly obliterated during the Fascist period. The sharp line of the Alps is, in fact, in rather few places a language frontier, for French and German stretched over it until very recent times, and do so even today, in many parts. In Ticino, indeed, the watershed can be called a frontier, but in Grisons, as usual, it loses its sharpness when regarded in detail, and there are even small encroachments of Italian north of the Alps (e.g., Bivio).

These complexities are recorded because they are very Swiss. They are boundaries that became fixed at a moment of time (usually 1850 for the language boundaries, 1798 or earlier for the religious ones) for reasons of political wisdom. In detail, they have been shifted here and there, but with reluctance, for Switzerland is a land of detail. To generalizations there are exceptions, and these exceptions are cherished. Switzerland is not a country of co-ordinated anarchy, like Britain, it is a country to be understood in terms of laws (such as the territorial *principle*, or the *principle* of governmental determination of religion of the old regime), but of laws which are complex and overlapped by other laws, so that 'exceptions' to any truncated statement are numerous. A large part of the interest of Switzerland comes from this rationality and this variety, which is not confined to the linguistic and the confessional spheres.

Much more could be said about language. There exist principles of extraterritoriality for officials in capital towns, on both the federal and cantonal levels, for example, and subtle rules regarding villages whose names differ in two tongues. Such rules are hard to formulate, but are as well understood as the laws of grammar itself and as faithfully obeyed.[9]

II. Religion

Christianity, it is to be presumed on rather patchy evidence, survived even in Swiss Alemannic territory from Roman times. It is really only Coire that has a quite unbroken heritage in place and extension, and it claims to be the oldest bishopric north of the Alps. The earliest history of Geneva and of Constance has many points of doubt, and Constance, whose enormous bishopric included most of German-speaking Switzerland, has remained in Germany and its see allocated to newer centres, whereas Geneva lost its nominal centre to Calvinism. The see of Basle had been in Augst in Roman times, and that of Lausanne seems to have retreated to Avenches from Vindonissa, before again retreating to Lausanne, a city which it lost at the Bernese conquest to the Reformation. Sion became the capital of the prince-bishopric of the Valais, and thus usurped the original see of Martigny, but here there is assuredly a continuity from late antiquity. South of the Alps, Riva San Vitale, if its baptistry is really of the late fifth century, bears witness to an undoubted continuity. Nevertheless, when the 'Irish', that is to say Hibernian, Scottish, and Anglo-Saxon, missionaries came from the north to German-speaking Switzerland, they found a pagan countryside, with a recollection of Christianity only huddling in the remains of the urban settlements. Their memory, mixed with stories that suggest an older cult of bears, is to be found at St Gallen and St-Ursanne and other places.

Rechristianization spread also from Burgundy, and may have been able to uphold a continuity in such centres of very early monasticism as Romainmôtier (Vaud) and St-Maurice (Valais). The cause of the church became that of the Frankish (and later of the Carolingian) supremacy and, one may say, of civilization itself.

No institutions, I think, survive from pagan times on Swiss soil in the manner of the English monarchy. Folklore doubtless retains some relics of heathendom, and various features – types of buildings, for example – are called 'heathen' because they were considered in the seventeenth century or earlier to be of unremembered antiquity.

The activity of the church in the spread of civilization and the imposition of order is not different in Switzerland from Germany, though much of Swiss history derives its interest from a revolt against this originally Christian order, a revolt of peasants against abbeys in the democratic cantons, of towns against the ecclesiastical foundations from whose patronage they sprang in Zurich, Basle, Geneva, and St Gallen, and, in the case of Grisons and Valais, a reduction of the absolute power of prince-bishops into a constitutional power. The revolt, however, does not seem to have originated in or given rise to heterodox ideas, unless there is a hint of albigensianism or Italian communalism overlooked by historians intent on the germanic background. When the Reformation came, it split the church, but fastened a more dogmatic confessional sentiment upon each part. The Enlightenment of the eighteenth century brought the two sides together in a somewhat rhetorical deism, and in this Enlightenment Zurich and Geneva played an important role, while Neuchâtel provided a location for refuge and publication. Europe's reaction to the French Revolution pushed the heirs of this Enlightenment into the anti-religious camp, and it required doctrinal socialism to push them back again.

The history of non-Christianity stems from this deism, which merges imperceptibly into a protestant atheism. During the half-century 1841–91 a self-conscious anti-clericalism provided the ruling political party. It would be a fertile theme for an essayist to discuss in what sense Switzerland is to be called a Christian country today, and one which would require separate treatment for protestant and catholic, and urban and rural, environments.

PROTESTANT AND CATHOLIC

It is the division between catholic and reformed which has marked the church life and dominated the history of Switzerland for four and a half centuries. The division might be called the tragedy of Switzerland, had it not bitten so deep that Switzerland cannot be imagined to be herself without it: the most characteristic Swiss achievements, neutrality and federalism, derive directly from this apparent weakness and actual strength.

One would like to understand more about the Reformation in Zurich, an event of international importance, and one which changed the moral basis of the Zuricois state and generated a new social order as well as marking a shift of power within the ruling oligarchy. Is this to be regarded as a religious movement (or a cultural one) with the spirit of the times as its hero, and is Zwingli himself at the centre, or is a faction among the ruling families? In 1519 reform was not detectable, though some priests had been touched by humanism; in 1523 it had been decided upon, though discussion was encouraged, but by 1525 an immemorial order had been destroyed and a new order established in permanency, due to have a profound effect on individual character, to create a new sort of person with a new ethos.

It seemed too that Zurich had not only established a new sovereignty at home, but was going to absorb the greater part of east Switzerland into a unitary, protestant, state, subject to Zurich. To this development the 'second battle of Kappel' put an end in 1531. It was a ridiculously small battle to decide so much, but this is true of some other Swiss battles, especially of confrontations of Swiss with Swiss fought in anger but without hatred. The peace which followed, 'the second *Landfried*' (replacing the first), established, very early, the principle that each 'sovereign' canton decided on its own religion within its own borders. This was a less easy principle than it sounds: for example, private landed property, especially of abbeys, extended over cantonal and even national frontiers and included manorial jurisdictions and rights of church patronage, and therefore room was left for intervention by the federal Diet. There was also in the *Landfried* the germ of a second principle, opposed to the state-primacy principle, namely 'parity' of the two confessions. This was needed in order to deal with the subject lands with rotating governors from various cantons: the principle, perfected in later centuries by subsequent *Landfrieden*, was that of a personal religion as a status recognized in public law, a second citizenship adjectival to the first.

The two religious confessions had a subsidiary difficulty, acute with the protestants, of dealing with heretics and dissenters such as the Baptists. The governments of Zurich and Berne proceeded against these with the savagery and inefficiency of their age in virtue of their sovereignty, and no other government protested at their rigour. In the remoter parts of Canton Zurich and parts of the Bernese countryside these sects survived, or were generated from certain social structures. In the story of emigration they have an importance, and they seem to be connected with early industrial (or sub-industrial) activity and with political disaffection, always on the margin of history rather than the prime material of it.

It is difficult on several counts to characterize the inner doctrines of Zwinglianism as opposed to Lutheranism and Calvinism. Zwinglianism derived much of its impetus from the humanists, from the classical revival and the critical attitude to texts and authorities, and much also from the uniqueness of the political situation of Switzerland, republican but inegalitarian and confident of her own legitimacy. Its religious crotchets were submerged by the intellectual force of Calvinism, which dominated the second Helvetic Confession of 1566. This Confession created a Swiss protestant religion without creating a Swiss church – the churches remained and remain cantonal. The formal statement of doctrine was important for the learned classes, but one gets an impression at various times that popular religion breathed a different air, derived from hymns (which were shared between cantons), from the Bible itself, and from more homely preachers than the official clergy. The clergy were almost to a man hereditary citizens of the ruling city, members of the outer fringes of the oligarchy, a discontented class within that citizenship, but bound to it by interest, the long arm of the *Landvogt* who was viceroy of the ruling Council. This popular religious feeling went, and goes, deeper and is more constant than the intellectual doctrines; it is very important for the understanding of Switzerland to grasp this religion-based ethos, but difficult. I would prefer as my source the Swiss novel rather than the Helvetic Confessions, or the incidental evidences, such as the pious quotations on peasant houses, which in some districts copy the very type-face of the Reformation Bible.

The Roman church is, grudgingly, recognized as being the true heir of the medieval church in Switzerland. It was partly in acknowledgement of this that catholic Inner Rhodes was granted the old banner and seal of Appenzell when the canton split into two in 1597, though it was the smaller and poorer part. Nevertheless, the Counter-Reformation produced such a change in the catholic church that it is almost unrecognizably different in atmosphere from the medieval church, and the social and intellectual life of the catholic cantons became dominated by the teaching orders, Dominicans, Franciscans, and Jesuits, the memory of whose successful proselytizations left a scar of terror on the protestant mind which has only recently healed. The church's moods followed those of Germany, apart from a republican and aristo-democratic content which is Swiss, and an idea of an all-Swiss loyalty which never quite disappeared, though occasionally forgotten in a passionate consciousness of a confessional bond with the former hereditary enemies.

By the end of the eighteenth century, the princely ecclesiastics who set the tone for the catholic church in Switzerland were breathing the air of rationality and (one cannot avoid the word) enlightenment, their latest flowering being in the person of Baron Ignaz-Heinrich von Wessenberg, a close connection of Metternich, who, deeply influenced by the febronianism[10] of the German prince-bishops, became, young, the episcopal administrator of Constance – last of this ancient ecclesiastical line. But the political defeat of the second battle of Villmergen (1712) had by then set its seal on a demographic and economic relative decline of the catholic cantons. From then, and in increasing measure down to the mid-nineteenth century, catholicism threatened to sink into the position and attitudes of a minority, poor, retarded, stagnant, unenterprising, spiritually infertile, to give one side of the picture; beautiful, tradition-loving, holy, to give something of the other side. But nearly all the great Swiss since the 1550s, in the popular renown of posterity, have been protestants, or have sprung from the protestant community.

The French Revolution came to Switzerland from the outside, and German-speaking Switzerland regarded it as something external, imposed. This was also true of most of catholic Switzerland except, paradoxically, Lower Valais and the French catholic Juras, both of which became bigots for clericalism later. So when the Restoration came (the word is said by some to have been coined by Carl Ludwig von Haller of Berne), protestant and catholic élites still had much in common, as they had had in the Enlightenment. Even the rise of liberalism in the 1830s did not at first divide them, but by the mid-century conservatives had become a minority among protestant voters (in normal years) and a permanent majority among the catholics, giving the impression (and something of the reality) of two opposed attitudes to life, protestant-liberal and catholic-conservative.

The opposition was exaggerated by the 'Swiss Kulturkampf'. In 1870, in Switzerland as in Germany, there was a revolt of educated and candid Roman catholics against the proclamation of papal infallibility. This revolt was strong among the highest academic pinnacles of scholarship and in the professional classes, especially those working in a protestant or a liberal-catholic environment. The rebels, in the flush of enthusiasm, declared themselves to be the true church, and the ultramontane majority to be the usurpers. This position is akin to that of many Anglicans and of the Jansenist church which had survived in Holland, and identical with the Old Catholic movement in Germany. Protestant governments, notably in Berne, Solothurn, Geneva, and Aargau, activated by idealism tinged with mischievousness, recognized the new 'Christian Catholic' church as the heir of the old, and especially to its churches and income. The romanist congregations, however, overwhelmingly rallied to the priests and the Pope after a first hesitation. Bitterness at times reached an almost Irish intensity, subsiding in the 1890s with the new grouping of forces on the federal and, in many places, on the cantonal level. The Christian Catholic church remains, but with a slender congregation and concentrated in a few places (such as the Lower Fricktal), largely descending from the founding rebels, and giving an impression of being closer to protestantism than to pre-Vatican II catholicism.

Today the two main confessions are again in friendly relationship. Protestant churches remain liturgically and pastorally somewhat chilly, a sermon of high intellectual calibre for the cultivated classes, with hymns that breathe a different, and earlier, religious climate for the simple. Catholicism has been deeply affected by recent changes, cultivating no more the rigid conservatism of the recent past, nor claiming political power nor even the political press, and now attempts to pitch its tabernacles in the ground between bigotry and indifference.

LEGAL POSITION

Because the religious settlement is the basis of Swiss federalism or, rather, of Swiss centralism, the Federal Constitution is much concerned with it. The fundamental assertion is the first sentence of Article 49: 'Freedom of conscience and belief is inviolable'. The constitution brings all the topics which it regards as 'mixed matters', such as primary education, marriage, registration of names and burials, holidays, oaths, church jurisdiction, under the law of the state. As religious oppression is the most likely form of oppression in Switzerland, the whole constitution may, in a sense, be said to be directed against it, and, more especially, against oppression by Roman catholics of protestants, and by Christians of agnostics. But churches, and especially the catholic church, claim to provide a rule of conduct for nearly the whole of life, and to this claim the state (which for long was equivalent to the Radical party) sets sharp limits. The constitution contained until 1973 articles banning Jesuits and the foundation or resurrection of monasteries, and still contains today an article requiring political consent to the alteration of bishoprics; these were provisions specifically directed against the Roman church. The cantons are free to create a single state church, or many, or none, and this original power residing in them gives cantonal politics a dignity, a savour of statehood, which marks them off from 'mere local government areas'. They have mostly opted for recognition of the two great confessions: the situation is described in greater detail below (p. 73). The social reality of what is locally recognized as the established religion in the main follows the outlines of the religious map of the old Confederacy, usually in detail, but occasionally with the outlines blurred.

RELIGIOUS DISSENT

The protestant sects of Switzerland do not impinge on the public eye. In Vaud, the Église Libre has a stirring history of non-compliance with the squalid tyranny of the cantonal government – small-town lawyers intent on humiliating Christianity as a centre and symbol of resistance to their day of power. The Bernese tradition of a state church passed after 1830 into the custody of doctrinaire radicals without the disciplined self-control of the Bernese tradition. But the individualism of the French civilization asserted itself, and courageous pastors left their big rectories and ancient churches to preach the gospel as the conscience dictated: the whole episode is of great socio-psychological interest as showing how much the Vaudois owe to the Bernese past and how much to the language fellowship with France and Geneva. In the Jura there are ancient settlements of sectarians, usually islands of German speech among a French population: in time these clans, descended from Anabaptist refugees, have become rich in the manner of certain old Quaker communities, preserving old simplicities of custom and maintaining connections with kinsmen in the United States. The Emmenthal is known for its Quietist sects, and some parts of the idiosyncratic Zurich countryside and the Toggenburg have pockets of old protestant dissent. There are also some nineteenth-century religious importations that continue resolutely, especially in the Vaud – Methodists and Darbyists. There is the Salvation Army, persecuted in the last century and the hero of a number of leading cases in constitutional law, and there are the Jehovah's Witnesses and other similar groups who are the heroes of cases today, pre-eminently in connection with military service.

Taking all these into account, dissent is nevertheless weak, and has not forced itself on popular respect against the strong traditions of an absolutist state church. One can live long in Switzerland and never encounter it: it cherishes a secret life and (outside Vaud) is not really a historical force. The nonconformist, and indeed the Anglican and episcopalian, churches of Britain have no close Swiss parallel, and are regularly misunderstood for this reason. As regards conscientious objection to military service, Swiss legal practice shows little tenderness towards it, though there is a reluctant recognition that religious objection should only be punished once by a prison sentence. For objection on other grounds[11] a prison sentence for the first offence is followed by a second call-up notice, with a more severe sentence for the second offence: conscientious, or any, objection is (one observes) exceedingly rare. But it occurs, and that it does occur is part of Switzerland's democratic legitimacy. Cases involving Jehovah's Witnesses sometimes catch the eye.

Although the social atmosphere of Switzerland has long been inimical to religious deviation, atheism and indifference are as respectable as the main confessions, but it is important to fall into some recognized category. This is not so very difficult, because each church contains varied 'directions', liberal, collectivist-social, and traditional, which enable the churchman (especially the catholic) to live the full spectrum of socio-political passion within the framework of his own church.

THE LEGAL STATUS OF CONFESSIONS IN THE CANTONS[12]

The following cantons are reckoned as traditionally catholic.

The former Sonderbund cantons: Uri, Schwyz, Unterwalden (both halves), Lucerne, Zug, Fribourg, and Valais. Of these only Fribourg has a traditional protestant minority, in a small district around Murten/Morat. Appenzell Inner Rhodes can be reckoned among these for practical purposes.

Solothurn and Ticino are also traditionally catholic, though Solothurn has a traditional protestant minority in the Buchegg district, under Bernese protection.

All the above recognize the Roman catholic church in public law. Nine of them recognize (in 1971) also, often in not quite the same terms, the Evangelical Reformed church, and probably all will in the next few years. Lucerne and Solothurn also recognize the Christian Catholic church.

The following cantons are traditionally protestant.

Zurich, Berne, both Basles, Schaffhausen, Appenzell Outer Rhodes, and Vaud. Berne has an important catholic traditional minority in the Juras, Vaud a small one round Échallens, Basle *Land* a very small one at Arlesheim, Schaffhausen in Ramsen, and Zurich has a tiny one (Rheinau and, theoretically, Dietikon), but also a large untraditional minority of factory-workers who have immigrated from catholic areas. All these cantons accord the Evangelical Reformed church a public law status. They also (but with complications) recognize in a comparable manner the Roman catholic church: in the case of Basle *Land* and Berne giving it parity of recognition with the protestant church.

Geneva (with a substantial traditionally catholic population) and Neuchâtel (with a tiny one) recognize no church in their public law.

The following are traditionally *paritätisch*, bi-confessional:

Glarus, St Gallen, Grisons, Aargau, and Thurgau. These recognize both the main churches in their public law (in general) in the same terms. Aargau gives full, St Gallen partial, status to the Christian Catholic church.

But Aargau, Thurgau, St Gallen, and, especially, Grisons are not really distinguishable from Berne in that they contain districts where catholicism is the traditional church, and other districts where the reformed religion is dominant and in possession of the ancient church buildings.

RELIGIOUS AND LINGUISTIC POLICIES COMPARED

It is to be observed that the old regime dealt with the religious problem on the territorial principle, and the language problem on the personal principle – the Bernese spoke French to their Vaudois subjects, and the administration of the Italian bailiwicks was chiefly in Italian. But the Roman religion was unlawful in the protestant territories, as was the reformed in the catholic ones, and these laws were strictly enforced. Since 1848 the position is neatly reversed: in religion the personal principle prevails over the territorial, while with language the territorial takes precedence of the personal. The lesson seems equivocal. Both systems, as well as persecution and tolerance, worked flawlessly in their day, and worked equally well when reversed.

The exception is the Bernese Jura. The lesson of Swiss experience is, perhaps, the avoidance of half-measures, either total expulsion of minorities or total integration. What exacerbates is the assertion of total rights to oppress in theory together with a wide tolerance in practice – the Bernese policy in the Jura, and the British in North America and Ireland.

NOTES

[1] This is the traditional date. Probably 1157 was the real date. See Pierre de Zurich, *Les Origines de Fribourg*, 1924.

[2] Hermann Weilenmann, *Die vielsprachige Schweiz*, Basle and Leipzig, 1925. An excellent book.

[3] The Walsers had already forgotten their own origin by the sixteenth century. The antiquarian Aegidius Tschudi, discovering them at the head of remote valleys, assumed that they were the original inhabitants of the land, driven to these fastnesses by the invading Rhaetians speaking a latinate tongue. Their true story was pieced together from documents little more than one hundred years ago.

[4] The word *Vogt*, bailiff, regent, is hard to translate. It derives, like the kindred English word 'advowson', from *advocatus*, advocate for, protector of, ecclesiastical foundations, a relationship which passed effortlessly into exploitation. For some uses of the word 'warden' is the translation (*Kirchenvogt*, churchwarden, while *Armenvogt* is beadle). In confederal practice the element of exploitation was uppermost, and the word retains hateful memories.

[5] Capitulations, 'heads of agreement', in this technical usage, were the treaties cantons made with foreign princes concerning mercenary service. They usually granted a monopoly of recruitment for a stated number of soldiers for a term of

years. Good conditions of service were stipulated. The monies received were a fulcrum of the political and social structure, and probably also of the economic and demographic structure – providing capital and restricting the Malthusian effect – but in detail this is a difficult hypothesis to maintain. They were forbidden by the Constitution of 1848, and individual mercenary service evaporated after 1875: supply and demand failed, and it was made unlawful. The *Pensionenbrief*, mentioned in the next paragraph, was an attempt to control mercenary service (and thus to make possible a national foreign policy).

⁶ That is to say, without contradiction from *German*-speaking scholars.

There is some suggestion that collusion between Romansch and German scholars has gone far in purifying the alpine language of its Italian loan words and elements, and increasing its links with Provençal-Catalan, and with German tongues. The matter is of some importance for South Tirol and Friuli districts annexed by Italy when the Hapsburgs left Austria in 1919, in which Ladin, a language akin to Romansch, is spoken, since germanic nationalists derive justifiable glee from the continuance of the Ladin idiom, and the Italians are said to wish to assimilate it. It is not necessary to discover the truth here, for my theme is that language is intimately connected with politics, and this is perhaps established. There is an interesting discussion of Romansch in Guido Calgari, *Die Vier Literaturen der Schweiz*, Olten, etc., 1968.

⁷ The Malans-Maienfeld district, *Die Herrschaften*, the Lordships, were, by a complexity typical of the old regime, subjects of the Confederacy while at the same time members of it, providing their own governor when their turn came in rotation.

⁸ The pronunciation in a bleating manner of *Bern*, the transformation of the *oy* sound into a doubled prim-lipped *ü* in High Alemannic, but into *ee* in Basle, and the treatment of 'd' and 't'.

⁹ My source for much detail in this section (Dr Schäppi) is acknowledged below, in note 12.

¹⁰ The movement to establish, as it were, a catholic church 'of Germany' minimally interfered with by Rome, under the leadership of German bishops.

¹¹ As I write this, I look at today's Swiss paper to confirm the impression. 14 November 1971, *Neue Zürcher Zeitung*, p. 36 (foreign edition). 'Ein Zürcher Rocker vor Militärgericht', an exceedingly provoking young man refusing to obey or serve from a generalized recalcitrance, sentenced to seven months. The notice ends 'Next year he will again be called up'. This is not a case of severity. Occasionally one notices one of real cruelty, such as a student with conscientious objections, jailed, when released writing about the prison concerned and its abuses, and then on the next occasion being sent back to that same prison.

¹² I have taken much detailed information about religion here (and also a good deal of what I say about the language frontier) from Peter Schäppi's dissertation called *Der Schutz sprachlicher und konfessionaller Minderheiten im Recht von Bund und Kantonen*, Zurich, 1971, an excellent, and now indispensable, work on the law affecting language and religion. (Since it was written, Basle Town recognized the Roman catholic church, in December 1972: this is one more example of how quickly a statement of detail becomes out of date.)

CHAPTER 3

In the Old Regime

THE SENSE OF HISTORY in Switzerland was, until recently, overwhelming. This awareness and its manifestations were partly natural, because there is a real continuity, and partly artificial, because the sense of continuity was for a generation officially cultivated and especially during the period between the National Exhibition in Zurich of 1939 and the similar Exhibition in Lausanne of 1964. There are thus two reasons for being interested in Swiss history: the observer is interested in what happened because there is a continuing chain of cause and effect, and he is interested in the Swiss image of themselves, self-consciously fostered as a part of an agreed cultural policy. The aims of this policy have been partly as an extension of foreign policy – to insist on the nationhood of the Swiss as against, for example, the Germans – and partly (and connected with this) to emphasize certain political lessons, order, democracy, localism, and the need for an army.

Such a use of history has its internal cause of weakness, because explicit lessons from the distant past tend to break down in the hands of the professional historian. On both accounts, therefore, the observer is interested in the events which underlie the official legend: the continuity is from what actually happened, and the legend itself is influenced by the conscience of historians who see the lesson of the events recorded in the documents as being a little ambiguous in its application to the present and the future. In the politicians' hands the lesson of history has been distilled into the verb 'conserve': the historian sees that there is also a lesson in the word 'change'. However, it would need a whole book to give the accepted version of Swiss history, and another to criticize it, and a third one to restore the balance by a non-historical treatment of problems. A convenient solution is to take some incident in Swiss history connected with a particular year and to suggest some of the difficulties of interpreting it. The space at my disposal is insufficient for a continuous narrative and the reader would find that the story told was a repetition of what had been told at the same length elsewhere: short histories of Switzerland have a marked family likeness, are freely available, and are more tendentious than is apparent at the first look.

I. 1291

In 1953, young conscript soldiers were asked 'In what year was the Confederation founded?', and also, 'In what century was 1476?' 87 per cent got the first question 'right', that is to say 'in 1291'. 65 per cent got the second one right.

The questions, as well as the answers, are typical of the state of orthodoxy and of the efficacy of education and of propaganda – the date 1291 is carved under countless statues, often set beneath the Federal Cross, referred to in speeches every First of August. An older generation would, indeed, with equal confidence and approach to unanimity have given the year 1315. It is since the centenary celebrations of 1891 that the earlier year has received the stamp of total orthodoxy. The significance of the year, of course, derives from the document in the archives of Canton Schwyz now simply called the *Bundesbrief* – the first Federal Charter. But the document was virtually unknown during the whole period of the old regime, though discovered and published in 1758 by a post-doctoral student in the course of submitting the dissertation for his professorship at Basle. It was printed in full by J. E. Kopp in his *Collection of Documents Illustrating the History of the Confederal Leagues*, in Lucerne in 1835 – a work that starts the modern period of historiography in Switzerland – and entered gradually the national consciousness as the really significant document, to be taken up by the nationalist renaissance of the 1890s which culminated in the construction of the present buildings of the Federal Assembly in Berne.

Three problems arise on looking at the Federal Charter of 1291. These are: (i) Is it genuine?; (ii) What is its connection with the saga of William Tell, the Oath of Rütli, and the Burning of the Castles?; (iii) What is the message of the Charter for us today?

THE AUTHENTICITY OF THE *Bundesbrief*

It is not possible any longer to have doubts about the genuineness of the document in crude sense: it has been too closely examined by the most distinguished historians, even if it is not externally validated in any way, and is, as it were, its own evidence for itself. It is, however, still possible to be sceptical of the date and the intentions of the parties to the agreement: they were conspirators, and there are other examples of charters being backdated. 1291 is a somewhat embarrassing date for many reasons, and one could reasonably suggest a later date, down to about 1315.

The provenance of the document is somewhat obscure: very confident opinions are held by eminent scholars on this question, but these opinions are not easy to harmonize. It is a document in elegant, slightly affected, Latin: some phrases (e.g., *accipiamus vel acceptemus*) were assuredly thought in German and then put into Latin: the German in this case is that of the Treaty of 1315 (*nemen noch haben*). It is penned in a clerkly hand and apparently is a fair copy – one word is omitted in evident error. It bore three seals (whose order is not that of the parties to the document itself, but corresponds to the order in the Tell saga); the seal of Schwyz has broken off, Uri's comes second, and Unterwalden's is put on to the bands the wrong way round.[1]

The document is endorsed in an early fifteenth-century hand. It may have been in Hapsburg possession before that, and been re-captured at Baden in 1415 – though it is not in the inventory of Hapsburg documents. Aegidius Tschudi, looking through the archives of Schwyz in the sixteenth century, did not set eyes on it, nor, indeed, on its translation at Stans: had he done so, his history would have been different. It had no historical consequences, is connected with no burning of castles or movement of troops or with any other document of 1291. I myself cannot help thinking that the date the document bears is indeed not above suspicion, that 1307, for example, is as likely a date for the composition, and that for some reason or other a date may have been set upon the document earlier than the real one.

CONNECTION WITH OTHER STORIES

The traditional narrative of the Swiss rebellion against the Hapsburg overlords, in the story of Tell and the Oath of Rütli, was the basis of the older histories of the revolt, which placed it in 1307–08.

Tell

Modern historians jettison Tell. His story is first recorded in an age of the boldest falsifications. It may even derive from atrocity stories circulated during disputes with the Hapsburgs when they acquired the Tirol around which old memories[2] crystallized and which touch a chord in the subconscious. The wicked *Vogt* bears a genuine name for a bailiff, but of a later age and a different place.

As to the historical basis, the inner Swiss political rebellion was followed up to a half-century later, by an inner Swiss social revolution, about which very little is known. The ruins of castles show signs of violent overthrow, seemingly not quite simultaneous, and the nobles disappeared, with a few significant exceptions. The ideas inspiring this movement are also obscure, and we are short on, as it were, the political theory of this peasant republicanism, though it is tempting to derive it from Italy or even from albigensianism. If this undocumented social revolution indeed took place, then it only partially succeeded, and the leading families of the cantons – descended from the franklins of an earlier period – continued to hold the life of their tiny states in a grip which has relaxed only recently: they have been called 'the oldest ruling families in Europe' by a somewhat exaggerated paradox.

The first printed version of the Tell story was in Etterlin's *Chronicle* of 1507. This in turn seems to derive from the manuscript in the State Archives of Obwalden known as the White Book of Sarnen, apparently of 1474, which weaves together the Tell saga with the story of the Oath of Rütli, the Hapsburgs' bailiff's outrages, and the burning of the castles. The White Book itself was 'rediscovered' by two illustrious Zurich historians, von Wyss and Meyer von Knonau (the archivist, not the professor), and the latter, a shade sharply, stole the credit for the first publication (in the *Neue Zürcher Zeitung* of 22 May 1854).

Three Tell ballads occur also shortly after 1480, and there soon grew up a veritable Tell cult, with curious manifestations. The local peasantry gave him a religious aura, the saviour of children from torrents. The ruling families, themselves *Vögte*, seized on the legend with the same innocent delight whereby Arthurian legends were Normanized or whereby the children of an eighteenth-century squire may have played Robin Hood in the park, ambushing their father's tenants. William Tell even appeared one year as the frontispiece to the *Almanach de Gotha*. But he also lived a darker life which seems to us more true to the content of the story, the cult figure of successive peasant rebellions, and he reappears among the socialists and anarchists of the nineteenth and twentieth centuries – at the time of the General Strike of 1918, for example. There is the conservative State-Tell and the revolutionary Social-Tell, and they fight it out for a half-millennium of Swiss history.

The name Tell (possibly meaning 'clown') suggests a *nom de guerre*, the asker of oversimple subversive questions. The saga calls him 'a young man of respectable family', but the name is unknown in the locality – although by a pious fraud parish registers were later falsified to include it. The legend, told in the fifteenth century of events in the thirteenth–fourteenth, is almost a double contemporary of Robin Hood – a sort of folk-hero around whose name fairy tales gather.

Tell now bears a rather nineteenth-century air, and has been dropped from commercialized pathos, postage stamps, and advertisements of modern products, though his crossbow survives as the mark of 'Made in Switzerland'. The semi-religious cult has been transferred to Niklaus von Flüe, and the patriotic symbolism is now attached to the Three Confederates taking the Oath at Rütli.

Rütli

The same generation that laughs at Tell, and banishes him to the nursery, takes the Rütli story,[3] and the symbol of the three hands raised in the corporeal oath, with complete seriousness. The story has now become firmly attached to the *Bundesbrief*, and to the year 1291 about which it was never told. The *Eidgenossenschaft*, the Oath Fellowship of the Confederacy, conjures up this picture and gives it a geographical location on a clearing in the wood above the Lake of Lucerne. Here, as we shall see, General Guisan stirred the nation by a moving allocution to his officers in the darkest days of the war (1940), and gave the sanctity of the legend to the policy of defending a central redoubt rather than the frontiers. Most Swiss will tell one that the charter of 1291 is actually dated from the Rütli, and will give the names of signatories – even though it mentions no place of solemnization and bears no names as signatures.

It is interesting to speculate on the nature of the society and the legal institutions revealed, if the date on the document is accepted at its face value. On the one hand, there are suggestions of communal democracy: the parties are 'the men of Uri, the corporate body (*universitas*) of Schwyz, the community or commune (*communitas hominum*) of the lower valley of Unterwalden'. On the other hand there are three or more *conspirati* meeting secretly in a remote meadow, who seem to have the matter so much in their own hands that they can commit the valleys to a course of action in perpetuity, without telling the folks back home until afterwards if at all. Meanwhile, in 1291 imperial troops were at Baar, blockading the valleys as a quiet pressure in favour of their claimant, but, if provoked, keeping remarkably cool. The claim is made today that the document was illegal, that is to say defiant, and democratic. But it is difficult to visualize a situation where it can have been both until the final and effective independence had been secured by military victory. And if the course of action had been publicly resolved upon at four *Landesgemeinden*, what was all this secrecy about? The document, too, contains confederal penal provisions, the death penalty for this offence, banishment and confiscation for that, by virtue, we would say today, of federal law to be applied by the local courts of the valleys: one wonders what was the machinery for this.

THE MESSAGE OF THE *Bundesbrief*

Memories of Schiller lead us to expect the *Bundesbrief* to proclaim 'We shall be free even as our fathers were, a united folk of brothers', which may still be its inner meaning, but the document itself is more soberly concerned with preserving the peace in the three valleys, during an imperial interregnum. It refers to an earlier (*antiquam*) alliance, but whether this means a contract drawn up a day or two earlier and now formalized, or whether it refers to the last time this dangerous situation occurred a generation or so ago, is disputed. There is a declaration that every man shall serve his rightful lord. It then suddenly changes its style from the declaratory third person to the first person plural[4] and asserts that 'we' shall not retain or accept a foreign or mercenary judge. The meaning now attached to this change is that here is a declaration of independence, unilateral and illegal like all such declarations worthy of their name. It is this native and revolutionary root of confederal liberty which is exciting. A charter of liberty from above is a concession or an agreement, but here is defiance with a military ring, and it is this which the Swiss celebrate annually on the First of August. Other overtones are an assertion of antiquity and of man-to-man equality: it is a declaration purporting to come from communities of free men. It is irrelevant that the gauntlet flung down before three parties in a remote meadow seems to have been unnoticed, and that the actual root of Swiss liberty cannot really be taken as stemming from here. It suffices that here is this parchment, and here is the fact of liberty, and here is this evocative and legend-haunted field in the heart of Switzerland.

II. 1315

In 1314 the herdsmen of Schwyz sacked the abbey of Einsiedeln and carried the monks into captivity. They had for many years been in conflict with the abbey, attempting to annexe certain alp pastures to which the monks had good legal title. The abbey had appealed to all available authority against this encroachment, to the Pope, to Austria, and to the emperor. But the imperial crown was just then being disputed between the Hapsburgs and Ludwig of Bavaria. To aid Einsiedeln, and to assert his other claims, Leopold of Hapsburg intervened at the head of a large army. At Morgarten, his forces were crushed. The battle was the first of an astonishing series of Swiss victories, which recurred during the ensuing two centuries, victories to which Switzerland owes her legend and her existence.

The military victory of 1315 can at first sight be attributed to accidental causes, the Austrians made this and that mistake, the Schwyzers adopted this and that tactic. But the event was later repeated so often that the Swiss victories seem to have a character of necessity, like those of the British in India in the eighteenth century, victories of a small force so technically and morally superior that a handful can prevail over thousands. Various explanations have been given. The superiority of herdsmen over ploughmen? But the pastoral economy of central Switzerland possibly dates, in its full form, from a little after independence, rather than before it. Democracy? But why, and exactly when and how, did this state of affairs come about, and did it also not follow rather than precede Morgarten?

The word 'democracy' is an anachronism, but can be replaced by 'a love of freedom' or more realistically by 'a love of privilege', of a feeling of privileges and exemptions, a passion more widely shared than in the invading armies. This does not quite agree with what we know of the course of the battles, where it was often the armoured cavalry, as much in love with its own social position as the free peasantry of the valleys were with theirs, which was defeated by an inferior number of confederates. Similarly, courage on one side cannot be postulated as less than on the other, for the lesser 'Austrian' nobility may be expected to have embraced a chivalric cult of unconditional physical courage. It may have been the prosperity of the valleys which gave them an economic basis in consequence of the opening of the Gotthard approaches so that they possessed a sort of dispersed urban economy, or it may have been the poverty which made them tougher and more lightly armed. Such speculations cancel each other. The actual nature of the terrain, where the decisive battles were fought, is not mountainous, but forested hills intermixed with settled cultivations and lakes – lakes scooped out and formed behind the moraine terminating a glacier, where it paused some centuries before withdrawing to its mountain roots.

There is a suggestion that the victories were due to a relatively simple but entirely effective tactic, passed on by the Schwyzers to the men of Glarus, and then to those of Appenzell, backed by a weapon, the halberd, as well suited to the social condition and the economic potentialities of the valley yeomen as the longbow to the English infantry in France. To this tactic there was a valid answer, learned by Count Frederick VII of Toggenburg in the 1420s, but apparently not by others. To ask 'why the local nobilities were so unintelligent' brings the enquiry back to the social background, and it is complicated by the recurrent military superiority of the Schwyzers over the Zuricois, for example.

The first suggestion that it was just a run of luck, that the great battles for a moment hung upon an accident and the die could have fallen the one way as the other, is always a possibility. It raises a further problem still, the moral problem. In Switzerland one sees a country which has enjoyed felicity for two-thirds of a millennium, and one asks why, and seeks a reason in some particular moral quality, courage, justice, conservatism, adaptability, pacifism, according to one's own prejudice. Or, on the same basis one sees the superiority of constitutionalism over feudality, of democracy over hierarchy, or of oligarchy over a mob's rule or a noble caste. The question is complicated in detail when one comes to look within Switzerland. Unterwalden has scarcely performed a noble deed, but enjoyed a status of equal privileges with Schwyz and Uri throughout the old Confederacy, and as a reward still has a grotesque over-representation in federal affairs. Other valleys, the Haslital, the Entlebuch, the Freiamt, started as promisingly as Unterwalden, fought valiantly, had similar original social conditions, but were for centuries oppressed and show today the signs of that oppression. Of the towns, Zug also seldom performed a noble deed. Its decisive battles were lost, and it took for preference the side of the Hapsburgs and was reluctantly puffed up by Lucerne and Zurich into formal equality with the valiant Schwyz which had seemed destined to absorb it. Other towns (Werdenberg, for example) fought for liberty, seemed in sight of it, but just failed to achieve the status and were ground down by a ruthless exploitation for centuries. The human mind is prepared to accept accident as giving a transient advantage, but the fourteenth-century windfall that fructifies through five hundred years and pays dividends today is hard to accept: one seeks a moral justification and finds it with difficulty. The student of Swiss felicity cannot avoid this problem. The problem has two stages – the facts and the deduction: before saying 'Swiss happiness derives from democracy' one must determine whether it *is* a democracy or, for example, a close oligarchy, and then one must ask whether happiness indeed derives from this source or from another one, and whether the reward is appropriate to the deed. It would be very hard to argue a strictly moral causality, the Schwyzers, for example, were assuredly in the wrong when they claimed the abbot's alps, but they possess them to this day.

The treaty between Uri, Schwyz, and Unterwalden concluded after the victory is known either as the *Morgartenbrief* or as the Pact of Brunnen. It lasted until the end of the old Confederacy, and there were attempts to revive it in 1813–15. It is in German, but follows closely the provisions of the Latin document dated 1291, discussed above, entering deeply into the legal system of the republics between whom it was made. It soon took on more the character of a constitutional document than of a treaty, and became the nodal point of the whole Swiss Confederacy, for the three (or four)[5] contracting parties acted as a sort of collective state when they entered into treaties of union with the later cantons.

The interpretation of the pact as a basic law rather than as a mere treaty became important in the conflict known as the Old War of Zurich which ended in 1450 (as wearisome a subject for Swiss schoolchildren as the English Wars of the Roses). The treaty which concluded this struggle is impregnated with the idea of Law – a law which Zurich had broken and to which it was right and necessary to return. Law implies Arbitration.

The two great institutions of the Swiss League as it expanded after Morgarten were confederal arbitration and the federal Diet. The roles of arbitration, mediation, and decision-making cannot be distinguished from each other: the *Morgartenbrief* itself was often consulted in ensuing centuries when arbitration was required, as a law rather than as a treaty, and the very document shows signs of wear from having been so frequently consulted.

The Diet was not provided for in the *Morgartenbrief* or in any other federal treaty. It obtained a customary and moral authority from successive situations when the confederates were called upon to mediate or decide and, in later years, when they came to rule conquered territories in common. The Diet was the day-session (*Tagsatzung*) of the ambassadors of the confederated republics, two representatives from each canton casting a single cantonal vote. At various times, especially before the Reformation, it was more than this. It was (when opinion was united) almost a sort of governing body of the whole Confederacy, and it seldom can be thought of as a mere private congress of ambassadors: more often it is to be thought of as a peace conference in frequent session and with no formal limits to its powers. For the weak cantons, the Diet's decisions were almost always of the greatest importance, and such decisions often entered deeply into the inner life of the component republics – even at times of the more powerful cantons such as Zurich.[6]

III. Growth of the Confederacy, 1315–1515

The following is the order of precedence of the cantons, and the dates given in works of reference (e.g., the *Annuaire statistique de la Suisse*) as the dates of entry into the union.

Zurich	1351	Zug	1352	Grisons	1803
Berne	1353	Fribourg	1481	Aargau	1803
Lucerne	1332	Solothurn	1481	Ticino	1803
Uri	1291	Basle	1501	Vaud	1803
Schwyz	1291	Schaffhausen	1501	Valais	1815
Obwalden Nidwalden } 1291		Appenzell	1513	Neuchâtel	1815
Glarus	1352	St Gallen	1803	Geneva	1815

Nearly every date is arguable. Thus, for example, Zurich finally joined in 1450, or 1454, but the treaty was backdated to 1351. 1315 would be the strictly defensible date for Uri, Schwyz, and the two parts of Unterwalden. Glarus could as well read 1450 or 1473, Lucerne and Zug could be given the same late year as Zurich.

Appenzell divided in 1598, Basle in 1833. The dates of accession of the later cantons are also arguable on various theoretical and definitional grounds, especially Grisons, Valais, and Neuchâtel. On the other hand, most dates could also be placed earlier, the union of Berne with Fribourg of 1243, for example, could be argued as according these cities a priority. But the concept of a date 'of joining the Confederation' is a lawyer's one rather than a historian's, and has served since 1803 to justify an order of precedence: this order is not in dispute in any way, and is anchored in the Federal Constitution itself.

The theory of voluntary joining a pre-existing perpetual league by a mutual contract is important for federalism. It seldom quite reflects the historical facts, nor is it easy to trace the modern Swiss state beyond 1813–15 without the aid of some prevarication: the social and the emotional case is easier to argue than the legal one, but produces different and vaguer dates when one comes to detail.

After the battle of Marignano in 1515, no new members were admitted to full rights as cantons until the nineteenth century. The nucleus, the Thirteen Cantons, did not expand its conquered territories after the Bernese (and Fribourgeois) occupation of the Vaud in 1536. Switzerland thereafter entered her long static period in international affairs.

IV. Constitutional Development

After Morgarten, federal and confederal law developed on two levels. On the one hand were the treaties of union whereby new members acceded, the parties being the three original cantons and the new member, and, often, other existing members. These treaties are different, that is to say, they have different provisions to one another and also are between different parties and are not the same in respect of the various parties – the obligations of Berne to Zurich at a certain period are not the same as the obligations of Berne to the three-canton nucleus or the obligations of Zurich to that nucleus. One can speak of this element as a loose but perpetual confederacy. The second level is a sort of mild federal law. In 1370 the document called the *Pfaffenbrief* provided a uniform federal law on certain matters, and asserted the jurisdiction of the civil power over the clergy. In 1393 the *Sempacherbrief* (following the battle of Sempach of 1386) legislated on other specific matters. The series was completed by the Agreement of Stans of 1481.

The Agreement of Stans plays an important part both in Swiss history and in the mythology of the Swiss state: it is regarded as a symbol of the will to national unity and alluded to at times of national crisis. Its durable practical result was the inclusion of Fribourg and Solothurn in the Confederacy – marking the expansion of

Switzerland to the west, and the replacement of the Hapsburgs by
the dukes of Burgundy and Savoy as the principal enemies. In
internal affairs, it provided the legal basis for mutual help by cantonal governments threatened by their rebellious subjects. But its
symbolic value arises out of the timely intervention by the hermit
Niklaus von Flüe, who appeared just as the conference was breaking
down and by his mediation secured agreement between the contend-
ing parties.[7]

The secret of the long duration of the Confederacy was its double
nature. Against outside enemies it produced a sufficient unity of
peoples. Against internal rebellion, it produced a sufficient unity of
oligarchies. If peasants rebelled, as they did three times or so in every
century, then differences would be put aside and the governments of
other cantons would lend their assistance, mediating, often but not
always in favour of their fellow ruler. Before the Reformation, this
intervention of the federal authority, this mediation of other cantons,
produced an intrusion of federal law into the cantonal sphere: having
mediated an agreement between the peasants and the ruling city,
this agreement took on a little of the character of federal law, though
the ruling city would strive to deny this. After the Reformation, having conceded the right of the rulers to determine the religion of their
subjects, the tendency was to push these agreements aside and allow
the ruling oligarchies to determine lesser matters (e.g., military
service and taxes) also. But a rebellion against the established
sovereignty and ruling class would be met by joint force irrespective
of religion. Berne and Lucerne would help each other against the
peasantries of the two Emme valleys, and Berne would help Uri to
dominate the Leventina: Berne was itself in a strong position, because
after the mid-sixteenth century French- and German-speaking populations could be used to suppress areas of different speech.

Federal law, after the Reformation, can also be found in the
successive peace agreements (*Landfrieden*) following the religious
civil wars, which penetrated the autonomy of the cantons most
notably in the 'parity' canton of Glarus. The subject territories of the
sovereign cantons were also ruled by federal law: here a simple
majority vote of those members who had rights in that district
decided. This is why it is important that the majority of cantons were
catholic, even though Berne and Zurich were protestant and dominated larger populations.

V. 1499 and 1648

In 1648 the disastrous Thirty Years War in Germany was concluded by the Peace of Westphalia. The peace introduced a new
principle of international society and a new order in the empire

which lasted until the *Reichsdeputation* agreement of 1803 and the renunciation of the imperial crown by the ruler of Austria in 1806. To the conference in Westphalia went Burgomaster Wettstein of Basle, in order to try and represent the interests of his city, primarily, and then of the reformed cantons, and eventually, after long manoeuvres, to represent and hold the credentials of the whole Confederacy of the Thirteen Cantons. Among the matters he hoped to regularize was the position of Basle, and of the Confederacy, as against the Holy Roman Empire.

To describe these relationships it is necessary to go back to the Peace of Basle of 1499 which concluded the Swabian War. The classic interpretation of this war by Swiss historians is that it is the dawn of the consciousness that the Swiss are not Germans. Hitherto the Swiss cantons had been proud to be estates of the empire; thenceforth they stood upon their own feet and, for the last four and a half centuries, have been German-speaking non-Germans. In reply to the question why over almost every city gate in Switzerland the imperial eagle surmounts the cantonal shield and why the device is repeated in all contexts, stained-glass windows, carvings, paintings, during the whole time that the old fortified towns were being built and decorated, the Swiss reply is that here is a piece of sagacious conservatism, a reminder that freedom in its first stage was Imperial Immediacy, the right to stand under a powerless emperor with no intermediary, the historical form of full (or quasi-) sovereignty in Germany, as in Italy and Burgundy.

Modern re-evaluations make this 'nationalist' interpretation unfashionable: it has a core of truth, but is clothed in a pathos which owes much to the political creeds of the historians concerned. However, the Peace of Basle relaxed the bonds which attached Switzerland to the empire. The concrete achievements of 1499, from the Swiss point of view, were the exemption from the jurisdiction of the *Reichskammergericht* (and therefore the abolition of the right of appeal to that court), exemption from the new imperial reforms, and recognition of the legitimate supremacy of the cantons in the Thurgau. It can be said that Swiss membership of the empire was thenceforth for practical purposes only nominal. But Basle and Schaffhausen were not yet members of the Confederacy (they joined in 1501), so their inclusion within the treaty was very doubtful.

Basle in 1648, therefore, had a special interest in obtaining exemption from the jurisdiction of the imperial courts, to which appeal might be laid from its own decisions. The larger German principalities already had such an exemption, which did not imply secession from the Reich. This goal was now obtained. The two treaties of Osnabrück and Münster stipulated that Basle and the other cantons of the Confederacy were 'in possession of, as it were, complete liberty and exemption from the empire' (*in possessione vel quasi plenae libertatis et exemptionis ab Imperio*). These two words, *vel quasi*, have given rise to much learned discussion, and to assess this would involve distinguishing between Swiss history and social pressures on Swiss historians. There is certainly an effect on the convention of heraldry: the imperial eagle disappeared immediately from new work in the reformed cantons and, as a general rule, in the catholic cantons.[8] Some other relics survived longer: in Solothurn and in Schaffhausen the oath to the emperor continued, it seems, until 1712. Basle continued to belong to the German university community, and this system was quite naturally extended to include new Swiss universities founded in the nineteenth century, with students and teachers moving freely from place to place, and the Confederation continued also to be included in the Germanic fellowship of handworkers and apprentices who moved from town to town freely, and whose customs, the wander-year and so on, were widely recognized. Until 1798 or a little later there were complicated overlappings of manorial jurisdictions and high jurisdictions and rights of church patronage on both sides of the later German–Swiss border. The curious eye can trace other links, the name of a sword at a *Landsgemeinde*, the colours of the postal monopoly (black on gold, the imperial tinctures), the title of an office (*Schultheiss*, for example), some connections between nobilities, and so on. Probably everywhere in Switzerland, if one pressed, one would have received until 1798 the explanation for the right of governments to impose the death penalty that it was a grant from the emperor in the beginning. But from 1648 this type of explanation met very severe competition from the new natural-law theories of sovereignty which came to displace the old explanations derived from the Common Law of the Holy Roman Empire.

Throughout Swiss history, one may say, there have been two theories of authority, one of legitimate power, welling up from the people below, and the other descending from above, from the emperor, for example, or, conveniently, from God himself. This dualism is present even in the existing Federal Constitution, which proceeds at once from an invocation of the name of God to the decision of the peoples of the two and twenty cantons. It finds a modern form also in federalism and in communal autonomy, a source of power conceived of as antecedent to that of the union itself. It finds another modern form in the conflict between the historical principle and the democratic – as in the case of the Council of States. 1499 and 1648 are two stages in a progression, representing a shift of language and of symbols rather than being in themselves a shift of power, but they are landmarks on this account.

VI. *1712*

There are certain parallels between the history of west European states, and therefore between Swiss and British history. In 1653 occurred the greatest of the peasant rebellions in Switzerland, followed by a reassertion of the established regime, thenceforth more self-conscious as to its own principles and values. During the seventeenth century, institutions took on a form designed to be permanent and laws began to be looked upon as unalterable constitutions, a development which drew sympathetic attention to the institutions of Venice, in this field a pioneer. Then between 1712 and 1715 there was a final disturbance, a shake-up, which established a balance between the underlying facts of power and the institutions. The long middle-period of the eighteenth century lacks picturesque events in Switzerland and has not imprinted itself much on the national consciousness, except on a local level.

Yet this eighteenth century fixed on the countries of western Europe their specific national character. The reason why the characters who play the drama of European history are so different today is, it sometimes seems, because their eighteenth centuries were different, their remembered old regimes on the last day before revolution or reform were different. But it is the structures, the form of government, the religious allegiance, and the social systems, but not the events of the eighteenth century, which remain in our consciousness of history.

The shake-up in Switzerland was the second battle of Villmergen, 1712. This was between, on the one side, Berne and Zurich as protestant cantons, and, on the other side, the cantons of Inner Switzerland as Roman catholic. It ended (unlike the three earlier religious civil wars of the Confederacy) with the victory of the richer, more populous, more sophisticated, protestant cantons and fixed their leadership permanently on the country. The constitution of the Confederacy was readjusted to give effect to this realistic new balance of power, but with no attempt to make life intolerable for the catholic cantons or to shift the actual religious frontier in their disfavour. The result was the old regime of the Confederacy as it became remembered and as it enters into the life of the country today as a social and political factor.

The rubric of this date seems, therefore, the occasion to describe summarily this old regime in its last phase.

THE OLD REGIME ON THE FEDERAL LEVEL

Here the old regime is characterized by a stalemate or, rather, a sort of draw-by-repeated-check, a game that can be perpetually

repeated without achieving a decision: this is a balance every constitution should ideally achieve, but which usually becomes shattered
after a single generation.

The confederative structure was on three levels. First, there were
the Thirteen Cantons (Zurich, Berne, Lucerne, Uri, Schwyz,
Unterwalden above and below the forest, Glarus (protestant and
catholic), Zug, Basle, Fribourg, Solothurn, Schaffhausen, and the
two Appenzells (the Inner and the Outer Rhodes). Then there were
the *Zugewandte Örte*, the permanent allies. Finally, the Subject
Territories. These levels must be considered in turn.

The Thirteen Cantons

These, as we have seen, were doubly linked, by the treaties of
accession and by the successive confederal agreements of the middle
ages supplemented by the four *Landfrieden* of the period since the
Reformation, as well as the all too rare (but rather important)
unanimous agreements between the sovereign cantons (of which the
poor law, and the law of settlement based upon it, was the most
important). In the law of the Confederacy, federal and confederative
(treaty) elements were subtly mixed, but after 1715 the dynamic
element, the element of innovation, was overwhelmingly confederative: that is to say, no perceptible change was made in federal law
in this period. (There was little change in the British constitution in
this period through legislation either.) The machinery of this union
was the *Tagsatzung* (in French, *Diète*), composed of two representatives from each whole canton. This met fairly often, in Frauenfeld
(after 1713) for its formal annual meeting, but frequently in its old
place of assembly in Baden for subsidiary meetings, and sometimes
elsewhere. For innovations unanimity was now required, which did
not exclude pressure on weaker cantons by more powerful ones.

The catholic and the reformed cantons were also joined in separate
unions which almost acquired separate international-law personalities (because they had separate foreign alliances for long periods).
These, too, had their Diets and agreed on concordats among themselves
and upon what attitude to take in the pan-confederate Diets: in these
Sonderbünde, also confederative elements are mixed with federal ones.

Over the subject territories, a Diet, composed of representatives of
the cantons directly involved, ruled as sovereign, and these cantons
acted as a unitary state so far as these subject districts were concerned.

Decisions overruling the government of a canton were taken under
the form of a mediation, a sort of judicial decision as between dis-
putants, applying federal law. The modern distinction between law-
making and judicial law finding cannot be pushed back much beyond
the French Revolution.

The Permanent Allies

Among this group, various levels can be distinguished according to the closeness of the alliance and the number of cantons with which territories were allied. Two, the prince-abbot of St Gallen and the imperial city of that name (whose territories were intricately enclaved within each other's), were so invariably present at meetings of the Diet, with vote and voice, that they can be considered almost as cantons enjoying an inferior precedence and without participation in the government of subject territories.[9] Biel, a tiny city, was in nearly the same position. Less closely and universally allied were four important territories which have now become full cantons: Grisons, Valais, Neuchâtel, and Geneva. Mulhouse and Rottweil, two imperial cities, were also considered *Zugewandte Örte*.

In a loose way one can also include other allies, notably the prince-bishop of Basle, in connection with some of his territories. There was a motley crowd of abbeys and towns and communities under the protection of two or more cantons which can with difficulty be classified as they hover between the status of subject territories and protected allies, the abbey of Rheinau, the abbey of Einsiedeln, the town of Rapperswil, the town and territory of Frauenfeld, and so on.

The Subject Territories

Finally there was the sad group of lordships subject to the Thirteen Cantons or to several of them. Their status was infinitely complicated, and is of great local interest in detail. By and large, the present cantons of Ticino, Thurgau, and (much of) Aargau can be thought of as being chiefly made up of little bits and pieces of land in this category. The Rhine valley from Sargans to where it enters the Lake of Constance also held a group of these little territories, and is now within Canton St Gallen. The Grisons had subject areas of its own (Valtellina, etc., now in Italy), and the Upper Valais governed the Lower Valais and (in a sense) the Lötschental.

The practice was for those cantons which had the rights to govern the area to send representatives to a special Diet, and this assembly exercised rights of sovereignty and decided by majority vote (except in matters of religion). The governorships (*Vogteien*) went in rotation among the ruling cantons, often for two years at a time and in order of precedence: this means that a series of protestant governors followed a series of catholics, a fertile source of discord. The larger and more aristocratic cantons were reckoned to send good governors, but the small peasant democracies might send atrocious ones.[10]

The lot of the subjects was sorry, but not intolerable. In the end they usually set as their ambitions to remain Swiss, but to liberate themselves from this political servitude: only the Valtellina chose

Italy. The social structure of the former subject territories remains different, and the ancient status still affects today's voting patterns and political comportment.

THE OLD REGIME WITHIN THE SOVEREIGN CANTONS

If we look within the sovereign cantons the design becomes still more intricate. We can distinguish first the *Landsgemeinde* cantons – Uri, Schwyz, the Unterwaldens, Glarus (both confessions), Zug, the two Appenzells. Each of these was normally under the imperious influence of a few great families who enjoyed patrician status, and therefore they can as easily be called aristocracies, oligarchies, or pure democracies. Each of these peoples at one time or another broke the bounds of order and spent a period under the tyranny of a mob directed by a leader from outside the closed circle and then relapsed after a reign of terror into the accustomed ritual of acclaiming the decisions of the old-established oligarchs. Such events were often accompanied by decapitations, sometimes also by torture, regularly by bribery, although, one must add in fairness, in nine years out of ten the democracies were happy and well ruled. The proportionate success of pure democracy in Valais and Grisons must be set rather below this figure. By no means all adult male inhabitants of these cantons had political rights. Catholic and protestant Glarus had subordinate *Landsgemeinden* of their own, which exercised most of the rights of sovereignty. The government of Zug[11] exhibited a dizzy complexity.

The remaining cantons were under the rule of cities, and the sovereign body was normally a Council of Two Hundred or Great Council, which had usually in the past derived this right from the whole body of the hereditary freemen of the city, and which had invariably in turn lost its effective exercise to a smaller executive council. At the head of this Petty Council was a single figure (as was the case in the *Landsgemeinde* cantons) whose term of office was short and whose power was limited, but who could be re-elected – and usually was in alternate years. In some cities, the selection to the larger council was in the hands of guilds, in others there was a sort of self-perpetuating system. Berne, Lucerne, and Fribourg were frankly reckoned as aristocracies, and Solothurn could be as briefly classified. Basle, Zurich, and Schaffhausen had somewhat more open constitutions. Both Rousseau and Voltaire are at hand to tell us about Geneva. In general, one can talk about concentric circles of privilege: at the centre, a dozen families, around them sixty or so families of lesser privilege, then as many citizen families[12] fobbed off with minor posts or lean parsonages. Among the unprivileged were various grades: denizens, permanent inhabitants, inhabitants, and, for we are a long way from the bottom, ultimately the *Heimatlos*, the sturdy beggar and the gipsy. Each district and township, moreover, had its own status, historically determined, its own hierarchy, and its own dialect and dress. Through this complexity a thread runs of legitimacy based on custom and on status: each person has his own right.

Throughout the eighteenth century there were outbreaks of discontent – the ideas of the nineteenth century struggling against those of the seventeenth, or sometimes the ideas of the fifteenth century against those of the sixteenth – which came to much the same thing, namely the claim for freedom against an imagined or a moral usurpation. But what struck foreigners about Switzerland increasingly throughout the eighteenth century was the dignity, prosperity, and felicity of her peoples, and this is especially the case with the countryside of Berne – namely Vaud, much of Aargau, and especially 'the old canton' of German-speaking Berne. This happy society was in great part the product of tradition, republican virtue, and the protestant and aristocratic ethos, but behind this lay an unperceived economic revolution, of enclosure and early industrialism, of forces looking towards the coming century rather than back at the previous one.

This exceedingly complicated regional and governmental structure of the old regime has bequeathed to Switzerland, among other rich endowments, the extreme and delightful complexity of a country whose interest the observant traveller never exhausts. The lineaments of the old order have, here and there, been bulldozed by total urbanization, but otherwise are everywhere to be found. The remaining ethos of the old regime has the unfair quality of moral beauty, and the visual remains have compelling physical beauty, for the Swiss landscape, villages, and towns owe their appearance to this old order.

NOTES

[1] This last seal may afford an important clue. Unterwalden has during almost all of its history been divided into two parts, now called for convenience Obwalden and Nidwalden. It is Nidwalden that is mentioned in the document as a party to the contract, while the seal bears words added to the matrix including also the upper valley, that is to say Obwalden. Obwalden, in fact, came to own two-thirds, not a half, of the rights of the fictitious whole canton, and Nidwalden's position was somewhat precarious as against its neighbour: it was therefore Nidwalden which had an interest in the document, and in fact there is an early (fifteenth-century) translation into German of it among the archives of Nidwalden, and it was cited in a lawsuit there in 1616.

[2] There is an English tale of a certain William of Cloudesley, hero of an arrow story which is possibly also connected with the Baldur legend. The Swiss Tell may

have derived his christian name from this source. The same Hapsburg names, Rudolf and Albert, play a part in the Tirolese events of 1363–79.

³ The traditional story of the Rütli (or Grütli) ran something like this. At dead of night on 10 November 1307, following a series of outrages and threats, Walther Fürst, baron of Attinghausen in Uri, Werner Stauffacher of Steinen in Schwyz (egged on by his wife), and Arnold of Melchtal in Obwalden, undaunted patriots, met in this secluded meadow to take a solemn oath that they would live and die in the common cause of resisting innovations and defending the inherited liberties of their valleys. The incident of Tell came just after this oath, which led to the burning of the castles. In this story there is nothing inherently improbable, if it be set in 1307. But when the story is referred to in conversation or public speeches today, it is always set in 1291.

With the real decisive event, the battle of Morgarten, neither the ballads nor the chronicle in the White Book of Sarnen are in the least concerned.

⁴ As does the *Morgartenbrief* of 1315.

⁵ Unterwalden entered as one unit, but comprised two states. Note how difficult it is to find any moment of time when three independent states voluntarily decided to associate in a confederal union. At one moment they are rebellious subjects, the next moment they are in a union which deeply compromises their independence of one another. Their freedom as republics is the result of this union rather than prior to it. This is the usual case with confederal unions, and it seems time that the theory of federal government was modified to take account of it.

⁶ As in the mediation of 1489 by the seven cantons between the peasantry of the countryside and the city of Zurich.

⁷ Niklaus von Flüe (or von der Flüe) had his hermitage at Ranft, Obwalden, conveniently situated not far from his family's house. His family was an influential one, and he took a lively interest in politics, as a Swiss saint should. Even in his miracles he showed something of the character of a saint keenly concerned with the affairs of his spiritual constituency, for whom no commission was too small: was there a village on fire, then a message was sent to Brother Claus who, in a trice, communicated with the right quarter and the wind miraculously veered. He was canonized in 1947, at some expense and amid much enthusiasm, in which pro-testants shared. The presence of his saintliness is still to be felt by visitors to Ranft, and among older catholics there is a certain feeling that it was the Blessed Niklaus who averted the threat from Germany in 1940.

⁸ If my memory serves me right, it is in the town museum of Lucerne that I have seen an inner-Swiss *Standesscheibe* of the eighteenth century with the *Reichsadler*. On the other hand, in Wangen an der Aare, a town gate-tower has what is meant to be a fifteenth-century town arms with the Bear of Berne as supporter wearing the imperial crown: I much fancy that this is a modern conceit (as it looks like a re-placement) and that it was originally a lion.

⁹ Both the prince-abbot and the city of St Gallen originally took precedence of Appenzell as allies, but when the latter jumped into the dignity of a full canton in 1513, its representatives sat in the abbot's place and force could not dislodge them. Appenzell had formerly been subject to the abbey, and was interested in ridding itself of its suzerainty, and in sharing the pensions paid by France to the cantons, and other fruits of full membership.

¹⁰ It was sometimes the practice to choose a *Vogt* by lot among those entitled to attend the *Landsgemeinde*, so an illiterate alpine cowherd of sixteen could suddenly find himself governor of an Italian-speaking province. Usually a simple man sold the lucky ticket to a rich compatriot, probably to a member of one of the great oligarchic families, and all was well. Among the pillaged subjects might be digni-taries like the Count Riva, himself also a manorial lord in the territory of a sovereign canton, and able to obtain revenge or restitution.

¹¹ The other city states subjected their dependencies to their rule, but in the case of Zug, the town of that name never succeeded in subordinating the three rural communities of Aegeri, Menzingen, and Baar to its power, and they continued to share in the governance of 'Stadt und Amt Zug'. The *Landsgemeinde* only undertook the business of elections: it had developed out of an oath-taking assembly, and retained this character to the end. The little walled town of Zug never quite made

its patrician families into a closed caste, as did Berne, Fribourg, Lucerne, and Solothurn, nor, on the other hand, was its government based on the power of the guilds, as was the case in Zurich, Basle, and Schaffhausen. It is thus an exception to all rules, neither urban nor rural, neither patrician nor guild. But since it remained throughout its history resolutely insignificant, it need not trouble us further.

[12] Rousseau belonged to such a family. His plea for the rights of citizens does not stretch to the right of denizens to become citizens. It is a plea for the race of hereditary outer-citizens who are excluded from lucrative jobs by the race of inner-citizens. In the same way, the Declaration that 'all men are created equal' excluded slaves.

CHAPTER 4

In Modern Times

I. 1798

IN THE LAST DAYS of 1797, revolutionary France took the Vaud under her protection, employing the excuse of an old treaty, and a little later sent troops to effect its liberation from Berne. The news reached the confederal Diet, which was holding an emergency session at Aarau, destined to be its last. The delegates dispersed to their home cantons: on 25 January 1798 they had solemnly and publicly resworn the federal oath – a ceremony too long intermitted on account of religious strife – but even in this situation they could not bring themselves to afford effective military help to each other. Their journey home was illuminated by blazing castles, but the embarrassed countrymen had first asked the ruling bailiffs and their families residing in them to leave lest they suffer personal damage, for the atmosphere was of confusion rather than of hatred, and a great nostalgia was in conflict with a feeling of a blissful dawn — especially blissful for educated and enterprising men not members of the closed circles of the hereditary patriciate.

Basle had already defected before the Oath of Aarau. Aarau itself waited decently until the delegates left its walls and then itself set up the tree of liberty that very evening. Other subject lands also constituted themselves as free territories: in Weinfelden, to choose one example from many, the 'patriots' met and then proclaimed the freedom of the Thurgau from the steps of the Gasthaus zur Traube where the bailiffs had formerly held court. On all sides the old order disintegrated. Sovereign cantons, to rescue their dignity, declared their subject areas, already lost, to be freed.

Meanwhile the French troops, welcomed in Vaud, marched on a trifling pretext to conquer Berne. Berne fought unaided, but surrendered, having lost a small pitched battle not far from the city. Schwyz too fought. There was, later in the year, a wild resistance in the miniature republic of Nidwalden: the French replied by a massacre in its villages. But by this time the old regime had passed for ever.

The French troops had brought with them as a propaganda pamphlet a draft constitution, which they distributed. It had been devised in Paris, or rather composed by a renegade Basle patrician and submitted to Paris for correction and alteration. This, 'the satanic booklet', was again amended and moderated in April 1798 at a new assembly at Aarau (attended by representatives of ten cantons) which took the powers of a constitutional assembly.

This was the 'Constitution of the Helvetic Republic, one and indivisible'. It was a brilliantly daring argumentative document, a work of abstract and non-historical reasoning, not without a strong tinge of the ridiculous and destined to go into effect for the briefest period and in a limited territory. It abolished, as being a relic of feudalism, its own financial basis, but went ahead nevertheless to legislate for expensive schemes. We laugh, but the ambitions of the *Helvétique* have also been the goal of many subsequent generations, and the dearest of its ambitions – the reorganization of the areas of the cantons and their reduction to the status of administrative districts – may well be finally attained before the year 2000.

In constitutional law, manhood suffrage was introduced with a system of indirect elections, and there was provision for a constitutional referendum which was actually held when the constitution itself was replaced by its (equally short-lived) successor. Later constitutions introduced a property qualification, and this restriction continued to be the rule for the next half-century. Manhood suffrage, of course, was a reversal of the idea previously held that citizen rights were a prized and strictly hereditary privilege of a minority. A Swiss state with a Swiss citizenship was created for the first time, with a Great Council or national assembly to represent the citizens and act as a sovereign legislature. There was a Senate, representing the newly created or reorganized 'cantons', of which districts some bore the old names, but none contained quite exactly the old areas. There was an executive college called the *Directoire*, of five members, and ministers for twelve departments of state responsible to it: the old Diet knew no separation of powers and had no separate executive or judiciary. In her institutions, in fact, Switzerland was at a stroke brought completely up to date: the shock was enormous, and has not been repeated on the federal level.

The achievement of the *Helvétique* in legislation was equally astounding, even though this legislation also seldom took effect when it required positive measures. The negative, destructive, legislation was the most successful. The surviving institutions of feudalism and of neo-feudalism were abolished, a miscellaneous collection – manorial jurisdictions, tenures smacking of servitude,[1] customs of forced labour, privilege of chase, and also the vexatious monopolies of the towns and the guilds. This negative achievement was enormous, and proved for the most part irreversible. But in some instances it went too far, it destroyed certain organizations of workers and of employers, for example, which had to be reconstituted under new forms.

On the positive side of the account, the whole catalogue of modern freedom rights was proclaimed – freedom of movement and residence, of the press, of conscience, and, most important, of trade and commerce. The principle of equality, the king-pin of the liberal state and society, was also proclaimed and permeates the constitution. To education the *Helvétique* paid particular attention. It was to be universal and cheap, and to be crowned, it was hoped, by a federal polytechnic college and university. The old land-taxes (tithes) were to be redeemed for a small sum, and their place taken by direct and indirect taxation on modern principles.

The law of citizenship was established on lines which continue today, though its history is not quite continuous. Citizenship of Switzerland became based on the hereditary citizenship of a commune (township) which was now granted in wide terms. This simple arrangement was later complicated by the reintroduction of cantonal citizenship, which (under the restoration of the old regime in 1813) came to be regarded as primary. By the side of this commune of those who had the right of citizenship (*droit de bourgeoisie*) was set up the political commune which included those Swiss citizens who resided and therefore voted there.

The economic and social effects of these legal changes were large, and permanent. An active new middle class created itself and asserted leadership, dominated at first by lawyers, innkeepers, and traders: this class was destined to be the vehicle of Swiss civilization, the driving force of political life, and to give the tone to other classes of society. Machinery and factories were set to work and a new industrial basis of the country quickly established: a pioneer spinning machine, of French manufacture but copied from an English model, was located in the buildings left vacant by the monks of the dissolved abbey of St Gallen, a symbol and portent of the new order. The development of trade was greatly assisted by the abolition (for the time being) of customs duties within Switzerland, which became a single economic area.

II. *1815*

By 1802 the Helvetic Republic was bankrupt, despised and fugitive: having taken over a treasury containing 6 millions of francs, it was now 12 millions in debt. It was weak from internal factiousness and replacements of its rulers and it faced military defeat at the hands of Swiss soldiers led in insurrection by supporters of the old regime. During the four years of the *Helvétique* French, Austrian, and

Russian troops had marched and skirmished and countermarched over the whole land. Napoleon, master of the continent, intervened. The constitution he imposed in 1803 bears the name of the 'Act of Mediation'.

Napoleon's title of Mediator was well chosen, for a procedure of mediation had been the nub of confederal power in the old governance of Switzerland, and Geneva, formerly an ally but under Napoleon a French provincial town, had accepted the king of France as mediator in her internal disputes during the eighteenth century. The idea of mediation, too, owed something to Rousseau's 'legislator', the wise man from outside who established the fundamental law of a state and then withdrew, as Lycurgus had done in Sparta. Mediation places both parties under obligation to comply with the arbitral judgement, without too much offending pride or doctrines of sovereignty. Napoleon, in Switzerland's case, had some sympathies with each contestant, and was in a position to arbitrate fairly. His authoritarian inclinations played to the side of the old regime and he had an interest in a paralyzed Switzerland: both these factors inclined him towards cantonalism and reaction. But, on the other hand, it was Swiss liberal and centralist opinion which was pro-French, and the patricians who took Austria's side. The new cantons formed out of the subject territories, moreover, contained almost one-third of the population and fervently supported France and liberalism against Austria and reaction.

The Mediation Constitution, in the event, suited all parties for the time being. It recognized the new cantons, and established the cantonal boundaries nearly as they have survived until today. Within their new borders, to all cantons was restored the title of sovereignty. A Federal Diet was re-created and furnished with more effective powers of reaching decisions within its narrow authority. An office of *Landamman* of Switzerland was created, to be held by the chief magistrate of the canton which held the primacy that year, since the capital, the *Vorort*, was to move every year around the six largest cantons. The backing of force, the weak point of confederacies, the Mediator could in emergency provide, though this did not require to be stated. Forms of government were presented to the cantons, historically based, which would give power to liberal patricians possessing the confidence of an electorate based on wealth rather than on the hereditary citizenship of the capital city. In the event, the successive *Landammans* were all from old privileged families.

The conduct, too, of the Mediation regime was tolerable, and it receives the praise of both liberal and conservative[2] historians. The student of federalism can examine this interlude with profit, since for a time it was a successful confederal union: the term 'union', as always, must be taken with caution; for a state has neighbours, but it does not choose them, and one can find no moment of time when the states of Switzerland were individually in a position to choose whether to stand alone or to enter or depart from a union. Certainly in 1803 the grant of 'sovereignty' and the incorporation into a 'union' were simultaneous – if anything, the union came first, and the name of sovereignty followed it: before the Mediation the Helvetic cantons (in different boundaries) had been not much more than administrative districts.

In 1813 Austria and her allies, Russia, Britain, and Prussia, again dominated Europe. They did not claim to mediate in Switzerland, but left her the fullest freedom to form her own constitution, adding that they would only recognize Swiss neutrality and guarantee the constitution if it followed certain very definite lines which they laid down: the difference to Napoleon's course of action was not great, but it plunged Switzerland into two years of confusion. The new cantons (Vaud, Aargau, Thurgau, St Gallen, and Ticino) were to be received as equals. Geneva, Valais, and Neuchâtel were added as cantons, and Grisons retained as one. Berne got the prince-bishop of Basle's lands in the Juras, but Grisons lost the Valtellina with Bormio and Chiavenna.

The settlement was not concluded until August 1815. This date is a staging-point in the forward journey of history, but it has even more importance looking back. The present constitution of 1874 was made under the forms of the Constitution of 1848. The Constitution of 1848 was made by the Diet under the forms (it might be said) of that of 1815. Under what forms was the Constitution of 1815 then made? Was it a new start, an act of revolution, or did it carry on from the old regime, or from the Mediation, or what? From what root, what 'basic norm', does Swiss constitutionalism spring? The matter is important for the ideologies of liberalism and conservatism, and pressing consequences follow from the reply to this question, notably a theory of federalism and one of neutrality (a topic discussed in a later chapter). If the cantons were already on the scene and then, willingly, came together in a conditional treaty of union, then they have rights which can hardly be destroyed without their consent. But if the central power of its free will granted them charters, then it can take back what it gave under the forms it prescribes to itself.

By the end of 1813, then, Austrian influence was felt, and Napoleon's protection removed. The anti-French coalition, however, was prepared to recognize the Federal Diet, and Reinhard of Zurich as 'Landamman', addressing him as such. Then there was a legitimist *coup d'état* in Canton Berne. This succeeding Diet effected a *coup* on the federal level, continuing to sit in Zurich, rather than move to Lucerne as the Mediation Constitution provided, and soon after Berne insisted in addressing Reinhard not as 'Landammann', for the Napoleonic title and constitution were usurpations, but as 'Bürgermeister der Klein' und Grossen Rath der Stadt Zürich', Burgomaster of the Town of Zurich, the personage who was wont to convoke the Diet under the old Confederacy. The legitimist attitude was the same as that of the English Restoration of 1660, in that the period of usurped power had simply not, for legal purposes, existed. In Canton Berne itself this was not easy, for Berne had lost Vaud and the Lower Aargau, and gained bailiwicks in the Juras, and quite a story can be told (though beside our purposes) of the recognition and non-recognition of the new cantons, and the dates accepted as the 'joining' of the union.

For nearly two years the Diet acted vigorously (for it had money and troops), intervening to suppress trouble in Nidwalden, St Gallen, and Ticino and exercising the power of life and death in these interventions. Finally, it succeeded in giving itself a constitution, abdicating its powers and calling the cantons 'sovereign' and declaring that it was they who had made the union. The pact stated as its purpose 'to maintain their [the cantons'] freedom, independence, and security against attacks of foreign powers, and to preserve peace and order within'. If it acted for this purpose, it seemed that it could do as it liked, using a simple majority of cantons, and (this was the crux) the same majority decided whether it was acting legally or not.

In virtue of her historic legitimacy, Switzerland joined the Holy Alliance. As supreme ruler of the union, the Diet in 1816 introduced press censorship and control of the movement of refugee foreigners (the equivalent of the Carlsbad Decrees) and when a cholera epidemic threatened, it acted vigorously to close the frontiers. For none of these actions was there constitutional authority. 'A simple congress of ambassadors', the Diet has been called, but no reader of its acts and resolutions can maintain this verdict.

After 1830 there was a series of cantonal *coups d'état* by liberals, setting up during the course of the next few years new cantonal constitutions 'legalized' by virtue of plebiscite. But during the ten or fifteen years after 1830 there was a short-lived democratic conservative reaction almost everywhere and so the Diet became at each stage divided between cantons with conservative and those with liberal governments. It is of this time of freebooters, of assassins and usurpations, of adventurers and fiery speeches, of *Putschromantik*, that the memory has survived and has branded the Diet and confederalism as an impossible form of national government. Posterity rightly condemns the revival of cantonal commercial discrimination at the

Restoration, but praises the establishment of a federal army and the founding of a national military tradition: in this field at least the Confederation acted as a state. There was also a lively Swiss patriotism on the level of voluntary societies, shooting clubs, choral societies, student corps. These societies mostly survive today and are of some local political significance. In the past they told in favour of the Radical party, but now they are pillars of the established order.

III. 1847–48

'We are going to have a federal civil war, then an armed intervention, then God knows what, some castigation we shall remember for life, a brandmark that will last as long as our skin', wrote Gotthelf to a friend in Basle in June 1846. The Sonderbund War of 1847 did indeed mark Switzerland for a generation, for a century one might say, even though the country was spared an intervention by foreign powers who, in 1848, had troubles enough of their own. The political map of Switzerland even today bears marks of this event: in referendums (until the most recent years) the cantons defeated in 1847 (and Inner Rhodes) could regularly be found on one side, their adversaries on the other.

In the years between 1830 and 1848, the Federal Diet had been very narrowly split on important occasions, but in detail cantons had changed sides according to the current putsch back home. Zurich, normally radical, had for a time been conservative, and Lucerne, conservative today as for the last century, had for a spell been radical. Not only was the Diet evenly divided, but certain cantons which held the balance became successively very evenly divided, so that on one occasion the fate of the union depended on a few dozen votes in one rural commune of St Gallen.[3] But it was the division on the eve of the civil war which became imprinted as a permanent fact of political geography, the situation whereby on the one hand were ranged the catholic-conservative Sonderbund ('separate league') of Lucerne, Uri, Schwyz. Unterwalden, Zug, Fribourg, and Valais (with the sympathy of the isolated Appenzell Inner Rhodes), and on the other the remaining cantons (with Basle Town and Neuchâtel attempting to remain neutral).

This 'period of the Regeneration' (1830–48) deserves a romantic novel, or rather an opera, to depict it, but an abbreviated account of the moves of the successive players would seem tedious. The Sonderbund War itself can be viewed in several ways. First, as a conflict of personalities. The cantons were sufficiently like sovereign states, and the ideological issues were so cosmic, that public life bred vivid personalities – one in four of the most colourful being foreign refugees, usually liberals at the outset but moving comfortably through the political spectrum from *Carbonari* to reactionary or, bitterly, from a serene liberalism to a sour radicalism. Some cantons produced two or three of these romantic characters – Siegwart, Zschokke, Baumgartner, Ochsenbein, Frey-Herosé, James Fazy, Casimir Pfyffer, the confusing Snells and Schnells, Segesser von Brunegg, the pious Joseph Leu 'of Ebersol', and most brilliant and enviable of all, Pellegrino Rossi,[4] with a pyrotechnic career in four states and two sciences.

Second, as a conflict of foreign princes. The emperors of Austria supported the catholic conservatives and cantonal sovereignty. Louis-Philippe was under various temptations, liberal and reactionary, while the young Louis Napoleon sported liberal colours as a private citizen in Canton Thurgau. Prussia had special interests in Neuchâtel, while Britain was, according to one's point of view, concerned with the balance of power, helpful, or merely mischievous. The Federal Pact of 1815 was a part of the settlement of Vienna, part of the same settlement as Swiss neutrality and the position of Savoy. However, when civil war erupted, Ticino happened to be in the grip of its liberal faction, and Austria (in Lombardy) therefore had no common frontier with the rebellious cantons and afforded no military help.

The revolutions of 1848 temporarily neutralized the kings and emperors, but their influence (and especially Britain's) was felt in the moderate and rational exploitation of the liberals' victory. It had been feared that a united Switzerland under radical leadership would be a centre of sedition and have expansionist tendencies and an active foreign policy, but in the event the new Switzerland fitted the European scene almost better than the old. With a relatively strong army, Switzerland never became as an easy victim a cause of war, and though the Confederation sometimes did have expansionist ambitions, the stalemate within the liberal political family and in the confessional field made the political ruling classes reluctant to add new cantons (Chablais and Faucigny, Valtellina, Vorarlberg, or Liechtenstein) which could only be Roman catholic.

Third, as part of a European ideological battle, with liberalism (free competition, republicanism, nationalism) on the one side facing historical legitimacy (paternalism, divine right, the common law of Europe) on the other. In the event this overlapped with an older dualism of protestant and catholic, but there is an element of the accidental in this. Governmental force in 1847 was overwhelmingly on the side of the liberals, but opinion in the country as a whole was probably rather narrowly divided on the ideological issue.

Fourth, as a conflict of social and economic 'sub-cultures'. Already before 1848, protestant society was lawyer-ridden and partly industrial, and catholic society was priest-ridden and rural, and 1848 strengthened an existing contrast. The complicating factor was a strong conservative movement among protestants and a liberal movement among catholics, and a sympathy of like-minded across confessional boundaries. Basle Town, especially, had strong sympathies for the Sonderbund, and so had the old Calvinist and aristocratic Upper Town of Geneva.[5] Jeremias Gotthelf can be said to have held, in the eye of the law, the same faith as Gottfried Keller, but the former came to sympathize with the Sonderbund and the latter to throw in his lot with the volunteer corps of radical would-be liberators, and to found his career as an official on this allegiance.

It shows the good judgement of the rulers of the Twelve Cantons who were the victors in the war that they chose as their commander-in-chief Guillaume-Henri Dufour, who came from this conservative protestant group. His is a recurrent type in Swiss history, steadfast in character, disinterested, of an honesty beyond reproach or suspicion, the natural mediator and symbol of unity – figures such as *Landamman* Aebli of Glarus or Schultheiss Wengi of Solothurn at the time of the wars of religion, or Max Huber and Walter Stucki in the 1920s and 1930s, or General Guisan in the second World War, who played the sort of part in cantonal or national affairs that Switzerland herself would wish to play in the affairs of Europe.

Fifth, as a trial of strength. Basle was traditionally a neutral under the old regime (for the three latest to be accepted as cantons were under the obligation to stay neutral in intra-federal disputes). Basle Town in 1847 was under severe conscientious strain, its sympathies were with the conservatives, yet it had an obligation to comply with federal law, and possessed a train of artillery which gave the League of Twelve a decisive advantage. Its representatives therefore offered their mediation and obtained very fair terms for the Sonderbund League of Seven, which they refused, perhaps relying on foreign help, for Britain was the only power whose government supported the radicals. The Seven, too, thought they could win. In the event, the Sonderbund bungled its military plans, stood on the defensive, and lost. Dufour picked off Fribourg, then advanced from Aargau: the leaders of the catholics fled by the new paddle-steamer from Lucerne, and the campaign was over. There were 104 dead. The liberals set up puppet governments in Fribourg and Lucerne, for at that period the winner of a *coup* determined the new electoral law, and the master of the governmental machine won the subsequent election. The exercise of power by the liberals in the principal defeated cantons was not forgotten a century later, nor, I think, has any canton occupied as a consequence of the Sonderbund War ever since then, in a free election, returned any other than a catholic conservative or catholic social majority.

Sixth, as a constitutional issue. It is difficult to take the constitutional conflicts, and in particular the questions as between cantonal and national sovereignty and the right of the majority in the Diet, quite seriously, because parties changed constitutional sides and it was regularly the party with a majority that argued for majority rights. Both liberals and conservatives, too, formed separate leagues. One's impression is that the liberals have slightly the worse of these constitutional arguments, and that the conduct of Canton Aargau was intolerable. The invasions of Free Corps (*Freischaren*) still leave a sour taste after more than a century, but both sides had a burning sense of their own justice, and one can still recapture the enthusiasm of both parties. Inevitably it was the defeated party that brooded longest over its wrongs, and inevitably one's final sympathies are with the losing side: it is this residue of sadness which makes the story dramatically satisfying.

A Swiss liberal might consider the formation of the Sonderbund league itself as an attempted *coup d'état*. But my own interpretation is to set Dufour's campaign in the tradition of the liberal *coups* within the cantons. The course of such *coups* is always of a show of force rather than of a battle actually fought, and the Sonderbund campaign was a sort of symbolic or phoney war – like the revolt of Basle *Land* in 1831, or, indeed, all the Swiss civil wars of religion (except the second War of Villmergen, which had some cutting edge to it).

In a judgement on the war, most Swiss consider it a tragedy, but praise the triumph of liberalism as being moderately exercised on the central government level, and especially praise a settlement which did not rob the vanquished of hope, and which established a Council of States, on the model alike of the old Diet and of the United States Senate: this Council allowed the language – and the religious – minorities, taken together, to have a blocking vote in federal legislation. Beyond this, Swiss diversity and Swiss localism owe much to disunity, and could hardly have survived so vigorously without the long-remembered violence and injustice of 1847–48. In the morality of history an event of the importance of the Sonderbund War cannot be wished away, and if the final product, the final state of Swiss society and governance, is considered enviable, then the civil war was necessary for Switzerland to become herself.

IV. *1874*

The years immediately after 1848 were spent filling out the constitution with legislation, of which much remains, using the temporary unanimity of the victors to good purpose. The next quarter-century, however, really belongs to economic, rather than federal political, history. Economically, the country was transformed, and the commercial centres of large towns took on their modern visual appearance, the railway network system was established, banks and industries founded and expanded, but the period in modern recollection passed with events of anecdotal interest scarcely meriting record. On the cantonal level, there were heroic rhetorical feats. Fribourg and Lucerne fought to shake off the liberal tyranny and furnish themselves democratically with obscurantist clerical-conservative governments, in Zurich there was the drama of Alfred Escher, and in all the cantons prodigies of encapsulated politics – in detail these are intensely interesting, but the casual visiting foreigner may feel that all they have left behind is a statue on the Bahnhofplatz and a few street names, and this approach is here reluctantly humoured.

The year 1874 demands to be recorded on account of the adoption in a referendum, by majority of voters and cantons, of the existing Federal Constitution, a 'total revision' of the Constitution of 1848. The background to this revision includes the Franco-Prussian War, posing an imminent threat to a country with an army now relatively weak and a backward education, and also includes the *Kulturkampf* arising out of the papal declaration of infallibility in 1870, which set the liberal spirit and the Church of Rome at loggerheads. The institutions of the federal government, however, are considered at such length in later chapters that a consideration here can be foregone. Radicalism now revealed its interventionist potentialities (especially within the cantons), a sort of drift towards state socialism by anti-socialists, a development which exposed its inner contradiction when the issue of protectionism against free trade had to be faced at the end of the century.

The movement for federal reform had started in 1870, and been preceded by a large number of cantonal constitutional revisions. A first proposal ran foul of both the linguistic and religious minorities, and was rejected by the 'Romance language cantons' as well as by the cantons of the former Sonderbund. The 1874 proposal moderated the degree of centralism, but increased the degree of anticlericalism, and both these factors assisted in its adoption against an even sharper rejection by the catholic-conservative Sonderbund states.

V. *1891*

Since 1959, all aspects of Swiss government have been permeated by the spirit of proportionality – the so-called 'concordance democracy'[6] – which is a very different system from that of the early years after 1875, when the central power was firmly in the hands of a liberal-radical-democratic group. The foundations of the present system of full proportionality were laid in the 1890s. This is not merely a matter of the party composition of the executive, but of a whole infrastructure, a system of elementary education, a political aesthetic, a spirit of nationality and a view of history, and a structure of political parties, pressure-groups, the press, and higher education. All this was laid down in a foreshadowing of its modern appearance in (approximately) the years 1891–96. The cantonal changes indeed were a score of years earlier and were a necessary preliminary for the federal changes. By the 1890s some form of proportionality was usual in the cantonal Great Councils, but on the federal level it was only introduced in 1919. Similarly the federal changes of the 1890s had already been pioneered by the cantons with the same period of anticipation.

The choice of the year 1891 is somewhat arbitrary, but it happens that in, or very close to, that year a change of direction took place in many aspects of public life to which in retrospect a significance can be attached which was not really apparent at the time.

NATIONALISM

The year 1891 was the year of the great jubilee of the foundation of the Confederacy in 1291, that is to say in this year that date was finally and irrevocably declared to have been the instant of time when Switzerland was founded. The sense of nationality and the pathos of history were given their modern form, although the full fruition of the new patriotism came later, in 1916, or in the National Exhibition of 1939. The new historicizing spirit of the 1890s included the glories of the old regime within its sympathies, the mythology of William Tell and the verifiable triumphs in battle of the confederates in the years before 1515. The liberal-radical tradition was thus removed from its throne as the single embodiment of the Swiss spirit, and shared its claim with the conservatives and Inner Switzerland: 'we shall be free, even as our fathers were'. In this mood the divisions of the Reformation, the Helvetic Republic, the Sonderbund, and the *Kulturkampf* could be overlooked, and the new divisions arising out of the industrial revolution could perhaps lose their sharpness of outline. Rightly looked at, cantonalism is not a derogation of patriotism but a means whereby differences of language and religion can be bridged. A sort of cosmic optimism became the ruling interpretation of Swiss history and institutions, not entirely shared by the factory proletariat.

THE STYLE OF POLITICS

Liberalism had come into power in the cantons in the years after

1830 by a sort of veiled *coup d'état*, and the vice of its ambiguously legal seizure of power haunted it for half a century. It soon passed into the socially more broadly-based form called radicalism, but it is probable that radicalism no more represented the unfalsified will of a majority than it did in contemporary Spain or Italy. This thought is peculiarly wounding to a liberal. At first the difficulties were overcome by a high property qualification, and, before 1848, by indirect elections,[7] but then the party went over to subtler devices, still not fully elucidated, such as intimidation of employees, corrupt supervision of votes, exclusions from the register, misuse of judicial process, and 'electoral geometry' or gerrymandering. In the result it was the conservatives who perceived that they had an interest in pure and total democracy, and who welcomed devices such as the referendum which might either help them back into power or at least serve as a counterbalance to radical tyranny.

In the 1860s riot and intimidation ceased to be the normal means of transference of power in the cantons, and the last cantonal *coup d'état* actually took place in Ticino in 1890 (though there have been later attempts in Zurich and Geneva which might bear this interpretation). A sort of lawful deflection of the rules and 'electoral geometry' continued, however, until 1916, and was the normal basis of liberal-radical power at many times and places.

THE REFERENDUM

In the light of this situation, the referendum has a special function. The launching of a referendum, indeed, requires signatures and their attestation by local officials, and could be, and probably was, influenced by the possessors of office until 1919. But the counting of votes in referendums since, and including, 1866, seems (in federal matters at least) to have been honest. Working men, it appears, voted in referendums even when they showed little enthusiasm for electoral rights. More important in the period 1870–90 was that catholics also exercised their rights, and it was the repeated rejection of radical proposals at referendums by catholic and protestant conservatives which was the instrument of the eventual proportionalization of the Swiss executive, and (more difficult to trace) of the informal procedures of Swiss government.

THE FEDERAL COUNCIL

In this process 1891 was a turning-point. In 1884, after a succession of defeats in referendums, the experiment was made of electing a catholic-conservative as Chairman of the National Council. But this concession, though followed by some referendal successes of the radicals, was too small to bait the trap. 1891 started with an important legislative programme, including a law to provide pensions for federal officials (a small but important step in the transition towards a modern state based on a career bureaucracy). This was challenged to a referendum and rejected. At the end of the year a still more important law nationalizing the railways was also similarly rejected, and this rejection had a consequence unusual in Swiss public life, for the Federal Councillor concerned, the great Emil Welti, resigned.

The vacancy Welti left was filled by a catholic-conservative. For the first time since 1848 the vanquished of the Sonderbund War, the cantons of William Tell's Switzerland, came fully within the pale of the Federal Constitution. Switzerland thereby set her foot on a long path that was eventually to lead to the composition of the federal executive proportionately to the strength of the parties in the electorate, a pilgrimage which led to a different concept of state, not based on the dialectic of government and opposition but on universal participation. It is this election to the Federal Council (hitherto exclusively liberal-radical) which makes the choice of 1891 as a turning-point inescapable.

There had, of course, been a considerable number of Federal Councillors in the past who had been titular Roman catholics, born of catholic parents and presumably baptized with the appropriate rites, but they had all been liberals or radicals and in some form anti-clerical or lapsed. There had also, in a sense, been conservatives, right-wing liberals whose practical economic and social attitudes seem to us profoundly conservational – Heer, Hammer, Bavier, for example. But the catholic- or clerical-conservatives gravitated to a different pole, ultramontanist, social romanticist, expressive of the views of the defeated party. Josef Zemp was conciliatory and a moderate of this party, but nevertheless his election was an event opening a new age. Only a few years before, the Swiss *Kulturkampf* had been waged with extraordinary violence. Pope Pius IX, who died in 1878, had, it will be remembered, for his part denounced liberalism with a baroque ferocity verging on the demented: the eightieth of the 'depraved and impious doctrines (spread by the haters of truth and justice with extraordinary impudence, foaming out of their own confusion like the raging waves of the sea)', which he 'condemned, denounced, reproved, and proclaimed to be avoided as a pestilential contagion', was that 'the Roman Pontiff can, and ought to, reconcile himself and come to terms with, progress, liberalism, and modern civilization'.[8] Liberals, in their turn, had used nearly as extravagant language, and followed their threats by action. The desire for peace was felt simultaneously by both sides: patriotism, and the defence of property, were ideals they equally shared. 1891 was also the year of the progressive Encyclical *Rerum Novarum*.

THE CONSTITUTIONAL INITIATIVE

Two other referendums of 1891 raised topics of great significance. First, it was in that year that the constitution was altered to introduce the federal constitutional initiative, the procedure whereby on a petition of 50,000 voters an amendment to the constitution may be proposed which is eventually to be submitted to the referendum of people and cantons. Such a reform was made unavoidable by the availability of a procedure for initiating *total* revision of the constitution, and the experiment had already been made in 1880 of making a partial amendment under the forms of a vote for total amendment. The attempt failed, but the precedent was clear and dangerous. The introduction of the initiative for partial amendment was accepted by people and cantons, but the distribution of votes shows that the radical votes were thrown against it. The effect was to increase greatly the power of the opposition so scantily represented in the National Council, and the need to square this opposition by offering the clerical catholics a seat in the national executive was overwhelming.

THE LOBBIES

The other significant referendum of 1891, in the context of this discussion, was the one which sanctioned the revised Tariff Act. The debate over this law was innovatory in that it was the first one in Swiss history to be fought between interest groups rather than the historical parties – though it was only shadow-boxing compared with the campaign in 1901 over the act's revision, a campaign so searing that never again was tariff revision made in a form subject to referendum.

Modern Switzerland is constructed not only on the foundation of concordance and total proportionality, but also on the pillars of the four great interest groups. These came into existence in the years shortly before, or shortly after, 1891 in more or less their modern forms. The groups are: the *Vorort* (the *Handels- und Industrieverein*, the bosses' union); the *Gewerbeverband*, the union of small traders; organized labour; and fourthly the Peasants' Union. The *Vorort*, which the romantic left wing traditionally insist to be the concealed government of Switzerland, had been established on the federal level in 1870. The *Gewerbeverband* (*Union suisse des Arts et Métiers*) was founded in 1879. In 1879–80 a socialist leader was given an annual federal grant as Labour Secretary 'to collate statistics', which was the beginning of the official consultation of labour as a partner by federal officials in the preparation of policy. Finally, in 1898, a Secretary for the

Peasantry was similarly appointed. All four economic organizations received and long relied upon a fixed financial support from the central government budget, justified by the need experienced by the (very small) civil service for technical information to guide their new, tentatively interventionist, policies.

These organizations were slightly ahead, in time, of the political parties themselves. Indeed, parties were surprisingly late in forming national (as opposed to cantonal) organizations. The socialists[9] claim to have been the earliest national party, founded in 1880 (or, more arguably, in 1888), and the Peasants were the latest, in 1918–22. One can give various dates, widely apart, for the founding of the *Freisinnig* (Radical) party on a federal basis, but 1894 is usually accepted. The catholic-conservatives followed, on one interpretation in the same year, on another in 1905. These dates are all open to argument and depend on definitions, and the motives were rather the contesting of referendal struggles than parliamentary or electoral: the establishment of reasonably centralized party organizations was in any event much less significant than the formation of the great lobbies and interest groups, and it was not until the 1920s that proper party secretariats were employed by the historic parties, nor have the secretariats bred the dominating extra-parliamentary figures that the great lobbies have produced. Nevertheless, it can be said that it was in the 1890s that the leading modern political forces first step on to the stage of national politics.

VI. *1918*

In the opening years of the twentieth century, the Boer War was closely observed by the Swiss. Their self-identification with the Afrikaaners left a wound on relations with Great Britain. But German Switzerland stretched basking in the sunlight that fell on the vigorous Germanic empire. The Kaiser himself visited Switzerland, and was received enthusiastically, even obsequiously, and his visit left the impression of being more than just the courtesy visit of the head of a foreign state. The German-speaking Swiss were proud of their German-ness (especially the protestants in east Switzerland), and liberal travellers from the German principalities felt at home in republican Switzerland. Trade and investment scarcely noticed the frontier. Within the whole area of the tributaries of 'the German Rhine' the relationship was unselfconscious and relaxed, and was not confined to a particular class. The well-bred spent a year of their student period in Germany and, preferably, graduated there; officers learnt not only the arts of war but the military ethos from Prussia; aristocrats and professional men moved freely in both directions. Skilled workers disregarded, and socialists made use of, the frontiers.

These attitudes were not shared or comprehended in French Switzerland – where the attraction towards Paris somewhat resembled (but did not rival) their confederates' veneration for Heidelberg and Berlin.

As elsewhere, 1916 was a turning-point. The chasm between French and German Switzerland was recognized, and bridges thrown over it. Germany's defeat, slowly foreseen by those who at first had not doubted her victory for an instant, caused a painful and final disengagement from Prussian sympathies.

Combatants have smiled at Swiss war memorials, forgetting that the hardships of soldiers are not restricted to the instant of battle, but are felt in drill, sentry-go, camp, and marches, and in the whole artificial personality imposed by uniform, rifle, and knapsack – and felt more keenly if not culminating in real fight. The spontaneity of 1914 turned sour. Social cleavages became deeper. General staff, officers, corporals, and men carried social attitudes into army life and military resentments into social life. To these exacerbations were added an inefficient and too-long-postponed rationing system, a deep quarrel over the style of leadership (personified by the disputed election as General of Ulrich Wille – expositor of old and Prussian virtues), and at the end the scourge of a deadly strain of influenza.

Meanwhile, Swiss socialist leaders offered their country as a meeting-point for the conspirators of Europe, notably from Germany and Russia: Zimmerwald and Kienthal, famous for harbouring international conferences which seemed to mark the divergence of the ways of Marxism and democratic socialism, are villages of Canton Berne. It was from Zurich that the legendary 'sealed train' left carrying the despot, the committee men, and the victims of Bolshevist Russia. The new Russia maintained an embassy in Berne, together with (it was alleged but never quite proved) a network of sinister tentacles of subversion. On 9 December 1918 Germany was in full revolution, the Kaiser abdicated and fled, the republic was proclaimed in Munich, to be followed by the mutiny of the fleet in Kiel. The Swiss socialists had leaders, a revolutionary situation to exploit, and lacked only a revolutionary spark.

General Wille, disturbed by facts and alarmed by rumours, had pressed the civilian leaders for military mobilization to counter these civic dangers. The Federal Council seemed to concur, and (with diminishing ardour) implored him to remain at his post whenever he threatened to resign, but took no concrete action. The police power remained with the canton in Zurich (in whose government only one socialist, a Grütlian, sat) which had become used to the old man's emergencies. To force their hand (as it seems probable, for he had acted likewise before[10] for the same purpose), or for the obscure military urge attributed to the valiant duke of York, Wille moved the only usable full battalion from near Zurich to the Austrian frontier, ordering the battalion quartered by the Lake of Constance to Zurich: in the meanwhile the fermenting city was left almost defenceless.

The cantonal government, alarmed, called federal aid. Wille appointed the brisk young Colonel Sonderegger[11] to the local command, telling him to make maximum display of force. The spark found powder. A one-day protest strike was called in Zurich for Saturday 9 November, and this escalated into a nationwide General Strike on the Monday, Tuesday, and Wednesday. Plans had been laid on both sides, but the occasion was unexpected, and there was an element of accident and even of muddle.

When forbidden public assemblies took place in Zurich, the military intervened and proved master. A federal country has resources it can bring to play against any particular rebellious community: this is one of the secrets of the longevity of the Swiss state. Catholic troops from Inner Switzerland, French-speaking soldiers from Neuchâtel, peasantry from Thurgau, were in emergency available. But most effective in street-fighting proved the horsed cavalry, troopered by rich farmer lads, no friends of Bolshevism. There was a nasty rumour that in France troops of the victorious allies were poised to intervene: this has never been substantiated. Leadership of the workers' side was asserted by 'the committee of the Olten Conference', a body which had been kept in existence with just such an uncertain situation in mind. It represented the combined authority of the trade unions, the Social Democrat party, and the socialist parliamentary group, and it contained intelligence, courage, and resource. Whether its members hoped to overturn the established order and set up its own dictatorship is disputed: the allegation was denied, but gaps in the documents preserved suggest that both sides went farther with revolutionary and reactionary plans than they later cared to recollect.

The Federal Assembly was then called together: it stiffened the hitherto conciliatory Federal Council, and on the third day of the strike the President of the Confederation, with shaking hand, signed an ultimatum to be delivered to the Olten Committee: it wavered, and capitulated.

The Liberal-Radical party, to whom the duty had fallen of confronting and defeating the strike, could look back on seventy years of dominance. But under this dominance lay a bomb of which the fuse was already burning. In 1913 a 'popular initiative' for proportional election to the National Council had been handed in with due form, but voting was postponed during the war. On 13 October 1918, it was submitted to a referendum, and carried. The law was drafted quickly (with the aid of Emil Klöti, later socialist mayor of Zurich) and the new elections were brought forward. The National Council taking office at the end of 1919 was composed very differently to that of 1917.

The catholic-conservatives could no longer be considered unreconciled since their inclusion in the Federal Council. In Motta they now had a powerful minister, soon (1920) as President to take the office of Foreign Minister which he held to his death in 1940 – the best-known Swiss statesman of modern times – and at the same time (on the retirement of the conservative protestant Gustave Ador) they obtained a second member in the federal executive.

Finally, a rising tide of agricultural unrest provided a military and political backbone for the right wing. In Berne, Rudolf Minger had secured the defection of large numbers of radicals within the cantonal parliament, and it was these who formed themselves into a new political party with prospects of cantonal dominance and federal representation, the political arm of the Peasants' Secretariat, backed also by the financial support of the agricultural co-operatives. Farmers and industrial workers had interests in dearer and in cheaper food respectively, and during the hungry years of war their opposition had ripened into enmity.

The unions of French Switzerland had supported the strike unconvincedly. In the new realignment the chasm between French and German Switzerland closed. Some social bitterness between classes remained, to continue until the 1930s, when the issue shifted to the combination of the central democratic parties against the new extreme groupings – the final hard core of communists (now chiefly in French Switzerland) on the left, and the nearly or quite Fascist 'Fronts' on the right. To this reconciliation of the Centre, proportionality[12] greatly contributed.

To conciliate the workers, proportionality was also introduced into the executive council of Canton Zurich, the wielder of the police power in the most unruly industrial conurbation. The strike thus takes its place as the last successful cantonal *coup d'état*.

As with all great events, it is easy to see the strike as necessary, but difficult to evaluate its effects. It polarized some attitudes, to the right and the left. Others, having seen the abyss of civil war, reconciled themselves with their adversaries. In foreign affairs, it was convenient, and perhaps even justifiable, to blame the Russians. Diplomatic relations with the USSR were broken, and only resumed in 1945 – this is an incident that deserves to be recollected when discussing neutrality as a policy. The victors of the strike were the catholics of Inner Switzerland, and the peasantry, who had rallied to the established order: the debt to the horsed cavalry was remembered until its abolition in 1972. The defeated, however, were not the socialists, but the radicals, who for so long had 'been' Switzerland. But the strike was no one's legend. As soon as the trials which followed it were over (they were very fairly conducted, and with the mildest possible sentences), the parties to the struggle tried to forget the incident. It is only now, as the documents become available under a new fifty years rule, that it is being written about. From these dangerous archives the two contesting parties seem to have removed the fangs.

VII. 1937

Switzerland was a country of industrial unrest and strikes during the first third of the twentieth century. In 1936 the Swiss franc had to be sharply devalued. Fearing another outburst of economically senseless strikes, the government gave itself powers to 'adjudicate, without appeal, collective wage disputes which cannot be settled by agreement between the parties'. The employers as well as the unions saw with dismay that control of their destinies was being assumed by the governmental apparatus. Under the pressure of this threat, the employers and the principal unions of the metal-workers' industry came together, on the unions' initiative, with an agreement of their own, the Peace Agreement of 19 July 1937.

This agreement obliges both parties to resolve differences and disputes *nach Treue und Glauben*, in good faith, during the lifetime of the contract and to maintain industrial peace unconditionally, and in particular to avoid all recourse to strike or lock-out. To settle differences, there should first of all be agreement attempted at works' level. If that failed, then there was to be a conciliation board of three members to attempt an agreed settlement. If both parties agreed, then the decision of such a board could be made binding. But if they did not agree, then on the application of either party a special arbitration board was to be appointed whose decision would be final. There was further provision for a special arbitration board to fine one or other party who broke a condition of the agreement. Both employers and labour were to deposit a quarter of a million francs in the National Bank from which such a fine was to be paid.

The agreement was for two years in the first instance. It was then renewed by mutual consent for five years, and has been renewed for this period ever since, and is still (1974) in force. The Swiss believe that this agreement is the foundation and condition of their subsequent unbroken prosperity. It took very quickly a place in the national mythology, being compared with the Agreement of Stans (above, p. 85) and the mediation of Niklaus von Flüe. But it could equally have been found a niche in the mythology of another nation.

The time of formation of the agreement was not in any way unusually propitious. In appearance it is one-sided, for 'lock-outs' have a place in the rhetoric of strikers but seldom occur in nature. The circumstances of its formation were different to those of its successive renewals, which are preceded by continuous bargaining; the renewal is never taken for granted, and is regularly opposed by the extreme Left – the official Moscow Left as well as the provisional intellectual Left. In one set of terms the success of the agreement cannot be doubted: it has stopped strikes. In some years there have been no days whatever lost by strikes. The usual statistic 'Strikes: negligible or nil' has in recent decades been followed by 'Unemployment: negligible or nil'. The only country that seems to have been directly influenced by the Swiss example, and to have pursued similar policies since 1948, is the Federal Republic of Germany. In some of the years of renewal a comparison of the atmosphere of management–labour relations with Japan is tempting, but not in 1937.

The Labour Peace is an achievement of Swiss rationality which could probably be transferred to Great Britain. Here are some factors which affected it. First, there was no doubt of the resolution of the government to impose its will if the parties had not come to an agreement. It monopolized physical force, and was prepared to use it – against labour. Its weaknesses were in its opening to the extreme Right. Second, the fate of trade unions in Nazi Germany was known to all parties. Third, there was a parallel movement in the political sphere, the *Richtlinienbewegung* of Walter Stucki, intended as a collaboration among all democratic parties, but which would probably have turned out as a centre-left coalition. Except in the Socialist party, no politicians saw much in this for themselves, though there was considerable support at constituency level among liberals, radicals, and Peasant party members. On the level of practical day-to-day politics, the movement failed. Though it shared some emotional backing with the Peace Agreement, it was really independent of it. Fourth, apart from this sort of rallying against the common danger from Fascism, times were perilous. Switzerland was less far from civil war than she usually is. Concessions were made to the Right rather than to the social democrats. Fifth, Konrad Ilg, the signatory on the labour side, was extrovert and combative. He had been vice-president of the Olten Committee that led the General Strike of 1918. His difficulties within his union came from the communists. Ernst Dübi, on the side of management, was shy, introverted, and non-political: the abiding interest of his life was in grey cast-iron. Like most employers everywhere, he was in principle social-minded and ready to co-operate with workers and to treat them with fairness and courtesy. He had the cast of mind of a liberal conservative, with a larger touch of liberal-mindedness than one might expect. Sixth, the dates of renewal (1939, 1944, 1949, 1954, 1959, 1964, 1969) afford a great variety of circumstance and expectations, and do not suggest that the utility of the agreement to both parties was the product of transient circumstance (e.g., Nazi threats, expectations of slump, boom conditions, foreign labour). Seventh, the remarkable Swiss atmosphere of mutual co-operation and proportional distribution of the good things of politics, and the cult of a patriotic mythology, did not prevail before 1940, and has considerably weakened in recent years. It is consistent with the Peace Agreement, and in a very loose sense partly a consequence of it, but not a cause of it in the first instance. Eighth, it is arguable that some long-term disadvantage to trade unionism, regarded as an end and a profession in itself, has followed from the desuetude of the strike weapon. There may also prove to be some very long-term disadvantage to the competitiveness of Swiss industry or the liveliness of Swiss culture or social relationships. If so, these are indeed long-term phenomena, to be thought of in terms of a quarter of a century or more.[13]

VIII. 1940

During the years between the two World Wars it seemed for a time as if the Centre were going to fall out of Swiss politics, leaving a left wing dominated by the extreme Left, and right-wing parties dominated by the extreme Right. While the extreme Left obeyed a distant Moscow, the extreme Right was to look to closer allies, to Italy and to Germany. The Centre had to look to the League of Nations powers, Britain and France, and ultimately to the United States, irresolute and uninspiring friends from whom it was Swiss neutralist policy to maintain a certain distance.

The Left had its own difficulties. In 1919 the third Communist International had been proclaimed, followed by a congress in Moscow. Twenty-one conditions were drawn up, which were to be accepted without qualification and which can be summarized as total subjection to the velleities of the party in Moscow, making communism into an extension of the foreign policy of the USSR. After long argument, the majority of the Swiss Socialist party, with reluctance, rejected the conditions. The minority went forward to establish themselves as the Swiss Communist party. The social democrats, the majority, moved at various paces during the next twenty years towards an understanding with the social wings of the bourgeois political parties, first at local level, then at industrial level, and finally, by 1939, at the federal political level. For most social democrats the turning-point came in March 1933, with the establishment of a Germany ruled by a National Socialist party holding full powers.

Meanwhile defections from among the communists continued to refresh the socialist membership and leadership.

The Right was in part a reaction against the extreme Left, which seemed stronger and more revolutionary than we think today it was. The Peasant party was from the outset visualized as an anti-socialist party of the middle classes as well as an agrarian pressure-group. In catholic Switzerland there was a strongly anti-socialist bloc, and the Roman church was still engaged throughout the period in a friendly dialogue with Italian Fascism: the church saw socialism as anti-religious, anti-traditional, anti-family, and anti-authoritarian. The Right was further stiffened by certain very powerful military and financial groups and, more dangerous still in a climate of violence, by youth movements in the various parties – Young Peasants, Young Conservatives, Young Liberals, who had ideologies and slogans strongly reminiscent of their equivalents in Austria, Italy, and Germany.

After 1933 these groupings of the Right were joined by 'the Fronts' which mushroomed in the spring of that year. Of these it is not altogether easy to distinguish between the two sorts, the destructive and the harmless or positively healthy movements seeking a much-needed national unity and revival. Unfortunately the distinction became blurred, and many respected personalities of today look back with apprehension at things they said or sympathies they displayed in the 1930s: one cannot imagine, for example, that the *Freisinnige* of the city of Zurich look back with nostalgia on the torchlight procession they shared with the National Front in September 1933 – to celebrate the establishment of joint party-lists in the municipal elections – or that the honorary doctorate which the University of Lausanne conferred on Mussolini in 1937, on the occasion of its centenary celebrations, added in fact as much honour to the university as the *Gazette de Lausanne* then claimed.

The numerical strength of the extreme Right is difficult to gauge. The referendum for a Total Revision of the Constitution in September 1935 showed 197,000 in favour, that is to say winnable for the extreme Right, and 512,000 against.[14] The referendum against Freemasonry of November 1937 showed 235,000 for the proposal and 515,000 opposing it. Both referendums were designed to gain support from the catholic-conservative Right as well as from the Fronts. In local elections, the National Front (Fascist) party sometimes attained 15 per cent of the votes, but usually only about half this proportion even in districts particularly suitable for them. It happened that nationwide elections for the National Council fell at a time when the Fronts were not at their height: they only ever elected one member (1.5 per cent of votes, in 1935: the communists had 1.4 per cent; but these parties did not put up candidates in many cantons). To have been the largest party in Switzerland, and thereby to have attained power in the existing international situation, they would probably have needed 20 per cent of the votes – depending, of course, at whose expense they gained these votes. But the strength varied remarkably from one month to another. Only in 1933, the first months of 1935, and in 1940, did the Fronts seem a menace inside the democratic system.

But the gross of the Swiss people (especially in German Switzerland) held firm and, more important in the short run, so did the main newspapers, no doubt with minor aberrations not now much celebrated. To these defenders of democracy was added an informal resistance group, of people who took part in politics with some reluctance, university teachers, young officers, journalists, pleasant middle-class men and women up and down the land: these in the last resort saved their country, together with solid trade unionists and unsung thousands who scorned the new movement just because it was new.

The rallying-point of these ordinary people was the National Exhibition, the *Landesausstellung* (*Landi*) in Zurich in 1939. The modern history of Switzerland can be written in terms of such exhibitions, and the tone set by that of 1939 lasted until the exhibition held in Lausanne in 1964. It was a serious affair, expressing itself visually in the *Heimatstil* mode (the arts and crafts, rural industries, flowers on natural wood, home-weave style). It placed an emphasis on democratic and military traditions and on localism – it was then that every commune in the country granted itself a coat-of-arms. It was clean, historicizing, rural, nice, healthy, with no hint of self-mockery, and this was the picture the Swiss presented to foreigners until the 1960s. The exhibition was master-minded by the socialist mayor of Zurich, Emil Klöti: this socialist patronage is significant. In the values the *Landi* expressed, kinships in taste with National Socialism can be found, but it was a rival and more durable ideal that was presented; even if it was in retrospect a second-rate ideal, it was sincere and valid, attainable, and self-consistent.

In this mood, when war broke out, Switzerland found a symbol: with the support of Federal Councillor Minger (an archetypal lowland working-farmer from Berne, who was Minister of Defence) Henri Guisan was elected as General-in-Chief of the Army. He was a gentleman farmer from Vaud, son of an upper-middle-class family, *charakterfest*, unassuming but with a quiet sense of drama, the picture of a professional officer. His photograph was for a generation in every inn, and in most homes: his rare (but highly-placed) opponents preferred that of General Wille-von Bismarck.[15] Guisan represented the concept of neutrality as a quality of the soul, not pacifism but stead-fastness.

The other members of the wartime Federal Council, apart from Minger, however, also represented permanent Swiss archetypes which are less compellingly attractive. There was Motta, soon to die, who had a touch of the Lloyd George; Pilet-Golaz, talented but labile; Wetter, vice-president of the *Vorort*, and elected because Klöti was, after all, a socialist and could therefore not quite be trusted; the lightweight Celio, who succeeded Motta; Etter, the model pupil of a catholic seminary – and so on. Such Federal Councillors gave not the same impression of steadfastness as Guisan. In retrospect, some of them seem fellow travellers of the dominant continental power, Hitler's Germany, while Guisan represented Switzerland in her aspect as being spiritually on the side of the Allies.

On 9 April 1940 the Germans attacked Denmark and Norway, on 10 May they invaded Belgium and Holland. Holland capitulated. Belgium capitulated. Dunkirk was evacuated by 4 June; on 10 June Italy entered the war, and on the 17th France capitulated. On 22 June 1941 the Germans invaded Russia, relieving Switzerland of immediate pressure.

The events of 1940 within Switzerland, much argued over, have entered into the canon of history as follows: (i) on 10 May 1940 there was an outward suggestion of panic as a large number of families, the prudent and, conspicuously, the more wealthy, decided to transfer themselves into safety in Inner Switzerland, by car and by train. (ii) On 25 June, Pilet-Golaz, President of the Confederation, delivered a radio address suggestive of a future Swiss capitulation. (iii) On 25 July, General Guisan delivered an equally famous allocution to his senior officers on the Rütli, initiating the new strategy of the Alpine Redoubt. (iv) On 10 September 1940 Pilet received a deputation of the Frontist movement. (v) On 15 November, 173 prominent Swiss submitted a Memorial suggestive of defeatism ('the Submission of the 200') to the Federal Council. (vi) Finally, on 19 November 1940, the National Movement of Switzerland – the combined Swiss Frontist movement – was declared illegal, and dissolved by an ordinance of the Federal Council. Two other events, less discussed in the literature, may be added: Guisan's own attempts at appeasement (a suggested mission of Carl Burckhardt under cover of the Red Cross to Hitler[16] of 8 August and 9 November), and Minger's resignation in December.

The policies between which these acts oscillate are termed in Switzerland *Anpassung* – adaptation; but the word has acquired ugly overtones in the subsequent controversies – and *Widerstand*, resistance.

All these incidents deserve further discussion. Indeed, they are ripe for re-evaluation, but it will here suffice to say more about Pilet's wireless speech, and Guisan's Rütli *Offiziersrapport*.[17]

There is neither reason to doubt Hitler's latent intention some day to annexe Switzerland, nor his advantage in doing so, nor his capacity to do it. There is equally no reason to doubt his preference for a peaceable annexation, other things being equal, over a warlike one. For most of the period of the war, he was occupied chasing greater game; but from time to time there were occasions when the matter would have been rather easy in terms of logistics and tempting in terms of advantage. It was Switzerland's good fortune that moments of *Anpassung* rather coincided with moments of maximum threat. Each time invasion was convenient for Germany it seemed that, within a brief delay, the country would surrender itself willingly. One speaks in this context of good fortune, and it does seem not to have been a result of deliberate contrivance, but possibly one should rather praise the institutions of government and society that made this good fortune possible. As regards personal judgements on states- men and soldiers, it is hard to separate a justifiable non-moral ex- pectation that Germany was destined to win from a weakness of character or a disloyalty to the fatherland. In retrospect, compliance and defiance were applied in exactly the correct proportions, though one sometimes finds oneself wishing that a very small extra dose of defiance had been risked.

PILET-GOLAZ'S RADIO TALK OF 25 JUNE 1940

When France fell, Pilet was asked (it seems) by military, and other, circles, through Minger, to give the nation a lead by a talk on the wireless. Pilet's speech was written by himself and bears his personal style; it contains echoes of Nazi rhetorical clichés, parti- cularly in the German translation.[18] It was broadcast by himself in French, and by Federal Councillors Etter and Celio in German and Italian, and, it seems, approved by the full Federal Council after being broadcast, so there can be dispute about how far it was a personal or collegiate action.

Pilet's speech does not now seem so very bad. It has a disagreeable air of double-talk, not of a message of compliance concealing the opposite intention to those in the know, but of a message of crocodile tears concealing underlying delight at the fall of France and the victory of the New Order: 'it would be dangerous to abandon ourself to illusions of careless happiness', for 'peace is not yet achieved and the British empire proclaims its resolution to pursue the war on land, sea, and air.' In internal affairs, the Swiss are adjured

to give up their cosy, folksy ways, drop their habits of inter- minable discussion, and act or, rather, close their ranks behind the

Federal Council, be calm as it is calm, firm as it is firm, following it as a trustworthy and devoted guide. So let all show the true solidarity of action, not of words or processions, action which cements the national community in confidence and unity, by work and order, not worm-eaten formulas, etc., etc.

To read it today is to be depressed and to find distasteful the mixture of slang, jargon, and scraps of piety. One realizes that the outdated formulas and folksy ways are constitutional law and democracy, and the references to 'Europe' are to Hitler's Europe. There was included a promise of partial demobilization, 'now that war no longer raged along the frontiers' (as if the threat had all along been from France) and this was, in fact, the only action that followed.

The echo was unfavourable, except from the Fronts, from Germany, and from sections of the Peasant party, but it was some days before the revulsion of ordinary people imposed itself fully on their representatives or the press.

How are we to interpret the speech? As an act of averting the anger of Germany and fending off the immediate danger[19] it was successful. In internal affairs it would have made sense if a *coup d'état* by the President or the Federal Council had in fact been prepared or imminent. But the trial flight of authoritarianism was not applauded. A group of officers laid plans for a counter-*coup* if there were a surrender to the Germans, and desperate resistance so as to save the honour of Switzerland – and their country's resurrection should the Allies after all win the war. The Pilet affair has the same ambiguity as the General Strike of 1918, paddling in the Rubicon and then, because the water is turbulent, paddling back.

GENERAL GUISAN'S ADDRESS TO HIS OFFICERS ON THE RÜTLI, 25 JULY 1940

Within a week after Pilet's wireless talk, there was a partial demobilization, coinciding with, and perhaps facilitating, a change of strategic concept by the army. The number of men under arms was reduced from 400,000 to 150,000, and this at a time – the only time during the whole war, as it was to prove – when the German army could have annexed Switzerland without taking any troops from another active front. Demobilization offered the advantage of propitiating the Germans, but also of enabling the Federal Council (if it were carried through) to get rid of an awkward commander-in-chief, such as Guisan was proving, and then asking the parliament to elect a more compliant one, Däniker or Ulrich Wille, General Wille's son.

Guisan had other intentions. With the assent of Minger, and probably of the Federal Council as a whole, he formed a strategy of withdrawing the whole body of the defence force into the alpine *réduit*, based on Urseren and its four approaches, straddling the Gotthard and immediately above the railway tunnel which was the key to Germany's links with northern Italian industry. To announce this strategy he summoned all officers exercising a command, about six hundred in number, to the Rütli meadow, embarking the whole lot of them on a single paddle-boat to cross the lake from Lucerne – a risky venture with a resolute and swift enemy not far away. Of the allocution there is no authentic text – the General spoke extemporaneously for half an hour and in German. The political message was unambiguous, *Widerstand*, resistance, not *Anpassung*.

There are three aspects of this speech to notice and of the policy resulting from it.

As addressed to the officers and to the army and people of Switzerland, it was a message of uncompromising clarity, to fight it out till the end against all comers. This was probably the resolution of the people at large, in any event, but now it was announced by the natural leader of the nation, and it became unquestioned orthodoxy – at least, in retrospect. An order of the day which concluded the speech was transmitted to every soldier in the army, and appeared in the press. As addressed to the Federal Council, it must have seemed to announce an alternative policy to its own 'wait and see', and to set up the General as an alternative leader. Thenceforth he would have the army under his immediate hand, and in the event of actual invasion he would have been the legitimate head of that part of Switzerland which remained free. From the standpoint of the Federal Council, the Rütli demonstration was a sort of quiet *coup d'état*, or rather, a counter-*coup* to Pilet-Golaz's claim to total authority made in the wireless speech of exactly a month before. From the standpoint of Swiss foreign policy, the speech needed to be disavowed in the presence of the German and Italian diplomatic representatives, but it was welcomed in Britain and the United States, in whose eyes it made the case after the war for considering Switzerland as a colleague rather than as a fellow traveller of Hitler.[20] Finally, in its psychological effect on Hitler it was masterly, for it established Switzerland as different from those other neutrals which had allowed themselves to disintegrate at, or before, the first attack. Its psychological effect on the people of Switzerland was more complex, for they saw nine-tenths of the inhabitants and two-thirds of the land abandoned to the enemy in the event of an invasion, and it was a strange experience for a soldier to sit in the mountains in relative immediate safety, behind his family and the undefended cities in the plateau.

It is this experience, of political resistance and of the Alpine Redoubt, which has 'made' contemporary Switzerland, in the sense in which revulsion against the Nazi occupation has made modern Austria. Having started some years too late, the mood of the Rütli survived its necessity for a generation, and it was only in 1964 that it started to crumble: today it divides the older generation from the prevailing civilization of the young. It has left a permanent addition to the Swiss mythology. As in 1815, and at certain other periods of crisis, the history of Switzerland was partly made in Britain and Russia, but partly also by the Swiss people themselves, who powerfully assisted fortune by their courage.

IX. *1964*

The year 1964 was the year of the Expo, the National Exhibition, held in Lausanne. The Expo caused a wave of horror in German Switzerland, and the delegation planned from Aargau refused to take part. Traditional Switzerland had expected a re-enactment of the *Landi*, the Zurich Exhibition of 1939, but the mood was an entirely different one, owing something perhaps to a late echo of the Festival of Britain of 1951. There was an air of gaiety, even lightheartedness. The symbol of the three hands (the Oath of Rütli) was in iron, jagged, like a halberd – entirely appropriate in reality – while, on the other hand, the Tell story was alluded to with a light air of mockery. The drums of triumphalism were silent, the Switzerland presented was the young persons' technology-based country, concealing an intensely deep sentimentalism for the past at which the young people seemed themselves to be smiling, but from which they were unable to free themselves. When I visited it, the Expo seemed to me to hit exactly the right mood, and to be by no means too *avant-garde*, but my German Swiss friends found themselves surprised at their own, eventual, acceptance of this new picture of themselves. For them, it was like looking at a passport photograph and seeing oneself ten years younger, and really becoming younger. Or, in another simile, it reduced Switzerland's culture-lag by ten years.

At the same time as the exhibition there was another event as destructive of the old order. The Vaudois statesman Chaudet was being pilloried in the National Council for his part in the 'Mirage affair'. It was a strange spectacle, to one used to the rather ineffectual appearance of this assembly, to see the chamber and the galleries full, to feel the spectators' tenseness, and hear the philippic of National Councillor Fürgler (now in the Federal Council) directing the lightning of the storm cloud towards Chaudet, the Minister of the Army. By international standards, the Mirage aircraft scandal was not a very terrible matter, not as bad as its contemporary Blue Streak affair in Britain. But it started off a mood of criticism and procedural reform in Swiss government which has still not quite spent itself.

The Expo and the Mirage affair were positive and negative shocks causing a profound change of mood. After 1930 Switzerland had stood still, even gone quietly backwards, under the influence of a historicism typified by the writings of Gonzague de Reynold. The classic of this mood is Reynold's *La Démocratie et la Suisse*,[21] where the two parties in the title are represented in some kind of dialectical relationship. After 1964 (or some such date, for this one is only chosen as a sort of symbol) Switzerland modernized her attitudes and, in catholic Switzerland, this coincided with the shattering of the picture of the world set by Pius IX in the Roman church's great counter-revolution of 1848 to 1870. This modernization is the gift of French Switzerland to German.

With change, as with economic development, there is a sort of take-off stage, after which people lose attachment to existing institutions, and to change things still more is a little easier than leaving them alone. Switzerland is nearing that stage, and the project for a total revision of the constitution (originally a seminar project at Basle) is undermining confidence in the parts of the constitution which are distinctively Swiss. Of this movement it is convenient to take 1964 as the start. In retrospect, also, it seems (what was not clear at the time) that around 1964 the struggle to preserve the peasantry had become hopeless, and the ethos of the country had taken the decisive step from being land-based to being city-based, as the economy of the country had been for a century or more. Some such year as 1964, too, may be taken as the point of no return for another sad progress. The old political and social structure had been given its tone, not only by the landowning peasant, but also by the owner-manager of very small commercial and industrial enterprises. The future lies with a different structure of society, where the tone is given by employees of very large enterprises, enterprises in which the visible managers are themselves employees too. In such a society, nominal ownership may be diffused among elderly members of the upper professional classes, but the effective control is with a technically highly qualified, but rather small and inconspicuous, managerial élite. It is interesting to see how far the old values can be adapted to the new reality.

NOTES

[1] Physical personal serfdom had almost everywhere disappeared, except as a liability to certain taxes, for the most part as early as the Reformation, and in the democratic cantons a century or more earlier.

[2] A collaborationist regime in 1940, with Gonzague de Reynold as *Landamman* of Switzerland, would not have looked very different from the Napoleonic Swiss Diet.

3 The village was Amden: on a sunny terrace above the Walensee, it is now a tourist resort. In the election of 1845, there were 75 liberals and 75 conservatives in the cantonal parliament of St Gallen. In the next election, 1847, the district known as the Gaster (from Latin *castra*) in which Amden lies returned a clean liberal ticket of six members, thanks to the vote of that village – where the two leading families had quarrelled. There was dark and justified suspicion, but the parliamentary majority decided the disputed election in its own favour with the result that the parliament came to hold 77 liberals and only 73 conservatives. With the majority of one canton the Federal Diet then was able to declare the Sonderbund unconstitutional, whereupon the civil war became unavoidable. Had some fifty peasants' votes been transferred to the other side, the decision could have been different.

4 He came to Geneva as a refugee in 1815, having as a young professor of law at Bologna supported Murat. He obtained so great a reputation in Geneva by his lectures on Roman Law that citizenship was conferred on him, and by 1820 he was elected to the Great Council. He represented Geneva at the Federal Diet in 1832. In this capacity he nearly endowed Switzerland with a federal basic law, *le pacte Rossi*, a project which left its mark on the Constitution of 1848. However, it was rejected, and Rossi went to France in dudgeon and despair, but rapidly found a post as professor of political economy. By 1836 he had been elected member of the French Academy, and in 1839 ennobled as Count Rossi. In 1845 he was sent as ambassador of France to Rome and then, when the July Monarchy fell, Pope Pius IX took him into his service as Minister of the Interior of the Papal States. In this capacity he was assassinated by a soldier while inspecting troops. He wrote books on Roman Law and on Political Economy: the latter brought him fame. What a life!

5 An environment which influenced the French Prime Minister, Guizot, a protestant who had lived in Geneva.

6 Or, as more accurately characterized by Professor Gruner, a 'consensus democracy steered by interests' (*Verbandsgelenkte Konsensus-Demokratie*).

7 In 1837, it is reckoned, 2.5 per cent of the population of Berne canton had the vote, and they voted for an electoral college.

8 Papal Encyclical *Quanta Cura* (The Syllabus of Errors).

9 In 1890 the first socialist was elected to the National Council, and in the years following, increasing numbers of social democrats were elected to the cantonal Great Councils.

10 On 15 June 1918. 'I told you that if Herzog was not arrested you were to tell the government of Zurich I would withdraw the troops from there' (my paraphrase). Letter from Wille to Colonel Reiser, 17 June 1918. This is one of the *trouvailles* in Willi Gautschi, *Dokumente zum Landesstreik 1918*, Zurich, etc., 1971, 90. As the instructions themselves have disappeared, this letter is a crux for anyone who maintains the documents have not been selectively weeded, in this case carelessly.

11 Sonderegger, hero of the Right, was later promoted to the highest military post, from which he resigned spectacularly. He drifted into frontist company, but found no Colombey.

12 The National Council before and after P.R.: In 1917 it contained 120 radicals (with liberals and democrats); 42 catholic-conservatives; 22 socialists; and 4 independent members (unclassified). In 1919, 76 radicals (with liberals and democrats); 41 catholic-conservatives; 41 socialists; 29 Peasants' party; and two independents. (Figures from Erich Gruner, Karl Frei, *et al.*, *Die schweizerische Bundesversammlung 1848–1920*, Berne, 1966. Slightly different figures are given in other sources, because of a different interpretation.) The new constellations proved permanent.

13 A translation of the text of the agreement is given in *Swiss Pioneers of Economics and Technology* (no. 2 in the English-language series), *The Peace Agreement in the Swiss Engineering and Metalworking Industries: Konrad Ilg and Ernst Dübi*, Verein für Wirtschaftshistorische Studien, Zurich, 1967. (It was renewed in 1974.)

14 These figures should be doubled to allow for men-only suffrage, and then multiplied by ten for comparison with Britain.

15 It is the Swiss custom, dating from the 1840s, to hyphenate the wife's name with that of the husband. It often produces rather distinguished-sounding combinations, for it runs parallel with the older, and now German, custom of hyphenat-

ing the name with the ancestral seat of noble families. There is an amusing tale by Gottfried Keller about the custom when it was an innovation. In this instance, it was of course General Wille's enemies who used the wife's name in this manner.

[16] 'Monsieur Burckhardt ne serait-il pas particulièrement qualifié pour tenter un apaisement et instituer une collaboration?' (9 November 1940). 'La Croix-Rouge internationale pourrait servir comme paravent' (14 August 1940). See Bonjour, *Geschichte der schweizerischen Neutralität*, 2nd ed., 6 vols., Basle etc., 1965–70, IV, 237, 229. The authenticity of this letter has been doubted. For Minger's resignation, see ibid., 241. Minger, and Pilet, saw the dangers to their country of such an initiative.

[17] The French words *réduit* and *rapport* have passed into both High German and dialect as technical terms in this context.

[18] French text in Bonjour, op. cit. As Bonjour points out, the French word *guide* is translated *Führer* in German. The student of the Swiss Constitution should notice the role of the President as President, often understated, and recollect the similar role played by the President of the Confederation in the General Strike. The emergency power is still his.

[19] In the German military plan for the invasion of Switzerland, Code Word *Fall Tannenbaum*, less than 48 hours were allowed between crossing the border and the occupation of Berne, Zurich, and Lucerne. This was before the Alpine Redoubt.

[20] The heads of indictment against Switzerland would be: the economic vassalage to the German war-machine, profitable but dishonourable, and various incidents such as the return, direct to Germany, for use against the British, of war material brought by the defeated French army to neutral soil or the dispatch of medical missions to the German front against Russia, or the return of Polish soldiers to Germany, or the diplomatic non-recognition of Russia, and so on. The reason for these transgressions of strict neutrality was not ill-will, but pressure from Germany. However, a neutral has the obligation as a part of its neutrality to defend itself from un-neutral pressure.

[21] Berne, 1929. It is dedicated to 'My Father, Alphonse-Marie Baron de Reynold de Cressier, my Uncles Arthur de Techtermann and Rudolphe Baron de Reding-Biberegg, and my first cousin Jean-Joseph-Georges Baron de Montenach, who have made me the Swiss that I am'. This is a book to be read with astonishment, to see a Switzerland not usually presented to the foreigner. But for pleasure, I would recommend Reynold's *Cités et Pays suisses*, Lausanne, 1914–20 as a book to accompany a visitor who is travelling in order to enjoy what he sees. Since the publication of this classic work, the Swiss themselves have come to know their own country much better.

CHAPTER 5

Government and Institutions

I. Direct Democracy

SWITZERLAND MAINTAINS an honourable position in many fields
of activity, but it is generally agreed that in the field of government
she holds a light to the world which justifies her independence and
material comfort. This especially applies to the institution for which
Switzerland is best known, that is to say to 'pure democracy' – the
referendum in its various forms.

The other peculiar institutions of Swiss government are (ii) the
collegiate executive cabinet ('The Federal Council'); (iii) federalism
(with which we may bracket subordinate local government); and
(iv) neutrality.

The modern Swiss federal referendum draws one tap-root and its
name from the federal old regime. The word is an abbreviation of
ad referendum[1] 'for referring back' or 'subject to referral back': in the
Confederacy of the Thirteen Cantons it was connected with the
'instructions' by which a delegate to the confederal Diet was normally bound by his government back home, so that decisions were
often delayed while members took back questions *ad referendum et
instruendum* and obtained the advice and instructions of their own
councils in their native cantons. Such instructions are forbidden by
today's constitution. In retrospect, the whole institution of instructions is regarded as undemocratic, but when it had been practised in
the allied republics of Grisons and Valais, themselves confederacies
with unchecked democratic sovereignty, the institution had had a
democratic content in that the assent of all free men enjoying full
rights was involved. There had been a similar institution even in the
city cantons in the fifteenth and sixteenth centuries, but it had been
driven into disuse (though never quite into oblivion) by the arrogance
and absolutist tendencies of the patriciates.

In its modern form, however, the main root of the referendum is
in the constitutional plebiscite, first used, and misused,[2] in the Helvetic Republic to provide a new revolutionary legitimacy for the usurpers. This legitimacy was again claimed by the liberals for their *coup
d'état* constitutions of 1830–35, though they only ventured upon a
restricted franchise and sometimes wisely instituted on a publicly

spoken vote, recorded by an electoral committee itself politically composed with some care. In 1839 a new discovery was made with large implications, that there lurked behind the enfranchised notables a substantial array of simple people who were by no means liberal in their political opinions, and whose unfalsified vote would ensure power for the conservatives of a religious tinge. The cause of democraticness was then taken up by the Right, both protestant and catholic, to mobilize the silent forces, if not of conservatism, at least of negativity.

Under the Restoration (1813–31) in the Swiss cantons, the cantonal Great Councils were held in check by their own conservatism and by a traditional respect for the executive Petty Councils, but with the Liberal Regeneration (1831–47) the full possibilities for mischief of a sovereign Great Council as legislator in a sovereign canton could be realized all too easily. Sometimes the Great Council (the parliament) was held in check by a dynamic leader who could treat his canton almost as a tiny monarchy, sometimes the ambitions of the members of the legislative council could be channelled into the quiet waters of jobbery and patronage. But in the absence of a pre-existent monarchy, the best check was appeal to the people, an appeal, moreover, which could pre-empt a *coup d'état* or legitimize a usurpation. The negativing device of a referendum, moreover, can serve not only to check a particular mischievous innovation, but also to express a general unease with government, striking down a needed law like a blind goddess, without apparent reason.

Cantonal history shows one style of rule succeeding another; at times there has been intense ideological activity, but for long periods the rewards of office have quietly spilled over into economic life, recompensing the politician but also forcing men into politics who would gladly have spent their lives within the confines of the spinning of money. That so many entrepreneurs in the nineteenth century served in the office of communal president, is not entirely due to disinterested and widely dispersed public spirit: until recent generations local political activity was a necessity of life. Even on the federal level, Gottlieb Duttweiler would not have founded a Federal party, the *Landesring*, unless life had been made commercially intolerable by cantonal (and ultimately, Federal) legislation directed against his firm 'Migros'.

The ambition of the masterful leader sometimes itself fostered the institution of the referendum. The ambitious outsider can use the call for one still more democratic device in order to make his entry into the ranks of the privileged on the shoulders of the people – it is extraordinarily difficult to *oppose* a democratic device, especially if it has a good chance of being adopted eventually – and the ambitious

man will find in 'the people' a more receptive audience than his own
legislative council. Nearly every canton has had its period of a
dominant personality, a tribune who used federal power (through a
seat on the National Council, and an ability to deliver the goods of
cantonal acquiescence in Berne), but who had a secure base in
referendum democracy, communicating with his electors preferably
by his own newspaper and, usually, with his left hand trailing in the
waters of economic activity, a big hotel, a railway, an electricity-
works, or so on.

It is now necessary to come to the detail of the referendum, though
the detail is less important than the general possibility of appeal to
the people, and this in turn is less important than the implied threat
of such an appeal as a permanent factor in daily life. First, historically, came the *Constitutional Referendum*. There being no other source
of legitimacy available, amendments to the constitution, federal and
cantonal, are submitted to a referendum. In the case of the Confederation, this (as has been said) is the double vote of people and
cantons, whereby the majority of those casting valid votes is taken
into account, and then the same votes are reckoned according to the
cantons within whose boundaries the votes were cast.[3]

In the case of the cantons, there is no equivalent of the double
majority, and in fact the Federal Constitution by implication pre-
vents a canton from anchoring its constitution in a qualified majority
or a majority of districts, so there is in a sense no greater sanctity to
be attached to a cantonal constitution than to a cantonal law, unless
the two conflict, since they are amended and made by the same
college.

In the second place, there is the *Popular Initiative* of an amendment
to the constitution, the device from which the other institutions of
immediate democracy have spread. In the case of the Confederation, if 50,000 voters' signatures can be collected and authenticated
within six months, then this is a valid constitutional initiative, which
'must' in due course be submitted to People and Cantons. The
financial cost of doing this varies, a petition with the right sort of
backing may cost rather little and the initiators can send the form of
words to voters with a post-prepaid reply, and ask for financial contributions to the good cause at the same time (as with the Schwarzenbach Initiative; below, p. 211). A million francs, or a bit more,
should suffice to launch the most mischievous and unmeritorious of
petitions (even though, in 1971, a federal amendment was successfully initiated at little expense by a thoroughly nice-minded group of
idealists, chiefly schoolmasters, to moderate persecution of conscientious objectors to military service). But most amendments are
initiated by interest groups or parties from motives where high-

mindedness is sharpened by a more direct advantage. The extreme Left find it a regular and convenient vehicle of electoral propaganda, and in the past the extreme Right have used it for the same purpose.

Thirdly, there is the federal *Legislative Challenge*. There is a delay of ninety days after publication of a 'Law' (a technical term in Switzerland – there are other forms of legislation), during which it may be challenged by a petition bearing a modest number of signatures (30,000). This was an innovation of 1874, based on cantonal precedent. There have been various methods used to evade this provision, successful in their day, which have now been halted by further constitutional amendments. If the requisite number of signatures (duly authenticated) is collected within the time limit, then there is (or should be) a votation.[4]

What usually impresses observers is the direct negative effect of this referendum procedure, striking down laws passed by the parliament and therefore having a conservative and delaying tendency. The positive effect is equally significant. In time, institutions adapt themselves to the referendum and are formed by it: the great political pressure-groups which give Swiss public life a corporative quality were called forth by the legislative referendum as well as by the constitutional initiative. In its early years, after 1874, a series of great negative decisions by the alliance (on a referendum level) between catholics and socialists threatened to bring federal political life to a standstill, until, in 1891, the catholics were bought off by a seat in the executive. Organized minorities can use the challenge to improve their bargaining position. The shadow of the challenge reaches very far back into legislative procedure, and the threat of it may be uttered at the early stage before the draft law has reached parliamentary debate: the art of legislating is the art of avoiding the legislative challenge.

TREATIES

The same procedure was adapted to International Treaties in 1921, though the subtlety of constitutional lawyers has here also introduced a possibility of evasion. As with Laws, a petition of 30,000 citizens is followed by a simple majority votation (i.e., not reckoning the cantonal vote). Indeed, to reckon the cantonal vote goes clean against the greatest attainment of 1848, which was to remove the cantons completely from foreign policy. However, partly to reward the catholics for their help in suppressing the General Strike of 1918, the decision to join the League of Nations was taken through the double majority of people and cantons. In theory, therefore, entry to the League was a constitutional amendment, but it was not treated as such when Switzerland left. This unconstitutional procedure was repeated in 1972 when Switzerland associated with the EEC. This procedure was adopted by a simple fiat of the government, assented to by the two chambers. It was done partly because it is thought to be vaguely more 'democratic' (i.e., more negative) to count Unterwalden and Uri as equals of Zurich and Berne, and partly because of a widespread impression that somewhere or other in the constitution there is a provision obliging the Confederation to be neutral, or that neutrality and sovereignty are so indistinguishable that any restriction of sovereignty must have a constitutional amendment.

The referendum is even more highly developed on the cantonal (and communal) level, where there is also a *Finance* Referendum, and a *Legislative* Initiative. The legislative referendum is sometimes compulsory for all cantonal laws, as is the finance referendum above a certain sum – below that sum being 'facultative', i.e., dependent on a challenge. Strange institutions such as the Recall (to remove a cantonal executive councillor from office) have been tried, usually only once. For a century the tendency was to increase such rights, and many a cantonal political career has been founded on increasing them. But saturation has now been reached, and they are gradually being diminished.

II. The Federal Executive

The Federal Council is a cabinet of seven members, which can either be regarded as the executive of the federal parliament or, more realistically, as simply 'the executive'. The constitution lays down (Article 103) that 'The business of the Federal Council shall be divided into departments and one of its members shall be at the head of each. Decisions shall be in the name and by the authority of the Federal Council'. The wording is very careful. The seven departments are: Foreign Affairs ('The Political Department'), Interior, Justice and Police, Military, Finance, Public Economy, Posts and Railways. The problem remains of who takes the decisions, the Federal Council as a body and the majority thereof, or the individual ministers subject to the ultimate sanction of the whole Federal Council? It might be thought that the question is the more pressing because of the composition of the council in a rough proportion to the strength of the parties in the country. In practice the disagreements seem to have been more bitter in the nineteenth century when the liberal-radical majority in the National Council[5] monopolized the federal executive council, and at present there seems to be general acceptance of the rules of the game, rules which are still not quite identical with the rules of the constitution, as expanded by legislation. A great deal of decision-making is left to the discretion of the individual minister, but that is to say that the decision is drafted by a senior federal official, whose attitude and background is likely to be close to that of the Establishment in general, and of the heads of legislative committees, judges and cantonal office-holders in particular, as well as of the liberal press and, indeed, of the paid officers of the vested interests. So when the official's advice is sought, and taken, it is likely to be found consistent with the policies of other departments. The problem for the individual minister is rather what happens when the Federal Council as a whole decides against his firm convictions or (a rather different matter) against the convictions he is supposed to hold as the nominee of a particular party, and whether by a wink or a nod or an express statement he makes known his disagreement. Biographies and newspapers and parliamentary proceedings afford material for a wide-ranging discussion of this point, which must be reserved for specialists.

The mode of election of the Federal Council is by the two parliamentary chambers in joint session.[6] The constitutional tenure of office is for the full period of the legislature, four years. In practice, the first important business of a newly elected National Council is to meet (with its 200 members augmented by the 44 Councillors of States) to re-elect the former members of the Federal Council who wish to stand. There may then well be a vacancy or two vacancies, occasionally more. But it is not a question of looking around to see who, in an abstract way, would be most suited to the job: there are certain political constellations which narrow the field to a particular party, confession, canton, and language, and there may also be a departmental requirement, an expert in finance or foreign affairs, though it is surprising how versatile statesmen are when in reach of high office.

The constitution here only lays down that not more than one Federal Councillor shall be 'chosen from the same canton', a provision that has lost much of its meaning. Cantons Zurich and Berne are large and important enough always to have had a Federal Councillor, and Vaud has nearly always had one. The German and French languages must be suitably represented over the years, and Italian must have a fair look-in. Catholics will have at least two members. The main regions of Switzerland must be propitiated in turn, which especially means some respect must be paid to east Switzerland.

Above all, the claims of political party are to be satisfied. Since 1959, the 'magic formula' has prevailed, two radicals, two catholics, two socialists, and one Peasant. It is normally expected that a good candidate will have sat in one or other house of parliament and have some basis of power back home, high cantonal office, a position in the party hierarchy, or the mayorship of a city – positions he will, of course, have to sacrifice on election. All in all, when these and some other requirements[7] have been met, the number of possible candidates for a particular vacancy is seldom large, varying from two to half a dozen.

Who elects? A great man sometimes imposes himself. Not only the historical parties, but even the socialists, usually manage to choose their own Federal Councillors themselves. Distinguished and impressive as is the hall of fame of those elected, the list of those who on one or another occasion stood for election and were not elected, or have refused election, contains names not less illustrious. In this century, for example, Emil Klöti was twice a candidate: the election of a socialist would have redeemed a promise made during the General Strike, but in 1928 an editor of the *Neue Zürcher Zeitung* was preferred to him, and in 1938 the chairman of the Employers' Federation. Neither of these two gentlemen made a positive mark on the history of their country while in its supreme magistracy. Of course, to include a social democrat, even Klöti, is a great political decision which lies beyond concerns for persons or private morality, but within a political party, also, the more distinguished candidate has often been passed over in favour of the routine personality. In the long run, this leadership by the second best has had consequences for the way in which others see the Swiss, and the way they see themselves and the possibilities afforded by the life of politics.

In the cantons, executive councillors are now 'chosen' by the electorate at large (with the exception of Berne, and the complication of election by the *Landsgemeinde* in certain tiny cantons). This probably increases the authoritativeness of the executive council as a body, but it is hard to generalize. There is also the possibility that the majority, or the compromises, in the legislature may be different from that of the executive – so that in the legislature the minority may act 'as an opposition', while in the executive 'its' member bears a collective responsibility with councillors from the majority. This leads back to the problem, what are the relationships between executive councillors and their political party?

On the federal level, Federal Councillors attend party meetings, not only in general, but also on each important item of business, without quite binding themselves to a particular line in general policy and much less one within their particular ministry. But it is essential for them to retain the overall confidence of their own parliamentary party, and more particularly of their own cantonal party.

So long as this trust is maintained, a Federal Councillor can be fairly confident of re-election. It is a century since a Federal Councillor failed to be re-elected when he was officially a candidate, and this has led commentators to assert that a Federal Councillor will be re-elected at the start of every legislature so long as he chooses to stand. Studying the lives of individual ministers, I am myself much less confident of this generalization. In the cases of nearly one-third of the number of Federal Councillors who have resigned there is a plausible story that the suggestion was urgently made that the statesman concerned should do so or should not again stand for election. In one famous case, indeed, (Arthur Hoffmann in 1917) two colleagues called at the house of a Federal Councillor and demanded a written resignation on the spot, to which he weeping, assented. This distressing little scene should dispose for ever of the legend that a Councillor can always remain and is re-elected automatically. There is a further means of pressure in the hands of the parliament in the customary rotation of the offices of President and Vice-President of the Confederation; the disgrace of not being elected in one's turn is a threat which has caused even the most immovable of departmental heads to seek honourable retirement. In the old days, indeed, positive inducements could be used, jobs in the World Postal Union, in embassies, the Red Cross, and even in private or semi-private industry, but nowadays this is a step down, however cushioned, rather than promotion. The express refusal to re-elect would be a sort of political atom bomb, inviting retaliation in kind, but such catastrophes can still enter calculations in a situation of conflict.

The office of President of the Confederation, as said, rotates. The constitution provides that it shall not be held in two successive years by the same person, but the constitutional practice of the last hundred years has been that it is normally held by the senior Federal Councillor in office who, having held it, goes to the bottom of the list. It has often been held thrice in a lifetime by the same man and there is an expectation that it will be held at least once. The office, or title, of Vice-President is that of heir-apparent to the Presidency next year. The Presidency now comprises little more than the highest titular dignity in the land and the chairmanship of the meeting of the heads of departments. In times of emergency, 1918 and 1940, the office has seemed on the brink of meaning very much more, but this brink has never been transcended. Originally, the office was combined with that of 'the Political Department', which became the Foreign Ministry of Switzerland: this automatic combination was given up, finally, in 1920, but has not quite been forgotten. It is the Federal Council itself which allocates the particular ministries, giving the choice of department (in practice) to its members in order of seniority, and it is felt that if the headship of the Political Department should fall vacant, the President of the day can lay claim to it – there is room for a little manoeuvering in this matter.

THE PARTY COMPOSITION OF THE FEDERAL COUNCIL

Until 1891, the Federal Council was entirely composed of the extended political family of the liberal-radicals (*Freisinnige*). In saying this, one does violence to the complexity of the political situation and the relationships with the parliamentary body: reading biographies one realizes that political bitterness was more extreme during the time when the executive was held by statesmen of different shades of liberalism (e.g., free-traders, Kulturkämpfers, federalists, democrats, moderates, and interventionists). This was the time of the revolving Political Department (except for a period under Numa Droz) and therefore a time when the other ministries necessarily revolved too, and the Federal Council as a college had sufficient time to interfere with the departments of its members. Thereafter, the council was composed as follows:

1891 Six *Freisinnig*, one catholic-conservative
1919 Five *Freisinnig*, two catholic-conservative
1929 Four *Freisinnig*, two catholics, one Peasant party
1943 Three *Freisinnig*, two catholics, one Peasant, one socialist
1953 Four *Freisinnig*, two catholics, one Peasant
1955 Three *Freisinnig*, three catholics, one Peasant
1959 Two *Freisinnig*, two catholics, two socialists, and one Peasant: the 'magic formula, 2:2:2:1'

The underlying *Freisinnig* majority in the National Council lasted until the introduction of proportional representation in 1919.

III. Federalism, Regionalism, and Local Government

FEDERALISM

The Swiss cantons regard themselves as having been there before the Confederation, and as having created the Confederation by a voluntary act, by a treaty of a very special sort, even if it be one by which they have in a sense been deceived, because the central power has slowly infringed the autonomies the cantons had expressly reserved from it. In most cases this is historical nonsense, and in every case this is historically dubious. If one looks at Swiss history from the point of view of the gradual aggregation of its members, then (with a different argument in each case) the joining into the Confederacy was the acquisition of an autonomy not as fully possessed before. The day when Appenzell joined, one might say, is the day when Appenzell attained its liberty rather than the day it lost it. As for the 'new cantons' (nearly half the number), some were wished onto the union, or carved out of it, by the federal power under the imperious influence of the victors of 1815. But the theory of a voluntary and conditional union is expressed in certain prominent passages of the constitution itself, together with allusions to a rag-bag of alternative theories – to the descending authority of God, to the ascending authority of 'the Swiss nation', to the dual sovereignty of centre and of components, to the residual sovereignty of the cantons, and so on. The document is rich in passages affording argument to the constitutional metaphysician.

As a fixed point in the arguments about Swiss federalism,[8] the assertion can be made that the Confederation and each of the cantons have attributes of statehood. The cantons may, and do, establish state churches, though religious toleration is enforced by the central power. The adjectival criminal law is cantonal (with considerable variation in the quality of justice), though the substantive Criminal Code, since 1942, is federal. Most of the law concerning language is cantonal, a matter that goes to the root of the union. In determining their own governmental structure the cantons appear to be autonomous, though the limitations of the Federal Constitution in fact bite deeper than a superficial reading might suggest. Residual powers are said to be cantonal: but in a concrete case it is not easy to attach a far-reaching meaning to this statement, for unexplored fields for legislation do not frequently reveal themselves, and would assuredly be subsumable under some federal heading (national security, rights of property, freedom of trade and industry and so on) if the central government wished to intermeddle, for no court can tell the federal government nay, and a federal law prevails over cantonal law. But in the silence of this federal law, a canton can certainly take the first step, under a general police power, in a way in which an English local authority cannot.

In daily life, the cantons call themselves 'states', and this is not an expression which has lost its edge in Switzerland to the extent that it has in the United States. It has not become a mere technical term for a province, but keeps the terror of the word, and alternates with 'Republic' (but with a little feeling of antiquarian affectation here) or the older *Stand*[9] (Estate). The tendency is the other way: the word 'canton' has no overtone of princeliness, except as applied to Switzerland, and under the old regime the flat word *Ort* (place) became a term kings respected, because the Thirteen Cantons used it for themselves. It being established that state co-exists on two levels, local and national, the constitutionalist is willing to recognize that federalism exists, and he enquires on two planes, the static and the dynamic, how matters are organized.

Concerning the statics of Swiss federalism, I have already mentioned that 'federal law prevails over cantonal law' (Article 2 of the Transitory Provisions of the Federal Constitution), and that no

court can, in express terms, adjudge Federal 'Laws' to be unconstitutional (Article 113 of the constitution). But the constitution
guarantees the citizen a proud panoply of rights: these can be
secured against the cantons by the courts, and indeed go into effect
as positive law in so far as they deal with matters in the *cantonal* com-
petence. The freedom of the press, the liberty of establishment, the
free practice of religious ceremonies, and so on, from the standpoint
of federalism these are so many shackles on cantonal government.

Nor is this all. One card in the constitutional hand, Article 4, is a
legal Joker, taking on the value which the Supreme Court may choose
to allot to it in a particular case. The clause, seemingly platitudinous,
runs: 'All Swiss are equal before the Law'. The lawyer can argue that
all unfairness is inequity, inequality. Justice treats all *equally*, attri-
buting to each man his own. But the provision does not mean that
man and woman, old and young, rich and poor, are to be treated the
same; indeed, to treat unequals equally is the height of injustice. In
short, the supreme tribunal has the choice between two principles,
sameness and equalness. Can children be excluded from obscene films,
available to adults? Equality can say no, equality can say yes. The
provision is used, much more open-handedly than in Austria or
Germany, to give a free jurisdiction in equity to the supreme, that is
to say the Federal, Tribunal over law, that is to say over cantonal
law.

Because they are states, cantons found universities and confer
professional qualifications. They establish their own police forces,
fly flags, make their own constitutions. They establish within their
own territory local government (though inner cantonal *federalism* is
impossible under the Federal Constitution), and those units may be
denied or given autonomy in a way in which the Confederation
would not dare treat the cantons.

With all this power for anarchy, all cantons in practice do much
the same things: their style is recognizably Swiss, and the differences
are regional rather than strictly cantonal. Only Grisons and Valais
really have a cantonal style in keeping with their history and unintelligible to other cantons.

Though there is still a lively, even a passionate, cantonal political
life, it is losing its total credibility. Some twenty years ago the appellation 'statesman' could still be earned by distinguished service on a
cantonal executive council: it has now receded to a national level. A
cantonal Great Councillor would now often be contented with the
honours of a county councillor rather than with those due to a
member of parliament. The old-style social powers are the ones that
are cantonal – the protestant churches, the political press, the bourgeois political parties – while the pressure-groups, the television and

even the wireless, are either national or attached to the linguistic regions. The heyday of the cantons was the age of gaslight and horses, but their vitality has given them an extra lease of life of half a century or more.

The cantons have their roots in localism and history, but beyond this a place is reserved for them as a constituent part of the national government, in the upper house of the legislature, in the amending process, in the electoral procedure for the lower house, and (tenuously) in the executive. The Swiss parliament is bicameral, and one of its chambers, the Council of States, represents the cantons in the same manner as the Senate of the United States represents the states.

To have a lower house (as we would say) constructed upon a principle of mathematical equality is defendable. To add to it an upper house with equal powers based upon historical principles which involve violent inequality (some cantons being thirty times larger than others) negates this principle. With the referendum to amend the constitution there is a rough justice, for the two majorities required (cantons and voters) rarely clash. But with the Council of States there is no rough justice: the bourgeois parties, liberals, radicals, peasants, catholics, always dominate and sometimes monopolize the Council of States. That this injustice does not produce a revolutionary situation is due to the nature of Swiss parties, and to the somewhat administrative (rather than political) attitude of the Council of States, and partly, also, because the socialists are in a minority even in the lower house.

Again, in daily life, the Council of States is not a cantonal, but a political-party, assembly, composed of two members from each 'whole' canton (one from the cantons regarded traditionally as 'half-cantons'). It is only when there is a threat to the federal bargain, including the implied regional bargain (in which east Switzerland is deeply interested), that the cantonal representatives do vote as such.

The cantonal structure of the States was deliberate, but has not worked quite as it was intended. In the National Council (i.e., House of Representatives) a cantonal element was adopted absentmindedly as an administrative device, but has worked to strengthen cantonalism: the cantons[10] are the constituencies for proportional representation. This does not greatly affect the proportions, but it has a profound influence on cantonal political life, and can be regarded as a key decision in 1919 for the subsequent half-century. It has kept party organization *cantonal* (except for the socialists). The names, the styles, the alliances, the inner life, of the historic parties are cantonal – the matter of alliances enters because of a PR device to count also the superfluous votes, not quite enough to elect one more candidate.

Although the councils are in law as near equal as makes no difference, the popular house is politically the more authoritative: the States is sometimes called the *Stöckli*, the 'wee dower-house' of an Emmenthal farm, not quite inaptly.

REGIONALISM

Related to federalism, but not corresponding precisely to it, is the underlying socio-economic and geographical factor of regionalism.

In the geography of Switzerland, there are four main regions: (i) the Oberland; (ii) the Mittelland (and Seeland); (iii) the Juras; and (iv) the country south of the Alps. The first is the real mountain district, geologically much varied, where the rock protrudes and reaches out into the sky: its economy has been discussed above (pp. 22–5). The Mittelland and Seeland are the areas between the mountains and the plain. Here what dominates is not the living rock, but the alluvial and glacier deposits – composed of big stones near the true mountains graded farther down to pebbles (packed into a stone resembling a rough concrete, called *Nagelflur*), and sand (packed into an easily worked sandstone). The agency that shaped these deposits was largely glaciers, and these, receding over the ages, have scooped out great lakes. The southern slopes of these lakes, and of the great rivers, exposed to the Föhn, make little patches which are almost like Italy, vine-terraced and fecund. The Juras are the bleak limestone parallel folds, of the same height as the alpine foothills, but very different in appearance and structure, stretching along the western borders of Switzerland.

The southern slopes of the main chain of the Alps (Ticino, the Italian valleys of Grisons, the Engadine, and the Valais) are climatically so different, so Italian, that one must make them into a separate region.

The dynamism of the Swiss states – the cantons as well as the Confederacy – is partly to be explained by the attempt, or the necessity, to include all four geographical areas in a political structure, for the areas are economically complementary, the cow-pastures and the cornlands, the towns and the passes, the wine and the cheese. Because the cantons are states, they also typically strove to include a bit of three areas, and even the communes (apart from bridgehead communities spanning a river and urban in character) strove to include a bit of valley, of intermediate area, and of alp.

The social-political areas do not quite correspond with these geographical areas. The religious map has already been discussed: it is cantonal, but does not sufficiently correspond with the area-structure to be called regional.

Above all, there is the split between east and west Switzerland.

This does not correspond with the language frontiers, but for many purposes lies along the river Reuss. Between east and west is a cultural and economic divide, of varying importance and sharpness throughout the ages, but always latent. West Switzerland radiates economically from Basle and Geneva: politically and culturally it is dominated by Berne (and its Roman catholic rival, Fribourg). East Switzerland centres for most purposes on Zurich, with subordinate centres in Winterthur, St Gallen, and the German Constance. When one thinks of the Swiss civilization, too often it is west Switzerland of which one is thinking, for it is politically and (for us) culturally dominant.

The Grisons and the Valais can also be considered as sub-regions of their own, symmetrically disposed around the central Gotthard axis, but very different in character from each other.

LOCAL SELF-GOVERNMENT

In size, the cantons are comparable to the old English geographical counties, and can be compared with them also in variety of number of inhabitants. In powers they are to be compared with the government of Ulster until its annexation by Westminster in 1972. In size, the communes are comparable to English parishes (though a city may in law be only a commune), but in powers even the smallest somewhat exceed the traditional (pre-1974) English county. Swiss experience sheds doubt, one might say derision, on any claim that British local units (in 1973) were too small. It suggests that they are far too big, and that the degree of central control in Britain may be one cause of the United Kingdom lagging behind the fully developed countries of western Europe and North America.

Regulation of local government is largely a cantonal matter, and systems vary within wide limits from canton to canton. The form of government of a commune is that of a canton in minature: an executive council and a legislative council (or public meeting). Communes use, in legal documents, language which suggests sovereignty (*Hoheit* and *Autonomie*), and this is far-fetched, but not ridiculous. At their best the communues are schools of freedom and exemplars of it, at their worst they are – or have been – instruments of a stern social discipline: one does not have to go too far back to find examples of oppression by communal oligarchies of the impoverished or the unpopular. Some of the freedom is less great than it at first appears, for there are doctrines of administrative law and practices of financial and political control which take away with the left hand some of what has been so largely granted by the right. The traditional system, too, is breaking down. Communes are too small, many are tiny (in 1960 two-thirds contained under a thousand inhabitants) and are unable to cope with really overwhelming pressures such as total urbanization or massive depopulation: they reached their zenith of effectiveness and satisfyingness between 1940 and 1960 – but this is true of Swiss institutions as a whole.[11] In general, one gives full marks to the Swiss system for democracy, half marks for liberty,[12] and independently of such moralizing judgements, top marks for administrative excellence and care for the physical environment.

Further comparisons and contrasts can be made with England. The process known there as 'the substitution of general purposes for *ad hoc* bodies' has not taken the same form in Switzerland. In both countries, indeed, the original church nucleus, the ecclesiastical parish, has hived off into a separate existence – but the Swiss cantons have kept their church rate (in general) as the basis of church finance. Some cantons have a rather wide range of communes for this purpose and that, others have fused the functions as much as possible. Peculiar, nowadays, to Switzerland is the distinction between the citizenship commune and the residence (or political) commune – the first being the legal corporation of those with the 'right of citizenship' of the commune, on average, about one-third of the inhabitants; the second being the corporation of those Swiss citizens with 'rights of settlement' (*Niederlassung*) and therefore voting rights, who are resident for legal purposes in the commune.

History of the Commune

The historical development of the commune (manor, township, parish, etc.) in Switzerland was not very different from the rest of Europe down to the end of the old regime. As elsewhere, there was at the outset the threefold structure of the manorial fief – the petty criminal jurisdiction, the economic organization of the alp or open fields, and the ecclesiastical parish – frequently within the same boundaries. In Switzerland the lordship of the manor (the Low Jurisdiction) had usually passed at some time previous to the Reformation into the hands of an urban patrician, or into the hands of the city itself or of a monastery due to be secularized: the squirearchy (the lesser nobility) usually, therefore, faded out of the picture rather early. The economic organization of the lowland village ceased to be necessary with the abolition of the three-field system, but survives in the alpine economy under various names and forms such as the Alp Corporation. The parish's ecclesiastical function has passed to the Church Commune, while the tithes disappeared in the first half of the last century: they had normally passed to the ownership of the state, which considered them as a tax on land and the most important and reliable source of public revenue.

In the sixteenth century, however, the village community was given the new function, heavy with consequences, of the maintenance of the poor. This was rendered necessary by the dissolution of so many monasteries and the increased control over beggars and vagrants exercised by more rigorous governments. Villages now became tiny republics, careful of their joint property in woodland and waste, and took to exacting ever higher fees for the 'right of settlement' on the citizenship which carried the corresponding duty of the village to maintain those admitted, should they or their descendants become paupers.

The Helvetic Republic abolished the manorial organization, and separated the two communities – the commune of those with the hereditary right of settlement and enjoyment of communal property, on the one hand, and those with the bare right of residence, on the other hand, who had taken advantage of the new freedom of movement. This distinction was reintroduced in the 1830s, however, wherever it had been abolished, and is taken in the Constitution of 1848 to be the universal rule throughout the country. This citizenship commune is the basis of a tight police control; the home commune holds the dossier of everyone with its citizenship, and records each change of residence. The 'document of origin' provides a sort of internal passport and identity card which the citizen must constantly produce and without which he never travels. The Swiss are astonished and incredulous that no such control is exercised, or needed, in Britain.

IV. Parliament and Legislation

PARLIAMENT

The word parliament is used informally in Switzerland to denote the bicameral federal legislative body. Officially its name is the Federal Assembly. It is composed of two houses, a Senate called Council of States, and a popular chamber called National Council. These two houses are constitutionally quite equal.

The Federal Assembly occasionally meets in joint session of the two houses, but the only important business it thus transacts is of elections, and the most important of these elections is that of the Federal Council, every four years.[13] But it also makes other elections, including that of the Chancellor.

The National Council has two hundred members, elected every fourth year (December 1973, etc.). Women have had the vote in federal matters since the elections of 1969, and a few sit in the parliament as members. They had had the vote within certain cantons some years earlier. Emancipation started in the French-speaking cantons, then spread to the larger and medium-sized

German-speaking cantons, and ultimately has conquered the fastnesses of conservative democracy in innermost Switzerland. The long delay in according the vote to women is typical: Switzerland was behind comparable European neighbours in many innovations – railways (1846), emancipation of the Jews (1866), motor traffic, television, as well as the political equality of women. (This latter is still not fully or universally secured within the cantons in 1973.)

For elections to the lower house, the constituencies are the cantons, which have to elect a number of councillors proportional to the size of their population, which works out as from one to 35 members, but mostly means between 3 and 10 members. Within this structure the elections are held 'under the Hagenbach-Bischoff' system, in principle proportionally to the number of party votes, but with opportunities for deleting names or giving two votes to particular candidates, or cross-voting between lists. These opportunities determine the actual choice of a member within the party lists and do not fail to deliver the occasional surprise. The effective selection of candidates to appear on the list is made by the (cantonal) party. At all stages the support of an interest-group is helpful, and it may prove decisive. The people elected can, in fact, be divided into three classes – members of cantonal or communal parliaments and executive councils; representatives of interest-groups; and prominent individuals of personal distinction, the latter, of course, being rather small in number. In form, all are elected on a party ticket, but in actuality there are a handful – the fingers of one hand suffice to count them — elected on their own merit as persons.

The Swiss vote often. There are also elections for the cantonal and communal parliaments and executive councils (under cantonal law), and usually elections of other high officials, such as judges, but perhaps even of schoolmasters and clergy, and of the council of the *bourgeoisie* if the voter lives in the township of which he possesses the citizenship. Added to this (but, mercifully, simultaneously with this) there are the various aspects of the referendum, which exist on the federal, cantonal, and communal levels. All in all, a Swiss citizen will go to the polls as often in one year as an Englishman in a lifetime, and on many more issues. It is this institution of continually voting, together with the extreme devolution of local government, which makes a Swiss feel that his country is the aristocrat of democracies and the preceptor of nations.

LEGISLATION

The interplay of executive and legislature, and of party and interest, can be illustrated by the procedure usually followed in passing a law.

1. The Tremola, Canton Ticino. Southern approach to the Gotthard Pass

2. Scattered farmsteads, each amidst its own fields and woods. Emmenthal district (Napf). Borders of Cantons Berne and Lucerne

4. Undamaged very small town. Le Landeron, founded in 1325 for military purposes. Strip cultivation. Canton Neuchâtel

3. The third Devil's Bridge, Gotthard Pass, built in 1830. The ruins

6. Site of the battle of Morgarten, 1315. The Austrians advanced from the right: their way was barred where the tower is visible.

5. The vineyards of Lavaux, Lake Geneva. The village houses are tightly pressed to economize land. Canton Vaud

7. Watchmakers' town in the Juras. The regular and artificial plan dates from a fire in the late eighteenth century. La Chaux-de-Fonds, Canton Neuchâtel

8. St Gallen. The line of the old walls is visible in the street plan. The great Abbey in the centre was formerly part of a different sovereignty. St Gallus was buried there in 650

9. Chapels at the site of the Hermitage of Niklaus von Flüe, Ranft.
Canton Unterwalden ob dem Wald
10. 1832. Handloom weavers set fire to factory at Uster. Canton Zurich

Verletzung angemessen sein muss. Die Konventionalstrafe und die auferlegten Kosten sind innert Monatsfrist nach Zustellung des Urteils zu leisten, andernfalls die obsiegende Partei den Betrag der von der andern Partei geleisteten Kaution bei der Schweiz. Nationalbank entnehmen kann. Die betroffene Partei hat alsdann den Fehlbetrag innert Monatsfrist zu ersetzen.

Art. 9.

Diese Vereinbarung tritt mit dem Tag ihrer Unterzeichnung in Kraft und dauert bis zum 19.Juli 1939.

Z ü r i c h , den 19.Juli 1937.

Arbeitgeberverband schweiz.
Maschinen- & Metall-Industrieller
Der Präsident: Der I Sekretär:

A. Sulzer   *H.A. Dostle.*

Schweiz. Verband evangelischer
Arbeiter und Angestellter

Zentralvorstand
des Schweizerischen Metall- u.
Uhrenarbeiter-Verbandes
Konrad Ilg   *Stainer*

Christl. Metallarbeiter-Verband
der Schweiz

Müller / Hans Schmid Walther, Nil Hs.

Der Zentralpräsident

11. The White Book of Sarnen, source of the William Tell saga
12. Signature page of the Peace Agreement of 19 July 1937, basis of modern Swiss prosperity

13. General Ulrich Wille in 1915. Portrait by Ferdinand Hodler
14. General Guisan (*left*) and President Pilet-Golaz in 1940
15. 25 July 1940. The Rütli meadow, Canton Uri. General Guisan addressing military commanders: a turning-point in Swiss history in historic surroundings, the traditional site of the Oath of 1291 (or 1307)

16, 17. Two photographs (probably the first ever taken) of the same meeting of the Federal Council – the Swiss Cabinet – in 1939. Top: President Etter (*left*); Federal Councillors Motta (Foreign Affairs), Baumann (Justice), Wetter (Finance) – *along wall left to right*; Chancellor Leimgruber and Vice-Chancellor Bovet (*at table, facing and back view*). Bottom: Federal Councillors Obrecht (Public Economy), Minger (Military Department), Pilet-Golaz (Posts, Vice President) – *along wall left to right*

18. Cantonal Direct Democracy. *Landsgemeinde* at Hundwil, Appenzell Outer Rhodes, *c.* 1946. Facing camera are the members of the cantonal executive council

19. Direct democracy in village affairs. Communal assembly in the Engadine, Canton Grisons, *c.* 1946

20. Communal assembly meeting at an inn. Canton Berne, 1865. Painting by Albert Anker, much-loved genre artist

21. Landscape with farmhouses, Franches Montagnes, Jura. Broad upland ridges such as this are separated by long, deep valleys. This countryside is a centre of the separatist movement. Canton Berne

22. The conurba-
tion of
Geneva,
where the
Rhône
leaves the
Lake just
above the
junction
with the
Arve.
Cantons
Geneva
and Vaud,
and a part
of France
(Savoy)

24. Medieval fortified city: Fribourg, cantonal capital. Town
hall and tower of cathedral. On skyline, right, new apartment

23. Mountain scenery. Soglio, in the Val Bregaglia, Canton

26. Sion. Canton Valais, about 1965, on the eve of being ravaged by industry, roads, apartment blocks. The twin hills are crowned by ruined castle of the prince-bishops and fortified church respectively

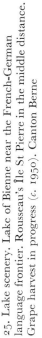

25. Lake scenery. Lake of Bienne near the French-German language frontier. Rousseau's Île St Pierre in the middle distance. Grape harvest in progress (*c.* 1950). Canton Berne

27. Chemical factories (Hoffmann-La Roche and others) at the place where the Rhine finally turns northward. Basle, looking into France

29. Romanesque village church (one of four) at Giornico, in the lower Val Leventina. In the foreground, 'two-level cultivation', vines sheltering another crop. Canton Ticino

28. Early twentieth-century engineering: the Landwasser railway viaduct near Filisur. Canton Grisons

30. Interior: country church in Italian Switzerland. Frescoes (1459) in church of Santa Maria del Castello, Mesocco. Canton Grisons
31. Interior of a great abbey church. Cathedral of St Gallen as recently restored. Canton St Gallen

At the start of every legislative period of the National Council, every four years,[14] the governmental parties within the Federal Parliament work out a programme of legislation: this has hitherto been couched in rather general and harmless terms. A little later, and without any connection between the two, the Federal Council publishes its own 'outline plan' for the period, which is debated in the two houses. These are new procedures, first tried in 1970, which have not yet embedded themselves firmly into public life and, indeed, lack a sanction; for while it is possible to maintain that individual Federal Councillors can be got rid of, no one asserts that a procedure is available for driving the whole Federal Council out of office. The projects are shopping lists, not directives, and their function is to introduce a certain rationalism into a hand-to-mouth activity.

The ultimate initiative for a project of law lies, of course, in society itself, but it surfaces usually in one or other house of the legislature as a 'motion' or 'postulate', in reply to which the Federal Council may (through the mouth of the minister concerned) promise a Report and Project of Law. Such a project is elaborated within the department, and submitted to the Federal Councillor at its head: this is the first stage.

The second stage is the 'consultation of interests': here, the pressure-groups are asked to make submissions, and as wide a range as possible is consulted. This merges into the third stage, which is the 'committee of experts': representatives, chosen from outside parliament, of the principal opposing interests predominate in this committee. The interests of capital and labour are usually represented, as well as narrower interests more particularly involved. Officials who make the selection keep a wary eye on the need to propitiate language-groups and regions as well as political parties. A record of the discussions is kept, and the draft is discussed clause by clause. An interest-group which feels that too little regard is being paid towards it may, even at this early stage, threaten the referendum. On the basis of this discussion in the committee of experts, the final draft will be made.

After this, the draft goes to the Federal Council as a body, together with a draft of the Message (i.e., the governmental explanation) which accompanies all such bills. Here other departments (including that of Finance) have their last say – there will have been consultations beforehand – and may approve or alter both the draft and the Message. Decision may be by majority (but is not likely to be other than unanimous), yet all Federal Councillors henceforth take responsibility for it, subject only to what is felicitously termed 'a loyal indiscretion'.

The draft and the Message now go to whichever legislative council has 'priority', being first submitted to an *ad hoc* committee of that council, and then to the whole body. Party discipline is somewhat lax, but each party will by now have considered the draft and taken up a position upon it – expressing its views if necessary through the mouth of its members on the *ad hoc* committee. When passed by both houses, it becomes law as from the date expressed in the draft, which will assuredly be some months in advance in order to allow the three-months delay during which the Referendum Challenge may be set on foot against it. The courts do not entertain appeals against the constitutionality of federal laws.

The Rule of Law

Switzerland claims to be a *Rechtsstaat,* a state permeated by legality. In many fields this claim is most amply justified. The protection of the property of individuals is meticulous, and accorded a high ethical value, that is to say the protection of property within Switzerland and under Swiss municipal law. The courts and public, or newspaper, opinion are very conscious of the economic value of this Swiss atmosphere of integral property rights. The framework of society, the wellbeing of the economy, the very sovereignty of the state are involved, it is felt, and for good measure there is sometimes a vague allusion to neutrality: the use of this sacred word precludes further discussion of where property came from and for what use it is destined.

In another field, this very concept of neutrality implies a certain legalism even of foreign policy, for neutrality is felt to be most safely protected when regarded as a legal concept, and one especially tailored for Swiss self-interest. Most high officials, not only in the foreign services, have a legal training, though a somewhat less all-embracing training than the German *Volljurist* and one which leaves a less deep scar on the mind. That is to say, lawyers in private practice, high officials, many businessmen and politicians and those who embark on the career of judge, have an identical training and, if of the same age, will very likely know each other and meet in societies and in military service. The spirit of law spreads wide, so wide that it may become a little contaminated by the areas into which it spreads. In particular, the worlds of politics, of officialdom, and of the judiciary are not sharply differentiated.

Judges are elected for a term of years. This avoids the worst abuses of the English system, the tyrannical, idiosyncratic, or sadistic High Court judge, and the usual practical result of election is to secure a balance of party forces on the bench: the party nomination is seldom contested. The judicial calling is a career like any other, a branch of the public service entered young, and it carries no overtones of majesty. There are, of course, occasionally cases with a political or a nationalist flavour, and in the latter type one sees reported cases that cause a slight raising of the eyebrows,[15] even some judgements of the tribunals of large cantons containing international airports. In criminal cases, moreover, there are certain medium-sized cantons where the reputation of justice may come under discussion. Criminal procedure is based upon interrogation in solitary confinement, and this process, for which special prisons are constructed, may last eighteen months without arousing public comment, and the prisoner may on occasion be charged for the expenses of lodging him in prison. Readers of Max Frisch's novel *Stiller* will observe that the interest of the novel in no way lies in the problematic of this method of questioning.[16] To retain a suspect in prison for a period of months, and then to sentence him for some lesser period, would give rise to all sorts of difficulties – the time spent under interrogation is subtracted from the sentence – and so there may be a certain temptation to award a sentence slightly longer than the time already served. The imputation that thereby sentence is passed after punishment grossly underestimates the skill and experience of interrogational judges and of court judges. Yet one sometimes gets the impression that it is best to avoid even being accused and, failing that, there is advantage in having money, local political connections, and access to the press. It must be added that penal conditions are sometimes a little old-fashioned; occasional reports and allegations concerning prisons and approved schools make the sensitive observer rather sick: but this is a field where the truth is difficult to find. The modern youth-culture, which sees the children of the well-born and powerfully-connected on occasion sent to prison, may prove the instrument of arousing a national consciousness which is less sensitive to the fate of the poor, of the feckless, or of the foreign immigrant worker accused of a crime against a Swiss. But the terror of the law is valuable and goes deep into private life and relations with fellow citizens, giving a sharpened edge to the importance of maintaining good relations with the whole of one's environment and of avoiding eccentric behaviour not in keeping with one's place in society. For those of good reputation, Swiss law can be very lenient, and especially in the matter of suspended sentences. The discretionary area of law is thus an element in the Swiss style of life even more important than the law itself, at least as important as legality itself.

Taxation

It would be idle to pretend that a foreigner not liable to Swiss taxation understands this matter: it is clear that there are numerous ways of, to use a euphemism, reducing the personal burden of taxation in Switzerland. The principle laid down by the clear implication of the constitution is that indirect taxation, notably customs duties, shall belong to the central government, and direct taxation to the cantons, and, under them, to the communes. Since the first World War, however, this has only for the briefest of intervals proved to be the case. For long periods, direct federal taxation has been levied 'in derogation of the constitution', for shorter periods Temporary Articles have been in force sanctioning these derogations. The temporary nature of these provisions ensures that the matter will be frequently and passionately discussed, but mostly under the heading of 'federalism'. What strikes the foreigner, and fills him with envy if he is rich, is the light progression of Swiss taxes and their general kindliness to accumulations of property, their use to fortify the social system rather than to weaken it, even though total taxation as a proportion of the national income is not very different to that of other countries.

In outline, the broad situation is as follows. The federal customs duties, the federal turnover tax (and various excise duties), and the federal direct taxation (of income, etc.), yield approximately equal sums. Of this federal direct taxation, the most important is the Defence Tax, *Wehrsteuer*, which serves the function of a sort of surtax. Cantonal and communal taxation, in addition to this, is partly on income, partly on capital, and there are many small taxes: the tax load varies considerably from canton to canton and commune to commune. Of expenditure, about one-third is by the central government, more than one-third by the cantons, and less than one-third by communes. Considerable sums yielded by federal taxation are surrendered to the cantons, whereby certain inequalities are in part compensated.

Federalism, as well as the weakness of the socialist parties on the federal level, accounts for the principal characteristics of the Swiss system. The towns which are also cantons, Geneva and Basle, are very close to frontiers, cantonal and international, a consideration which must always limit their possibilities (apart from federal law) of discriminatory taxation of one social class. This is an important matter, but somewhat tedious, and subject to constant changes.

V. *Neutrality, Army*

NEUTRALITY

Finally, there is the distinguishing feature of neutrality. Neutrality, one may say, created Switzerland in her present boundaries, and Switzerland in turn has done much to give an agreed content to the word neutrality. Swiss neutrality depends on the Swiss army.

The very word neutrality was first used in a formal treaty (it is said) in respect of the temporary[17] neutralization of Burgundy and the Franche-Comté in 1522 by France and Austria, through the intermediacy, and under the promise of intervention, of the Swiss. Such neutralizations frequently had led to absorption by the guarantor, and claims to be considered a part of Switzerland (and the present boundaries in detail of the Confederation) have often depended on the boundaries of the old confederal neutrality.[18]

As late as 1861, Switzerland very nearly annexed the Chablais and Faucigny[19] (south of the Lake of Geneva), in consequence of the position she held as guaranteeing the neutrality of Savoy: only through ineptness (on her part and Great Britain's) did this opportunity finally slip. Liechtenstein might one day be covered by Swiss neutrality, as the penultimate step in absorption. On the other hand, the largest Swiss acquisitions since the old regime – Geneva, Neuchâtel, and the imperial territory of the Bernese Jura – were only fully and formally covered by a guarantee of their neutrality when it was too late to do so effectively.

The content of neutrality has often been decisively influenced by Swiss practice. Until 1635, for example, it was not inconsistent with the peaceful passage of armed forces in wartime over the territory of a neutral: the turning-point in the development of the modern practice which forbids such passage was a resolution of the Swiss confederate Diet. The long continuance of regiments in foreign service was partly due to the bad Swiss example.[20] The idea of neutrality itself, of course, is scarcely less old than the idea of legitimate war, and was a necessity in the quarrels within the old empire in Germany.

Various dates are given by writers as the real beginning of Swiss neutrality, according to the requirements of their theme and their ideological fetters. The Convention of Stans (1481), the Defensional of Wyl (1647), for example, can be chosen among many intermediate dates. Edgar Bonjour favours 1674 as the date of a formal declaration of the Diet claiming recognition of Swiss neutrality as a permanent part of European international law. In diplomatic practice 1815 is given as the operative date, but a case can be made for 1848.

The most universally accepted date, however, is 1515. The quarter-century preceding that year had been a time of wild military activity, with Switzerland on the verge of becoming a republican great power. But after the defeat at Marignano came a change of direction (see above, pp. 53-7), partly explained by the high cost of artillery, partly by internal discords (soon to be greatly exacerbated by the Reformation), partly by the Perpetual Treaty with

France (1516 and 1521) combined with the *Erbvereinigung* with Austria, renewed in 1511. Switzerland after 1515 withdrew from the European scene as an entity – there was no Swiss national army and only a shadowy Swiss international personality – and the collectivity of cantons could therefore follow no course except neutrality. Swiss writers sometimes introduce a certain pathos, that this was a willed decision, not imposed from outside nor conditioned by internal division and indecisiveness. However, it was also French policy to keep the Confederacy neutral: the motivation is of some doctrinal importance, because being 'neutralized' by others is a derogation of sovereignty, while choosing to remain neutral is a very high assertion of statehood. In the event, the successful preservation of neutrality until the 1790s seems a miracle. The protestant cantons formed an inchoate state of their own with their own Diet and foreign policy, favouring France, and occasionally Sweden, Venice, or England, while the catholic cantons also formed a group with institutions and international personality of their own, favouring Austria or, occasionally, Spain. The tiny canton of Appenzell split permanently into two on an issue of foreign policy in 1597.

However, the continuity with an old tradition that had kept the territory guaranteed by the Thirteen Cantons (but not Grisons) out of the Thirty Years War and later conflicts was decisively shattered in the struggles following the French Revolution. After August 1792 (the massacre of Louis XVI's Swiss Guard) neutrality was frequently ignored, and from 1798 until 1815 it was scarcely ever observed.

The present status is always referred back to 1815 and the Treaty of Vienna. This is not quite satisfactory. There were three guarantees of neutrality in 1814–15, the first two conditional, and the third definitive on fulfilment of the conditions. The conditions have since been broken. The guarantee by the Swiss of the freedom of the catholic religion in the new territories of Geneva, indeed, has been sufficiently observed, but the guarantee of the unchanged religious status of the Bernese Jura has been flouted. More significantly, the changes of 1847–48 (when Switzerland was created as a new sort of state through the Sonderbund War) broke the conditions. This, in a sense, strengthens the Swiss case. The defiance of the treaty in 1848 was recognized as a fact, and Europe swallowed the fact, incapable of intervening. Neutrality shifted from its historical and conditional basis to a natural-law basis, as a manifestation of sovereignty whereby the country declared itself neutral and had to be recognized as such; the status was not a grant petitioned for by Switzerland, as in 1815, but a conquest.

In another sense, neutrality as understood at present is even more recent.

In peacetime, neutrality is a policy followed by a country in exercise of its sovereignty. In wartime, it is a legal status in the law of nations. But the wartime status profoundly affects the peacetime policy. Though her status as a neutral is uniquely old, Switzerland has only rather recently come to her present understanding of the content of that status, especially in its peacetime implications.

One may take it that there are three, or perhaps four, cardinal points in Swiss neutrality: first not to engage in a war of conquest, and therefore, second, to shun military alliances and, in extension of this, to treat all powers equally, so as not to prejudice in peacetime the conduct of the neutral state if war should occur. Third, to defend one's own territory. This is really an extension of the above, since others could only effectively defend the territory of a neutral on its behalf if there were agreements beforehand, and the defending power, invited in, might be tempted to remain. To these may tentatively be added a fourth point: to take part in and foster international works of benevolence, and to support institutions tending to preserve peace, to a greater extent than non-neutrals do.

With regard to the first of these cardinal points, the last invasion of a foreign country which Switzerland undertook was the expedition of 1815 into the Franche-Comté, two weeks after the battle of Waterloo. It was not a success: the failure was due to desertions rather than to meeting any military opposition, and what remained of the expeditionary force withdrew as soon as Louis XVIII was safely on his throne again. The incident is an inconvenient memory, now largely forgotten.

However, the Swiss General Staff have played with aggressive plans on other occasions. It is not surprising that this should be so. The country is too small to have a military literature entirely of its own, and its soldiers were brought up on maxims of 'offensive action'[21] and the primacy of the attack, just like those of other nations. Indeed, it is difficult to maintain a military spirit on any other terms. In 1848–49 there was talk of intervening in Italy on the side of the liberal insurrectionists. In 1856–57, Dufour had plans to invade Baden, arising out of the incorporation of Neuchâtel (of which the king of Prussia was titular prince). In 1860 there were plans to invade Savoy, which were narrowly defeated in the Federal Council. In 1866 there was a proposal to invade Italy and thereby regain the lost territories of the Valtellina. In 1870 there was again talk of marching into Savoy. In the 1890s and until shortly before 1914 there were repeated plans for either operations in Savoy or a pre-emptive *coup de main* on Milan, towards which Ticino points. In the same years there were plans, apparently quite detailed, of co-operation with Austria in an attack on Italy still with some eye on the Valtellina. Probably these ideas were only finally given up in 1916,[22] when von Sprecher, the centre of these negotiations, got dangerously close to involvement in the 'affair of the colonels' (who were caught supplying Austria with military information).

Such talks and agreements are natural. Until 1918 it was rather assumed that the main danger came from France and Italy – it was the Jura front that was manned in 1914 and has entered into the imaginative literature of the first World War in Switzerland. Staff talks, entering into details of co-operation, were therefore held with Austria and Germany, not with France. In 1939 the position was reversed, and staff talks were held with France, and not with Germany. The record of these talks fell into German hands at La Charité-sur-Loire in 1940. Had a pretext been needed for an invasion of Switzerland, these would have furnished it. There has been speculation in recent years as to talks between Switzerland and NATO. The surprise is rather that the Swiss themselves admit one-sided talks to be un-neutral rather than that they take place: they can be seen to be necessary as soon as one reflects on the concrete situation that might arise in a war.

The great period of Swiss neutrality was that between 1920 and 1935. In 1920 Switzerland joined the League of Nations. The federal government decided (quite unconstitutionally) to submit the proposal to the double referendum of people and cantons, and it was passed – by a large popular majority centred in French Switzerland, and a very small majority of cantons. The League took up residence in its magnificent buildings in Geneva (completed just before its final defeat) and so did the International Labour Office, which is still there today. When the crisis came in 1935–36, over the Italian invasion of Abyssinia, Switzerland started clambering out of her engagements. In the civil war in Spain, Foreign Minister Motta took up a position of neutrality towards the legitimate Spanish government in a form which suggests an ideological sympathy with Franco and the insurgents. Motta had always felt close to Italy, and this ripened to a feeling of friendship towards Mussolini. He admired German culture, and in more favourable times would have been a friend of Germany's too.[23] He had no sympathies whatsoever with Anglo-Saxon civilization, of which indeed he had no more knowledge than one would expect of an Airolo innkeeper. In May 1938 he got Switzerland released from effective obligations towards the League (with no referendum this time of people and cantons).[24]

This movement after 1935 has gone down in Swiss literature as the 'return to absolute from differential neutrality', but it also bears the opposite interpretation. Motta (who never had to suffer a social democrat colleague in the Federal Council) never had to have diplomatic relations with Soviet Russia. During the whole time of his rule, and Pilet-Golaz's, there were no diplomatic relations between Switzerland and the USSR.

Remembering the League of Nations, Switzerland has not joined the United Nations, though the project is always being discussed and has wide support, especially (again) in west Switzerland. Switzerland even refused in 1944 to contribute money to the United National Relief and Rehabilitation Administration (UNRRA, the predecessor of UNICEF) in case it should endanger her neutrality. For many years she made no government-to-government aid to undeveloped nations, counting, however, in her favour the investments and loans made by commercial enterprises. The present contribution is rather modest. Yet there is probably no nation which has so high a reputation for international solidarity: this solidarity (or expression of solidarity) is the positive side of neutrality, giving it a touch of idealism. The International Red Cross, with its seat in Geneva and its former connections with the Genevese patriciate, is counted on the credit side, and so, with less conviction, are the other international bureaucracies of Geneva.

If there is anything the Swiss do not want to do, or want to do, an argument from neutrality is readily forthcoming. Even the Swiss arms industry allegedly helps neutrality, for it is scrupulously fair in supplying both sides, and the equipment for the Swiss army is a spin-off from it and is necessary to preserve neutrality. Joining EFTA, and not (quite) joining the EEC, is a debate conducted in public in terms of neutrality. When the enquirer presses, he is reminded there is a unique Swiss form of neutrality, unlike, and better than, all others. The metaphysics of this approach sometimes are dubious, a genus is posited which is inherently incapable of having more than one species, while denying that there is also only one of any other sort of neutrality, Swedish, Austrian, and so on. However, it is convenient to be able to invent rules as one goes along in the international game, and the Swiss approach sometimes verges on the assertion 'Whatever *we* do, is neutral'.

The backing of Swiss neutrality is the Swiss army, and this is a very important institution.

THE SWISS ARMY

Switzerland, neutral, has been in a state of war every week-end since 1945. Every year, to the irritation of late autumn tourists, the Gotthard is stormed and successfully defended, the progress of the rival armies being reported in the press. 'Nuclear weapons' are exploded (until recently among the real life of horse-drawn artillery). The railway stations are full of young soldiers, piling into trains;

call-up notices are on the public boards. There is a latent suspicion that spies are around. The valleys are crossed by barriers against miniature tanks, and if one looks along the line of these barriers, one sees among the grey or pinkish rocks an area of concrete painted in triangles of military green and khaki, and a sinister iron door and small square holes. Education reiterates the presence of a threat from abroad, and monuments and frescoes remind the citizen of a glorious, if mercenary and remote, military past. Sunday afternoons are enlivened with the crack of rifle-fire, the normal accompaniment of a week-end picnic in the open all over Switzerland.

By virtue of the Federal Constitution, every Swiss male is obliged to military service, and few are exempted on health grounds: these have to pay a special extra tax. In principle, it is entirely a militia, conscript, force. After the initial call-up period, there are repetition courses and firing practices throughout the best part of adult life – until fifty (in 1973) although the last ten years may be treated somewhat lightheartedly. Units keep together to a large extent, so military service is the basis for lifelong comradeship of people of different backgrounds, and the shared experience of extremely arduous physical activity sets a brandmark on the national character. Until recently, the army was nearly coterminous with the electorate, and this gave a deeper sense to manhood suffrage and direct democracy. Rifles, and occasionally ammunition, are taken home.

The training of militia officers is even more exacting than that of soldiers, depriving a young man of most of his holidays (and thus prolonging university education). In the last few years officer trainees have, it is claimed, ceased to be selected on social grounds, as they once were. Becoming an officer is still the expression of a certain civilian ambition as well as of public spiritedness.

Inevitably, there is some atmosphere of indoctrination in this military service, for military values have a counterpart in civil life, and this civilian counterpart falls within the ideology of the right wing. The working of Swiss democracy is not to be fully understood without this background of military discipline and fellowship, nor is the open-airness of the Swiss culture (an open-airness, be it understood, strictly kept out of doors).

At the centre of the military machine is a small, highly trained regular professional corps of instructors. The fixed underground defences are said to be impressive. The expenditure on mechanization, on air support, and on technology generally, however, seems relatively light.

About 1970 a silent and unanimous mutiny forced the army to sanction relatively long hair. The spirit has spread: there is a visible relaxation in discipline and strenuousness, a pervasive spirit of mockery, and a loss of confident swagger. For the moment, the result is a more intelligent team of pressed men, but there are signs of a deeper incompatibility with the contemporary youth-culture. An attempt has been made to siphon off the most unco-operative spirits into a *Sanitätskorps*, but a large company of drop-outs is even more difficult to manage than a single specimen. Here, as elsewhere, Swiss civilization is fraying at the edges.

Paradoxically, the army has been at the peak of efficiency during a generation of profound peace in Europe. At the one moment of danger, June to September 1940, it had been partially demobilized and in the process of moving to new, ill-prepared, defences. But from 1945 to 1965 it was razor-sharp and keen. One is reminded of an historical parallel. The town of Zurich had rather weak medieval defences throughout the period of the Thirty Years War, but felt that in wartime it was rash to make extravagant expenditure on them. But as soon as the war was over in 1648, Zurich set to work and constructed enormous modern ramparts around the whole city, with water-defences, zig-zags, and redoubts.[25] One hopes that the final decay of the Swiss military spirit will not coincide with the third World War.

NOTES

[1] i.e., a gerund not a gerundive. It does *not* mean 'a thing meet to be referred'. The plural is therefore referendums rather than referenda.

[2] It counted non-voters as acceptors of a proposal, a precedent followed by liberals in many cantons in the first half of the nineteenth century.

[3] It is important to keep in mind that the two minorities, non-German and catholic, taken together, comprise $11\frac{1}{2}$ cantonal votes, out of a total of 22 – the reader will remember that there is an overlap in the case of Valais, Fribourg, and Ticino – which gives them a blocking vote. (Solothurn, also catholic in religion, tends to cast its sympathies with liberalism.) The politically catholic cantons, in fact, used almost invariably to vote on the same side and still often do, and the ghost of the Sonderbund haunts nearly every map of political opinion.

[4] The word votation is used in Switzerland for a vote on an issue rather than for a person. In this discussion I have left out many technical niceties of constitutional law. The details in my *The Federal Constitution of Switzerland*, Oxford, 1954, remain largely correct.

[5] There are two Houses of the Federal Assembly (parliament) – the National Council of 200 members elected by the people at large, and the Council of States of 44 members chosen by the cantons (see pp. 139–40 and 143–6).

[6] An absolute majority, more than half the total number of members, being necessary in each election of each member of the executive, several rounds of voting may have to be held when an election is disputed.

[7] There is a discussion of the grounds of choice in Dr Klaus Schumann's brilliant book *Das Regierungssystem der Schweiz*, Cologne etc., 1971, 179 *et seq.*

[8] In this book I follow the ordinary English usage which makes no distinction between 'federation' and 'confederation'. I do so on doctrinal grounds, but also because this is the way in which the words are used in the French version of 'the federal Constitution of the Swiss Confederation'. But the word 'confederacy' has

kept its sharp edge, and I reserve it for the older, looser, form of perpetual league of confederate states, *Staatenbund* rather than *Bundesstaat*. The expression 'confederation' also sometimes covers this, for it is really the only possible translation of the German term *Eidgenossenschaft*. An attempt is sometimes made in German to distinguish between *Bund* (a general term) and *Eidgenossenschaft* (a term only applied to Switzerland, but applied to successive regimes in Switzerland which were certainly not all of the same sort, and a term which in ordinary speech has historicizing, patriotic, affectionate overtones). The usage in south England of the terms English and British has some analogies in that they have very different emotional overtones, and are used without juristic precision, but not interchangeably.

9 The heirs of the old Republic of Berne (Canton Berne, Aargau, and Vaud) retain most the feeling of state, while Valais, Grisons, and Geneva merit the appellation republic. The archaic word *Stand* brings to mind in the first place the pure democracies and Inner Switzerland. 'Canton' just asserts a fact.

10 In 1972, there were proposals to break up the large cantons into electoral districts of six to eight members. The reason why this was not done in 1919 was a fear of the recurrence of the gerrymandering (*Wahlkreisgeometrie*) which had dominated life for seventy years.

11 Communal government is too large a subject to discuss here but the subject is an important one. The literature is not easy to handle, as the systems are so multifarious and there is a folklore and a reality which are not quite in harmony. In English, I can recommend two modern works: *Government by Community* by Ioan Rees, London, 1971, and *Politics in Swiss Local Government*, Boulder, 1967, by G. A. Codding. These are based on observation of Grisons and of the commune of Veyrier (Canton Geneva) respectively. For an evocation of what it is like to live in a community where so much power lies in practice in the hands of the local notables – school, church, police, fire-brigade, newspaper, taxation, expropriation, licensing, hospitals, and so on – one must turn to fiction. In novels, Gotthelf is well informed on the old (1820–45) village life of the Bernese Emmenthal and Upper Aargau. The picture given of a commune in Valais of (I presume) about 1900 by Maurice Zermatten in *La Montagne sans Etoiles*, I find quietly horrifying. The picture of provincial life in Canton Zurich in immediate post-1945 years by W. M. Diggelmann in *Die Hinterlassenschaft* is also, deliberately, horrifying, but is based on an actual incident. Biographies, of the eminent, give another and more favourable side of the story, especially in cities, and so do formal studies such as those by Professor Adolf Gasser of Basle.

12 I think local tyranny everywhere now belongs to the past. Its existence may be suspected in communes where one hundred per cent belong to a single religion, or there is unanimity in elections or at a referendum. Local taxation contributes to the sharp distinction between town and country which until recently prevailed in Switzerland: a rural commune has high taxes and poor services, and if it opts for expansion, has to urbanize itself quickly and decisively once and for all. The social effects of this are very large indeed.

13 The other elections it makes are: the President and Vice-President of the Confederation, annually; the Federal Chancellor, and the members of the Supreme Court (Federal Tribunal) from time to time. It also elects the General who is Commander-in-Chief of the Armed Forces when the army is mobilized under threat of war.

The Federal Chancellor is a dignitary of subordinate importance, a sort of Lord High Chief Clerk. He is secretary of the Federal Council and has other lofty but politically inconsiderable functions. His is an ancient office, dating back to the Napoleonic regime and, in a sense, to the old Confederacy; until 1848 he was virtually the only federal civil servant, and the office was retained in the expectation that out of it the whole federal civil service would grow. But actually this was not how it worked out. Modern officialdom derives from the secretaryships to the individual Federal Councillors. From time to time attempts are made to exploit the latent possibilities of the magnificent-sounding office of Federal Chancellor – and such an attempt was made in the early 1970s.

14 In *The Parliament of Switzerland*, London, 1962, I examined these procedures at

some length. But the Law on the Relationships between the Councils, *Gesetzver-kehrsgesetz*, has now been changed.

[15] My own eyebrows were raised by the *Mattmark* Cases (1965–72) in the Valais.

[16] Nor is the description of the pre-trial process in Paul Erdman's *The Billion Dollar Killing* (1973) inherently quite impossible.

[17] The status was frequently renewed, and in a sense lasted until 1674, when the Franche-Comté was finally annexed by France.

[18] The reverse of this is that places whose neutrality was under Swiss guarantee normally had to contribute troops to confederal military expeditions. This may be illustrated by a particular case, Arbon in Thurgau: here, under the old régime, the High Jurisdiction (the right of life and death) was with the bishop of Constance, and Arbon was therefore still reckoned a part of the empire, but the right to levy troops lay with the ruling cantons, and the town has remained within Switzerland today. A similar situation occurred with some Schaffhausen villages. On the other hand, when the boundaries of Switzerland were finally drawn in 1815 (or, very occasionally, later), natural-law thinking adjusted boundaries to run along geographical features, rivers and watersheds. The new, post-revolutionary, doctrines of sovereignty cut through many a tangled historical knot, conflicts of high and low jurisdictions, rights of levying troops, and rights of taxation.

[19] For the vexed question of the Vallée des Dappes, and indeed for further reading on the subject of neutrality, see the monumental 2nd edition of Bonjour, *Geschichte der schweizerischen Neutralität*, 6 vols., Basle etc. 1965–70. (It is also available in a French translation. The first edition is relatively worthless. For the period of the second World War, the 2nd edition is a source of unique importance and value.)

[20] Every effort was made to see that Swiss did not fight other Swiss: sometimes, as at Malplaquet, in vain.

[21] For the history of Swiss military thinking, see Alfred Ernst, *Die Konzeption der schweizerischen Landesverteidigung 1815–1966*, Frauenfeld etc., 1971 – written by Switzerland's foremost intellectual soldier.

[22] In 1919 the people of the Vorarlberg in a referendum expressed the wish by a majority of four to one to be accepted as a canton of Switzerland. It was a proposal with a considerable history behind it. The Vorarlberg has a kindred dialect, and the same racial (if one may use the word) mix as the Grisons (Alemannic, Valaisan, and Romansch), of which it would round off the territory geographically. Had Switzerland accepted Vorarlberg, she would have been involved in the second World War, and survived it, and the Vorarlberg would by now have become a canton. In the Swiss rejection there was an element of timorousness, and of anti-Roman catholic feeling. The incident raises some rather interesting moral problems about 'the mission of Switzerland': in some ways it is profoundly depressing. But it also documents the end of expansionist illusions.

[23] To take an extreme (and slightly unfair) example, when the Nazis took Austria under their wing in March 1938, Motta expressed his 'admiration of the way in which the Führer had acted' to Köcher, the German minister in Berne, who further reported 'an almost happy atmosphere with Motta'. But Motta had a notable line in blarney, and Köcher could at times be a bit untruthful, and some qualification was added (Bonjour, op. cit., 2nd ed., III, 235–6). The happy atmosphere was not widely enjoyed in Switzerland.

[24] During the war, the ILO took refuge in Canada.

[25] They were never used when the French came in 1798. New trenches had to be rapidly dug in the woods around, and also proved unavailing. The liberal government of the 1830s removed most of the defences, but the zig-zags can still be traced and the remaining rampart is rather charming.

CHAPTER 6

Politics

I. Political Parties

THE POLITICAL PARTIES of Switzerland have adopted the habit of changing names rather often, a process whereby innocuous and even laudatory adjectives such as democrat, republican, Christian, liberal, social, and popular, temporarily take on a hard and sinister meaning and are applied to persons whom a coarse observer might in conversation term clerico-Fascist, social reactionary, or *laissez-faire* nationalist. Moreover, the cantonal parties sometimes bear names other than the federal party they support, and there is a slight variation even between the electoral party and the party group within the parliamentary assembly.

The inner nature of political party varies sharply from place to place, and is now changing. Parties are a product of democratic or representative institutions, and therefore in a loose sense one can talk of parties at various times and places in the old regime of Switzerland. Since 1798, one can say, a little arbitrarily, that the liberals were the first on the scene, compelling those who were old-fashioned or aristocratic or religious to become conscious of themselves as 'conservatives'. This primitive dichotomy sufficed until the seizure of power by liberals within the cantons after 1830, when it became necessary to make place for successive parties on the left wing, at first radicals, then democrats, then socialists. However, a simple left-right classification breaks down in use: an anti-clerical party may stand 'to the left' on the religious issue, but to the right on the issue of private enterprise, or a clerical and socially conservative party may stand to the left on constitutional issues, demanding full plebiscitary rights for the ignorant, dispossessed, but wonderfully bigoted poor. Moreover, the federal political stage seems destined by nature for a deadlock between three great parties of equivalent strength. But the cantonal stage sometimes lends itself naturally to a dominant party system.

Traditionally, Swiss parties were of the type of the 'political family', what the Belgians call little 'worlds', the Austrians 'camps'. At the beginning, in the 1830s, their devotees did not see themselves thus, but as like-minded individuals choosing the way of light by intellectual effort and called by an inner voice to oppose the sons of darkness. But this choice and call were so predictable on grounds of class, economic ambition, and place of residence that a post-Marxian age is inclined to regard party as being crudely predetermined. It is when one comes to the detail of biography that one sees choice and calling reappearing: could not (apart from personal factors) Augustin Keller have led the clerical-conservatives, and Josef Leu[1] of Ebersol the liberals?

Once formed, that is to say, once the steady connection of members of cantonal parliaments of like mind and interests had given itself a name which spread to the leaders of electoral opinion in towns and villages, party soon took on aspects of a clientele group, a ladder for social and economic promotion of individuals. A child after 1848 found himself born into a particular political environment which offered all he needed in career prospects and intellectual and social surroundings, and even offered a lively political life within the political extended family itself, for the great party groupings too had a left and right wing and a Centre. A young man could rebel from his father and make a name within his party's Left and move back gradually over the whole inner-party spectrum with the feeling of having made an interesting political pilgrimage. Reading a localized party-political press and with friends from the same party, intermarrying, clubbing together, giving and receiving patronage, a citizen would have the impression that his party was a city state for itself which happened to coexist with various lesser political breeds about which curious legends circulated. Even the young Socialist party took on this atmosphere, and one could be 'fifty years a heretic' wobbling between left-wing radicalism, Gruetlianism, social reformism, Trotskyism, Stalinism, and, breathtakingly, back. The difference from (most parts of) Great Britain is the all-embracingness of party life, shattered only by the great events of each generation, a *Kulturkampf*, a war, the death agony of the peasantry, the insurgence of the organized working class, or an emotional fermentation over some happening abroad simplistically reported by the Swiss news agencies – sparse events which nevertheless recur during a long lifetime and may coincide with some private personal crisis.

This long tradition is fast breaking down. It only survives with full force in traditionalizing districts, or where parties are very finely balanced. Many sections of the population are now more mobile, the political press is in financial difficulties, and the rewards of political activity are much diminished. A non-political frame of mind on the one hand, with a utopian leftism on the other, are blurring and bleaching the old political map, to explain which it was necessary to delve far back into the old regime. Swiss democracy could not now work without pressure-groups, but the present tendency seems to be in the direction of relying rather less upon parties. The tendency is ambiguous, because there is a personal connection and a connection in ideas and in the public served, between parties and these underlying interest-groups, church, trade unions, employers' unions, farmers' union, for the catholics, socialists, radicals, and Peasants respectively.

LIBERALISM

The spiritual, and often the genealogical, ancestry of liberals derives from the Helvetic Republic, from the French Revolution on Swiss soil. A current of Young-Hegelian thought flowed into it, a veneration for the state and *Sittlichkeit* which is difficult to disentangle from a native Swiss ethic that may, conceivably, itself have influenced the young Hegel more than he acknowledged, during his tutorship in Berne. During the 1840s liberalism already had become a centre party, and gradually became the typical allegiance of conservative-minded protestants and of the notables of the great liberal professions and of high industry and big finance.

In Berne liberalism has become cheated of its position by the Peasant party, which absorbed the urban conservatives. East Switzerland (east of the Reuss) has a somewhat different political past from the west: there the radicals have retained their extreme right wing under pressure from a left wing, that is to say of the various parties there called Democrat. In consequence, liberalism is now west Swiss, the creed of a small but highly influential and intellectually distinguished class, dominating the serious political press, and with a disproportionate governmental weight. There has long been a catholic (or rather, renegade catholic) liberalism in Solothurn, St Gallen, Lucerne, and Aargau, which is aesthetically rather attractive: it forms a political bridge between the two confessional camps and notably with the protestant conservatives.

RADICALISM

The radical parties of the cantons bear many names – liberal, progressive, radical, democratic, and, especially, *Freisinnig*: this last name is borne by no other party. Radicalism has had a conspicuous place in Switzerland during the last century and a half and it is not much overshooting the mark to say that the character Switzerland bears in economic, cultural, and social life is due to *Freisinn* and to the underlying interests this party represents. Most of the Swiss of whom one has heard in any sphere in the last century and a half were *Freisinnige* – or liberals – but they are the party of less than a quarter of the population.

Modern Switzerland is the creation of the radicals, and the other parties have their justification in correcting and supplementing or resisting their attitudes. The radical in consequence finds it difficult to perceive in himself any political prejudice: he himself is above party, independent, factual, believing in truth, justice, patriotism, and virtue and representing no vested interest. The societies to which he belongs are open to all fellow countrymen of goodwill, and composed exclusively of radicals. The good urban, protestant or atheist, middle class erected into a doctrine and believing in itself, this is 'radicalism' in Switzerland and for most purposes *is* Switzerland.

As for ideology, a radical or a liberal can claim almost the whole of political theory and the life of politics itself as his own; he can claim most parts of the controversy as well as the belief that free controversy is itself a basis of legitimacy. Rousseau (especially in French Switzerland), Kant (and neo-Kantianism, especially in German Switzerland), Hegel, classical political economy, the tradition of natural law superior to state law as well as the opposite doctrine of the supremacy of the majority for the time being, and a sense of nationality – these all find a place in radicalism, and local situations have added anti-clericalism to the list. If this seems to include much, it must be added that it does not readily include what in British politics is called Liberalism, and thus the words radical, and radical-democratic, ceased to be descriptive about eighty years ago.

CHRISTIAN DEMOCRACY

The liberals of the 1830s professed a facile deism, but sneered at priesthoods and mysticism in a manner which time has not robbed of its repulsiveness. They proceeded to active despoliation of monasteries in the same lighthearted manner as they flattened medieval city walls and gateways. But the times turned against them. The churches, and especially the Church of Rome, became dyed with a new romanticism at the same time as the gothic acquired young defenders, and, at the end of the 1830s and the beginning of the 1840s, this movement joined with the genuine conservatism of pre-industrial rural society and of those suffering at first hand or indirectly from factory work. The liberals were pushed to further excesses, and, especially in Aargau, the clerical-conservatives to self-defence. The civil war of 1847 was an easy military victory for radicalism, but left a deep scar, as deep as the American civil war upon the old South, clearly visible in the centenary year of 1948 and only now healed. From this conflict, catholic popular conservatism emerged as a recognizable party, to be given a socio-political doctrine by papal encyclicals, especially *Rerum novarum*, which was to some extent conceived on Swiss soil and moulded in the light of Swiss experience.

In Fribourg, Valais, and Lucerne the catholics had to struggle after 1848 for the rights of a conservative catholic population disfranchised by the contrivances of a liberal minority. The settlement of 1815 had furthermore left a rather large number of ancient catholic minorities in radical cantons, as well as leaving the catholics a number of tiny cantons they would regard as being entirely their own. These circumstances made the catholics enthusiastic for decentralized federalism, for popular voting rights in referendums and in elections. They became, in greater measure than others, an all-class party, accommodating very large differences of emphasis within a single Christian party. They were, and are, democrats by self-interest, and local necessity, though there is little (except the doctrine called subsidiarity) in catholicism's professed doctrines or in the traditional structure of the church to bind the party to democracy. This has led to a certain atmosphere of shifting alliances, of tactics rather than strategy, of small advantages. This opportunism sometimes seems at variance with the magnificent system of ideas derived from St Thomas Aquinas and developed into a modern philosophy, a match and more for Marxism and of equal standing with the ideological inheritance of liberalism.

The Swiss *Kulturkampf* of 1870–90 consolidated rather than weakened the catholics' position, and they successfully traded support in referendums for a first seat on the Federal Council in 1891. Their help in the General Strike of 1918 gave them a second seat in 1919, each seat being at the cost of the radicals. There was a discernible tendency in the 1930s to perceive the positive aspects of Fascism, especially during the Spanish Civil War, and to be clear about the negative aspects of Soviet communism. During the whole inter-war period foreign policy was in the agile hands of Federal Councillor Motta, a catholic-conservative whose sympathy was ambiguous in the confrontation between Fascism and western European parliamentarianism.

The second Vatican Council has led the church to disengage itself from right-wing politics and this, in its turn, to a change in the whole ethical attitude of the catholic cantons, a change outwardly visible in a feverish industrialization and commercialism. The old confidence is gone and the old barriers have fallen. The party apparatus survives, and so does much of the society built around it. If a reaction were to occur in world catholicism, it would find in Switzerland that the foundations still remain to rebuild the catholic camp, but beyond this, catholic democracy can be no surer of its political future than radicalism can.

THE PEASANT PARTY (SVP)

Town and country are traditionally distinct in Switzerland: even today the classes of society are sometimes described as burghers, peasants, and workers, the peasantry being thought of as a class of society for itself and not a trade of which the members are to be classified as employer or employee. The idea is accepted that for each class the powers-that-be should have a policy, a policy for the peasant class, a policy for the lower-middle class, a policy for the upper-middle class, a policy for the workers. This is strange for the Englishman, used only to the concept of the working class as an object for policy, the owners of the policy being presumably the upper classes whom, in their turn, the defenders of the workers regard as fat lowland cattle to be raided in wild sorties of punitive taxation from time to time – with no care for how such fine cattle are to be raised, milked, and cropped.

This type of *ständisch* idea, this idea of society being composed of 'estates', numerically unequal but each with an inherent right to exist, is generally received, but the Peasant party have made it peculiarly their own among the protestant parties – the concept being, of course, entirely acceptable to catholic thought. The Peasant (or Farmers') party formed itself during the first World War, at first in Zurich and then in Berne. The way for it had been prepared by pressure-groups, themselves the product of a basic conflict of interest between the countryside and the urban working class – the former interested in protection and high prices for food, the latter in cheap food from abroad. This conflict had arisen from tariff policies, but was sharpened during the siege conditions of the war, a brief period when the land could hold the towns to ransom and shift some of the burden of debt from its shoulders. The party became the basis of parliamentary government in Canton Berne, and with proportional representation it became a national party able, after 1929, to claim a permanent member in the Federal Council. Its relations are close with the underlying interest-group and the Farmers' Secretariat in Brugg, but it early set out to give itself a wider basis – at first in the groups dependent on agriculture, country lawyers, and traders and so on, and then in the *Mittelstand*, the intermediate estate, generally. The party has proved attractive to salaried officials and to conservatives generally, both to state conservatives believing in the role and authority of the state, and to traditionalists enjoying a romantic fellowship with the past. Pursuing these relationships, the party widened its name to 'Party of Peasants, Traders, and Burgers' (BGB) and now has extended it still further as 'the Swiss *Volkspartei*' (SVP). Wherever it treads in the field of doctrine it is poaching on ground claimed by other ideologies, catholic, liberal, conservative, evangelical, socio-Fascist, and so it depends on local political circumstances, whether these views are represented by the Farmers' or one of the great historical parties.

SOCIALISM

The oldest political organization of the working class is taken to be the Gruetli Society, founded in 1838 or a little before, but this is a field in which it is artificial to disentangle workers' unions to improve conditions, and mutual sickness and unemployment funds, and societies of ideas. The Gruetli was not in origin, indeed, specifically 'socialist', but it became so on account of its membership and character as a self-improvement society. Because of its moderate and rational character, after the middle of the nineteenth century it increasingly obtained the confidence of social Christianity and left-wing radicalism, and proved the stepping-stone between the forces of revolution and the Establishment, which was marked by the federal, salaried, post of Workers' Secretary, started in 1887. The Gruetli officially adopted socialist doctrines in 1893, and became a member *en bloc* of the Swiss Socialist party in 1901, but continued as a society with a life of its own until it dissolved itself in 1925.

The other root of the party is more narrowly political, though here also difficult to disentangle from the trade union movement, from the party political press – the *Volksrecht* – and from the personalities involved, especially Hermann Greulich. The first united organization was in 1873, but this fell apart, and one can either take the Congress of Olten in 1880 as the founding date or, reserving this for the trade union organization, take the definitive establishment of the Swiss Socialist party of 1888 as the relevant date of foundation. The referendum of 1877 on the Federal Factory Law (which established a federal regulation of hours and conditions of work and, above all, an effective inspectorate) proved the culmination and justification of the earliest federal grouping: the party, it may be said, thus had its origins in the politics of the referendum and not in those of representative government.

The same arguments that might lead one to state that the task of trade unionism (or of socialism, or of liberalism, or of conservatism, or of Christianity) in Switzerland was particularly difficult, might also be used to argue that it was peculiarly facilitated. The typical Swiss worker has only since the beginning of this century been seen as quite divorced from the land. Industry arose in the late eighteenth century as a product of the minute subdivision of land among heirs and in those countrysides where this subdivision was practised. As the share of land became smaller, its productivity was increased by the introduction of potato culture: it followed that a worker long retained a portion of land upon which he could rely for food in hard times.[2] The location of industry strengthened this reliance: using water-power, the mills are to be found in long narrow strips curling deep into the countryside. In other parts, the textile industry was

long based on the *Verleger* system, the travelling agent collecting
finished products from 'farmhouses', then loaning the raw material
or perhaps the machines, so that a factory might in effect be dispersed over a rural-seeming landscape. These workers had a certain
economic independence. In addition, they had the fullest political
rights, cantonal power was entirely within their reach: even if they
never mastered the representative system, the direct democracy of
the referendum (or the *Landsgemeinde*) was available after 1875, and
had been available from time immemorial in Glarus and Appenzell.
How could workers be organized? What need was there to organize
them, when the normal political processes and parties (until one
comes to the detail of the law, the position of non-resident citizens
and those receiving poor relief, the publicity of voting, etc.) seemed
to place power in the hands of 'the people'?

This socially and politically democratic environment is peculiar
to Switzerland, but any socialist party must labour under certain
necessities: it must continue as a party, it must proffer a criticism of
the capitalist society among which it lives, it must obtain certain
definite objectives in the short run (progressive taxation of income,
official control of certain aspects of economic life, etc.), and it must
depict an ideal state of affairs where peace, justice, material and
spiritual enjoyments reign – for the doctrine presupposes that social
justice is also technically more effective as an economic system than
capitalism. These necessities intertwine and contradict in a curious
manner, for there are several doctrines which rightfully call themselves socialism (Marxism, for example, or interventionist radicalism, or religious socialism). To continue as a party, the Marxist and
revolutionary wings can usefully be conciliated by a wild negative
attack on capitalist society, while the sober wings can be given charge
of the reformist objectives, cheap milk, social insurance, etc. The ideal
can be pictured in misty outline and agreeable colours, pleasing the
left wing because of its difference from present society, and the right
wing because of its unattainability. Thus a conference of socialists can
work out an acceptable programme. The trouble comes when this
programme is read by the unsympathetic eyes of the property-owning
classes, who take literally the carnage and thunder which the steady
majority of the party inserted in a spirit of brotherly conciliation.
One is astounded by the moderation of the Swiss socialists and by
the persecution they often underwent, but the bourgeois attitude is
also intelligible. The programme of the Swiss party in 1888 can be
read as an extreme radicalism, that of 1904 is already Marxist. The
programme of 1920 is a violent one. 1935 was a certain retreat from
this class-battle violence, but it is only since 1959 that the party has
had a programme which justified socialism's opponents in taking

socialists into their confidence in any way. There is still a certain ambiguity about what happens in practice to anti-socialists, if socialism attains power. Democracy as a means to power is accepted: does it survive, or wither away on attainment? There is also ambiguity about certain practical problems: neutrality, the Common Market, foreign workers, and the balance between industrial activity and an agreeable environment.

Switzerland plays an important part in the history of continental social democracy, but chiefly as a refuge and a meeting-place on account of the cantonal police power: throughout the nineteenth and early twentieth centuries one or more cantons have tolerated fugitives and conferences on Swiss soil. The native Swiss contribution has been rather small. This is not to say that socialism is a foreign import and anti-Swiss; though this is an accusation which can be made concerning Swiss political doctrines throughout the centuries – Switzerland contributed to the development of ideologies here and there, but did not originate or form any of them. The sources of socialism are the same as for working-class organizations generally: (i) the survival of pre-industrial ethics which were critical of industrialisms; (ii) societies of apprentices and journeymen, mostly German (but sometimes French) in Swiss towns with some Swiss members; (iii) the strange anarchic ideas of the back-room workshops of the Juras; (iv) late on the scene, the modern type of dispossessed factory-workers in Zurich, and a few other towns. To these are to be added the constant presence in Switzerland down to the 1930s of one group or other of refugee.

Extreme localism might be thought to be favourable to Swiss social democracy. Two cantons, Glarus and Appenzell Outer Rhodes, are highly industrialized and have had majorities of exploited handworkers. Basle Town and Geneva are (at first sight) city cantons where industry dominates. The town of Zurich enjoys very extensive powers of local self-government. All these could have been enclaves of socialism in a liberal environment, had not such freedom worked both ways and disarmed and deflected socialism into constitutional and historic channels. And even in these citadels, capitalism has fought back with success and usually kept the reins precariously in its own hands against the apparent odds.

THE ALLIANCE OF INDEPENDENTS (LANDESRING)

This is a small party, founded to give expression to the social and economic programme of the founder of the Migros co-operative, and still with its base in that excellent firm. As it is not represented in the Federal Council, it sometimes takes on the role of being a vehicle of opposition to the ruling parties, whose conspiracies it breaks. The centre of its power is in Zurich, but it has been making successful forays to get support, usually from the lower-middle classes, in other cantons. It has a useful function as expressing the views of a non-élite which might otherwise become politically dangerous.

The *Landesring* is now a permanent part of the political landscape, on the federal level and in many of the cantons. In 1972 there were also two small federal parties which collected votes from the large body of anti-immigrant opinion which at one time had as its leader Dr James Schwarzenbach, a Zuricois from a famous textile family, sometimes referred to as 'the Swiss Enoch Powell'. It is not foreseeable whether these will survive as political forces or not. It is not uncommon to find parties which have some success in one election not surviving beyond a single electoral period: this is commonly the case with 'youth parties' which every now and then appear on the cantonal or municipal level, Young Peasants, Team of 1967, Young Radicals, and so on.

COMMUNISM AND FASCISM

Between 5 and 10 per cent of Swiss adults are normally winnable for parties of the extreme Right and Left, whereby over the years a rough symmetry is reached. On the left, there is the usual division between the hard-line Stalinists taking orders from somewhere east of the Iron Curtain, a sober and dedicated group with whom other parties can come to terms from time to time, and, on the other hand, various colourful brands of hippy-politics, students of sociology and architecture suffocated by the Swiss political atmosphere (for example) or emotional anarchists of one sort or another. Political and cultural fashions in France, in particular, are very faithfully followed in French Switzerland and give a tinge to youthful politics.

The extreme Right may, according to circumstances, be a deviation from political catholicism or arise from the general xenophobia and the taste for order widely felt in Switzerland. There are many aspects of Swiss life which, exaggerated, can be seen as having some potentiality towards a rational Fascism – nationalism, the military ethic, Calvinism, anti-communism, a certain tension of feeling concerning Jews and anti-Jews, the cleanness and tidyness and veneration of *Ordnung* that manifests itself in work and school, garden and house – these and other phenomena can assume a distorted form in particular circumstances, but are counteracted by the intense variety of Switzerland, and by a justified satisfaction with the existing order and an appreciation of its adaptability to change.

II. Pressure Groups

Switzerland is governed by the People, that is to say in the last resort, and by those who have the power to create majority opinion.

Switzerland is governed by the political parties, who work not only through the federal and cantonal legislatures and executive councils, but also in a sense through the judiciary and the civil service and education and, one might say, the newspapers and organs of mass communication. Unanimity of parties, however, by no means secures a majority of the People as transmitted by a referendum. Thirdly, Switzerland is governed by certain very powerful organizations and by those who control them and speak for them. These are known as the *Verbände*, the professional and economic organizations, the pressure-groups.

The most formidable, and the oldest, of the *Spitzenverbände* – associations of associations – is the Confederation of Swiss Industry, the famous *Vorort des schweizerischen Handels und Industrievereins*: the name *Vorort* (by which it is usually called) derives from its early period when its headquarters rotated from one commercial centre to another, as did the capital of the Confederacy before 1848. It had its origin (like the other great *Verbände* here considered) in the deficiencies of the Federal Civil Service, and their need for a consultation-partner. A Federal Department of Trade and Customs was set up under the Constitution of 1848, and the businessmen of Basle suggested forming a pan-Swiss organization with which the department could consult: this came to nothing. Until 1863, moreover, no official was appointed to the trade side – the department's activity concerned customs and its policies were free-trade and non-interventionist. Custom duties were therefore levied for fiscal purposes only. The foundation of a national organization representing trade and industry took place only in 1870, in response to a desire expressed by the federal executive. The impetus, significantly, came from Glarus, pioneer in social legislation, and from St Gallen. The association provided a focus for the cantonal employers' organizations, some of which have a broken continuity with institutions of the old regime founded in the sixteenth century – notably the *Kaufmännische Directorium* of St Gallen and (with a short break in its continuity) the *Kaufmännische Gesellschaft* of Zurich. The *Vorort* quickly became officially recognized by the central government, and in 1881–82 the Confederation paid it a subsidy.[3] From that year two Federal Councillors have regularly taken part in its Annual General Meeting. Germany, it must be remembered, had gone over to protectionism in 1879, and France in 1881: trade had entered politics decisively.

Founded to assist and influence the government, the *Vorort*'s justification came with the referendum, and with the disputes over the custom tariffs of 1891 and 1901. Soon a certain anti-collectivist trend became noticeable, and the *Vorort* took on its character as the defence of capitalist enterprise against socialism, for example, in the campaign against the Factory Act of 1877 (which introduced the eleven-hour day in factories) or the long-standing and successful opposition to social insurance schemes. When other political parties entered the government (after 1891), the *Vorort* became manifestly linked in the public mind with the liberal-radical faction, but without any formal connection.

The public may regard the *Vorort* as the left hand of reaction, but in the *Vorort*'s own eyes, things look different. It is conscious of the difficulty of finding any line of action agreeable to the whole of industry and commerce: faced with the great issues of the day – inflation, the Common Market, immigrant labour – the *Vorort* is forced to adopt a strict policy of objectivity and accurate information, of intelligence guided by the national interest (considered in materialist terms).

Swiss public life, with its unchanging personnel, its shared background of attitudes, provides an ideal field of influence for the grey eminences of wealth – and it is certainly the case that in a particular historical situation the student of Swiss affairs takes into account not only the seven Federal Councillors but also the Chairman or Secretary of the *Vorort* (as well as the editor-in-chief of the *Neue Zürcher Zeitung*, the President of the Peasants' Union, and, in wartime, the General of the Army).

The forces which the *Vorort* represents give a certain tone to Swiss affairs, a logicality, an ability to strike free from ideology, a concentration on limited, but real, material benefits. In the absence of these forces, Switzerland would be even more inward-looking, nationalistic, xenophobic, illiberal, shortsighted. The *Vorort* is railed at, but what it represents retains an overwhelming prestige, and it is respected and delivers the goods from which its adversaries – organized labour and agriculture – benefit.

The counterpoint to the *Vorort* is the Swiss Trade Union Association (*Gewerkschaftsbund*, SGB; *Union syndicale suisse*). Formerly, one could refer to the two as adversaries. However, since the famous Peace Agreement of 19 July 1937 (the *Arbeitsfrieden*; discussed above, pp. 115–17) the two have also been in some sense partners.[4] This agreement is the cornerstone of modern Swiss industrial relations: by it strike action was renounced as a method of settling disputes. Since 1945, the Swiss standard of living has crept up to, and surpassed, the standard of countries which resort to strikes. The agreement (it sometimes seems) has changed the whole problem of Switzerland; for the problems of poverty it has, in a quarter of a century, substituted the problems of overflowing prosperity: for the problems of discord it has substituted the problems of complacency and satisfaction.

The agreement must indeed be renegotiated periodically, and inflation (running between 2 and 7 per cent in a year)[5] provides a dynamic for discord, so the Swiss trade unions are by no means made superfluous: nevertheless, they are an organization for wielding a sanction which they never exert, they are an army which never fights. Because, apparently in consequence of industrial peace, there is no genuine unemployment whatever in Switzerland, the problem is of limiting excessive temporary immigration of foreigners trying to obtain work there.

In this context we are concerned with organized labour as a pressure-group and political factor. Three-quarters of union members belong to the *Gewerkschaftsbund*. Of the minority unions, only the Catholic Union (CNG) is important: there is also an Evangelical Union (SVEA) and a liberal one (LFSA), which are of symptomatic interest. Needless to say, the SGB, though nominally without party or religious allegiance, is closely connected in its leadership with the Socialist party (with some overlap of grass-roots membership), while the CNG is connected with the Christian-socialist wing of the Catholic party. Workers with Swiss nationality are almost 50 per cent organized, foreign workers much less so, so the total is normally about one-third organized. The leading union in the SGB is the Metal- and Watch-workers' Union (SMUV), the union which is the party to the Peace Agreement.

The standpoint of the unions on the main problems (wages, prices, rent control, social insurance, factory laws, progressive taxation, immigration) contains few surprises except for the rationality of approach and the moderation of claims.

The influence of the SGB is felt in four ways. First, according to its statutes, the SGB is non-political and non-confessional, but nevertheless in practice about one-half of the socialist members in the federal parliament are union officials. Although there is no institutional connection between party and union, there is a strong personal connection, and in particular the chairman of the union is a member of the managing committee of the Socialist party. The union wing of the party is, as elsewhere, social reformist rather than doctrinaire intellectual. Secondly, the union has direct access to means of influencing public opinion. Often in Switzerland this is done by participation in a referendum campaign; occasionally by launching a referendum, frequently in opposing one, for the SGB (like the other big lobbies) is not quite strong enough to carry a proposal for constitutional amendment, but is easily strong and rich enough to make its opposition to one decisive. Thirdly, since 1919, the SGB has been in constant direct contact with government departments. Nowadays its contact with the important sub-department called colloquially

BIGA[6] (Federal Office for Industry, Trade, and Labour; in French, OFIAMT) is especially close, and it is regarded as a regular and essential consultation partner in the formative stage of legislation. Fourthly, an agreement with the other 'social partners', the *Vorort* and the Peasants' Union, is a combination which overawes government and could if necessary supersede the constitution, and can assuredly carry a referendum. This is what makes the big four (*Vorort, Gewerbeverband,* SGB, and Peasants' Union) so powerful and respected.

The Swiss Peasants' Union, with its Secretariat at Brugg, was founded in 1897. It was long dominated by the personality of its creator and Secretary, Ernst Laur (1871–1964). There had been older associations on the cantonal level (deriving from the physiocratic movement), notably the *Oekonomische Gesellschaft* of Berne founded in 1759: these, which still survive, represent primarily the gentleman farmers.

The interests the Peasants' Union represents enjoy wider support than is apparent at first sight, notably from small traders and employers in the *Gewerbeverband,* and from traditionalists in general. In some cantons these wider interests are politically organized by the Peasants' Party (SVP), but in others the peasantry still support older parties, radicals or catholics, and so the union's catchment area is not identical with that of the SVP. Its membership is wider, in some ways, for it spans the confessional boundary, and narrower in that it pushes exclusively the claims of the land. But the claims of the land are more bound up with the permanent national interest than the claims of the employers or of the workers in industry, and the ethos of the Peasants' Secretariat is patriotic, historicizing, corporativist, and localist: it has close affinities with the official, August-Bank Holiday-speech, ethos of the years 1940–64. In the 1930s, perhaps, the Peasants' youth wing veered a little close to the social-Fascist Fronts, but the movement recovered itself and settled for a patriotic and military ethic. Its friends on the right have never quite forgotten the support the yeomanry gave the established powers at the time of the General Strike in 1918. The left wing (while also not forgetting this) is conciliated by the memory of the increase of agricultural production in beleaguered wartime Switzerland.

The firm position which the peasants' lobby has in the scheme of government of an industrial society seems, at first, out of place. The old ethical basis, traditionalism and the values of rural society, is eroded, but the cult of the environment is taking its place. Having let slip the chance which the peasantry had in the last century (1831–71) of dominating the country, the peasantry has more than recaptured its proportional position. It has done this by the combination of industrial organization (the Peasants' Union) with statistical and scientific data in support of its claim (the Peasants' Secretariat, with its admirable library at Brugg), and has been skilful in the use of the referendum, and of cantonal pressures. It is not fanciful to see the very landscape of Switzerland as the product of this combination of pressure politics and referendum institutions – the cow-bell-image landscape which extends into peasant-dominated Austria, but which abruptly ceases in France and is doomed in Italy. By intelligent political action the farming community has given itself half a century's reprieve from its death sentence, and this is largely due to its political comportment and effective organization.

NOTES

1 The reader must forgive me 'dropping names'. There is a class of statesmen who never obtained the highest federal rank, but who in their day and age stood for an important principle or represented an important political type. Other names might be cited, Jakob Baumgartner, James Fazy, Alfred Escher, and so on. Citing such names means that the alert reader may recognize them when he again hears them mentioned in St Gallen, Geneva, or Zurich. The stuff of politics is not only ideas, but politicians, and I should gladly have dropped more names than fewer, to avoid distortion.

2 This is what impressed foreign observers, such as Bowring. Although it gave a specific character to Swiss working-class movements, connection with the land, statistically speaking, at most times since industrialization may well have been confined to a minority of factory-workers.

3 The subsidy, continued until 1941, was then 7,000 francs (£350): it had suffered successive reductions as a result of federal economy campaigns. The *Vorort* renounced its claim in 1941, in order to help the national finances in an hour of need. These details remind one of the minute scale of Swiss life until very recent years: the 'mini-Great Power status' is more recent than foreigners, or the Swiss, remember.

4 Strictly speaking, the partner of the unions in such negotiations is the *Arbeitgeberverband* (Union of Employers, ZVSAO). Originally (1908–09) this was based on a different, vertical, principle to the *Vorort*, which was at the start a union of cantonal employers' societies (i.e., constructed on a horizontal principle). Time has erased this difference on both sides. Both associations represent many of the same enterprises, sometimes differently grouped, the *Vorort* having the wider coverage and the more dominating position in the public mind. For completeness, one must also mention the *Gewerbeverband* (SGV), the Union of Trades and Crafts, which represents the small employers in retail trade and industry, and thus has a different centre of interest. It must, for example, protect its members *against* the great concentrations which the *Vorort* represents: it shares a belief in private enterprise, but is prepared to be protectionist on occasion and to maintain internal prices by means of cartels. The present SGV dates from 1879, but had predecessors. Between the three great patronal associations the demarcation is not quite logical.

5 In 1973, however, exceeding 10 per cent.

6 There are a dozen offices of which the holder is referred to as the (unofficial) 'eighth Federal Councillor'. The civil servant heading BIGA was the most recent candidate for this unsought title, until it was conferred on the Swiss diplomatic representative in Brussels (in 1973).

CHAPTER 7

Industry

I. The Swiss Economic Miracle

SINCE 1930 the standard of living in Switzerland has risen from relative poverty compared with Britain to relative prosperity, and this conspicuous prosperity spreads to all sections of the native Swiss population (with the possible exception of the elderly in a few rural communities). The impression must be fortified by statistics, but it is that (with some exaggeration) from a country half as prosperous as Britain, Switzerland has become one twice as prosperous. How did this come about?

The Swiss have no doubt that the foremost cause is the wisdom of the trade unions, which renounced the strike as the day-to-day instrument of policy in July 1937 by the famous Peace Agreement of the engineering and metalworking industries – a date felt to be as much a subject of commemoration as the Pact of 1291. The spirit of this agreement has become part of the national ethos, and the British way of managing these things is regarded with the sort of disgust and fear which a primitive people feels for leprosy.

This agreement was not in return for any measure of socialism. The second, but connected, cause of prosperity is thought in Switzerland to be the adherence to a market economy: to a sound currency, free trade, and free competition. These matters must not be overstated: the German mark has regularly proved stronger than the franc. The financial system has the strength that comes from quick-wittedness, secrecy, and mutual support rather than the massive and brutal strength of vast resources. Free trade and free competition are not absolute. Matters are often arranged as between cousins. There are mergers,[1] inhibitions, cartels, tacit conspiracies, winks of the eye, and nudgings. The very law is subject to social and political influences, and there are practices which have survived from wartime, with vague legal backing, double markets (as with shares, which may cost a foreigner twice what they cost a Swiss), and the collusion of the planning authorities and the aliens' police. But having said all this, there is still freedom, with an occasional Japanese-type deflection of the rules. It is the great service of firms like Migros to have set limits to the reign of non-economic considerations, and of enterprises like

Landis & Gyr to have demonstrated that an industry can survive publication of accounts and the rule of ordinary market forces based on full disclosure.

As regards the relationship of finance with technology, there is a parallel with public life. Politics are based on a sort of treaty between ideologists and manipulators, whereby the ideologists get the outward show and sufficient real rewards to make life tolerable, while the manipulators enjoy low respect and have the consolations of power. Financiers, one imagines, rule industry, but the Swiss work-ethos gives respect and possibilities of social mobility to technical excellence, together with a sufficient reward to perpetuate this quality.

Since Swiss economic life is such a success, its characteristics are considered the causes of its success. If it were to be a failure, they would be held to explain this also, and rather convincingly. The recipe is old-fashioned, socially conservative, static, and intellectually unsound. This is one reason why it is interesting: condemned by all rational standards of criticism, it sheds doubt on those standards.

Switzerland is a highly industrialized nation, a country where industry provides its own momentum, a source rather than a recipient of the industrial culture. In history, indeed, Switzerland appears as a secondary pioneer of the industrial revolution, perpetually apprenticed to the pioneer of the day, England, France, Germany, or the United States, but internalizing the lesson and incorporating it into the fibre of her national culture, and able to compete with her master of the hour in certain chosen products and even to surpass him. This remarkable economic achievement has always been given a distinctive colour by the Swiss political structure, by neutrality, for example, by liberalism, or the hegemony of the protestant middle class, or by cantonalism, or the survival and political power of a landowning peasantry.

That industry should be so much at home in Switzerland requires an explanation, and a further explanation is needed as to why it is at home in some parts of the country, in Glarus, for example, but a recent intruder in the other parts, in the Valais, for example, or in Fribourg. In seeking these explanations a pattern emerges which is shared by the great Swiss industries.

A DOMESTIC HANDWORK TRADITION

In the first place, there is an origin in a domestic handwork tradition, often connected with an agricultural or political pattern going back into the middle ages. A long, snowbound, winter or a custom of division of land between heirs, has at various times and places made a secondary occupation necessary. The political dependence of the countryside upon a town in the old regime often led to a concentration of industry in the former, and trade and capital in the latter. A handwork tradition resulted, in which a sort of crisis occurred at the time of the Reformation. There is a faint suggestion that those territories which were marginally more industrial before 1520 accepted the Reformation, and a rather strong suggestion that the territories which rejected the Reformation became less industrial (in a handicraft sense) after 1520, or some later date, than they had been before. In some ways cutting across this tendency was the division between those cantons with a military and a non-military ethos. Basle and Zurich, non-military and with early industries, seemed destined for the Reformation and for future mercantile and industrial prosperity, and events bore out this expectation. But it is difficult to be certain whether Berne or Fribourg was the more industrial before the Reformation. Both retained a military ethos into modern times. Berne became protestant, Fribourg a seat of the Counter-Reformation, but neither industrialized wholeheartedly: Berne slightly increased its medieval rural industries after the Reformation, Fribourg sharply diminished them. Today, Berne has modest enterprises scattered in a rural landscape, while Fribourg remained until the 1950s a pre-industrial community. The most interesting cases are those of the two divided cantons – the catholic Inner Rhodes of Appenzell and the protestant outer parishes; and Glarus, with its protestant commercial families and its catholic and military ones, who long led two inchoate demi-states. In both cases, the protestant areas became the industrial ones, and the catholic remained agricultural and military.

FOREIGN MILITARY SERVICE

The part played by foreign military service in the old regime is ambiguous. Zurich founded its early tendency towards industry on the rejection of mercenary service abroad, under Zwingli's influence, while Appenzell found the capital for its first steps into domestic industry through its share in the confederate military pensions when it became a full canton.

In general, however, the military ethos was unfavourable to industry, and the protestant ethos favourable. The decisions over the places of concentration of industry were largely taken at the Reformation. The workers from the catholic cantons tended, after 1830 or so, to play the part in industrialization that the Irish played in Britain, a source of cheap labour for the new factories – although early industry also sometimes established itself in catholic cantons, in Zug, for example, or Schwyz, to tap the cheap labour at source. In general, however, in catholic territory industry is relatively new, or very new indeed. Uri, Fribourg, and Valais, are countrysides of new dynamic enterprises, imported fully formed from a basis in other cantons, while Solothurn industrialized relatively early. The existence of a particular ethos, non-military, non-catholic, is a precondition of industrial take-off, and this was present in many parts of Switzerland. It is complementary to, but very different from, the William Tell ethos.

A PARTICULAR FORM OF GOVERNMENT

Thirdly, and connected with this, is a particular form of government, a combination of strict legality with a certain blind eye to exploitation, and a power structure whereby industrial success can obtain either the ear of power or a share of it. It is significant that the two pure democracies, Outer Rhodes and protestant Glarus, industrialized early. In a way, however, it is also curious, for the ultimate political power might be seen as lying in the hands of the exploited proletariat. A certain laxity in government, in the countryside of Zurich and Basle, for example, also assisted industry (especially in some processes or branches of enterprise that were not subject to the old guild regulations), and the weak or rather uninterested governments of the Jura chain may have contributed more to industry than the conscientious paternalism of Berne.

PEACE AND NEUTRALITY

Above all, there was peace, neutrality, unbroken (except for somewhat stylized battles in the occasional civil wars between the protestant and catholic cantons) from the 1530s until 1798, and again from 1815 until the present day. The young industries in those parts of modern Switzerland over which the Thirty Years War did rage (the prince-bishopric of Basle, the Fricktal, Grisons) in fact suffered for a century as a result, or went under. Superficially, at any rate, neutrals seem to profit by the wars and troubles of neighbours. There were profitable exports during the Thirty Years War and, following it, a certain financial depression. Other large troubles brought other small profits, the red kerchiefs, for example, worn by the Paris revolutionaries were woven in the Toggenburg and Appenzell. War remained external, but some of its indirect stimulus to economic activity was felt. The influence of the Napoleonic Wars, and of the Continental Blockade, was more direct: the first take-off, the first independent flight, of textile production and of machinery for textiles, took place as a consequence of war and the interruption which Napoleon made in the supremacy of England.

LEGALITY AND REPUBLICAN ETHOS

As for strict legality, in the republics of Switzerland this environment was reserved for the privileged classes, pre-eminently but not exclusively the inner patriciate of the sovereign cities. Especially the great banking dynasties of Geneva benefited from a relative absence of arbitrariness, and the locally important financial power of Basle and St Gallen, and later Zurich, owes much to this secure basis which enabled the protestant ethic to take the form of production of wealth. Republicanism brought also a trend towards equality which worked in two ways: on the one hand, it made extravagance politically dangerous and thus encouraged saving, but on the other hand, it discouraged accumulations of too great a size. Such personal extravagance as has left traces in private buildings seems, by comparison with other countries, relatively modest – the Freuler Palace at Näfels, the Schlösschen A Pro near Flüelen, even the relative megalomania of the Stockalpers in Brig and elsewhere, the Gonzenbachs' house at Hauptwil, the Zellwegers' houses at Trogen, and so on, are not extraordinary by German princely standards, though such follies can be found here and there throughout the land. In the catholic parts, superfluous private wealth might finish up as a rebuilt abbey or an ambitious church.

A SUPPLY OF CAPITAL

Furthermore, capital was available. It seems in the late seventeenth century and throughout the eighteenth to have been difficult for a prudent Swiss to find an investment for his capital beyond keeping gold in a chest. The rate of interest obtainable was often low, less than, and sometimes much less than, the 'natural' rate of 5 per cent. Churches and governments inveighed against the practice of only paying 2 or 3 per cent. When it was impossible to lend on the security of rent-charges or mortgages on land, loans were made by the sovereign cities, and by individuals, at low interest to Britain and at high risk to France. Already in the late eighteenth century the (old) *Zürcher Zeitung* was reporting the stock market – but exclusively foreign stocks. There was no Swiss or cantonal public debt.

Some, but perhaps not a large proportion, of capital from this source of private saving found its way into those forms of industry where there was visible security, such as the loan of yarn for weaving or the purchase of looms – either directly through the middleman, the *Verleger*, or via banking enterprises. In the mid-nineteenth century the railway industry found local capital insufficient, but German, French, or other foreign capital was then available, and occasionally British and, nowadays, American. Direct investment in risk capital by individuals unconnected with management, however, is rather rare, late, and undeveloped in Switzerland. Yet non-risk capital has frequently been lost, especially loans on the security of hotels (an industry which has twice systematically gone bankrupt) and in railroads (and at one time, in banks). Often in the history of a Swiss enterprise one is surprised by the pre-industrial source of the original capital, the prudent marriage, the family holdings, the act of political sharp practice, the saved pittance, or the source abroad. There seems, in the literature, a gap between showing that capital was available and showing how it was channelled into the new enterprises which changed the face of the country. In this formation of capital, the generally low taxation of Switzerland (sometimes the product of underexpenditure on defence or social welfare) is a perennial factor.

AVAILABILITY OF A LABOUR FORCE

Next there comes the availability of a labour force. Switzerland is traditionally (but not today) a land of emigration. The landowning yeomanry with political power limited its own numbers, and so did the privileged citizenries of the towns. But there was a small true proletariat at the base of the social system everywhere, and there were the catholic districts with a population surplus. Industry was physically decentralized and mopped up many local pools of starvation near their source. There were patterns, too, of temporary or permanent migration which may at one time have helped industry, and fluctuations in the availability of foreign mercenary service. At most times there was a shortage of work rather than of workers, though there have been wild fluctuations in particular industries, in watches and textiles for example. The distress caused by the successive agricultural revolutions of the Swiss lowlands, the enclosures of the eighteenth century, the switch from a corn to a milk economy, and the crises of the nineteenth century due to imports from the New World, were timely in that they brought labour resources to the new enterprises and factories when they were most needed.

A FOREIGN IDEA

Then there has been a foreign idea. Neither watches, mechanical spinning or weaving, steam-power, railways, aniline dyes, electricity, banks, nor insurance, after all, were invented or pioneered in Switzerland. It is regularly at the end of the initial period that Swiss technical conscientiousness or organizing ability comes in and chisels out a share in the market. A quarter or half a century may elapse between the exploitation of an idea in the West and its development in Switzerland. There is some inhibiting factor to inventiveness in the social and ethical system. To copy, smuggle, even to purloin an idea has been held reputable: to perfect an idea is admirable; but Switzerland is a hard place to pioneer or to sell a really new idea. I think this generalization applies to the cultural sphere as well: hippies, Hell's Angels, protest, the Environment (to take trivial recent examples) appear as imports, as foreign seeds which flower on Swiss soil.

SWISS CREATIVITY

But though the seed be foreign, it is introduced into Switzerland by a native hero of genius. Derivativeness on the evening of the first day does not mean that there are not Swiss giants of creativity. Nearly every Swiss industry has its creative hero, without whom it would never have been implanted, and who has a genuine inventiveness – often a secondary but a crucial invention, sometimes in technique (such as mini-mass production of watch parts). Swiss industrial and commercial history is often the biography of colourful individuals.

THE MARKETS

Finally, there are markets. Neutralism has commercial advantages. A small country is not feared. It can intrude into its neighbours' markets, and it can weave commercial webs inside the colonies of naval powers without being much resented either by the colonizers or by the colonized. The cotton-printers of Glarus must have devastated village industries in the Dutch Indies, in India, and in Siam: the story is told (too often for credibility) of the son of the factory-owner, sent out by the firm to the East to buy samples of the best local designs, who returned after a strenuous year with his purchases, only to find the samples were all the products of the paternal mill. The Swiss have been very ingenious in penetrating markets, and in recent years in new techniques of doing so by establishing daughter-firms beyond tariff barriers. The doctrine of free trade, too, was forced upon the centralizers of the Helvetic state, and is part of the ideology of the anti-cantonalists, and the anti-patricians. In some respects the geographical position of Switzerland has proved favourable, though it is a geography improved by man, by roads, railway tunnels, oil-pipelines, and the now navigable Rhine.

Having said all this, there is still a mystery. Swiss industries have regularly had one fairy godmother fewer than those of other countries. Iron is present, and the handicraft origin depends on this, but it is scarce. Wood is there as a fuel, so is water and hydro-electric power, but in relatively small quantities, sufficient for take-off, but not for flight. There was native wool and flax, but the industry was founded on imports of raw material. Silk and cotton had to be carried by pack-ponies over the Alps, and sometimes carried back. Even in agriculture, the raw material for cheese exports could only be home-produced at the cost of the raw material for bread. The country is too small for a proper stock-market, the home basis by itself is rather small for a traders' currency or a banking industry or insurance. Wherever one looks there is some deficiency, which may indeed have acted as an incentive, but could, in other circumstances, have acted as a total preventive. There is an economic miracle, wrought by native courage and inventiveness and the viability of the native ethic, which is of the same cloth as the Swiss political miracle.

II. Textiles

The first industrial revolution – the movement from primary production (agriculture, forestry, mining, and so on) to secondary production, the application of water, steam, and electric power, the employment of borrowed capital, and the new organization of work in factories – was pioneered by textiles. When one looks at a piece of cloth, and imagines the spinning of wool or cotton into thread between finger and thumb, and the weaving of thread into cloth by throwing a shuttle of thread the yard's length between the left and the right hands, one visualizes the drudgery of creating textile fabrics to clothe mankind before the age of machinery. With mechanization of textile operations, human life was changed and the old society overturned.

Today, Switzerland (like other countries of the West) is entering the third, the post-industrial, phase. The number of workers engaged in secondary production remains constant, and of those in the tertiary (service) sphere has increased by an amount which compensates for the diminution of numbers of those in the primary sphere. Immigrant labour, and this also is typical, has in some cases almost taken over the primary sphere from the native-born, and is infiltrating into the secondary. But in detail the categories break down and become meaningless: what is significant is that the great service industries, and especially the management of money – banking, insurance, and financial management – are becoming more important, and honest toil in the open air producing a product one can see and touch and use immediately, is decreasing. Textile production itself has long seemed on the verge of deserting western Europe. This shrinking of the textile industry is the sign that Switzerland has entered the post-industrial stage of development, just as her expansion had been the sign of entry into the industrial age.

The handwork origins of the weaving industry can be found everywhere. Each ancient city in Switzerland has its weavers' guild. Linen manufacture was widespread in the east of Switzerland at the close of the middle ages (eclipsing that of the town of Constance, where it had probably started), but there were minor locations elsewhere: after 1800 the industry retreated into one of these outlying centres – the Bernese and Lucerne Emme valleys. Wool has been woven for export in many places, especially in west Switzerland, to be sold at the Zurzach fairs and Geneva. Silk manufacturers of specialized types were introduced, and reintroduced, from Italy into Geneva, Basle, and Zurich, at various times.

Spinning in the middle ages was not so much an industry as a predicament of the female sex: in fairy stories even princesses spin, and in no other way could the need for thread for weaving be met. There are no spinners' guilds. And until spinning was mechanized there was only a limited justification for the mechanization of weaving. Factory weaving in Switzerland therefore comes rather late. From the beginning of the eighteenth century an early capitalist organization was widespread in the Swiss countryside, often originally based on loans by cities to patrician families on the security of their land and houses, and as a result of their political influence. In various times and places a capitalist organization had appeared in earlier centuries, but it was shortlived. Italian and French refugees brought successive industries to Geneva and to Basle. In Zurich, a handful of families from Locarno and Lucca provided an impetus and added a few names to the patriciate of later centuries, von Muralt and von Orelli in particular (the Pestalozzi were not refugees, as their Italian name suggests, but came from a Grisons territory). Huguenots, too, brought an impetus, but were less generously treated and seldom received into citizenship: in the town of Zurich none were, for when their secrets were learned, the refugees were expelled. The workshops set up to pursue such introduced crafts had capitalist characteristics, but the old guilds were jealous and usually limited expansion. The only attempts at mechanization using water-power were in the twisting of silk. Some eighteenth-century industries were based on foreign, sometimes English, cotton-yarn or cloth, as was the cotton-printing industry in Glarus. The general picture is one of constant change, so that a district might move the whole way through the processes of textile-making in less than a century, starting with a specialization in spinning, and ending with printing and finishing of cloth. Periods of prosperity alternated with periods of depression and unsuccessful competition.

With an increasing division of labour in the eighteenth century, many operations needed only a fairly generalized skill – habits of punctuality, exactitude, conscientiousness. But a few operations, on the contrary, needed education and alertness, and artistic capacities or inventiveness, or a modest capital. Thus, in the pure democracy of Glarus, for example, a class system of the modern type was created, a hereditary proletariat, and a hereditary middle class ready to take advantage of the liberal revolution. Here and there small factories were constructed, for the textile operations higher up the chain (such as dyeing or printing) need a dozen or so operatives working together.

Similar developments can be followed elsewhere in east Switzerland, a movement from hand-spinning of local products to hand-machine spinning of an imported product, cotton or (locally) silk, or silk wastes, and from thence to products such as colour-weaving or embroidery. The progression was to repeat itself during the next century, moving from mechanical spinning, for example, to mechanical embroidery. The changes this implied were painful, even agonizing, preceded by intense poverty and accompanied by social readjustments between families – and such crises were frequent, every fifteen years or so. Export-oriented, workers were the prey of foreign decisions, of import taxes, of wars, changes of fashion, and competition from England, France, and Germany. It may be recalled that a very considerable part of east Switzerland (notably the protestant part) is in fact an industrial landscape, in spite of its superficially pastoral appearance, a landscape of home industries and very small factories, where wages are supplemented by an acre or a potato patch, a cow or two, and a share in the communal forest. By about 1800, this part of Switzerland was considered the most heavily industrialized part of continental Europe. Goethe (in *Wilhelm Meister*) regarded Appenzell for this reason as idyllic.[2]

The revolution in industry in Switzerland, it is generally agreed, coincided with the political revolution of 1798, and was organically connected with it. Symbolically, it opened with the establishment of English spinning-machines in the empty halls of the great monastery of St Gallen, which had been secularized – the 26 spinning-mules installed there started production in 1800. In that same year the spinning factory of Hard was founded near Wülflingen (Winterthur), and this entered production in 1802. For a time it was the largest on the mainland of Europe. Then factories were opened in Rapperswil and Trogen (Appenzell, Outer Rhodes). In 1805 the famous firm of Escher-Wyss, a partnership of enterprising Zurich patricians, started manufacturing, and already in the next year had diversified into the trade that made the firm famous, into the production of their own copies of the machines they used – being forced to this expedient by Napoleon's Continental Blockade: the step from textiles to the machine-making industry had been taken. Another firm (still famous), J.-J. Rieter and Co. of Winterthur, took the same step into machine-making with their spinning-mill, founded in 1812: the firm also operated in St Georgen near St Gallen. They then moved into, and destroyed, the old convent at Töss near Winterthur, a Hapsburg foundation which had an important series of frescoes in its cloisters.

In 1814 Salomon Honegger used the water-power of the Jona (north of the Lake of Zurich, above Rapperswil) for a spinning factory. Under his famous son, Caspar, this moved upstream to Rüti and the small river became used for mills for much of its length. The long river Töss, flowing through the Zurich landscape by Winterthur into the Rhine, likewise became exploited for industry, as did the upper valley of the Linth in Glarus – a sort of industrial ribbon-development still rather remarkable to observe. The most startling character was the 'Spinner King', Heinrich Kunz (1793–1859), who started in Oetwil north of the lake of Zurich working in his father's attic, and died worth more than 20 million francs.

The application of powered (as opposed to hand) machinery to the process of *weaving* is another story.

The liberal *coup d'état* in Canton Zurich had started with an assembly in the township of Uster. On the first anniversary, another mass meeting was held in the same place in commemoration. But the meeting turned its hand to a matter of more urgent importance to the working class than the establishment of a high-liberal constitution: the crowd riotously burned down the factory of Corrodi & Pfister, the pioneer of mechanical weaving (as opposed to spinning) in Switzerland. This act of luddism was severely avenged in the criminal courts, but it postponed for some years the introduction of advanced mechanization into weaving. When introduced, two years later, it was over the border of Zurich in the catholic countryside of Schwyz (by one of the brothers Honegger, whose enterprises became famous). The fire of Uster is a sort of turning-point in Swiss social history – when the working class surfaced for the first time – but in the long run the gesture was ineffective to hold back mechanization, which was powered at first by water, then by coal and steam, and ultimately by electricity.

When one looks at the economic history of a district, rather than of a particular industrial operation, there is often a recognizable pattern. In the middle ages and until the early eighteenth century, it is usually a story of a new industry being introduced from abroad, usually from Italy, into a particular town, and flourishing there with governmental encouragement, or, as the case may be, flourishing in spite of the opposition of established local guilds. Then, within half a century or so, the new craft disappears. There is probably no particular textile industry which can trace back its origins in a district beyond the mid-seventeenth century, and very few quite so far. As regards individual firms, the only really old enterprises are paper factories which, anchored in a water-mill, can in a few cases claim a continuity into the late fifteenth century: an 'old textile firm' usually dates from 1830–60 at most. The only continuity in a particular place is a sort of proneness to textility, a background of enterprise and available labour, of capital and speed to take up a new idea. Apart from Basle and Geneva, the export-oriented textile industry is now chiefly concentrated in east Switzerland, and the important developments took place there – in the Zurich countryside, in Toggenburg, Appenzell Outer Rhodes, St Gallen, and, most remarkably, in Glarus.

The Glarus industry started around 1712, with hand-spinning of cotton introduced by a protestant clergyman to relieve poverty and to stay emigration. The raw material, of course, was entirely foreign. The industry was at first pursued in the homestead, often with the help of children, feeding a population with limited resources of land, and enabling holdings to be ever more minutely divided on inheritance. The introduction of potato husbandry in the 1770s enabled an increased population to be maintained. During the course of the eighteenth century, textile specialization rapidly ascended throughout the whole range of processes, from spinning to weaving, to finishing and printing. With the application of power to spinning, the whole operation repeated itself in the nineteenth century. In the 1970s, the textile industry is (once again) said to be moribund. Nowadays it is based on small, untidy, unhistorical conurbations which often have a certain period patina of the 1850s. The workforce is chiefly foreign, in some branches stiffened with a backbone of elderly Swiss matrons of a type which is dying out. The foreign workers, on enquiry, sometimes themselves come from villages in which a pre-industrial type of craft-work – spinning, for example – is still alive. The return on capital in these enterprises, one suspects, is often only about 5 per cent and probably the bank advancing the capital has the same suspicion. In any one district there is a traditional specialization – silk-weaving, for example, south of Zurich. Most branches are being undercut by Japan and other industrializing countries, and occasionally by still more highly capitalized industry elsewhere. As before, the Swiss retaliate by still greater specialization. The industry has so often been on the point of death that it is unwise to speculate that it will not survive this crisis: its absolute volume of export is still quite considerable, and its firms skilful and resilient.

III. Machines

The machine industry is partly, but not entirely, a side-effect of textiles. Sulzers, the Krupps of Winterthur, was self-started as a metal-working enterprise, an expansion of a small business of a locally respectable family in the early nineteenth century (the present firm was founded as such in 1834). So was Georg Fischer's, also a famous firm for heavy iron products. Later firms, Maschinenfabrik Oerlikon,

Bührle (armaments, a firm with a controversial record), and Brown-Boveri, have a different origin: they are secondary firms building on the success of the pioneers and sometimes taking over men trained in the earlier firms. Two Englishmen, Charles Brown father and son, brought their undisciplined inventive genius and imagination to Sulzers and Oerlikon as well as to the firm which bears their name and that of a German immigrant, Boveri, who introduced the necessary capital by a fortunate marriage. Brown-Boveri came to specialize in a new branch of the industry, electrical generating, which has proved of great importance. A spin-off from electricity has also been the great aluminium enterprise at Chippis in the Valais, whose parent firm mars the Rhine Fall at Schaffhausen with its intruding factory: aluminium requires vast quanitities of electrical current for its manufacture.

IV. Chemicals

The chemical industry also finds one of its ancestors in textiles, for the step into the industrial age was taken with the help of the cloth-dyeing industry. Its principal location is in Basle, but Geneva leads in the kindred industry of cosmetics. Unlike other Swiss export industry, its products are relatively 'heavy', in both raw material and finished product, though there is a typical Swiss pre-eminence in the lighter end of pharmaceuticals in which labour (or rather intellectual, i.e., research) costs are a very high proportion of the product. This reflects a change in the structure of Swiss society.

The predominance of Basle is due to geography, politics, the availability of capital, and the social environment. Basle is wedged between France and Germany, and lies astride the Rhine, which is with art navigable and which a primitive technology could use as a sewer for its poisonous wastes, and which is here easily bridged. It has a corner site on a natural crossroads. When the synthetic dye industry was born in Britain and France, and developed and flourished in Germany, Swiss sovereignty enabled these inventions to be pirated, at first for the local textiles and then for export. The raw material, notably coal tar, had to be imported, but Basle could do this for it had an advantageous position in the European railway system, and fought hard and successfully to maintain the advantages of the position within Switzerland: it was the first Swiss town to have a railway, and pioneered the first long tunnel on Swiss territory, the upper of the two tunnels beneath the (Lower) Hauenstein. Basle, like Zurich, had an interest in the Gotthard being made the centre of the Swiss railway system and recovering its position as a hub of mainland Europe. The pharmaceutical industries of Basle at first were also a by-product of tar distillates or dye-stuff experiments, and benefited from the intellectual processes developed in the production of dyes, processes which crossed the frontier between organic and inorganic chemistry.

The great names in the Basle chemical industry, Geigy, CIBA, Sandoz, Roche, have histories which typify its various origins. Geigy bears the name of a Basle patrician family, which in the eighteenth century traded in spices, including drugs, and dyestuff roots for the silk ribbon manufacture (which was owned by city families and exercised in the Baslois countryside). In the 1830s it moved over into silk dyes, and in 1856 into the new aniline process, for Swiss patent law allowed Swiss manufacturers to exploit foreign patents, while enabling them to patent their own inventions abroad – an example of the intelligent co-operation of government with industry which is one of the minor secrets of Swiss economic success. Other great firms grew out of private research and enterprise. Sandoz, at the other extreme to Geigy, was founded in 1886 by a capitalist who reckoned that there was a good future in chemicals, and invested his family capital in this rather than in textiles, hiring an experimental scientist of genius, Keller, to manage the scientific side. CIBA (Chemical Industries in Basle) derives from an enterprise started by a Frenchman to exploit anilin. The former Durand & Huguenin also demonstrated a typical debt to foreign inventiveness and enterprise, allied to native capital and seeking the protection of Swiss freedom from foreign patent laws. Hoffmann-La Roche, bearing a well-known local family name, specialized from the start in pharmaceuticals. It is a firm whose secretiveness is widely known, which reveals little in its company reports, and whose shares (at about £15,000 each) are monumentally 'heavy' and concentrated in few hands.

Geigy developed DDT, a winner, thought of as a mothproofer of textiles. It has now fused with CIBA. Roche and Sandoz have equally famous products, unexcelled in purity and quality. The three firms co-operate and compete in a very typical manner, having been linked informally since the 1930s by a sort of loose cartel. Their factory premises run in and out of each other, sometimes straying across the international frontier into France, so they are physically and socially in close contact while each preserves a distinctive style.

The export side of the light end of chemicals is the area of fastest growth of the Swiss economy, whereas watchmaking just holds its relative position, and textiles are declining. The ethos of the industry is perhaps now more typical of modern Switzerland than watchmaking is. Since the turning-point of the foundation of the ETH (Federal Institute of Technology in Zurich) in 1856 it has gradually become based on native Swiss research. Although still in great part located on Swiss territory, it shows a typical tendency to become a service industry, supplying the technology, organization, and much of the capital to a world-wide industry. The combination of benefiting and exploiting mankind, doing good with a calculating eye on the main chance, is as typically Swiss as the delicate combination of competition and collaboration within the industry, and its strongly localized basis in the distinctive atmosphere of the immediate environs of the old free city of Basle.

V. Prepared Foodstuffs

The prepared-food industry, soups, chocolate, condensed milk, and the like, also has a slender base in a native tradition, for natives of the Ticino and Grisons long dominated the confectionery trade in north Italy. It is more widely spread than chemicals are: it has historic centres not only in Vevey (on the Lake of Geneva), but also in Neuchâtel, Berne, Cham on the Lake of Zug, and the historic Maggi mill at Kempttal (by the side of the main road from Zurich to Winterthur). The great names, Nestlé, Suchard, Peter, Cailler, Lindt, and so on, are of mid-nineteenth-century pioneers. One of the historic firms, Anglo-Swiss Condensed Milk, was an American foundation: like many others, it has become a part of Nestlé. The greater part of the production is not physically exported, but produced in factories located abroad. Indeed, foodstuffs are the extreme example of this form of decentralized Swiss production, closely managed from Switzerland and bringing great financial reward to the country. The great names, such as Knorr and Nestlé, are on the most frequently bought products of the country and create much of the image of Switzerland in the mind of foreigners: this causes a certain tension among patriotic Swiss, typified by the chocolate on sale in Berne called 'Tradition' and advertised by the colours and the flamed cross of the eighteenth-century mercenary regiments. Swiss cultural diplomacy is at pains to counteract this sort of chocolate and yodel image, while not replacing it by banking gnomes or arms manufacturers or drug monopolists.

VI. Watchmaking

Clocks and watches are the essential instrument of Western civilization, necessary to science, and a symbol of regularity and rationality as well as of luxury and status. The larger part of the world's exported, high-quality, watches are still made in Switzerland: for a short time after the last war nine-tenths were. The Swiss see themselves, in one mood, as typical watchmakers, precise, reliable, industrious, producing goods of high individual quality, engaged in an industry where individualism and small scale are combined with mutual dependence and the service of mankind. And Switzerland could still, at a pinch, satisfy the whole world demand for watches – not the potential demand, but the demand at the traditional price.

The industry is traditionally concentrated in a very strange part of the country, the thinly grassed limestone ridges of the Juras which have otherwise no wealth to display. Agriculture there produces little, except horse-pastures and forest, for the limestone does not retain water. The country is seamed with deep parallel gorges along which the bitter north-westerly Bise blows, while the dividing ridges exclude the Föhn, so it is climatically the most disagreeable inhabited part of Switzerland, and has long, Siberian winters. Until recent times, also, communications were exceptionally bad.

Different parts of the range have specialized in different types of production – cheap watches and expensive, watches and clocks – from Basle through Neuchâtel to Geneva and into the prolongation of the Juras in eastern France. The watchmaking towns are artificial, and of relatively modern (eighteenth-century) foundation. Le Locle and La Chaux-de-Fonds appear suddenly in a sort of wilderness, to provide a test case against those who believe in geographical inevitability.

The making of big clocks, like the historic one in Basle or the Zytglogge in Berne, seems to have been in the late middle ages the work of specialized smiths, of armourers and locksmiths. The demand for these big monastic or urban clocks was intermittent, for they last for half a dozen centuries, so the craftsmen themselves were itinerant. Smaller clocks were also made for the wall or table of noblemen. Watches, on the other hand, were the work of the goldsmith or jeweller and came much later on the scene. After the Reformation, the goldsmiths in Geneva sought an outlet for their skill in secular rather than religious artefacts, and watchmakers from Burgundy were therefore welcomed in the 1570s and 1580s. The ethos of Calvin's theocracy, and Geneva's continuing importance as a market, encouraged a special skill. Politically, also, the craft fitted in well as a suitable avocation for the outer class of citizens, of families hereditarily privileged but kept at arm's length from the inner citadel of power by the patrician oligarchy. Jean-Jacques Rousseau was from this class, a class whose main privilege chiefly consisted in the monopoly of watchmaking which it preserved until the mid-eighteenth century. On this Genevese skill the watchmaking tradition of the Juras was built, spreading to Neuchâtel, famed for its elegant clocks, and thence (probably) to the Jura countryside.

Besides the ironsmiths and the goldsmiths, whose crafts overlapped, the third source of the industry is to be found in the Juras themselves. It was the latest area of present-day Switzerland to be settled: first had come monks, to Moutier, St-Imier, St-Ursanne, and

elsewhere. Much later came lay colonizers attracted by special privileges granted by the counts and princes of Neuchâtel, the counts
of Valengin, the prince-bishops of Basle, and others – chiefly in the
fourteenth century. As late as the eighteenth century there were still
empty places where Pietist and sectarian refugees could be settled.
Charcoal, iron, and glass were produced, and many homestead
names reveal this former activity. Under the protective influence of
Berne, the principality of Neuchâtel (and some outlying domains
of the prince-bishop where he could not exercise effective sovereignty)
adopted the Reformation. After the first multiplication of the settlers,
subsidiary employment became necessary, especially as the winters
are so exceptionally long and snowbound. This was, as elsewhere,
found in textiles – for the industrial take-off is even here through
textiles. Here it was the lace manufacture, needing delicacy and neat
fingers.

The introduction of watchmaking is accounted for in a traditional
anecdote, first recorded by a local historian in the 1770s. It is attached
to a genuine name, Daniel JeanRichard, but the date ascribed seems
somewhat too late, and Daniel was not in fact (as Tompion had
probably been) a blacksmith. The story is given by Archdeacon
Coxe (*Travels in Switzerland*, London, 1779, 1789) much as in the
narration by Osterwald. In 1679, it is said, a horse-merchant showed
Daniel's father, a blacksmith to whom the boy was apprenticed, a
watch made in London, and asked if it could be repaired. The son
volunteered to repair it, and managed to do so and also to record the
mechanism. After a year he succeeded in making a whole watch
himself, and then travelled to Geneva to learn details of the manufacture there. 'He continued for some time the only watchmaker in
these parts', says Coxe, 'but business increasing, he instructed several
associates; by whose assistance he was enabled to supply from his
single shop all the demands of the neighbouring country'. In this
saga, three stories may be conflated, and probably JeanRichard was
only responsible for some innovation in production: the district
specialized in turnip-watches of coarser and cheaper manufacture
than Geneva, with some approach to mass production. The absence
of guild regulation was here a help. Manufacture soon became
specialized – the spring, machine tools, case, balance, face, hands,
etc., being made in separate small workshops and assembled and
mounted by another craftsman still: the assembler tended to dominate the trade economically – but each stage held some sort of
stranglehold over the whole process.

The later history of watchmaking is of crises every fifteen years
or so, occasioned by changes in technique, although the basic principle was established in the classic mechanism of the early nineteenth

century, and only now is threatened. Some of these changes were initiated in Switzerland, and some cleared inconvenient rivals out of the way – the English industry, for example, was destroyed twice by Jura competition even though it had been at times the pioneer. Some came near to destroying the Swiss industry. The two most remarkable were the introduction of the cheaper, massive, Roskopf watch from the 1870s, and the shift to the wrist-watch in the years immediately before the first World War, to which the Swiss were a little slow to adapt.

The boom time immediately after the second World War led to a typical reaction into guild-type cartelization and protection of technical achievements and the prevention of export and import of parts, so as to get if possible the whole production physically on Swiss soil (providing work for Swiss to the exclusion of foreigners) with a typical encouragement to the smuggling of watches abroad so as to prevent rival industries being protected by import duties. A whole temporary pathos and myth were constructed, somewhat archaizing, to associate patriotism and watchmaking. 'C'est peut-être la plus authentiquement suisse de toutes les fabrications nationales', wrote André Siegfried in his admirable documentation of Switzerland smiling to herself in front of the mirror, *La Suisse, Démocratie témoin* (still today the most perfect single evocation of the country). Feather-bedded, with draughts excluded, the industry dozed. When it woke, prodded by Japanese, American, and other competition, it found itself becoming slightly out of date, with a bad image among young people, secretive where it should have propagandized, and a work-force predominantly foreign. Whereas other industries have taken native capital and techniques abroad, the most famous example being the Nestlé group, watchmaking has imported foreign labour to manufacture within Switzerland goods destined for export – occasionally even using foreign capital. The most recent healthy-shock has come from electronics, pioneered and developed outside Switzerland, but adopted in time and exploited to fit Swiss conditions and capacities.

Under such pressures, the atmosphere and structure of watchmaking have changed. There has been a great wave of concentration of capital and management. The *atelier*, the small master working with a handful of assistants (a cell of utopian politics, and anarchist or faintly dotty speculation) has nearly disappeared. Expenditure on research has vastly increased. Within the next decade one may expect a modern commercial structure with the twentieth-century style of shareholding and openness, because the restrictive legal network (designed by the industry to preserve its supremacy in the world market) has been largely removed. Perhaps what is ultimately needed is the disappearance of the watch industry as a special case, and its absorption into the machine industry in general: but this is just the sort of step which may have to be resisted – in this and other fields – if Switzerland is to preserve the distinctive civilization which gives it a reason for survival.

The present difficulties in the watch industry are not untypical in Swiss industrial history. Swiss industries in their origin offer a cheaper article of lower quality than their competitor. In possession of a market, their quality relative to other countries increases to meet technical advances by competitors. Faced with competition, there is panic among the small producers, now concerned to maintain quality, cartels and mergers are created, and government help is solicited. For a time this is successful, then the system breaks down, but a new Swiss or introduced invention at the eleventh hour saves Swiss industry and places it again on a competitive basis. The story of many minor industries – of shoe manufacturing for example – runs thus. What is now needed is the innovation which will allow Switzerland to enter the mass market for wrist-watches in competition with Japan.

VII. Banks

In the Swiss free cities of the high middle ages conditions existed out of which banks might have arisen – settlements of Jews, then Lombards and (probably) Cathars, who did a lively business as pawnbrokers, mortgagees, moneychangers, and the like. Meanwhile the town fiscs, and families of native or immigrated burghers, entered the business: much of the growth of the city territories has origins in the infinitely complicated financial transactions and indebtedness of the local landed nobility, which ended in transfer of the ownership of large jurisdictions to the town. But from the early beginnings of usury and fecklessness there is no significant continuity to modern banking; some patrician families (like the von Diesbachs of Berne and Fribourg) owe their origin to such business, but after the Reformation took up the new ethos which looked to civic office, military and administrative rank, and ownership of land and houses as the basis of respect. The new banking probably derived afresh from Italy, from Italian families fleeing the counter-reform, notably to Geneva. In the mid-eighteenth century, new banking families arose whose names are still powerful, chiefly in Geneva but also in Neuchâtel, Basle, St Gallen, and Zurich, and to a lesser extent in minor centres, Berne, Lucerne, Schaffhausen: the last five markets were probably in some way dependent on German centres such as Augsburg. These families sometimes played a role in French or even in English history. One may mention such names as Hentsch, Hottinguer, Thellusson,

Paccard, Ador, de Rougement, Iselin, La Roche: there are others. These names are still to be seen on discrete brass plates, in houses breathing quiet wealth.

Even a handwork textile industry locks up money in commodities for quite a time, and needs to be financed. One is surprised that so much was done on so hugger-mugger a basis, for the channels whereby the credit of the private bankers flowed to actual manufacture, if it did, are devious. The Swiss middle classes were, and are, bourgeois rather than capitalist in their manner of thinking, with superstitions about debt and a concern for status and stability. The world of the private banker is a place for the sophisticated or for large-scale financial expertise. Subsequent innovations in banking structure are probably best considered as imported from abroad, from France and Germany, rather than native ideas: in banking (other than the private banker) and in insurance, the big developments came rather later in Switzerland than one might expect.

The style of Swiss banks and the range of their activities is different from Britain. Until recent years (e.g., 1965) the banks were a little aloof from the ordinary middle-class citizen, who would use perhaps a savings account, but do his normal money transactions through the Post Office cheque system and confine his investments to fixed-interest stocks. In their activities in extending credit, banks were said to be ready to reinforce social attitudes of the established order: those who fell foul of society or deviated politically from the local norm (for example, by being conscientious objectors) could expect no kindness from a bank. On the other hand, the range of bank services is wide. Banks replace a range of what are in Britain independent professions – stockbrokers for example – and in their management of money for their clients will be prepared to exercise his voting rights in companies. Indeed, a bank's representatives will often be on the boards of companies (if it is a large company, and a Great Bank). Their general influence on the economy is very large indeed, and through this economic power, they influence political life.

The secrecy of Swiss banks has been widely known since the 1930s, and become a factor in international affairs, setting limits to the power of governments over their own citizens' wealth. In extremist politics, in large-scale crime, in the freemasonry of the very rich, the Swiss bank account has a place. Some of this fame is unjustified. In most countries, banks are secretive. The 'numbered account' is a fetish, for banks nowhere make a practice of publishing lists of clients. A nominee company is, for most purposes, as dense a cloak, and an ordinary bank account abroad (I take it) as little likely to be divulged to a foreign government.

We may reckon (for purposes of discussion) that there are five different sorts of bank in Switzerland: the Great Banks, the Cantonal Banks, Private Banks, 'Other Banks', Savings Banks. To these one may add the Swiss National Bank, with the monopoly of note issue.

THE GREAT BANKS

The Great Banks form the weightiest single element in Swiss banking.

(i) *The Swiss Bank Corporation*

The Swiss Bank Corporation (Schweizerische Bankverein; Societé de Banque Suisse – the names are somewhat confusing), is a Baslois bank in origin, and assumed its present form and title in 1895 when it had acquired banks in Zurich and St Gallen. The *Basler Bankverein*, its original centre, was founded in 1872. Its prehistory is complicated, going back to banks formed by associations of private bankers in Basle.

(ii) *The Swiss Credit Bank*

The Swiss Credit Bank (Crédit Suisse; Schweizerische Kredit-anstalt), on the other hand, was founded on a larger scale at the outset, in 1856 by Alfred Escher of Zurich. It was modelled on the French *Crédit Mobilier* and the Leipsic *Kreditanstalt* (which for a time claimed a certain tutelage), and was closely connected on the one side with Escher's railway projects – in particular with the Gotthard line – and on the other side with the founding of the great Swiss insurance corporations. It started with a bang, but unlike its parent in France and its relations in Geneva and St Gallen (and later in Vienna) did not end with one. It was oversubscribed in a dramatic manner when shares were offered for sale, but most of the shares were placed institutionally before public subscription was invited. In the event, investors could profitably have waited until 1935, when the shares were substantially below par. Only in 1905 did the *Crédit Suisse* (its usual, but not its official, English name) open branches outside Zurich. It spread in the next generation to the other financial capitals, Basle, Geneva, St Gallen, and Berne, and to the secondary centres (Lugano, Lausanne, Lucerne, Neuchâtel, Coire, Zug) and is represented all over Switzerland and, of course, abroad; but it remains a Zurich-based bank, and one of the causes of that city's modern pre-eminence.

(iii) *The Union Bank of Switzerland*

The Union Bank of Switzerland (Schweizerische Bankgesellschaft; Union des Banques Suisses), as its French name indicates, was the product of fusions of a very great number of small local banks, some with a long history. At its centre was the Bank in Winterthur, founded in 1862 as part of a megalomaniac project to make Winterthur the entrepôt-trade centre of Europe. A big storehouse was erected as part of the same project, which has long been used as a barn by the railway station of that town. The Union Bank received its present name in 1912 on fusion with the Toggenburger Bank, which had collected many smaller enterprises of east Switzerland in its career.

(iv) *The Schweizerische Volksbank*

The Schweizerische Volksbank, founded in 1880, was supposed to be the 'people's bank', just as the ill-fated *Nationalbahn* had been intended to be the 'people's railway' – as opposed to the millionaires' banks and railways, radical rather than liberal. It attained its present recognition between the wars. It started with a capital of under 3,000 francs in Berne in 1869 as a co-operative venture. Though it has now moved its headquarters to Zurich, it still retains traces of its co-operative structure: it is far smaller than the three big Great Banks.

(v) *The Bank Leu*

The Bank Leu is reckoned as a Great Bank by a traditional courtesy. A bank of that name was started in 1754 as an agency of the Republic of Zurich, which found difficulty in investing its citizens' money to enable them to receive the 5 per cent that was thought to be the 'natural' rate of interest. In 1798 it became a private bank of the ordinary sort. It confines itself to Zurich, and is much smaller than the other great Five.

The Migros Bank, more important than Leu, is not reckoned as a Great Bank. It remains outside the bank cartel and refuses to conform with the restricted opening hours of the other large banks. It seeks to play the same role in the banking world that the *Landesring* party plays in federal politics, or as the Migros stores play in retail trade, the plague of the Establishment and its stimulus.

One must also not forget absent friends. The great *Eidgenössische Bank*, of Berne, whose name embodied its unfulfilled ambitions, has been taken over, and as recently as 1934 a Great Bank, the *Banque d'Escompte Suisse* of Geneva, broke. Such a catastrophe is now unimaginable: it is only minor or foreign banks that nowadays occasionally, every other year or so, pass from the scene in disgrace. In 1915 the cantonal Savings Bank of Uri went bankrupt, and many districts still remember a past disaster in which savings, as well as stockholders' money, were lost. The present complete solidity dates from 1936 (the last, indeed the only, time the Swiss franc has been devalued), or at least from 1946.

THE CANTONAL BANKS

The earliest of these (in the stricter definition) was founded in 1834, in Berne by the victorious liberals. As late as 1960 the combined assets of all the cantonal banks were about the same as the three largest Great Banks, but the Big Three have now collectively outstripped them.

Each of the cantons is represented in the association of cantonal banks, which means that, according to one definition, every canton has a state bank of its own, and two have two: it depends on this definition whether Geneva has two, or none. The student of the detail of cantonal politics and of economic decentralization finds them interesting.

PRIVATE BANKS

The traditional location of private bankers (a legal and administrative category) is Geneva and Basle, though Zurich, Berne, and St Gallen have each famous and ancient firms. The private bankers of Geneva have played a part in French social history since the mid-eighteenth century, and the long continuance of many French family fortunes is said to be due to the tax and inflation haven just over the border. A certain discrete mystery surrounds the Private Banker. His section of the banking system is the only part that is genuinely rooted in the old regime, and some of his traditions have been handed down to the Great Banks, and inspired the ethos which prompted the too famous law on banking secrecy.

This, the Law of 1934 (revised 1971), makes breach of banking secrecy a criminal offence. In itself, this law makes no history, but it is the announcement of a policy which has been of considerable importance for Switzerland and the world when taken in combination with the policy of neutrality and with the connected phenomena of economic success and a 70 per cent anti-socialist majority. The policy in its modern form started in order to protect the funds of nervous Germans from Nazi espionage, but it was soon found to have a wider clientele, among whom Fascists themselves were to be counted. In the years after 1945 when governments attempted to manage currencies, and to change the structure of society by discriminatory taxation, a Swiss banking account acquired new uses for the rather rich and the extremely rich. Complicated transactions can be arranged through a Liechtenstein-incorporated company and a Swiss numbered account which will defeat the investigation of any police force except the Swiss. The shadier banks, which are fairly numerous, may be expected to be prepared to handle rather dubious accounts. Legend has it that communist governments finance their James Bond-type transactions in this convenient manner, and that

Arab and Israeli assassins find the system equally convenient, while the petty tyrant of some underdeveloped country may salt away funds under his own name which were really intended for quite another purpose. The phenomenon itself, the illegal but untraceable movement of money, is clearly of some importance in the story of great private wealth, of rulers subject to *coups d'état*, and, one fears, of crime other than technical tax evasion. Whether it is really important now for the Swiss economy is doubtful; big though the sums may be, they are assuredly small compared with honest trade and finance. It is a sort of black market, a flag of convenience, of which governments everywhere have to take some account. It is by no means confined to Switzerland, but Switzerland is rather a large and strong country to indulge such practices. Medium and great powers feel more solidarity with each other in such matters than they feel sympathy with the monetary refugee. Very small 'states', Monaco and the like, can be coerced in a friendly manner – Liechtenstein is to be coerced only via Switzerland, and serves to corroborate the alibi.

The Swiss defence runs as follows. First, she has the right to do this as a neutral. Second, in reply to the objection that a neutral forswears intervention in the policies of other countries, the argument shifts to the value of the practice in general, and that it is Swiss policy to liberate trade and commerce, so the practice is really part of the noble Swiss tradition of humanity and freedom, protecting individuals against unjust governments. Third, when again the consistency of this policy with neutrality is pressed, the Swiss defender will patiently explain that sovereignty is involved, and that a neutral has a positive duty to defend this sovereignty. If the argument is pressed further, it rapidly becomes *ad hominem* or else returns to the starting-point. The alternative contention that it is essential to the Swiss economy or that it is irrelevant to the Swiss economy can be thrown in for good measure, and effectively. Some inkling that the argument is not quite watertight has seeped into the mind of the federal authorities, who have given in a little to United States pressure on circumferential matters.

'OTHER BANKS'

A slight distaste is implied by the name of this official category. The Private Banks have an aristocratic image, discretion combined with elegance, and the aspects of Swiss banking that are most reluctantly acceptable can be found in this 'other' class. It also includes some very respectable banks, of which some are foreign, and the implication (quite false) is that the shady sort of banks are the foreign banks, tolerated so that Swiss banks may operate abroad. The category is in fact extremely mixed.

SAVINGS AND MORTGAGE BANKS. LOCAL BANKS

The oldest of these go back to the last years of the old regime, when Berne set up an institution to look after the savings of industrious apprentices, domestic servants, and the like, an example which Basle followed. The 'Public Utility Societies' which sprang up in the last half of the eighteenth century, and played a useful role in dulling the edge of respectable pauperism during the early nineteenth century, helped set up savings societies in most of Switzerland. The Mortgage Banks started in order to fill rather the same function as building societies in Britain, though with a special emphasis on the needs of the peasantry.

'Local Banks' scarcely constitute a different category to the foregoing. There are rather a lot of little banks confined to a canton or a district, which share some joint services for matters requiring some considerable scale of operation. The survival of these institutions half a century after they disappeared elsewhere is typically Swiss.

THE NATIONAL BANK OF SWITZERLAND

This is the central bank, rather interesting in its details, which was set up in 1906 to have a monopoly of note issue. It has a control, whose strength is disputed, over the whole range of banking: officially its powers are limited, but with the federal executive decree at its disposal the government could if it so wished control the whole financial system of the country.

Also controlling the system are a series of cartels and associations. The most important of these is the *Bankiervereinigung*, dominated by the Great Banks but not an instrumentality of then. Most banks belong to this association – but the Migros Bank does not. It acts partly as a joint organization, trying to put its own house in order to prevent more central control, and used also to represent banking opinion to the National Bank and the central government.

Since 1965 the three greatest of the Great Banks (Union Bank, Bank Corporation, Crédit Suisse) have tried to penetrate the whole Swiss market. They are now in an absolutely dominant position. The cantonal banks, the foreign banks, and Migros, make it unlikely they will quite monopolize the scene, but the small banks no longer seem essential to the life of the country. Like the small newspapers and, indeed, the small parishes and smallest cantons, their years are numbered. The country is overbanked, as well as over-newspapered and over-communed. Another disquieting feature is the relative concentration on Zurich: even the Cantonal Bank of Zurich is bigger than the fourth of the Great Banks, which once was based on Berne. Basle and Geneva remain as counterpoises, but this repeats the familiar pattern of a preponderance of west Switzerland. In return, in place of a larger number of financially rather unsteady banks, the three giants are large enough to make a respectable showing in Europe, and can command enough talent to be able to let the country continue in business if the thirty-year boom should end.

VIII. Insurance

The insurance industry of Switzerland expanded as an offshoot of the banks, which means that it also became important rather late by western Europe's standards and took form as a fully fledged idea incubated abroad. It also, however, had a native origin in the societies started to insure against the fires to which wood-built (or roofed) villages are prone when the Föhn wind rages. When most of the town of Glarus burned in May 1861, the buildings had been insured – insurance had been compulsory in the canton since 1811 – but the reserves of the cantonal insurance institute were only sufficient for one-fifth of the liabilities incurred by that enormous fire. Some of the impetus to found insurances had come from the Public Utility Societies already mentioned. The old insurance plaques on buildings are usually of the Helvetia, founded in 1861 as a fire insurance. In 1885 federal governmental supervision over all insurances was initiated – a Swiss innovation. Foreign companies have been somewhat edged out in subsequent years, and since the last war ended, Swiss companies have had tremendous expansion abroad. Like banks, they are based historically in the regional financial capitals (Zurich, Winterthur, St Gallen, Basle, Geneva, Berne, Lausanne, and Neuchâtel), but with a certain predominance of Zurich.

IX. Transport

At first glance, the road map of Roman Switzerland looks rather like that of the railway age, and still more like that of the motorway system. But on a second look, important differences are apparent. The centre of the railway system is Olten, not Brugg. Here, at Olten, the line Basle–Gotthard–Italy crosses the line Geneva–Zurich. The Romans used the Nufenen, not the Gotthard, and preferred the Great St Bernard to the other passes. Their transverse diagonal skirted the Lakes of Neuchâtel and Bienne, whereas the railway was drawn by political considerations to one side of the geographically determined route, via the cantonal capitals of Berne, Fribourg, and Lausanne. The modern system is the result of a political tug-of-war, of history rather than geography.

Railways, typically, came very late to Switzerland. In 1844 Basle secured its link with Strasbourg, and breached the city walls to let in the railway: a special gate was constructed, to be carefully padlocked at night. In 1847 the line between Baden and Zurich was completed (connecting with the steamer from Zurich through the Linth canal and the Walensee), for which the first railway tunnel in the country was bored under the castle at Baden. The new Constitution of 1848 enabled the Railway Law to be passed in 1852, which established (until 1872) private enterprise under concessions granted by cantonal governments (subject to the sanction of the Federal Assembly) with a right of repurchase to the central government. A first railway mania started. By 1858, under Baslois leadership, the central cross intersecting at Olten was established and the upper Hauenstein tunnel built, and by 1862 one could travel from Geneva to Coire along the present route: indeed, except for a short stretch, one could travel back on a different line. There was a second fury of railway-building from 1870 to 1882, in which year the Gotthard railway tunnel was opened to traffic. Railways were nationalized in principle (but not in detail) in 1898. There are still very long lengths of line in non-federal ownership, especially in Grisons, and one internationally important link – the stretch from Berne to Brig via the Lötschberg – in cantonal ownership. For these great ventures, Swiss capital was insufficient, and there were borrowings from Germany, Italy, and France: on the strategic Gotthard line there were for a long time international servitudes in favour of Germany and Italy scarcely consistent with neutrality, in consequence of this former financial dependence.

The result of an almost uncontrolled development was, in some places, a wild duplication of routes, in other places a big gap in through lines. The failure of the line Zofingen–Lenzburg–Winterthur–Singen has left its traces in the modern timetable, and in the stunted development of certain small towns which were financially ruined by too great participation. The greatest casualty was east Switzerland, promised a through route and tunnel to Italy, but never given one: this drama has recently been repeated. However, though railway speculation proved eventually unremunerative to long-term investors, its result is an extraordinarily close network. Every substantial village in the country can be reached by a combination of railway and postal-bus, a factor which in the early years of this century played a part in delaying the motor age. Until 1926 there were no private motor-cars in the whole canton of Grisons, and other cantons could, until then, prohibit driving on the sabbath day completely. Electrification of Swiss railways (that is to say, the use of a native source of power) was started in the late 1880s and largely completed in the 1920s. The Burgdorf to Thun line (1899) was the first main line[3] to be electrified.

Late with railways, Switzerland was also late with motorways.

Cantonal sovereignty over road construction was a bastion hard to storm, particularly as the supremacy over road policing was necessarily bound up with it. Political considerations have again played a large part, every canton wanting some motorway, and every community through which it was to pass wanting it just a mile or so farther distant. Stretches of splendid road (two lanes in each direction) alternate with confusion, especially in and near the city of Zurich. Vaud has seen a frenzy of construction, while Berne has proceeded with slow wisdom, regretting the destruction of every farmhouse. But, as usual in Switzerland, a late start is outweighed by an ability to learn from others, and a technical perfection.

X. The Holiday Trade

There are ancient inns throughout Switzerland, as staging-posts along the routes over the passes, as resting places for pilgrims to the shrines of the country, or for the visit of the sick to mineral springs. Many of those we see today were established by the seventeenth century, and they have names from the old empire (The Crown, The Golden Eagle), the old church or the shield of the old sovereign (The Bear, The Lion), or from old functions such as The Post, The Balance. Districts have peculiarities, like the diminutive names of Appenzell, Schäfli (little sheep), and so on. After 1798 periods of liberal government coincided with the unrestricted licensing of new inns, too many of them, and some 'new' cantons which had a long spell of liberalism may still have more inns than can comfortably stay in business. Certain small towns on ancient routes, or with markets or law courts or places of pilgrimage, are quite dominated by ancient inns, for example Aarberg near Berne, or Zurzach. The old inns are still delightful to stay in for the individual holidaymaker, and they provide the tradition from which the modern hotel sprang. They have had their own political importance, for the innkeeper was a man of substance, powerful, well-informed, who could play a large role as local notable – usually in the liberal interest – at a time when the Swiss rural middle class was small in numbers.

The peculiar fame of Switzerland (among the unthinking travelling public), however, comes from the hotel or guesthouse specifically designed for tourists. This is a large element in the Swiss image abroad (though much less so than two generations ago) and still plays a part in the national economy. The yield of the holiday trade, after deducting what is spent by Swiss abroad, is traditionally given a place in the statistics which suggests that tourism enables Switzerland to balance (more or less) her trade. There are metaphysical difficulties in accepting this claim, but tourism is certainly effective in redistributing income geographically within the country: the

great honey-pots are in places which would otherwise be impoverished and perhaps depopulated, such as Zermatt, stuck at the
end of an apparently dead-end valley. This is not quite as true today,
for the workers at all but the most traditional (and agreeable) hotels
are foreign, and the mere presence of a hotel has a dispiriting effect
on honest labour. Tourists are no longer birds of such exotic plumage
that the grandmother laden with a cloud of dried hay does not
recognize them for her own species.

Such tourist hotels are relatively modern. The English in the last
part of the eighteenth century fanned out from Geneva on the Jean-
Jacques trail, found the south-facing Vaudois shore of the lake
climatically agreeable, and enjoyed, and enriched, its literary associations. Cultivated Germans found Zurich a sort of republican Weimar,
convenient for the tour to Rome. The waters of the Swiss Baden
softened the infinite delays of confederal diplomacy, those of Schinznach provided a meeting-place for Swiss aristocrats intent on the
regeneration of their own country, while the possibilities of Swiss
territories as a place of refuge from inconvenient laws or taxation
were early recognized and, at the upper end of the range, merge into
a resident tourism of a graceful sort. But voluntary journeys into the
mountains for relaxation started only after 1815. The complex lore
of simple folk lost its innocence and started to become folklore after
the first of the famous games at Unspunnen (1805), and from here
the nearby Interlaken and the Bernese Oberland became famous:
until 1939 it was the classic holiday-ground of the English middle
classes. Almost at the same time (1815) the mania for seeing sunrise
from the Rigi Kulm started, opening the delightful, but rainsodden,
Lake of Lucerne to the industry of pleasure. The milk-cure of
Appenzell became a rage in central Europe. These places are near
lakes, and the most pleasurable of all modes of travel, paddle-steamer,
was the first mechanized transport in Switzerland (1823, the *Guillaume
Tell* between Geneva and Ouchy; 1824, a steamer on the Lake of
Neuchâtel, later owned and captained by the Suchard famed for
chocolate; in the same year a steamer on the Lake of Zurich and
Walensee; 1837, steamers on the Lakes of Thun and Lucerne). The
railway age only opened seriously after the Federal Law of 1852, but
the roads had been improved before then, the country unified, the
town gates opened, the currency made intelligible. From Davos the
open-air cure for tuberculosis became known, the first exploitation of
the Swiss winter, and in the second half of the century mountaineer-
ing became of importance as a sport. The genus Grand Hotel started
in 1869 with the Interlaken 'Schweizerhof', and often bears this, or a
French name. The Palace Hotel is a little later, possibly to be dated
from 1896 with the hotel in St Mortz. Many of these pioneer buildings

survive, and mockery of them is now turning to admiration, and preservation. Some, with the unheard-of luxury of a bathroom and lavatory on every floor, are exactly as they were built (like the delightful hotel at the end of the road in the Fextal, above Sils) and still appeal to the same class of visitor. Others languish, or have been pulled down, especially that enviable sort of hotel which made the reputation of the Valais, to be reached only by mule or on foot, but with every contemporary comfort and excellent service at the destination. Many have come down in the world, filled with bargain trips, even on a do-it-yourself basis, as they await demolition. A few (in Lucerne for example) have been gutted and reconstructed internally, and in each decade have been abreast of the times, as have hotels with famous names in Geneva, Zurich, and Basle. In very recent years the concrete-box type of hotel, with American-style comfort, air-conditioned, insulated, anonymous, has appeared, a first attempt to meet the problems of the jumbo-jet age.

The typical financial structure of the earlier type of hotel is that management and ownership coincide. Already in the 1870s the Grand National Hotel of Lucerne saw a divorce between capital and management, and the manager became the most famous of all hoteliers, the great Caesar Ritz. Soon Swiss enterprise spread overseas: many of the most famous enterprises of the old world have been at one time in Swiss ownership or management.

Considerable political power was amassed by the heads of some of the great hotel dynasties, the Seilers of Zermatt and Ryffelalp, for example, or the Badrutts of St Moritz: the conditions of their enterprise demanded that they should dominate their commune and be influential in the canton and, if possible, also in Berne.

The trade requires a peculiar ethos. At first sight there is something unrepublican about hotel-keeping, for there is expectation of servility on one side and arrogance on the other. The ticklish problem of how to avoid this and maintain the dignity of the free man while putting the visiting potentate at his ease was well mastered in Switzerland: the old-fashioned hotel-manager is a pleasure to watch, moving from table to table with graduated respect, so one can estimate the relative social importance of one's fellow guests by the length and type of conversation, one rule for the native, one for the foreigner, time for the rich, and brisk but courteous treatment of the poor. In other countries one sees mistakes made, the traveller on foot with ancient wealth placed after the flash man with a car, but in the older Swiss hotel this is rare. The charges have the reputation of being high, but absolutely fair, and the quality excellent, but uninspired.

The contribution to local economic life varies in the two different societies. Basle, Zurich, Berne, and even Lucerne were famous places in their own right before hotels, which have a function in local life but are in a way a mere decoration of it: industry was financed from earlier industry and wealth, or from abroad, not from tourism. But parts of Grisons, Ticino, and above all Valais were until a century ago undeveloped countries. Luxury hotels were plonked in a sort of desert. Lugano as a tiny borough drew visitors from the Italian lakes, but hotels made it into a city. The Valais was bigoted, poor, and beautiful, and took to exploiting tourism as a hungry wolf falls on a chance-found carcase, sometimes almost with lunacy, enjoying seeing the lovely money spent so openhandedly, even if on others by others. The mania has recently overtaken impoverished parts of Grisons. The long-starved greed of such places has sometimes defeated its own purposes, water-power was sometimes sold for a small sum to city-dwellers apparently easy to overreach, so the valley is dry for all future; crude sewage runs into the waters of lakes, so that scarcely anywhere in Ticino can one bathe; vineyards in beautiful surroundings are sold to speculators; and so on. In a canton like Berne, long prosperous and with a tradition of good government, things are different: protective measures in some cases date from the 1860s, and waterfalls can still be seen in their old glory. The Lake of Zurich, with towns along both banks almost continuously, is crystal clear and bacterially rather pure. The Lake of Lugano is a vast settling tank for the town's sewage, and the Lake of Geneva, draining the Valais, is so dirty that soon its waters will not be able to clarify themselves naturally.

The really great years of tourism were before 1914. During the war, the great mountain hotels went bankrupt or, to use a euphemism, wrote down their capital. They were revived, but suffered in a disguised form the same fate during 1939–45. Once again there has been massive, but discriminating, injection of public funds in one way or another. Typically, Switzerland has been reluctant to cash in on mass tourism in Costa Brava style: she has tried to remain the refuge of the individual tourist, travelling by train and post-auto if possible. Since 1970, package tourism is becoming more common, notably in Inner Switzerland. The ethos of the totally impersonal hotel is available, and the ethos of the highly personalized hotel where manager and visitor are on terms of Mr This and Herr Doktor That is still easy to find, but there is an area in between, the tourist merely in search of physical gratification and scarcely knowing which country he is in so long as it is as much like his idealized home-country as possible. In this area Swiss hotel-keepers feel profoundly uneasy, in the same way as the manufacturers of the country resist producing cheap watches or untested pharmaceuticals. Indeed, in many respects the holiday trade follows a recognizably Swiss pattern

– the handicraft origin, the native ethos and source of capital, the successive importation of ideas from abroad, the native entrepreneur of genius, the urge to shift from a cheap to a luxury product, the time-lag in taking up new ideas (but the eventual brilliant exploitation of such ideas), and the spin-off in some circumstances to other industries and the concentration on export (which in this trade means the foreign visitor to Switzerland as well as the Swiss enterprise located abroad). The pattern must not be overemphasized as it conceals verbal traps, and because this is not a field in which it is very helpful to speak of industrialization or mechanization.

XI. The Effect of Industry on the Environment

Swiss landscape, apart from the high alps above pasture level, is in much of its detail artificial. Some landscapes, such as the Emmenthal or Appenzell, are on the surface predominantly formed by man: it was the industry of the seventeenth and eighteenth centuries which made Appenzell a toy paradise, a most charming and playful environment. Even the nineteenth century's scars are hidden by hills and trees, and green countryside is always within walking distance and view. There is no Swiss Black Country, in part because the twentieth century (or rather, the years after 1880) brought exploitation of electricity on a large scale. Since 1945, however, electricity production has deformed very extensive landscapes. The scenery of the Valais, the wildest and most original of Switzerland, has in places become an industrial and hydro-electrical landscape of grandeur, and often where it is untouched by the diversion and impounding of streams, it is devastated by modern apartment blocks and holiday settlement – also rather well designed in detail.

However, some sites of the greatest beauty have been needlessly harshly treated. It is difficult to recapture the poetry of the plague-chapel at Safien-Platz, for example, now that a continuous hum, and a floodlit basin on the water-closet system, have been placed immediately adjacent to it. The falls at Schaffhausen have been much prejudiced by factories; lengths of the Rhine itself are now stagnant (and Rheinau spoiled); the Hermitage at Longeborgne (one of the half-dozen most poetic sites in all Switzerland) has a rather attractive, cheerful, noisy, generating station just below it; and so one could moan on endlessly. The biggest damage has been done by the secondary effects of industry – the slopes of the great lakes (Geneva, Zurich, Lugano) that were pasture and vineyard and are now becoming a continuous, fairly attractive, conurbation.

In spite of these blemishes, there is very little of the brutality which makes the traveller prefer not even to visit the French and Italian Alps again; Canton Berne, in particular, has at times attempted to protect and enhance its natural beauty in a manner which (I hope) is a model for other administrations.

Water-power at least is a sort of strategic and moral necessity for Switzerland, a necessity to reassure the public that it can survive in wartime. Its contribution to the total economy is actually rather small – some 10 per cent of the energy requirement is the most that can be produced – and so the silencing of the rivers along most valleys is the jam, not the bread and butter, of Swiss society, a preference for one sort of comfort to another sort of consolation. Atomic energy faces other problems, notably that Switzerland is still rather small – too small to pioneer in this field, though large enough to benefit from the pioneering of others in due time. Already it is causing environmental difficulties, since its favourite location is in the very type of pleasing but undramatic countryside which hydro-electric power had left little disturbed. The railways have been there long enough to be accepted as a fact of nature, and have added courageous bridges to the scene, as have the mini-motorways.

The first tourist hotels were often situated so as to cause the greatest devastation, and gain a view thereby, and some are in places that are morally impossible – just above the Rütli, or within sight of the Ranft. Cable railways and ski-lifts are a modern nuisance, and are exceedingly intrusive in summer and more numerous than can be defended. For that matter, the modern mechanized pastoral and agricultural systems lack charm. As roads are built, the lure of urbanized society gradually destroys the old alpine culture in its entirety, and roads now penetrate everywhere.

Roads are in themselves a threat to the landscape their existence makes accessible. The motorway, in particular, is incompatible with the Swiss ethos, the localism, the miniature scale of the country, the sense of peculiarity. Even though it is usually only a mini-motorway and admirably designed, it is playing a noticeable part in the destruction of the Swiss civilization. Symbolically, in the last few years, road maps have ceased to mark the cantonal boundaries: in 1950 the communal boundaries (historically very interesting) were marked.

If Switzerland is a little small for motorways, the country is definitely small for aeroplanes. The airfields of Basle and Geneva have been pushed partly on to French soil. The big traffic lanes have been pushed so far as possible on to German airspace, to save the Swiss from being bothered by noise, but the whole triangle north of Zurich-Kloten is rendered objectionable by the roar and drone of planes. The big marsh west of Berne, towards the Lake of Bienne, drained and made fertile by enormous effort, was foreseen as a great airport, but the cult of the environment came just in time to rescue it. Swissair – the word-coinage is an early example, 1931, of a modern fashion – has cashed in on the expectation of Swiss reliability and created an entirely Swiss image for itself, even down to the penny bar of milk chocolate served instead of the food provided by other lines, and it is firmly established as an important international line. The Federal Constitution was virtually suspended to deal with the emergency when one of its planes was hijacked, and popular fury was vented on the Red Cross which attempted about the same time to raise funds for starving Arabs: Swissair has become a totem of national feeling.

Overall, however, Switzerland has been intelligent and concerned about the landscape. The inherent problems are crushing, every day witnesses some degradation. But the young people of good education, in particular, are conscious of the dangers of industry to the world around and prepared to defend the landscape of nature and to try to enhance the beauty which remains: some cantons and communes set an admirable example in preservation both of the natural-pastoral-agricultural landscape and the human landscape of ancient towns and local styles of rural houses.

Finally, the Forestry Law of 1902 has retained the proportion of woodland to pasture unaltered. Much of the forest land is in public ownership, cantonal, communal, or alp corporation, and many of these, like the Sihlwald near Zurich, have an international reputation for being well managed. At the time of the Helvetic Republic, much woodland passed into private ownership, but legislation has transferred most rights of management to the public power, together with sporting rights. This is one example out of many of the sort of socialism without socialism which is so typical of Switzerland. Early mismanagement of woodland often caused floods and erosion: the immense bog which once covered the land between the Lake of Zurich and the Walensee, now drained by the Linth Canal, was caused by ill management of woods in Glarus, and there are other examples (the Haslital, or the Urseren valley, for instance). The forests are mostly self-regenerating and, therefore, natural-seeming. The intelligent policy of the more enlightened cantons, moreover, has kept them full of game, and almost everywhere (except in Grisons) wild deer are plentiful. The woods are accessible to the public, there is an admirable network of footpaths, and the civilization of the country is favourable to enjoyment of the open air in general, and of walking and ski-ing in particular. The environment is appreciated, as well as protected.

XII. Immigrants

A book on Switzerland of today must contain a section on immigration.[4] This is a many-sided problem, a problem of population, but also of internal politics, neutrality, industry, and society, and a moral problem with a character of its own in a multinational state in the heart of western Europe. It is therefore difficult to decide where within this book to place a discussion of this question. The reason for inserting it immediately after a section on industry is that it is a problem arising out of industry, just as pollution of the natural environment arises out of industry.

In 1837 the proportion of foreigners on Swiss soil was already over $2\frac{1}{2}$ per cent of the total population and rose to over 5 per cent in 1870, and has never fallen below that number. By 1914 the proportion, which had risen steadily at each census, was over 15 per cent (in absolute numbers about 600,000). There is a flashpoint for xenophobia in all societies at around $12\frac{1}{2}$ per cent of population, and this had, of course, long been exceeded in some parts. The figures, however, are less remarkable when broken down: the greatest intermixture with foreigners was along the borders and with neighbours, with French in Geneva and Neuchâtel, with workers from Alsace and from neighbouring German states in north and east Switzerland, with north Italians in Ticino. Swiss borders are complex, and Geneva and Basle are large towns whose dependent countryside lies over these borders, and the pull of Zurich early reached into southern Germany. Certain trades had traditional links; there were Savoyard servants in Geneva, and everywhere Italian road- and railway-constructors. The numbers are also inflated by the quirk of Swiss law which makes 'settlement' for a foreigner a comfortable status, and one which was easily obtained from the 1860s until the first World War, but Switzerland makes naturalization rather difficult and citizenship strictly hereditary, not conferred by mere birth on Swiss soil – though the convoluted procedures of today are an innovation. Counted among the migrants is the contingent from the leisured class in semi-permanent residence for health or social reasons. In reality the foreign community lacked cohesion and was dispersed. Some sections of it had an important impact, however, on Swiss culture.

In the first place, immigrants have contributed much to Swiss middle-class civilization. This Swiss middle, or middle-upper-middle, class, derives much of its ancestry from callings such as innkeeper, lawyer, or teacher, and beyond that to some ultimate peasant or small burgher origin. It owes a debt also to the old privileged classes, especially to the classes that were on the fringe of privilege, such as the leading families of provincial towns. Thirdly, to a surprising extent (considering the small number of naturalizations), foreign immigrants are among its literal and spiritual ancestry. The universities were long dominated by foreign (chiefly German) professors, the first generation of ordinary professors at Zurich were all foreign, and there were many Germans and other foreigners in manufacturing and business enterprises. The immigration was, in fact, one from which Swiss life greatly benefited, as, in an earlier century, it had benefited from Huguenot immigrants. The reason was not dissimilar, for these nineteenth-century immigrants were often liberals who found life in princely Germany uncongenial or threatening.[5]

In the second place (one supposes that this is an advantage) immigrant handicraftsmen contributed to a rival set of ideas; they introduced social democracy and trade unionism. These movements depended, in the take-off stage, very greatly on foreign ideas and foreign instigators, but also on foreign workers. Both the artisan and the bourgeois immigrations were very different to the modern immigration, and they came at a time when Switzerland was not confident where her own cultural centre of gravity lay, and were therefore the more penetrating. At the same time, not to exaggerate, one must notice the countervailing phenomenon of what we may call cultural incapsulation: the citizens of Geneva, for example, like those of Zermatt, have an extraordinary ability to lead their own life-style as unaffected by the foreigners as if the intruders were ungainly birds, flapping, noisy, messy even, but irrelevant. The very small immigrations have often been more positively effective than the massive ones.

A socially interesting theme, and one which occasionally arouses public feeling, is the intermarriage of Swiss young people with foreign partners. The early tendency was for foreigners to marry Swiss girls: the later (overtaking the first tendency already in 1910, with a high point in 1934) is for Swiss young men to marry foreign girls. One reaches at once for a romantic and 'cultural' explanation. However, the statistics (as Professor Bickel points out) coincide over a long period with what one might expect from the proportions of male and female of marrying age in Switzerland, on the one hand, and in neighbouring countries on the other hand.

The *Ueberfremdung*, the excessive number of foreigners, of the pre-war period was not repeated in the anxious years of the 1920s. Treaties may have guaranteed treatment of foreigners 'with rights of settlement' not less generous in civil matters than those of Swiss citizens, but measures were taken to prevent foreigners staying long enough to acquire such rights. A special branch of the police, federal as well as cantonal, was expanded into an apparatus to dislodge foreigners who exceeded their stay as tourists without bringing into the country money or skills needed. This apparatus, not very agreeable for the foreigner and necessarily a little arbitrary in dealing with people without legal rights, remains today.

1933–45: THE REFUGEE PROBLEM

During the late 1930s and the second World War, refugees crowded at the gates of Switzerland. There is a long-standing legend, like windmills and clogs in Holland, that Switzerland recognizes a right of asylum. Jurists wrote learnedly to explain that this was not a subjective right enuring to the non-citizen, but a right of the Confederation to accept whom it will despite the protests of other powers, a claim, in fact, to unrestricted state sovereignty in this matter. However, it is a policy (loosely connected perhaps with the policies collectively called neutrality) to admit 'political' refugees. The trouble is that those guilty of political crimes have necessarily been guilty also of other crime, assassination perhaps, or failing to report to the police, or currency offences, offences for which no immunity exists. The executive therefore has a choice in the matter and, at the end of the day, those are admitted whose views are consonant with the inner views held by those in power.

In April 1939, for example, some defenders of the legitimate government of Spain had taken refuge in a neutralized zone of the harbour of Alicante, and through a Swiss deputy in the National Council asked for asylum, as facing death; private organizations were willing to see that no cost fell on public funds. After seven weeks came the reply, a refusal.

> With a population of only four million, Switzerland already sheltered between ten and twelve thousand refugees, of which three thousand were without private means and supported by private Swiss citizens. Switzerland had no colonies to which she could ship such people, and it might be difficult to get rid of them and, with unemployment in Switzerland, it would be impossible to permit them to work. Perhaps the work of the International Red Cross, supported by Swiss private citizens, etc., could unfold its activities so rich in blessings, equally, of course, to both parties and without the slightest ideological tinge.

This, the Red Cross, 'was a crusade against the distress and sufferings of thousands of men, of women, and of children'. Switzerland must set an example which could be followed with greater generosity by Belgium, Italy, Germany, the United States; and Switzerland sent immediate aid, in the sum of £400. Could Switzerland take one single refugee, however? No, not one. One cannot doubt that behind the official protestations of complete neutrality[6] was Motta's friendship with Italy and Italy's friends. Many of the refugees would be social democrats, or worse, and they were unlikely to be good catholics or they would have rallied to Franco's rebels.

With regard to Germany, Switzerland preserved a less absolute exclusivity, but it was clear to jurists that Jews as such could not benefit under the heading of political refugees. They were in concentration camps, and later being exterminated, for being Jews, which was not a political activity. It was, however, often difficult to distinguish Jews (as understood by Goebbels), who might, for example, only have a grandmother tarred with this brush; so the Swiss government entered into talks of which the outcome would be that the passports of Jews should be identifiable: in the most friendly way, Hitler's government co-operated by doing this, stamping them with a capital J (October 1938).

By such means, un-Swiss (*wesensfremd*) elements were kept at bay and, from the standpoint of demography, the influx of foreigners was kept within very tolerable limits. In 1910, there had been 552,000 foreigners, in 1941, only 224,000.

In the same year, 1941, Bundesrat von Steiger made his famous speech about the lifeboat in the storm, with the words 'The boat is full'. These words still lie heavy on the liberal and Christian conscience today, at a time when the boat does indeed show signs of fullness, with one million foreigners on Swiss soil.

But these policies were of course almost forced upon Switzerland, surrounded by the allies of Germany after France's defeat, and the total number of those assisted was very large, especially towards the end of the war. The reason why the black side is unfairly emphasized here is because a latent ill ease about the past is a factor in the present situation.

AFTER THE WAR: THE PROBLEM OF FOREIGN WORKERS

The war of 1939–45 left Swiss industry intact, indeed flourishing, amid the ruins of Europe. The duty and the interest of Switzerland were to expand production to the maximum until the world recovered and until the inevitable slump occurred. For the foreigner it was a privilege and delight to be allowed entry into the fat land where shops were full and life was sleek, where houses were undamaged, a land without rationing, without devaluations, where tax was light and society secure.

The boom, however, has continued for a generation, not for a few years. The problem of immigrants it created was recognizable in the 1950s, and by 1964 it had ceased to be easily curable. Successive measures and policies were introduced, each produced its own evasions and side-effects, and when the next reckoning came, the number of foreign workers had again increased. The matter entered politics, a referendum was launched, political parties formed which, as usual with such flies of a day, sent one or two members to a parliament dominated as to seven-eighths by the governmental parties.

Then in 1969 another referendum was launched, this time by Dr James Schwarzenbach, a rich Zurich industrialist, leader and sole National Councillor of one of these temporary right-wing extreme groups. The initiative, having gathered its signatures, came before parliament. Of the two chambers with their 244 members one single member was in favour, Schwarzenbach himself. The parties were against it, the interest groups were against it, the respectable press against it, the churches and men of education and goodwill against it. There was no one in favour – except 45 per cent of the electorate voting at the referendum, a close-run thing on an exceptionally heavy poll. The date of the vote, 7 July 1970, is acknowledged as a turning-point in contemporary Swiss politics.

The aftermath of the Schwarzenbach referendum is stricter controls, both of cantons by the federal government and of firms by the cantons, which impose a strain on a delicate balance of political power between central and local, and governmental and economic, groupings. The elections of 1971 have brought the opposition within the walls of the lower house of the Federal Parliament and impose a further strain, a temptation for governmental parties to leave the executive coalition so as to reap the electoral harvest of opposition for themselves.

Behind this explosive situation, psychological and demographic factors can be detected. First, a diffused expectation on the part of other countries that Switzerland, being a prosperous country, welcomes immigrants and treats them with the equal-handed justice appropriate to a model democracy. Fortifying this, within Switzerland there is a large body of cultured opinion wishing this to be so, and sensitive about the reproach to conscience afforded by the fate of Jews refused admittance in the period of Nazism. Second, there is a spirit of exclusiveness, reinforced by the citadel mentality of wartime and the need to define sharply the frontiers between the Swiss and the less than Swiss around Switzerland, so like in language and so akin in religion, and reinforced also by the confident official expectation that the events of 1920–30 would be repeated in 1945–55. Third, there is a rigid law of citizenship, appropriate to a Swiss race rather than to a Swiss Confederation, and of a special police regime for foreigners, both fortified by the needs of the 1920s and 1930s. Fourth, there are demographic factors. The years of pessimism were reflected in a low birth-rate. The normal graph of population classified by sex and by age is a silhouette of a pyramid: the uneven birth-rate had come to make it look like a haystack nibbled by cattle, until the expansion of the post-1950 years provided a new platform for the structure. When the waist of the age-structure corresponds with the working years, there is a demographic need to import young men from abroad whose work can support the old and the very young and to restore the stable-looking pyramid of age. The demographic case for immigration of young workers was strong.

In figures, the problem was that in 1970, in a population of just over 6 million there were more than one million foreigners, and there were over three-quarters of a million foreign workers. These are categorized by the administration under three headings: resident, seasonal, and daily workers who cross the frontier to work in Switzerland (*Grenzgänger*). Of this latter category there are some 70,000 and the number is felt to be the natural one, given the frontier position of Geneva and Basle and also, more questionable, the industries that have set up factories at the southern tip of Ticino in order to tap the Italian labour market.

The resident working foreign population, totalling around 600,000, is divided again into two categories. The aristocracy of foreign workers are those with rights of settlement (180,000 in 1970, but rapidly increasing). These have mostly been resident ten years and more on Swiss soil, and, as it were, pose no problem – even if they raise the question why they cannot be granted Swiss citizenship. The remainder have a yearly permit and are *kontrollpflichtig*, subject to conditions and regulations enforced by the *Fremdenpolizei*. The content of these controls has varied. Two policies conflict: on the one hand, there have been attempts to direct them to industries and places in particular need of cheap labour, and to attempt to keep them there; on the other hand, there have been attempts to have a market economy in labour, letting workers follow the best pay and conditions, not supporting dying industries in an artificial and eventually untenable manner, but employing the moment of prosperity to allow industry to adapt itself to the present needs. Inevitably, there have been compromises between the two views, such as allowing workers to move after a certain time, now one year, now three years – an arrangement which, while seeming a compromise, sometimes contrives to achieve the worst of both systems.

The seasonal workers are those who come for less than a year: the ideal picture is of an Italian building-worker, employed in Switzerland during the summer, and returning to his family in Italy to work his holding or his trade in his family's dwelling place in Italy during the long Swiss winter. The reality may be different. Building operations no longer need to be totally closed down during six months: they can be run continuously. The Italian worker then comes with his family, gets a seasonal permit, and after eleven months must leave Switzerland for a month, before returning for another eleven months-odd. One needs little imagination to visualize the sort of situation that results, with illness, childbirth, and so on, in a strange country with a vigilant and unyielding police spurred by a policy of keeping foreigners out.

The nub of the problem is the *kontrollpflichtig* resident workers, largely concentrated in certain industries – building, machines and foundries, textiles and clothing, and hotels and restaurants. In these industries one-third, or more, of the workers are foreigners: in particular workshops, of course, those engaged in one particular task may be all foreigners, with perhaps a Swiss supervisor.

One-half, and more, of these are Italians. In early days these were northern Italians from a social background similar to that of the Ticinese and speaking a kindred dialect, but now they are largely from southern Italy, less assimilable. There are about one hundred thousand each of Germans and Spaniards, and about half that number of French and Austrians. These have rather a different character as immigrants, younger, less likely to be married. Very recently more remote races have appeared: one aspect of the problem is that as the homelands of the migrants industrialize, Switzerland attracts from farther away among more backward and quite unassimilable peoples, to whom the Swiss worker refers contemptuously as 'semi-niggers' – the true negro being rare.

On the good side of this many-sided intrusion, there is the economic gain, and the economic guarantee for the future. If unemployed, the foreigner 'without right of settlement' is simply shown the border, and in no circumstances would a Swiss be unemployed, for is he not cushioned by a half-million tolerated foreigners? Socially, too, it has jacked up the whole population by half a social class. The unskilled Swiss of a generation ago is now the pampered leader of a group of Italians, or Turks or Jugoslavs, who, if not unskilled in fact, are doing a job of rather little skill. The skilled Swiss worker is a foreman, and so on up the scale, until one reaches the more remunerated or less energetic work where Swiss still meet only Swiss as in the past. This 'upward social mobility' has kept the working class content, without much affecting relative social mobility among Swiss: no one has moved down, hierarchy is undisturbed among the autochthonous population, even if social differentials are diminished in a democratic manner.

Industrial structure, nevertheless, has changed. The employer has labour which, if it be unionized, pays union subscriptions without much seeking to change the host society. An awkward worker is soon removed; a quiet word to the police suffices. On the other hand, cantonal or federal government can also use the mechanism in its own interest; an awkward firm might run into unexpected difficulty with its work permits. In its turn the federal government may come under a little polite pressure from the Italian government, an uncongenial situation for a nation that has become used to the appearance of unrestricted independence. Supposing the supply was suddenly withdrawn? The economic repercussions would not stop at lost production, at foundries without labour, at untended machines, but would echo throughout the service sector which feeds and houses the immigrants. How would Swiss society stand the restoration of class differentials in their old form, and the collapse of house prices?

The secondary effects of this permanent but unaccepted foreign society are still unfolding, and stretch in every direction. There is, for example, a religious problem. For the last four hundred years the confessional balance has been the most important factor in Swiss politics. The immigrants are overwhelmingly catholic. The Roman church is strengthened by their presence even if they do not have a vote. Moreover, the industrial and religious societies overlap, for there is a latent rivalry between catholic and socialist trade unions in Switzerland, and a struggle for recruitment would also be a struggle between the socialist and the catholic political parties. Just as the immigrants are not protestants, so they are not going to be Swiss liberal-radicals if they ever do become integrated into Swiss society – they will be communists, socialists, and clericals, unless they form parties of their own to counterbalance the anti-immigration parties. There is also an education problem. If the children of immigrants are not to be accepted into Swiss nationality, should they be educated to be Swiss and cantonal citizens, learned in the history of Solothurn and Zug and fluent in a local dialect, and then be dispatched back to Apulia when Father loses his job? As elsewhere in western Europe, the bomb ticks, and life goes cheerfully on.

As to the solution of the problem, it would be palliated by a freer naturalization process, perhaps even by the introduction of a modified *jus soli* whereby those born in Switzerland before a certain date had a claim to Swiss nationality. One wonders whether the picturesque principle of commune-citizenship, anchored in the old poor law, serves any practical or moral end other than as a means of extortion and humiliation of candidates for citizenship. The citizen commune can, after all, no longer choose which Swiss citizens can reside on its territory and so has lost its long cosy exclusiveness. I do not myself see that the cause of communal freedom is advanced by this relic. I am not sure whether even the idea that an applicant must first be integrated before he is granted political rights is sound, for the exercise of such rights is the best means of integration.

The system, indeed, has its positive side, which Britain and the United States must in different ways envy. Law must follow society in a free country and give expression to society's wants. Citizenship is not a mere legal status: it is also a word like 'friendship' describing an attitude, and acceptance of another as being equal and of the same sort. Varied evils follow from the legal fiction of citizenship where the reality is not there. The Swiss tragedy is that the assimilable and the assimilated are often not given political rights and that only the very new immigrants are of the types that will either take long to assimilate or are unassimilable. To the problem of the Savoyard, the Austrian, the northern Italian, the Swabian, or Alsatian immigrant, a 'Swiss' solution is possible, even if it is difficult to see a Swiss solution to, for example, the colour problem. Unless, of course, postponement is also a Swiss solution as it is a British one. Like Britain, Switzerland's greatest contribution to the sum of things is in her demonstration of good government, and the problem of *Ueberfremdung* is one created by government, by a government which assumed that all its people wanted was rising prosperity, while the people, as the Schwarzenbach incident showed, was prepared to sacrifice prosperity for national integrity.

The Housing Problem

It is often said in conversation or implied in speeches and articles that immigrants are responsible for the unsatisfied demand for houses, for the high price of land, or for the high rents demanded by landlords of tenants. There are really two allegations here. One concerns the need for immigrant labour to be housed somewhere or other, in huts and dormitories, or in working-class flats. The other concerns the idle rich who come to Switzerland or have a second home there, partly to enjoy the landscape and climate, but partly also to pay lower, and less steeply progressive, taxes than at home.

The problem of the rich is often discussed in a somewhat demagogic tone, 'the sell-out of the homeland', and can be used to direct social resentments into the more manageable channels of inflamed nationalism – speaking just loud enough to get cheers from a patriotic audience, but not so loud that other countries retaliate against Swiss residents abroad (who are organized by their home government in a way that would be bitterly resented if foreigners in Switzerland were so organized). Numerically, the rich non-Swiss settlers are not a problem, economically they are a source of large profit, culturally and scientifically they could, if accepted, be a source at least of sufficient benefit to out-weigh certain real disadvantages. The matter is a moral and psychological problem of the Swiss and of the foreigners rather than a problem of housing: the relationship lacks mutual respect.

The problem of the poor immigrant is alleviated by the exceedingly bad accommodation many immigrants occupy. It is a manageable but genuine problem. The secondary problem created by these immigrants, however, is a serious and perhaps insoluble one. The reason for the presence of these labourers is that they do the dirty work of the country, and the native citizens enjoy an upward social mobility. A consequence of this upward mobility is an increased appetite for housing. The former Swiss labourer demands the housing suited to an artisan, the middle class hitherto dwelling in rented flats demand to own houses, those with one house seek a second house in the Valais or Grisons for the weekend for increasingly long vacations. This demand is by its nature insatiable, until checked by price.

The increased prosperity is also, even in Switzerland, being accompanied by a gradual inflation. The two factors together – the demand for a commodity in short supply, and the increase in money-value of land and houses because of inflation – have meant a terrifying rise in house and land prices. This has created a dangerous social tension. The class of owners of houses enjoy an enormous increase (on paper) in their wealth. The class of renters of houses (and particularly of flats) suffer a large increase in rents. This is a social cleft that hardly existed before, and is politically very dangerous: in a democracy it is dangerous to belong to a minority enjoying unearned wealth gained at the expense of one's fellow voters. It may even affect the labour-peace (the agreement between management and trade unions) upon which Switzerland's prosperity totally depends. If it does, and workers strike for higher wages, the resulting inflation will make the social cleft intolerably wide.

The problem is especially acute in Vaud and Geneva, both because there is a somewhat above-average proportion of tenanted (rather than owner-occupied) property, and because of the inflammatory terms in which the problem is there discussed. The foreigner looks with interest to see how the Swiss political system will solve or attenuate the problem: the problems of nationality, of language, or religion, are after all phoney problems, but this seems to be in part a genuine one, and one to which it is difficult to visualize any solution not destructive of the values which the political structure of the country exists to preserve.

NOTES

[1] In recent years there has been a great movement towards concentration, which has increased the identification of the fate of big firms with the public interest. CIBA has merged with Geigy, Brown-Boveri with Oerlikon, Sandoz with Wander, Suchard with Tobler, Nestlé with Ursina. Such great firms determine for themselves what degree of competition with other Swiss firms is desirable, economically and politically, in the short run and the long: they are so big that the very situation imposes upon them a responsible attitude. Government is therefore not at odds with particular industrial undertakings, nor are these much at odds among them-

selves or with public opinion. There seems here to be a similar pattern to political life, where the parties share rule with each other. Industrially, as well as politically, such a pattern may prove superior to the British pattern of institutionalized bickering.

[2] The amateur industrial archaeologist will find much to interest him in Switzerland – not machines *in situ*, but old buildings of the early industrial revolution; Winterthur, and Canton Zurich in general, have good sites. Often one can see all stages of a factory with the successive buildings, beginning with the modest house in which it all started which now often serves as the management headquarters. In some districts the accessory accommodation is interesting, from the *Flarz* houses for the workers of the earliest home-industries (virtually peasant houses without the barns, stuck together in a continuous row, often dating from the last half of the eighteenth century or a bit later) to the *Kosthäuser* built for workers by the early factory-owners, whose own villas are nearby. The difficulty until recently was the unavailability of the sort of literature the traveller can conveniently take with him. But modern guidebooks are sometimes helpful: the new *Kunstführer durch die Schweiz* (Begründet von Hans Jenny, I, Wabern, 1971; II, expected 1975), and such books as the *Architekten Führer Zürich*, Zurich, 1972, by Lea Carl and, indispensable but bulky, the second edition of *Geographie der Schweiz*, Berne, 1958–69, by Hans Gutersohn. Apart from the (sometimes) excellent series of *Schweizer Pioniere der Wirtschaft und Technik* – only the ones in German are usually to be recommended – one is often left scraping round centenary celebration books in libraries. Libraries, however, are excellent and helpful.

Railway archaeology at first sight is rather better served, but I do not know of anything which is 'spot on' for the historian using his eyes, interested in the old stations and tunnels and the earliest bridges, and wanting to sort out the origins of the various lines he travels over.

[3] The tram Vevey-Chillon, 1888, being the very first, followed by a private railway in Basle Land, Sissach to Gelterkinden.

[4] The problem and its solutions change rapidly: the pages here were written in 1972.

[5] Paradoxically, the applicants for teaching positions from Germany today are refugees from undergraduate radicalism.

[6] 'I should be walking on thin ice if I touched on the question whether or not the regime of Madrid [Franco's insurgents] were or were not the legitimate power. Much less would I presume to examine whether or not the insurgent population of Spain be defending a just cause. Such a discussion I must scrupulously avoid. The only fact, and one which I have the duty and the right to establish, is that anarchist and syndicalist groups in Spain have taken upon themselves to exercise a considerable part of the force of the state'. Federal Councillor Motta, 6 October 1936. Quoted from Bonjour, op. cit., 2nd ed., 210, which is the source of the discussion of this incident. This is the attitude called by Swiss writers 'the return to absolute (as opposed to differential) neutrality'.

CHAPTER 8

Civilization

I. Major Arts

THE INITIAL PROBLEM when talking about the arts of Switzerland before 1500, indeed before 1800, is to give a meaning to the word 'Switzerland'. On the one hand, the boundary expands. Does one reckon Basle as being in Switzerland in respect of its works of art before 1501? When is Geneva Swiss? While 'Basle' and 'Geneva' have a meaning in this context, the union of these cities with the other cantons is scarcely relevant. Apart from this, before 1500 personal movement was very free throughout the imperial territories. To what nationality do we allocate Conrad Witz or Holbein or the humanists in the circle of Erasmus? Similarly, in the first half of the nineteenth century (and the late eighteenth) nationhood sat rather lightly on the shoulders of the cultivated middle classes: Madame de Staël, Fuseli, Angelica Kauffmann, Sismondi, Benjamin Constant, are they all Swiss?

Some of these difficulties occur in other places, but in Switzerland they are rendered acute by a factor nearly peculiar to the country, its polyglotism. The language districts are also art districts, much more lightly connected with each other than with their language-brothers over the frontier – Italian Switzerland more connected with Italy, for example, than with German and French Switzerland. It is only exceptionally, and mostly in very modern times, that one can talk of a culture that it Swiss and only Swiss, and when an artist transcends the language frontier (as a sculptor like Giacometti, or an artist like Paul Klee, or an architect like Le Corbusier may do), he often transcends the national frontier also, as in his day Rousseau did.

In the visual arts, Switzerland, like England, is characterized by an extraordinary richness of the agreeable, second-rank, works that heighten the enjoyment of daily life and make the country delightful and beautiful and interesting – castles and ancient churches, for example. Here and there are objects which are in the very first class, which take one's breath away and need to be approached with solemnity and awe, but they are rare. In this way, Switzerland is unlike France and Italy (north of Naples) but like many other

218

European countries. The country is rich in art, because it has been rich in money, and has been somewhat conservative and politically stable, and has avoided shellfire and bombs. Swiss art seldom attains the very highest rank partly because everything is localized – it is not just that Switzerland is rather small, but that Basle, Zurich, and even Geneva in their great days were very small indeed. The supreme works, the *Portail Peint* in Lausanne Cathedral, the glass at Königsfelden (to take two examples which will not be contested), are often[1] the product of pre-confederal days and larger political units.

There are some three Roman works of art of the first rank in Swiss museums. A rather large number of Roman sites – mosaics, walls, castles, arenas – survive: the most striking are Avenches, Augst (near Basle), and Windisch (near Baden); after this might come Irgenhausen, a reconstruction, in Canton Zurich. Lesser sites are numerous.

There are remains of many really rather early churches throughout Switzerland, some incorporated in existing buildings but mostly discovered in excavations while repairing a later church: they are usually dated from A.D. 600 onwards. There is much Carolingian art of very high quality: from about 800 to 1000, Switzerland is as rich in buildings and remains as any area outside Italy – whole churches, frescoes, and crypts of churches. St Gallen possesses notable manuscripts of this period, for it has a first flowering in the years after A.D. 720 and remained for two centuries a principal centre of European civilization north of the Alps. Notker, the poet, was a monk there. If the theory holds that the beginning of sculpture in the post-classical West is to be found in carved ivory reliefs on book-covers, then St Gallen possesses very early ones indeed. In these centuries, Switzerland (after Italy) was the equal of the Rhineland and parts of France, and is followed by England and north-west Spain.

After A.D. 1000, there are numerous works of the high romanesque, as many as one would expect in any part of Upper Germany, Burgundy, or alpine northern Italy. The influence of this style continued long in the Grisons, punctuating certain countrysides with variants of romanesque church towers. These towers dominate the valley landscapes of the Ticino also: Giornico has perhaps the best example in Ticino of a romanesque church of distinction, and is easily accessible for the traveller by rail. But to study romanesque art in Switzerland would be a lifetime's hobby. It is very strongly influenced by Italy (the church at Amsoldingen near Berne, for example, is one of many throughout Switzerland that might as easily be near Verona), but there are other influences, fascinating to trace, Eastern, or occasionally perhaps even Spanish (as in Zurich's Grossmünster).

While some of the masters who worked in Switzerland were foreign, many craftsmen attributed to Como (masons and inlay-workers) derived from villages now in Switzerland. The same import and export of artists continued into later centuries. Carona, near Lugano, is famous for the architects and sculptors from the village-republic who worked abroad. In the seventeenth and eighteenth centuries, German Switzerland was importing styles and architects from Bavaria and Vorarlberg, at the same time as Italian Swiss architects were working in Rome and Venice. The richness of the churches and lay buildings of the Mesocco is due to returning emi-grant masons. These worked far outside Switzerland for many cen-turies. In the eighteenth century, for example, they rebuilt Eichstätt, in Germany.

In gothic times Switzerland still was not a country distinguishable in its art from the areas adjacent to it, south Germany, Burgundy, or Lombardy, though she is intensely rich, and has her own local styles, and regional peculiarities. Frescoes (as at Rhäzuns and Waltensburg) and altars (especially in Grisons) are among the best of their time. What is also remarkable is their survival – sometimes protestant iconoclasm has preserved frescoes under whitewash which a greater piety would have destroyed to allow for more fashionable ones, and whole schools of fresco-painters have come again to light in recent years. Italian Switzerland contains marvellous painted church in-teriors, in late gothic and Renaissance styles.

The period from 1500 to 1650 has given an indelible character to the lay architecture of the Old Towns (*Altstädte*) of Swiss cities. Each town developed a variant of its own: even Biel has a Biennois style of late domestic gothic. For the traveller, these brilliantly preserved or restored old towns are a chief delight of Switzerland. Gruyères, Stein am Rhein, and Morat have become too pretty and too well known and self-conscious, but Vaud and Aargau (and parts of Berne) possess many examples which remain unselfconscious working towns in almost perfect preservation.

A word must be said about preservation. The visitor to Swiss churches has to reconcile himself to the restoration philosophy of the federal authorities. The effect striven for is boldness, whiteness, decorated with a few choice examples or naïve curiosities (as in a rich man's house of good taste). All stonework has the patina scrupu-lously removed to the depth of several inches, and is replaced with a sounder quality, tooled over nicely and with masons' marks and dates recarved on it. Sculpture is replaced by a copy which increases the boldness of effect – delicacy is considered rather old-fashioned and finicky, even if the original manifestly strove for it. The federal style of the last twenty years is imposing a swissness and unity on buildings which were very different indeed in total effect before this happened. Frescoes, in particular, owe effectiveness to the restorer. Before the war, protestant churches, even former cathedrals, were kept tightly shut. The visitor sought out the custodian, who enjoyed an afternoon's sleep (or, preferably, was undisturbed from Monday to Saturday). The custodian furnished himself with a Petrine key, turned a heavy lock, and busied himself with acts of tidiness, whistling, while the foreigner gaped: the prudent tourist saved his 50-centime bits as the smallest tribute acceptable by the guardian of a minor edifice. Today, churches restored at federal expense are freely open, but they have been stripped of the clutter of piety superimposed during three centuries. They are more striking, more available, in better structural condition than before, but usually now quite lack a devotional or picturesque atmosphere. When I first visited Payerne and Rüeggisberg, the ancient churches were used as barns, and Königsfelden (if I remember right) was little more: I was disturbed, but moved. Now they are show places; they have gained much, but what they have lost is saddening. There remain some unrestored churches, usually in unfashionable parts, Solothurn, Thurgau, which are still very moving, and there are other buildings, in Ticino and Grisons, for example, which desperately need saving from destruction. It is the scarcity of a middle way between perfectionism and dereliction that is Swiss.

The small towns, it is agreed, are delightful. Everyone has his favourite – Kaiserstuhl, Le Landeron, St-Ursanne, Saillon, Sursee, Werdenberg, Regensberg – but the big and famous towns have all kept the 'medieval' (usually sixteenth- and seventeenth-century) old town nearly intact. Zurich had an impressive number of dwelling houses from romanesque times, until a recent wave of restoration, and has kept the old town north of the river as a picturesque handworkers' and small-shop quarter as in former days: even the district frequented by the ladies of the street is the one where they traditionally plied their trade. Old Berne, on the other hand, is becoming an elegant shopping quarter. Everywhere in different ways the old centre is being kept up, and improved, and put to some characteristic use. The contrast with France is very great. If one compares Porrentruy, for example, with Montbéliard or Mulhouse, one sees that the Swiss town is delightful in quality as well as interesting to the connoisseur and the French town has just a few consolations remaining here and there, but in general gimcrack-modern has replaced what was ancient and derelict in a haphazard and ugly manner. As works of art, the French and Swiss towns were probably of equal quality down to the 1850s. To what century then is Swiss beauty to be attributed? Is Fribourg, for example, not a work of art of the preserver and restorer and sympathizer as well as of the late middle ages and the Renaissance?

It is a little the same story in the countryside. Because of just laws and light taxation the countryside is filled with delightful peasant buildings in wood or other local material, among which eighteenth-century work dominates. These buildings are mostly still used as farms, having in their time been converted from corn husbandry (needing many rooms for labourers) to milk husbandry (needing stalls), and recently modernized and adapted to electricity. Every district has its own style – the boundary of a style seldom coincides with political or linguistic or religious frontiers in detail. These houses have not been allowed to fall down, but kept and used – even if the period of genuine agricultural use is drawing to a close. One step over the border (of France or Italy) and the magic of the rural buildings has fled.

The eighteenth century in Switzerland has the same quality as that of England in that nothing very memorable happened between 1715 and the Revolution. It has left behind it a heritage of delightful country houses in protestant Switzerland, and important and beautiful abbey and parish churches in catholic Switzerland, many of them of astonishing loveliness – Fischingen (Thurgau), for example. During the same century Switzerland kept up, as it were, her end in literature, with a rather distinguished place held by Zurich as a sort of republican Weimar – Gessner, Scheuchzer, Bodmer, Lavater, Breitinger, to be followed by a generation of romantics, notably Pestalozzi and Füssli – while Basle, Berne, and even Schaffhausen produced quite distinguished writers and thinkers, Iselin, Haller, von Müller.[2] Geneva is as special a case in France as Zurich in Germany. But, again, there was no Goethe and only one Rousseau.

The nineteenth century in Europe is the century of historians, novelists, and lyric poets. There are many names one could pick out. Most German Swiss would probably say 'Gottfried Keller' first. For myself, an Englishman, I find this incomprehensible. Keller seems to me self-pitying, perverted, unobservant, incapable of telling a story with more than two characters, flat in his characterization, ugly in his politics (politics are part of a Swiss writer), and generally repulsive – but he does not seem so to his countrymen. The name I would myself pick out is Jeremias Gotthelf, whom I consider as great a novelist as I have come across.[3] One is getting here on to matters of taste and personality; the argument for the purposes of this chapter is that even in the nineteenth century Switzerland made a good showing in German literature. In Germany, provincialism is not an adverse judgement, for German culture is a decentralized one. But French civilization is less tolerant to localism, and in the nineteenth and twentieth centuries one could be well-read in French literature without ever much considering French Switzerland. A *Romand*, a French Swiss, it is said, has to go to Paris for his consecration: only there can he make a reputation that is respected at home, though Geneva has more self-sufficiency than other centres. From the standpoint of Geneva (and Lausanne, Neuchâtel, and Fribourg) the observer is surprised at the intense cultural activity, but from Paris, French Switzerland is an interesting little province, always and again producing delightful little writers: there may well be some injustice here, but I suspect it is not very considerable. A great Swiss writer might easily be undervalued in Paris, but it is not easy to point to a case where this has happened. Indeed, in 1973, for the first time, the Prix Goncourt was awarded to a book by a French-Swiss writer (*L'Ogre*, by Jacques Chessex).

Ticino, culturally speaking, is not a province of Switzerland but a part of Italy, a name for a bit of Lombardy. Francesco Chiesa, recently dead, has a fame which overshadows all others. As regards German Switzerland, since 1945 two of the most widely praised German writers have been Swiss, Dürrenmatt and Frisch – though this has now been repeated for a rather long time. In such matters German Switzerland can be reasonably seen to be (as in economic matters, and in political authority) a mini-great power. Assuredly, the English reader of German is as likely to find pleasure in Swiss German writing as in that of the main country.

As regards painting in this century and the last, Europe is in the shadow of France. There have been good Swiss painters, a Swiss met casually would usually name Hodler first of all, both because of his merit and his swissness. In galleries, the Swiss names make a creditable showing.

Switzerland is famous in the sciences as well as the arts. The story would start no doubt with the attractively named Theophrastus Bombastus Paracelsus,[4] and mentioning on the way the Bernoullis and Euler. There is reason to think the proportion of famous scientists is well above average for the size of population, and somewhat above average for national income at any particular date. Switzerland is a rich country, and the civilization is in large part an urban one. A favourite subject of speculation in the 1950s and 1960s among Swiss writers was which particular national virtues were responsible for the above-average award of Nobel Prizes to their countrymen: the controversy was never quite settled, but democracy, tolerance, individualism, goodness, and inborn genius were suggested, together with the spirit of 1291. To these I would add a certain uncontroversialness and political harmlessness, and the tribute due by one neutral to another, but the achievement itself is not deniable.

Just as she is a great country for preservation and restoration, so Switzerland has become a great country for collecting. In the past, she had a few strokes of luck, especially the Burgundian Booty, captured from Charles the Bold in the fifteenth century and divided among those who had lent help, or the Amerbach Cabinet, confiscated by Basle from the estate of a respected and wealthy settler who turned out to have been throughout the period of his residence the secret leader of the Anabaptist movement. But these acquisitions were matched by dispersions and sales of the Swiss cultural heritage – major losses, such as the sale of the Golden Altar of Basle to the Musée de Cluny in Paris, and many minor losses, evidenced by such collections as the Swiss stained glass and cartoons held by the Victoria and Albert Museum, or even by the glass in the parish church of Wragby (Nostell Priory, in Nottinghamshire). The serious Swiss collecting which has shifted the balance of connoisseur-power in Europe is a modern phenomenon. Many of these great Swiss private collections have come by gift or testament into public hands.

One cause of the collecting mania is the difficulty of being rich and satisfied in a country where the ultimate power is after all with the artisan class, and the climate of opinion is set against flamboyant waste. The rich buy Impressionists, or Swiss artists of any period. There are certain tax advantages in picture-collecting, not all quite official. But even this hobby can be a bore, especially if one does not particularly like pictures, and the point is, after all, quiet display, but display, of wealth and culture. So a rich man not infrequently makes them over to the commune where he lives: there may be further tax advantages in this also, and a spirit of mutual forgiveness for underdeclared assets and forgone exactions is engendered, and such generosity is balm for a bad conscience as well as tending to strengthen the existing structure of society while giving (or purchasing) the family a good name. For the donor too, there are the minor honours afforded by a republic, Honorary Citizen, Doktor, even Ambassador. Above all, to donate a collection is patriotic, and patriotism, especially localized patriotism, is as deeply felt in Switzerland as in nation-states. Whatever the psychological springs, Switzerland has recently become a home of the muses by purchase as well as by inheritance.

A minor pleasure of life in Switzerland is the abundance of good, and other, sculpture in public places. The sculptures which adorn fountains (whence the public used to draw water) prolong a tradition of the old regime – the earliest are in Basle, the most decoratively effective in the town of Berne. In Bernese territory figures of Justice are to be found with a vague political and ideological motivation typical of Switzerland. In rich towns such as Zurich modern sculpture is sometimes doodled round the place without any commemorative function, simply to relieve a wall (as my favourite, in the Seilergraben by Ernst Suter) or decorate a *quai*, and such sculpture is more enjoyable than the commemorative pieces, a militiaman heroically pulling on a coat, for example, or the Rütli oath again. These public works by good artists bring art into life in an unforced way. A more ephemeral extension of this is the very high standard of poster design.

II. Arts of Daily Life

Such a topic leads on to the minor arts of daily life. In these Switzerland is acknowledged to take a very high place, but one's assessment must needs be a personal one.

The custom of singing traditional songs on country expeditions (which used to capture the whole second-class deck of paddle-steamers, touched off by a school outing) is now nearly dead: it suddenly became unbearably old-fashioned around 1960. Song, with or without non-functional yodelling, may still fill an inn or a carriage-full of soldiers, or a family gathering, or come pouring out of the open window of a school. I have no ear, but find it delightful.

The Swiss have a high repute for gardening, and have developed sophisticated colours and breeds of flowers. To my mind, this reputation (entirely justified in comparison with Switzerland's immediate neighbours) must come second to that of southern England. The real specialism is in window-boxes, which used to be filled with carnations, but in this century most districts are now filled with geraniums. Even fountains are often adorned with these. Geraniums (red zonal pelargoniums) have become the national flower, sometimes locally replaced by cactuses or other tough and brilliant genera that can spend a winter in the cellar and enjoy the humid sunshine of summer and the smell of ammonia from the cow-stalls. The suburban garden, it seems to me, is thought of as an extended window-box. A little stretch of grass, elephant-step stones in a line across it, bedding flowers, and a tree (and rocks lifted on a weekend expedition): it is a pleasing formula, suited to a small country. And over it all often flies the national flag, the dumpy white cross on a crimson field.

Hospitality and indulgence take the form of 'eating out'. It sometimes seems as if the whole landscape only served the purpose of making lunch or dinner in a restaurant completely agreeable, the village, the lake, the cows, the mountains being there for ambiance and *Stimmung*. The first three days in Switzerland, before one has had to cash a traveller's cheque, are spent in paradise. At the end of that time, apart from anything else, the visitor has to start the *à la carte* over again and his digestion demands a sweet: there is an

excellent one, a mountain of cream and sugar, but already before
that stage he is replete.

As every Briton knows, Switzerland is the land for holidays – individual holidays in the open air, lasting a fortnight. Transport is
excellent, the hotels utterly reliable and clean, the pedestrian always
welcome, the relevant landscape is of intense beauty and brilliant
light. The Swiss themselves nowadays are there too, but they also
like to go abroad – one long visit to England, to learn English somewhere in north London (Lonndonn, not Lundun), and repeated
visits to France and Italy. As travellers they are a little less thorough,
a little less sun-mad, and much less obtrusive, than the Germans.

Cleanliness, we know, is a Swiss virtue. There are some indications
that it spread from Bernese territory to the protestant cantons of the
east, and from the middle of last century it has made strides even in
the catholic cantons, conquering, in our own times, even most of
Valais and Ticino. It has spread also from the house to the person – it
is no longer true that the English have a spring clean once a year
and a bath every day, while the Swiss do the reverse. By a familiar
perversity of events, just as cleanliness has finally established its
kingdom, a cult of apparent dirtiness is a vogue among the rather
young of the respectable classes. The first guidebooks complain
bitterly about Swiss dirtiness: the Swiss now complain about England.

The culture of the home, indeed, is also a Swiss art. Rooms are
more comfortable than in France, bearing out de Tocqueville's
generalizations about the relationship of comfort to democracy, and
with a more confident taste than Germany. The elements of status,
tradition, comfort, technology, individuality, and attractiveness are
usually nicely blended. But these are topics on which everyone will
have his own opinion.

The argument of this chapter and of this book is that Switzerland
has a peculiar and delightful culture, not too philistine, properly, but
not excessively, materialist, and with an agreeable balance of sensual
and spiritual. This is a first impression which abides, and returns in
full force when thinking about Switzerland in England. But this is
not how the foreigner always feels about Switzerland. There may be
times indeed when he wishes to be able to yell so loud that the whole
abominable place would collapse in ruins, a modern Gomorrah.
Foreigners may also become angry at the way in which Italians,
Greeks, and Spaniards are treated, for one might regard them as
symbols of cultures superior to the Swiss – even if one is in no position
to cast the first stone. Refugees in Switzerland have called the
country 'the chilly Paradise'. Swiss people living abroad have told
me with an impressive unanimity that they feel freer in (for example)

London than Zurich. And when the foreigner confides his moments of revulsion to other foreigners who have lived in Switzerland, they at once understand. Something of this mood of momentary revulsion at a certain heartlessness inherent in Swiss society is felt by Swiss themselves when they come to live in another part of Switzerland, and especially when they cross the language (and until recently, the religious) frontier. The Zuricois in Lausanne may well suffer from the same apparent friendliness but deep-seated lack of involvement which the resident Englishman or American observes, the hospitality (in which the guest often acts as host) in restaurants rather than the home, the *unverbindlich* courtesy, the hypocritical regrets, the skilful evasion. I am inclined to think this is more widespread in Switzerland even than in England, and that disinterested acceptance within a social group is slower in Switzerland than in most Western societies. It is the reciprocal of, and reinforces, the attachment of a Swiss to his own hearth and native village – the only place where he is totally sure of unforced acceptance.

More serious, but also more encouraging, is that this mood of revulsion is also felt increasingly often by young Swiss people, and especially by the most vigorous-minded and articulate. The mood dominates the undergraduate life of universities, not because of numbers but because of the strength of the emotion, and it is spreading to other sections of the community and other age-groups. The advantages of Swiss civilization, the low level of non-legal violence, the relatively stable currency, the virtues of craftsmanship, honesty, healthiness, the respect for social class, and the general rationality of the system are, it seems when in such a mood, achieved by the formula 'Be twenty years behind the times in moral attitudes, but keep abreast of technology'. As a virtue a culture-lag may be morally second-rate: what it creates is a first-rate ambiance to live in.

This environment and civilization is threatened by this type of criticism, and will not, in all probability, long survive. Switzerland is a problem, not a solution. Her civilization will not survive the implicit criticism of the other, greater, civilizations that surround it or with which it is in contact – Germany, France, Britain, the United States, even Italy and Austria. But Switzerland also constitutes a criticism of these countries, and each of them (but especially Britain) can learn a lesson for its own future from Switzerland's long-continued relative felicity.

NOTES

[1] The Great Luini fresco of the Crucifixion in Sta Maria degli Angioli in Lugano is from after the Swiss annexation; Luini's birthplace is a few miles inside Italy.

² These are famous names. But it is not concealed from me that one may be good and wise, but never have read Gessner (or seen his pretty pictures), or Scheuchzer, Bodmer, Lavater, Breitinger, Iselin, or Müller or even Albrecht von Haller. The works on which the contemporary reputation of Pestalozzi relied are today unreadable, and Fuseli's (Füssli's) pictures have so largely been repurchased by Swiss collections that his reputation in Britain is diminished, and Blake is far better known.

³ A most delightful writer, whose works have not been reprinted, is Ulrich Hegner (1759–1840) of Winterthur: a facsimile edition is urgently called for. 'Jeremias Gotthelf' was the pseudonym of Albert Bitzius (1797–1854), a Bernese pastor. Most of his novels are about the peasantry of the Emmenthal.

⁴ Also known as Philip Baumast von Hohenheim, and Aureolus. His sciences nearly outnumber his names: he was skilled in medicine, chemistry, philosophy, astronomy, and theology. Only his mother was 'Swiss', a copyholder of Einsiedeln. Theophrastus (1493–1541) was one of the great figures of the Renaissance: the motto 'Be not another's if you can be your own', *Alterius non sit qui suus esse potest*, is ascribed to him. Not much of his life was spent at Einsiedeln.

CHAPTER 9

The Cantons

SWITZERLAND IS A SMALL COUNTRY for the purpose of a young man unfolding his ambitions for a life within it, and this is one reason why so many have emigrated to the United States. But for the foreigner interested in the country, it is a very large one. He must start with the histories of two dozen sovereignties, and to every generalization he finds exceptions. The cantons, even the communes, still mean something essential to Swiss life today, and the Swiss past is unintelligible except in the form of localized history – not the local history of a municipality, but of a sovereign state, even if a very small one. It is therefore necessary to get some sense of this diverse personality of the cantons.

The usual way of listing the cantons is in the order of accession to the Confederation. The trouble with this 'historical order' is that in some ways it is not historical: history is concerned with events and with power, not with the ceremonial order of precedence fixed in the early nineteenth century. The arrangement which follows treats Berne and Zurich as the two centres of power, and radiates from these cities on mixed historical and regional principles.

Even a brief account of cantonal politics since 1815 dissipates the expectation that within the cantons a rational tolerance has been the rule for time out of mind – the political equivalent of the cowbell and chocolate image of Swiss life. To make it quicker for the reader to pick out what is distinctive in the life of a particular canton, a note may be helpful on the general pattern that is common to the cantons' political life since their appearance in their modern form in 1815.

The constitutions of cantons at any one time resemble each other (except for the allowances to be made for a *Landsgemeinde* – the open-air sovereign assembly of all voters held annually). The Great Council is the parliament, the Petty Council, or Council of State, is the executive. Cantonal government mirrors the institutions of the federal government, except that cantons only have one house of their legislature.

The cantonal political pattern is: (i) Restoration of a modified old regime in 1813; (ii) Liberal *coup d'état* in 1830–31; (iii) Conservative *coup*, with a lower level of violence, 1847–41; (iv) Transition back to liberalism at an election; (v) Radical rioting threatening a *coup*, followed by a radical victory, 1844–49; (vi) Radical rule with federal backing, 1848–54; (vii) Short period of conservative or liberal rule, accompanied by gesture of accommodation to the radicals, such as the offer of a ministry and place in the executive council; (viii) Final radical victory in election, gesture of conciliation with right wing (in 1860s or 1870s). Thereafter (ix) The gradual introduction of proportionality and, after 1891, (x) A regular pattern of minority representation in the executive council; (xi) After 1891, appearance of socialists in parliament; after 1920, in government. In 1920, loss of radical control of parliament, and soon after that, of the executive; (xii) By 1945, full proportionality in government as well as parliament.

In catholic cantons the pattern is different in that, after about 1854, in the above scheme one can substitute the words 'catholic conservative' for 'radical'. It is important to observe that the pattern had a slightly different timing everywhere, and therefore on the federal level the swings were not so violent, but nevertheless there was considerable national excitement at every cantonal change, because this at once affected the federal balance.

Until 1870–90 a change of regime usually meant a change of constitution, the mechanism for making short work of opponents being a constituent assembly elected under pressure, then a constitution designed to secure the future for one's own party. Turning-points in a canton's development are: the date when existing officials, including judges, are retained after a defeat; the date when an election, rather than a *coup*, changes government; the date when a constitution survives a party defeat; the date of fair, secret, and proportional elections (usually around 1910–20); and the date of full proportionality in the executive.

In east Switzerland, the 'Democrats' asserted a claim to power in the 1860s or later, as a party to the left of the radicals, and thus forced the radicals into the role of a centre party. So the liberals were squeezed out. In west Switzerland, the radicals kept their position on the extreme left until the appearance of socialist and communist parties. There was thus no room for the Democrats, and the liberals became at first the centre party, and then absorbed the conservative Right and became the party of the high-bourgeois, the great vineyard families and the wealthy peasantry of ancient descent.

I. Berne and West Switzerland

BERNE

Berne has imprinted its personality on its former territories, on those it snatched from the Hapsburgs in 1415, and those it con-

quered from Savoy in 1536; the former are now part of Canton
Aargau, and the latter are the greater part of Canton Vaud. (Aigle,
and some other bits, were acquired by Berne in 1486.) This inherited
personality has varied aspects – the reformed religion, a distinctive
conception of the state, a structure of rural society, a style of architecture. The territories themselves were lost by Berne after the revolution of 1798. The lands acquired in 1815 in their place, the
French-speaking Bernese Jura, have not (in their catholic districts)
taken on the Bernese personality.

Berne is a big, rather rich, and disproportionally rural canton. It
includes all types of the Swiss scenery north of the Alps, reaching
from the snow-clad peaks of the Bernese Oberland, through the
Mittelland and the Seeland, to a chunk of the Juras, protruding
thence into France.

The Bernese of the Old Canton feel themselves to be an imperial
race, conscious of tradition, and have a firm conviction that the
authority of the state is to be respected, but also that the native
citizens are a part of that state as well as owing duty towards it. The
spirit is perhaps strongest in the Seeland, the part from which
Bernese statesmen have most often derived since 1846. The Emmenthal has its own character, the Oberland a greater imprint of the
generic alpine character (and therefore less Bernese). But as one
looks round like this, Haslital, Simmental, Schwarzenburg, Oberaar-
gau, and so on, the canton falls into its historic parts, which kept a
sort of separate identity and their own laws until shortly before the
fall of the restored aristocracy in 1831. Only Bienne (Biel) has become
relatively characterless and shapeless, an urban agglomeration of
watchmakers and metal-workers which has islanded the tiny historic
centre of the old/free (or almost free) city, which came finally to
Berne in 1815. With the flood of French-speaking immigrants from
neighbouring parts of Switzerland, Bienne is one of the rare places
where the *de facto* language frontier has shifted in recent years.

Politically, the largest party in the canton is the Farmers' party –
now called SVP – which regularly provides a Bernese Federal
Councillor. Bernese institutions and traditions have left their imprint
on the ideology of that party.

A curious phenomenon is the way in which the Bernese peasantry
have colonized similar countryside all over the Swiss Mittelland,
especially in Neuchâtel, Vaud, and Thurgau. In *Suisse romande*, the
second generation of these settlers becomes French-speaking. In other
parts it picks up the local dialect at school, and the descendants are
only recognizable by their name, or their inherited cantonal citizenship.

'Canton Jura' : the non-canton

As one goes north-west of Bienne over the Col de Pierre-Pertuis (the pierced stone, where the Romans made a road tunnel), shortly after Moutier and the iron-works in the gorge at Choindez (a name derived from the German *Schwenden*) on the road to Delémont (or shortly after Tramelan if one is going to Saignelégier), the Bernese bear disappears from the flags in street and garden. It is replaced by the armorial flag taken from that of the old bishopric of Basle, with the episcopal crozier, red on white, in the first and fourth quarters. This is secessionist country, the French-speaking, catholic, Bernese Jura.

The story is complex, the literature too large, but some important matters (social structure, for example) have been left nearly uninvestigated. Here is a part of the canton which has suffered genuine grievances, especially during the years (1870–90) of the Bernese *Kulturkampf*, and which wishes to secede from Berne, and join with almost anyone else (if the worst befell, perhaps even with France), but above all to form a separate canton.

The reactions of this area, and the character of its folk-heroes (such as Xavier Stockmar in the last century), remain quite uncomprehended by the Bernese, much hurt at the complete failure of firmness combined with unswerving justness to command the Jura. At every turn one is reminded of the relationships of Great Britain with Ireland, though Switzerland is, of course, comparatively on a tiny scale. Even the quiet sympathy of the neighbour-state is not lacking. Here bombs have exploded, farmhouses been set on fire, war memorials damaged, sympathizers with German (protestant) Berne terrorized. Every reaction of the Old Canton, whether conciliation or repression, turns against it; and a body of conspirators is now firmly established whose living and notoriety depend on the regular perpetration of outrages, professional nationalists who are not to be conciliated.

The reader must be reminded that federalism within a canton is legally impossible, and that the creation of a new canton requires a constitutional amendment, and one which would raise very grave issues in view of the vague atmosphere of the Confederation being in some way a league of cantons. Where would such a movement stop, the dwarf cantons would ask? The solution of two Bernese half-cantons is inappropriate in view of the enormous size of the Old Canton to be left with half-representation in the Council of States.

The German-speaking catholic area of Laufen remains loyal to Berne, a sort of tiny Ulster, and so does the French-speaking protestant area, though this factor might later change or be accommodated by making a new Canton Jura into two half-cantons. Bienne is necessary to the economic wellbeing of the area, and its inclusion would be historically justifiable, but would put the separatists in a minority. The issue is now argued by the separatists that only old-established inhabitants of the area should vote (to the exclusion of settlers from German Switzerland), and that Jurassians in exile elsewhere in Switzerland should vote. A whole series of constitutional amendments would then be needed to allow this and they would be incompatible with modern concepts of the rule of law. The topic of the Jura is large, the controversy hot, and events are moving fast.

VAUD

Vaud is a canton formed in 1803 from the French-speaking parts of the old canton of Berne, together with some other little bits, of which the most interesting is a group of catholic parishes around Echallens, formerly a condominium of Berne and Fribourg: otherwise the canton (as having been Bernese) is protestant. Like Berne, it has samples of different sorts of country – mountains in the district centred historically in Aigle, the vineyard country along the north shore of the Lake of Geneva, the 'plateau' country and the Gros de Vaud (rich farming land of the Bernese type), and a portion of the Juras (the Vallée de Joux). The structure of rural society, the layout of farms, the dominance of the substantial peasantry, are typically Bernese, as is the appearance of the streets in the old towns. Like the Aargau, it is historically (in most parts) a country of castles and tiny boroughs, for here feudalism survived until the conquest by Berne, and thenceforth local and manorial rights were frozen in their then existing form until the end of the old regime – apart from the freeing of the serfs. For the Vaudois under Bernese rule were personally free, and bore arms; the peasants were not subject to the heavy and unfair taxes of the French monarchy next door, and the burghers, especially in the old capital, Lausanne, retained privileges and certain rights of self-government.

In very recent years the part of the canton between Montreux and Geneva has become heavily urbanized, around Lausanne frighteningly so. In general, the canton retains its typical character of seeming, from the standpoint of Berne, very French – the support of foolish causes, the quick reactions and reverses, the cultural enslavement to Paris, and the centralism of Lausanne as against the communes. But coming from France, the protestant religion, the attitude towards the state, and exercise of democratic rights, seem entirely Swiss. As in Berne, the state in this context means primarily the canton, and cantonal government is probably more authoritarian here (fortified by a system of *préfets* almost on the French model) than anywhere else in Switzerland.

The name Vaud is very much older than the present canton (it probably comes from the German *Wald*, forest) and the old Pays de Vaud when it belonged to Savoy included parts of what is now Canton Fribourg: this is why the canton has such a wasp-waist north of Vevey. But Berne took the greater part in 1536. Berne encouraged the church Reformation, through Guillaume Forel, an event which plays a certain part in the larger history of France and western Europe.

In the eighteenth century there were some movements of discontent with Bernese rule, which during the nineteenth century were built up to have been patriotic revolts: the most famous is that of Major Davel. Eventually, on 24 January 1798, with the backing of French troops just beyond its borders, a delegation of Vaudois towns declared 'la République Lémanique': the principal public act of this republic was to lend a substantial sum of money to the commander of the French forces at his emphatic request. On 9 February of the same year Vaud lost this new status, and became an administrative district, the *canton du Léman*, of the new unitary Helvetic Republic. Napoleon, however, in 1803 granted it cantonal sovereignty again under the Act of Mediation. In 1813–15, a whim of the sentimental Tsar Alexander of Russia secured that Vaud (which had heartily wished for his defeat by Napoleon) was accepted as a canton in the new Switzerland. In deference to the allies, Vaud adopted a form of government whereby a Great Council elected on a high property franchise was dominated by the executive. After the French 'Revolution of July' in 1830, the Great Council, intimidated by a large crowd armed with staves, decided on a Constitutional Assembly, which the next year worked out a Liberal Constitution, which returned duly a Liberal Great Council. In 1844, after riots led by radicals, a radical constituent assembly worked out a Radical Constitution, which returned a Great Council of the expected colour. The leader of this movement was Henri Druey: his government had an exciting programme, interventionist, almost socialist. It dealt with the church in such a way that more than two-thirds of the pastors threatened to resign their incumbencies, and a third did – the Église Libre of Vaud was the result. It is difficult, seeing the sleek and negative radicals of today, to recapture the exciting youth of the party. It is as if a government of the New Left were to be returned today after a *coup d'état* and were in a position to exercise sovereign power. From the 1840s until the 1880s Switzerland was a violently and exhilaratingly democratic country under the guidance of slogans that have become utterly boring clichés of big-business reactions. This exciting life was acted on the cantonal stage, in Vaud as elsewhere. The names of great leaders Druey, Ruchonnet, Cérésole, Ruffy, Secretan, echo through Vaudois history of the years before 1914 and still retain their local resonance. During most of the time since 1848 Vaud has been represented in the Federal Council, by a radical. Today radicals and liberals seem the same party, but for long they were so antagonistic that their followers could not speak with one another. At the time of writing (1973) it is represented by a socialist, Pierre Graber, of Neuchâtelois citizenship, a Foreign Minister whose travels to foreign capitals have caused delight abroad and irritation within Switzerland. The recent political and ethical *aggiornamento* of Switzerland in many ways started from Lausanne, and the 'Expo 1964', the national exhibition held there and bearing a Vaudois imprint, superseded the ethos of the confrontation, also between two Vaudois, of Pilet and Guisan. Lausanne has an alert intellectual and artistic life, and a famous university. This was founded in 1839, but – as in Berne, Zurich, Neuchâtel, and Geneva – it was developed out of a much older Academy. The Lausanne Academy had been founded by the Bernese immediately after their annexation of Vaud in the sixteenth century, with the function of training French-speaking pastors for the Reformed church, and of providing the preliminary education of administrators and lawyers. It was a distinguished school, and in the eighteenth century it produced a cultured Vaudois high-bourgeoisie of European renown. Because of the accessibility of the language, the three French-speaking academies account for a large part of the respect in which Swiss culture was held during the eighteenth century by France, Britain, northern Italy, and Russia.

In the nineteenth century also, for many people of English language, Switzerland practically consisted of Vaud, Geneva, and Neuchâtel, and traces of this attitude remain in the distribution-map of finishing schools for young ladies. The Vaudois tutor for young nobles and princelings can be found deep into the eighteenth century, and Vaud has on occasion been able to capitalize on its own behalf, and on behalf of Switzerland, a certain sentimental affection felt by the ruling classes of Europe for the homeland of these tutors.

The cultural magnetism of Vaud operates also within Switzerland. A German Swiss of established family will often send his sons for a year to Vaud to learn a decent French. Even big farmhouses used to send the young heir for a *Welschlandjahr*, to a farm in Vaud for a year, and the contacts there made might be later renewed during military service in the cavalry, and continue for generations. This old custom is now becoming folklore, but the swissness of German Switzerland is due to a French tinge that has its origin in Vaud.

Vaud and Canton Berne are of the same religious faith. The difference in history is not great, for most of Vaud fell to the rule of the city of Berne only a century later than some of the German-speaking lands, and this was so long ago that the century can be disregarded. One can almost say that the only difference is in language.

Nevertheless, this different lingustic civilization bites very deep. It puts a different interpretation on Vaudois and Bernese history under the old regime: the Bernese can look at this history with pride, but the Vaudois escapes from a certain humiliation only by dwelling on the attempts to revolt against Berne. This attitude to Berne is important even today. With all the circumlocutions for Berne which French rhetoric can devise, little distinction is made between the city from which Vaud at last broke loose in 1798 with the assistance of revolutionary France, and the federal capital of the modern Swiss state to which Vaud owes its liberty: the animosities that belong to one are transferred to the other.

As is well known, the intellectual style of the two languages is very different, and this affects both the press, and the whole attitude to politics and the state. The French-Swiss press is less factual, less serious, more inflammatory. Indeed, it hardly possesses the financial resources to be otherwise, since four distinguished newspapers struggle for the loyalty of a Vaudois and Genevese public which can hardly afford to support more than one in the face of the competition of French journals from France. The best newspapers of Zurich, Basle, and Berne keep a distinction between facts and comment, and give their ideological commitments free play only in the latter. But the French-Swiss papers frequently examine the problems and events of daily life only in sufficient depth to generate an emotion, and then immediately discuss it in the light of some fashionable doctrine, usually that of the more vapid Left.

Yet, though the fuel is stacked, and the flame applied to it daily, it fails to ignite. At base there is a healthy peasant instinct that things go very well in Switzerland, and the reason why life is so sweet is that the cold-blooded Bernese are in charge. Eloquence, not action, is the fruit of eloquence, and here Vaud is different from France. It is also different from the catholic Bernese Jura, whose grievances meet with disdain in Lausanne. The substantive of a Vaudois is Swiss, even though the adjective is French.

AARGAU

Swiss, even Argovians, speak of Aargau as a 'canton without tradition'. A moment's reflection suggests that the metaphysics of this assertion are doubtful. The name itself is an old one, and goes back to the Carolingian period, though originally it denoted a district much larger than the present canton and not coinciding with its present boundaries. The Aargau of today obtained a certain unity under the Hapsburgs, and still contains the castle from which they derived their name and the parts of Swiss soil they held longest – indeed the Frick-tal was only finally ceded in 1814. Geographically, Aargau is more rational as a unit than many cantons. One must also remember that a canton such as modern Berne had no particular unity under the old regime (except a shared relationship of subordination to its capital city): the 'city' cantons are creations of the nineteenth century as political *communities*.

Canton Aargau was created by Napoleon from districts whose common past had been interrupted by four centuries of confederate rule. This rule dated from the seventeen days' campaign in April 1415 when Swiss forces overran (almost unopposed) the Hapsburg territories in Aargau: in 1412 the Swiss and Austrians had concluded a fifty years' truce, but in 1415 the Hapsburgs had been declared out-laws by the emperor and the opportunity was not to be missed. Berne got most booty, Zurich and Lucerne got some, but the county of Baden and the Freiamt were made *Gemeine Vogteien*, shared juris-dictions of the cantons that had taken part in the invasion.

The result was that a narrow corridor of shared territories separa-ted Bernese from Zuricois territories. At the Reformation this became the 'priests' corridor', joining catholic Italy with catholic south Germany through catholic territory the whole way.

The new Aargau contains, therefore, three sorts of political tradition: the former Bernese lordships, which are protestant; the former *Gemeine Vogteien* which are catholic or *paritätisch* (i.e., with equality of confession, and usually largely catholic); and the Fricktal, ceded by Austria, which is catholic in a rather different tradition (and, curiously, proved very amenable to the arguments of the Old Catholics after 1870).

Aargau had declared itself free in 1798, and the centre of the Helvetic revolution was in fact its later capital, Aarau. When in 1814 Berne wanted its old lands back, Aargau raised forces to defend itself and, as Austria also supported the new canton, this resistance was decisive. Thereafter, it and Vaud distinguished themselves by their resolve to be independent of all authority except that of a federal Switzerland. The liberal notables kept control over the canton, usually with an anti-clerical policy, and in fact unleashed the Sonder-bund War through their quite unlawful secularization of the Aargau monasteries.

Aargau is typically a countryside of nucleated villages, formerly open-field, the scenery varied by a low and interrupted prolongation of the Juras (which are responsible for funnelling the rivers of Swit-zerland together in so astonishing a manner). On spurs of these hills are often castles, some spectacular, some ruined. But today the valley of the Limmat from Zurich until its confluence is fast becoming a long-drawn conurbation, and much of the flat land (such as the Birrfeld, where Pestalozzi's Neuhof stands) is due to be built over by factories and houses. Historically and architecturally Aargau is rich, but the villages seem still to show signs of the long period of exploitation under confederate rule. In politics it remains lively and unpredictable: through the nineteenth century it supplied a disproportionate number of federal (and local) statesmen, radicals, of high distinction, reared to politics by the extraordinary complexity of local traditions in the various component districts.

FRIBOURG

Before the Reformation Fribourg was industrially more prosperous than Berne, but by 1600 its industry had fled: Fribourg's choice of the catholic Counter-Reformation still determines its character. This choice was made under the fear of being absorbed by Berne, and in this sense has justified itself. Moreover, Fribourg, unlike Berne, did not lose its French-speaking subjects in 1798. Under the old regime it formed a big, square, catholic island in the midst of Bernese and protestant jurisdictions.

Until 1960, Fribourg stayed catholic, conservative, and clerical, with a trend to authoritarianism, in lively touch with the French Right, overwhelmingly agricultural and with an influential patriciate bearing names sonorous with the pageantry of the old regime.

The combined influence of the second Vatican Council, and of a powerful pressure-group within the ruling oligarchy – and the generalized Swiss atmosphere of cultural relaxation – has changed all this. Like Valais, Fribourg is in the grip of the early stage of an industrial revolution introduced complete from outside the canton. The capital town, one of the most astonishingly beautiful in all Switzerland, is surrounding itself with concrete high-rise housing (where beech-trees and meadows were), and roars with traffic. Other districts are also industralizing, notably around Bulle in the Gruyère country to the south. The least contaminated countryside of the whole Swiss Mittelland is losing its attractiveness before being ever discovered and the parts that have been discovered, near the small towns of Gruyères and Morat, are overrun with tourists.

The history of Fribourg is not unlike that of Berne: both were founded by the same dynasty – and both are set in Üchtland, the big boundary forest separating the Burgundians from the Alemannians. Both Fribourg and Berne developed a military ethos and an aristocratic form of government, in which the local minor nobility played a continuing part. In the late middle ages they were still on a frontier, first on that between the sphere of influence of Hapsburg and Savoy, and later on that between Burgundy and the Swiss Confederacy.

These influences they astutely played against one another, and expanded their territories, dividing the Gruyère between them, and picking up little fragments of territory along Lakes Morat and Neuchâtel as they became available, especially after the defeat of Charles the Bold in 1476. Morat (Murten) itself was a condominium with Berne, but passed to Fribourg in 1803; it has proved the Achilles heel of the canton, for it is both protestant and liberal. In 1847 Fribourg, of course, was on the side of the Sonderbund, but it yielded to General Dufour after a brief campaign of manoeuvring. The victors took revenge, pillaging convents and mansions, and set up a radical reign of terror, which was toppled in 1856 with the introduction of secret voting. Since then the canton has been solidly catholic-conservative, though this period is ending.

It comes as a surprise to learn that one-third of Canton Fribourg is German-speaking, for the language of public life is overwhelmingly French. The German-speakers on the Bernese border show what the Bernese would have been like had they remained catholic: 90 per cent of them traditionally vote catholic-conservative, but tradition is being disturbed even there as industry creeps south from Berne and north from Fribourg. Recently they have begun to make themselves more heard, for they are the largest language minority in Switzerland to be denied full rights.

The University of Fribourg is the only Swiss university located on traditional catholic territory (though there is talk of founding a university institute in Lucerne), and thus has played an important part in the last eighty years in the life of catholic Switzerland, and in the life of the Roman church in general, producing distinguished scholars and journals. The tendency today is for it to lose its confessional character, and become a university like any other, and within the catholic fold to become a nest of innovators.

BASLE

Basle was already a great city of the Holy Roman Empire when it acceded to the Swiss Confederacy in 1501, and it already had a famous university. Like other German bishopric-cities, it is on the left bank of the Rhine at a river-crossing,[1] the bridge over which much of the Gotthard traffic went. It is still a much more important place for trade in commodities (as opposed to industry and commerce) than Zurich. It has kept, too, the character of a Free Imperial City. There were many other such cities, which also had kept their character, in Germany down to the defeat in the first World War and the ensuing inflation, or even to the bombing in the second: today the parallel is only with Bremen and Hamburg. In many ways Basle resembles Geneva, but is without the froth of internationalism. Like

Geneva, its patriciate is descended from immigrants of the sixteenth century, rather than from native citizen families, and like Geneva it has managed to maintain its wealth and position, even if not its supremacy – for much of the industry, wealth, and intellect is in the hands of non-Baslois Swiss. Like Geneva, too, in being a sort of peninsula of Switzerland, it also has a sort of secretive quality, a family character, enjoying family jokes and festivals, decisively separated from France and Germany, but also rather separated from the remainder of the Confederation. Like Porrentruy, it is north of the Jura wall, on the edge of the Alsace plain. The old-descended citizens speak a dialect cognate with that of the Black Forest, and the delightful poet of Basle, Johann Peter Hebel (whose dialect, like Burns's, places him just beyond my reach), wrote in this, or a nearly kindred, dialect, though a subject of the margrave of Baden.

Basle and Zurich make unkind jokes at each other's expense, but they have traditions in common: neither was really a quite closed oligarchy under the old regime – their tradition was plutocratic rather than military and the structure of government was based on the guilds (*Zünfte*), which still survive (as in all the old ruling cities of German Switzerland, although only in Berne are they recognized in public law in that membership of a guild is a necessary part of citizenship of the town). As a city-canton, Basle fairly often has a socialist-dominated government or sends a socialist to the Council of States, otherwise the town has played rather little part in national politics. This is in part due to the tradition of protestant conservatism which coexists with its record as the canton most likely to be dominated by the Left: in the period of radical rule Basle satisfied its demands (for example, in keeping the Gotthard as the axis of Swiss communications) through the influence of its experts, rather than through the charisma of its politicians.

BASLE LAND

In 1832–33 the countryside that had formerly been subject to the city of Basle revolted, and the Federal Diet, with a Liberal majority, made it a separate half-canton, and allotted to it half the property of the city, or a little more, dispersing in this way some remarkable treasures. The two half-cantons have long made up their quarrel, and for thirty years have been trying to unite again. Apart from anything else, the city is now overflowing its boundaries, and the cantonal frontier running through the conurbation makes astute calculation of tax and educational advantages necessary for the private citizen. The original quarrel was political, for the countryside, like other former subject territories, was radical, and the town with a restricted franchise was, like the other towns which had lost their sovereignty, conservative. What was unique in Basle was the position of the capital city on the frontier which enabled it to stand alone. The centre of the insurrection was Liestal, the only town of the Basle countryside. The other parts joined a little reluctantly and the city, for its part, had no mind to remain within a democratic canton with a permanent radical majority.

The part of Basle Land which is well known to the traveller is the Ergolz valley, along which the road and railway pass on their way to Olten. It is now almost a continuous urbanization from Muttenz to Gelterkinden. Away from the main valley, it contains agreeable countryside ascending into the Juras. In the other corner of the little canton, the Birseck near Arlesheim is, unexpectedly, a traditionally catholic district, formerly in the prince-bishop's territories, but handed over to Basle in 1815. The only old borough, apart from Liestal, is the tiny Waldenburg, guarding the Oberhauenstein pass to Solothurn.

GENEVA

The early history of Geneva is not unlike that of other episcopal cities in the Holy Roman Empire (including Basle and Lausanne) in that it soon began collecting rights against its ecclesiastical sovereign. The propinquity of Berne and Fribourg was a counteraction to the immediate neighbourhood of Savoy and France. When Berne took Vaud (and some lordships south of the lake under the walls of Geneva, which it surrendered in 1567), it very nearly also annexed Geneva. But Berne did not do so, because it lacked confederal backing, and had to content itself with supporting the local protestant party (the Huguenots, either 'Eidgenossen', or 'followers of Besançon Hugues', a party leader). In 1541, the city called back Calvin to reform its church and civil life: the theocracy he temporarily established has given Geneva its place in world history.

For a long time Geneva, linked by treaties of *combourgeoisie* with Berne and Zurich – the treaty with Fribourg was broken off on account of the Reformation – was the largest city in the area of Swiss power. Geneva traditionally feared Berne (which had played with the idea of selling the town to Savoy in 1589), but the link with Zurich has always been a friendly one. After the repulse of the Savoyard escalade in 1602, the history of the town is taken up with the internal quarrels between the aristocrats in the upper city and the democratic small craftsmen of the lower city (and the St-Gervais quarter), a division which lasted until the 1870s. Geneva's cultural position in the eighteenth century is well known, and so is the influence of its banking families on the last years of the French monarchy. At the Revolution, it became a *département* of France, or rather, *chef-lieu* and *préfecture* of the Département du Léman, formed out of the Pays de Gex and part of the former Savoy. Geneva was glad, in 1814, to receive the troops of the Confederation, to which it had been allocated as a new canton by Austria, Prussia, Russia, and Great Britain.

By the Treaty of Vienna (or, more accurately, by the Treaties of Paris and Turin) Geneva received new territories, by which the various lordships it had held were no longer enclaves in Savoy, but a continuous bloc, which furthermore was thenceforth joined with Vaud by a land connection. These new territories were, of course, catholic, and the free exercise of this religion was guaranteed by the treaty: the Genevese statesman Pictet secured these for Switzerland while failing to push Swiss claims to the Valtellina. The republic lived an extremely active political life into the 1890s, the scene of many *coups d'état*, each followed by elections which confirmed the victors in power by an impressive majority. As before, the rivalry of the upper city and the lower was the substance of the battle. To these two combatants were added, as a third factor, the catholic and conservative rural communes received in 1815. These early quarrels have been superseded by a rivalry between radicals, socialists (ready to ally with a strong local Communist party), and conservatives as well as strange and short-lived new parties from time to time. In 1932 there were again riots and the last Federal Intervention in Swiss history took place – thirteen men were shot dead and some three score wounded, by Valaisan troops.

The three-cornered disputes among the old Genevese, the banking aristocracy descended from refugees of the fifteenth and sixteenth centuries, the artisans of equally old descent, and the new citizens of 1815, have been submerged by two new populations, the Swiss from other cantons, and the foreigners (politically without influence, but with economic importance and dominating the appearance of the town and its housing problems). Beyond this, Geneva is the natural capital of a large district which is now in France, the ancient Genevois, and as such it has a local market-town function which is facilitated by the survival of certain customs concessions, deriving from the old *Zones franches*, and by the daily cross-frontier traffic of French residents working in the town.

NEUCHÂTEL

Neuchâtel is distinctive among the cantons in having been until 1856 a hereditary monarchy, a constitutional principality where the real exercise of power had early passed into the hands of an oligarchy of citizens. The principality (the sovereign countships of Neuchâtel and Valengin) descended among various families, mostly German,

but the powers of the ruler were hollowed out by the local bour-
geoisies, under the influence of the nearby Confederacy. From 1512
to 1529 it in fact lived under the direct rule of the Thirteen Cantons,
and seemed destined to become a subject territory. However, its
former ruler, Countess Jeanne of Hochberg, succeeded by judicious
bribes in getting it back, and from her the principality passed by
complex vicissitudes to the family of Orléans, dukes of Longueville,
bastards of the French royal line. In the years after the departure of
the confederates, however, Guillaume Farel (the reformer of the
Vaud) succeeded in converting the country to the Reformation,
with the friendly assistance of Berne, whose influence after the seizure
of Vaud became predominant. Only two parishes near the Solothurn
border remained with the old religion: Cressier, and the tiny walled
town of Le Landeron.[2]

In 1663, Prince Henri II died; he had been an important man, the
French negotiator at the time of the Peace of Westphalia. The succession then passed to his nephew, the 'abbé d'Orléans', a nobleman
of weak mind. A half-century of intense complication ensued, but
finally the Tribunal of the Estates (having considered William of
Orange, king of England) chose the elector of Brandenburg, the
future king of Prussia, as prince. He had a remote claim to inheritance, he was of the Reformed Faith, and above all he was distant,
able to exert protection against France and the confederates, but
unable to interfere too much in the life of the country. For a time
the choice of the Prussian ruler caused difficulties with the Confederacy – the status of Neuchâtel was that it was linked in
combourgeoisie with four cantons, Berne, Fribourg, Solothurn, and
Lucerne, of which three were catholic. These difficulties were scarcely
settled by the end of the old regime, but the territory was eventually
received into the confederal neutrality in 1792. However, the protection of Prussia was the more real, and Prussia ceded Neuchâtel to
France in 1806. Napoleon, in a picturesque gesture, declared the
country a Fief of the Empire, and conferred the principality on one
of his generals, Marshal Berthier, 'Prince Alexander of Neuchâtel':
caught up in the defeat of his master, Berthier abdicated in 1814, and
Neuchâtel was received as a canton of Switzerland, but at the same
time was returned to the king of Prussia as a principality. After 1831
this double status caused difficulties, the liberals fighting for a
republic, the conservatives for the king. There was an attempted
liberal *coup d'état* in 1831, and a successful one in 1848, after
Neuchâtel had remained neutral in the Sonderbund War. In 1856,
the royalists essayed a *coup*, which failed. A war was nearly the consequence, and Prussia broke off diplomatic relations with the Confederation. The powers intervened, and under Palmerston's initiative

King Frederick William IV of Prussia eventually renounced his rights in 1857 (except for the bare title of prince). Some late echoes of the Prussian connection could be heard until 1914: General Wille, for example, was only too conscious of his family's historical connection with Prussia. Since 1918 all connection has been severed at its root: only romantics sometimes toy with proposals to revive the old flag of the royal past.

Neuchâtel falls scenically into two contrasting parts, the sunny vineyard country along the lake with its castles and tightly packed villages, and the desolate but beautiful Jura country, containing the watchmaking towns, themselves very handsome with their grid layout. This difference of landscape corresponds with a psychological and political difference, but the two parts are linked in religious tradition – Neuchâtel had a religious constitution reminiscent of Geneva, and at times seemed on the verge of becoming an intolerant Calvinist theocracy. It is altogether an interesting canton, living rather apart from the main current of Swiss life, and seldom coming on the national scene except in connection with its great and peculiar industry of watchmaking.

SOLOTHURN

It is a curious experience to enter a school in Canton Solothurn and see the map of the canton presented as if it were the Outer Hebrides, this tattered area, wasp-waisted, with outlying islands of canton strewn around. It is an exceptional canton in other ways: although catholic, it is liberal in politics and general tendencies; although formerly reckoned as aristocratic, few traces of this remain. It was long the residence of the French ambassador to the Thirteen Cantons, and conceivably a French influence has affected its character, though it is German in speech and, indeed, has seen to it that the cantonal frontier is (rather exceptionally) also the language frontier, thus pushing a little back the older line of demarcation.

Like Basle Land, its main valley is urbanized, a discontinuous chain of new houses and factories between the foot of the Juras and the Aare, linking the cantonal capital loosely with the other important town, Olten—linking (it almost seems) Bienne with Aarau, or Yverdon with Rapperswil. Because of this thin urbanized zone, the canton as a whole is reckoned as among the most highly industrialized of Switzerland, but large areas are lonely Jura country.

The little city of Solothurn claims to be 'the oldest town in the Germanies, except for Trèves': although this is only a verbal popular tradition in its source, it may well be true even though it cannot be vouched for. Like Zurich, Solothurn bears an ancient celtic name. In the town hall one sees the initials SPQS, the Senate and People of

Solothurn, as if claiming an equal pride with Rome. The capital town is one of the most delightful in this whole country of delightful towns. As elsewhere, the capital was the conservative stronghold, and the main provincial town, Olten, was the radical centre, and the radicals when they got power took care to demolish the capital's megalomaniac walls excepting only one main gate and a small corner. The Buchegg, a shred of country intermixed with Berne, is a landscape that is Bernese in character, whose population (under Bernese influence) adopted the Reformation, and whose parishes are by a concordat between the two cantons reckoned as within the Bernese territorial church. This is a rare exception to the rule that religion followed sovereignty. It is accounted for by the conflict of various claims to jurisdiction, and, of course, the military power of Berne.

Since 1831 psychological impediments against liberalism and the industrial revolution have been rather little felt in Solothurn. In 1848 the canton provided a radical member of the national executive, Federal Councillor Münsinger of Olten, and after 1870 it took up the cause of the Old Catholic resistance to the declaration of papal infallibility, though the eventual result of this was to rally the remaining latent resources of catholic conservatism. In general, Solothurn has followed the moods of neighbouring Berne, while Fribourg has reacted throughout modern history strongly against it. Indeed, Solothurn has perhaps a more open character than Berne today, and feels less the burden of its historical tradition, for it is a bridge between French (Vaudois and Neuchâtelois) and German Switzerland in its social and political structure, as well as a bridge between the protestant and the catholic attitudes to modern civilization.

II. Zurich and Central and East Switzerland

ZURICH

Zurich was the greatest and most famous town of the older Confederacy, of immemorial antiquity and early freedom – having grown rich at the gates of two great ecclesiastical foundations, the Fraumünster (one of whose outlying farms was the later Canton Uri) and the Grossmünster. Emperors visited it. In the middle of the eighth century it was chief imperial residence of the Zürichgau, to which Inner Switzerland belonged, and in the tenth century it was already called 'town'. On every account it took first place, except that it had joined relatively late. The final union was in 1450, but the document was backdated to 1351 when a short-lived first alliance had been made. Throughout the remainder of the Old Confederacy, Zurich had ceremonial precedence and certain procedural advantages connected with this. This precedence in the list of the cantons it retains, but the dignity of federal capital after 1848 was secured by Berne. Nevertheless, for commercial purposes Zurich is the undoubted first city of Switzerland, and the great *Verbände* (pressure-groups) of modern Switzerland prefer Zurich as their residence to Berne.

The canton is a large one, in population the largest of all, not mountainous, but with respectable forested hills in the Zurich Oberland. It was mostly stitched together piece by piece with purchases of lordships as occasion offered, or by secularizations, and only to a small extent by conquest. In its wars, Zurich was unfortunate and regularly lost out to Schwyz. Its greatest acquisition was the purchase of the county of Kyburg in the fifteenth century: the castle from which the county got its name is just south of Winterthur. Under Zwingli's influence most of east Switzerland nearly came under Zurich's suzerainty, in the same way that Berne acquired Vaud, but Zurich again lost the decisive battle.

In the nineteenth century, the recurrent political theme was the struggle of town against countryside within the canton, renewed in the twentieth century in different terms when the town had a socialist-dominated government. The town, as in the old regime, is again the senior partner. It is expanding at a frightening rate; the change in the landscape between Zurich, Kloten, and Greifensee is amazing. What was twenty-five years ago a rather lonely, but sweet and gentle, countryside is now under concrete. Yet there are still large parts of the canton where one can walk all day on footpaths and get lost in the woods. Except for Regensberg,[3] the small ancient towns in the countryside (Grüningen, Bülach, Elgg, and Greifensee) have lost their character in different ways, either becoming totally rural, or torn apart by traffic, or sinking into folk-museum. Winterthur is a proper town, dynamic, respecting its own past and enhancing it, as encouraging a place as anywhere in Switzerland.

URSCHWEIZ

The cantons of innermost Switzerland, Uri, Schwyz, and Unterwalden 'above and below the Kernwald', remain conservative, but are too small not to be profoundly changed by modern developments, such as the autobahn over the Gotthard. Because they were the nucleus from which Switzerland grew, they are collectively called *Urschweiz* – original Switzerland – or, together with Lucerne, Inner Switzerland.

Uri broke out of its isolation when the Gotthard pass was made viable in the thirteenth century, and again in 1882 when the Gotthard tunnel was opened, though the tunnel destroyed a way of living earned by the provision of services for horse-transport over the pass.

The isolation, however, was historically more apparent than real, for trading and transhumations of cattle carried Urners very far into Italy: it is typical that rice is a traditional basis for peasants' food in a canton which for centuries grew no corn of its own.

The tunnel brought citizens of protestant cantons into the territory, and changed attitudes. In 1925 the ancient *Landsgemeinde* was given up, but every cantonal citizen is a member of one of the two great alp-corporations which own four-fifths of the area of the canton, and these corporations, of Uri and Urseren, retain the old *Landsgemeinde* form: they were older than the cantonal meeting and outlasted it.

Around Altdorf there is now an industrial zone, and there are certain kindly tax practices that make Uri, with its good communications, a suitable place for firms of the Mittelland to set up subordinate factories. It is not the sort of community which in principle welcomes outsiders and absorbs them, but it is astute enough to be friendly when it needs them, and today it does.

Schwyz

This is the largest of the original cantons and gave up the *Landsgemeinde*, that had ruled it for centuries as many-humoured sovereign, in 1848. But the *Bezirke*, the heirs of its old constituent communities, hold their own *Landsgemeinden* still today. Schwyz was 'a pure democracy': it was ruled by the open-air meeting of those with the hereditary entitlement to attend, who acted as legislator, judge, and executioner. This privileged community was a relatively small proportion of all the inhabitants of the canton. Einsiedeln, with its famous abbey, can be regarded equally well as a subject territory to the valley of Schwyz or as the territory of an imperial abbey ruled by its abbot as sovereign, immediately under the pope and emperor. Gersau, now a *Bezirk*, claimed to be a sovereign village-republic. The Höfe, lands conquered from Zurich in the Old War of Zurich and bordering on that lake, were frankly subject, but with a large degree of self-government, so were the Marches, farther east. Küssnach, on the Lake of Lucerne, where Tell assassinated the wicked bailiff, remained as much subject to Schwyz as it had been to the Hapsburgs. All these in the 1830s started to claim the equality of free men: only later did their catholicism draw them together with the valleys of the old canton in a shared conservatism.

Parts of the canton near the Lake of Zurich are scarcely distinguishable from the rural landscape of Zurich, and near the church-village and capital of the old community (this village, like the Confederation itself, has also taken on the name Schwyz) there is urbanization and a degree of industrialization. Hoch-Ybrig is being developed as a holiday and play area for Zurich, and between the one fate and the other the old Schwyz is probably doomed, though it has far to go yet, and agriculture and forestry are still important. Much of the alp-pastures still belong to the two ancient corporations of which the lineal descendants of the old privileged citizens entitled to vote at the *Landsgemeinde* in the old regime are exclusively the members – so long as they continue to live within their canton: there can be few of these privileged families who have been within the closed circle for less than five hundred years.

Unterwalden

The half-canton of *Unterwalden ob dem Wald* has as its capital the village of Sarnen where, on the Landenberg, the *Landsgemeinde* is traditionally held: it will probably be moved, as the area is too small to accommodate the women voters recently (1974) admitted to the sovereign assembly. Obwalden was the home of Niklaus von Flüe, patron saint of catholic Switzerland: kinship with his family is a matter of pride in the ruling families of the canton. Besides the main valley and the Melchtal, the canton now includes the abbey and parish of Engelberg, which was a protectorate of the old cantons and an independent ecclesiastical principality. This island of territory which lies between Nidwalden and Uri was added in 1815 because Nidwalden refused for a short time to join the Confederation at all, and had to be occupied by troops to force it to adhere. It is not really clear quite how and when Obwalden and Nidwalden ever were a single republic – the matter is too complicated to justify discussion, and insufficiently important. Connoisseurs assert that the character of the two populations is quite different, the Nidwaldners being the more passionate and lively.

Nidwalden is financially more advantaged, having industry in the part near Stansstad. It holds a *Landsgemeinde* in Wil an der Aa near Stans, the capital village (there are no towns in the democratic cantons, on doctrinal principle). Apart from its niche in the history of the union, and the story of Winkelried, it is famous for its gesture of defiance of the invading French troops in 1798.

LUCERNE

The political attitudes of Lucerne have often had a wider interest, as if it were the function of the canton to be guardian of the conscience of Switzerland. From the start it hesitated between allegiance to the Hapsburgs and its destiny on the side of the pastoral cantons of Urschweiz.

At Morgarten, Lucerne supported the Hapsburg side, but in 1332 an attempted Hapsburg counter-revolution was suppressed, and the town entered its permanent alliance with Uri, Schwyz, and Unterwalden. After the battle of Sempach (1386) the independence of the town from Austria was assured, and the town rapidly increased its territory, until by the end of 1415 it was entirely surrounded by other Swiss sovereignties and had no more opportunity to expand.

The confederal alliance with Lucerne meant that for the first time a walled city entered the League which thereby consolidated its economic and military position. From Lucerne the traveller over the Gotthard usually set sail (unless he embarked in Küssnach or Brunnen) for, until as late as 1856, when the Axenstrasse was constructed, there was no road along the lake – it had been necessary to take William Tell by boat from Altdorf. The alliance meant that Lucerne took position against the feudal nobility on the side of the pastoral cantons, but that within the walls it could remain the type of an aristocratic town ruled by a closed oligarchy. The peasantry of the countryside it ruled were its subjects, not its equals, and this was especially resented by the free peasants of the Entlebuch – the Lucerne Emmenthal – who were exposed to the democratic infection of Inner Switzerland.

Apart from the Entlebuch, and the small town of Rothenburg which Lucerne destroyed (so it is to this day only a village), Lucerne spread into the southern Aargau, obtaining the two delightful miniature towns of Sempach and Sursee and the famous abbeys of Beromünster and St Urban: there was a little expansion along the lake (including the territory of New Hapsburg), but this was soon blocked by the sphere of influence of the pastoral cantons.

Lucerne might have chosen either side at the Reformation, but having made the decision in favour of the old religion, it became the capital of Romanist Switzerland, and the seat of the Papal Nuncio. Towards the end of the eighteenth century it became a town where the party of the Enlightenment was strong – it was in the see of Constance, then governed by the enlightened prelate Wessenberg. In 1831, as in the other city-cantons of Switzerland, the liberals got control, and this control of a leading catholic canton seemed of decisive importance in the plans for a revised Federal Treaty. But already the position had changed.

The revised project was accepted by the parliament of the canton by 71 votes to three, and submitted to a referendum. On this its fate depended, for the parties in the Diet were narrowly balanced. To universal surprise, the people of Lucerne rejected it decisively, by twelve thousand to one thousand votes. Even if the votes of those who had not gone to the polls were reckoned as being on the side of the parliamentary majority, it would still have been rejected. The proposal therefore shipwrecked, and had to be dropped. The cause of this volte-face was a movement among the catholic peasantry, led by

Joseph Leu 'of Ebersol' (so called to distinguish him from a colleague, Joseph Leu of Gumikon), which for the first time revealed to the liberals that they were in fact the party of a minority and that the simple people of the country were conservative. In 1841 Leu's catholic-democratic party conquered the elections to a Constituent Assembly, revised the constitution, and introduced direct and secret voting, and won the ensuing election held under the rules they had themselves laid down, reducing the liberals to only seven members. The new conservative government proceeded to introduce censorship – of liberal journals. Lucerne was now seen as the leader of catholic Switzerland once more, the centre of reaction, and when it invited the Jesuits to reconvert the canton, a shudder of horror passed through liberals in every protestant canton. Lucerne was the catholic leader, as it had in some sense been the initiator, in the Sonderbund War. Defeated, it and Fribourg were harshly treated by the victors. In the elections of 1848, the catholic-conservatives who stood for election were promptly arrested and deprived of civic rights, except (through the oversight of arrogance) Philipp Anton Segesser von Brunegg: von Segesser thus became the germ from which the whole constitutional opposition to liberalism sprang. In 1891, finally, this opposition saw its first Federal Councillor elected, also from Lucerne, and became a party of government again.

In the meanwhile, by gerrymandering constituencies and various dubious (and occasionally oppressive) means, the liberals continued to rule Lucerne until May 1871, when at last the conservative majority broke through. The electoral laws were revised, and in due time the constitution was remodelled to the taste of the victors, although they were wise enough to allow the liberals to retain a minority share in the cantonal executive cabinet. This reversal secured the catholics power for a century: the pre-eminence of Lucerne in catholic Switzerland had been recovered, and has been shown in various ways, for example by the extraordinary behind-the-scenes power which National Councillor Heinrich Walther of Lucerne allegedly exercised in the 1920s. Today the internal conflict within catholicism watches the fortunes of the Christian-socialist group in Lucerne with expectation. The politics of the canton are still of wider interest than might be supposed.

Economically, the canton remains largely agricultural except around Lucerne itself. The town reached the take-off stage through an early expansion of tourism, for which it still enjoys a classic fame, and in spite of which it manages to live a life of its own.

ZUG

Zug was lucky to be taken into the Confederacy as a member, and not treated as subject territory (for it had sided with the Hapsburgs), and it was only the jealousy of Lucerne and Zurich which prevented it becoming an outlying part of Schwyz. It is remarkable in that even within its own territory the town never managed to secure sovereignty, but shared power with the rural districts. Until the end of the old regime there was a cantonal *Landsgemeinde*, but it only had electoral functions, not legislative. The most distinguished act of the canton is negative, that it never secularized its monasteries. The town, the Lakes of Zug and Ägeri, and the countryside are delightful, with a large and cheerful industrial zone, and several scattered factory enterprises, some of which are famous. Perhaps the moral problem of Switzerland is here in microcosm: does one need to be heroic to be free, or is it enough to possess neighbours jealous of one another?

GLARUS

The interest of this mountain-locked canton lies in its combination of traditional *Landsgemeinde*-democracy and industrialization. Its industries continue to confront the difficulties to be expected of the illogicality of their existence, and it is the only canton which suffered a decrease of population between 1960 and 1970. Only the northern strip of the canton along the Walensee has good communications. But this might be dramatically changed if a railway or road tunnel were to be driven through the mountains at the head of the Sernft valley or under the Tödi. The dead-end geography of the valley has already been broken by the road over the Urnerboden and down the Schächental to the Gotthard, and the easy Pragel pass will soon have a road along it: some find these roads splendid, others horrible.

The main valley is interesting for its narrow string of factories (formerly they were all textile enterprises, but now only two-fifths are). There is only one large tourist resort, Braunwald, one of those delightful stations not accessible for private motor-cars but only by funicular railway. The canton is touched by autobahn and rail along the Walensee, but otherwise little visited by foreigners – one sees why.

The valley was originally a big farm owned by the nuns of Säckingen. Säckingen is one of the four Forest Towns (*Städte*, not *Stätter* – it is difficult to distinguish the name in conversation from the Four Cantons of the Lake of Lucerne – of which two, Laufenburg and Rheinfelden, have come to Switzerland and two remained in Germany. But the abbess's titles to sovereignty were squeezed out by the Hapsburgs who acquired a higher title than hers by becoming *Vögte* (Protectors) of the abbey, and a subordinate title by becoming reeves (*Meier*) of the valley. The process of the democratic revolution is as mysterious as that of the inner cantons. At one moment the inhabitants are contented serfs lightly taxed, then in a generation they are a well-armed and organized community of yeomen grumbling at new oppressions and claiming ancient rights, and winning them in a battle with the same tactics on both sides as Morgarten, and the same result, an easy and overwhelming victory for the peasants over armed and disciplined feudal nobility and soldiers (battle of Näfels, 1388). Thirty-five years earlier (1352) the valley had been overrun by the troops of Schwyz (and the inner Swiss cantons) and Zurich in the course of their feud with Austria, and had received a charter from them, a subordinate alliance such as might have led to the rank of *Zugwandter Ort* (permanent ally) and might later have led to subjection as a common bailiwick. But this had only been in effect for two years, and survives in the copy Zurich kept, from which the seals were cut as a sign that it was no longer valid. (Zug, conquered two weeks later, received more privileged terms, and indeed until 1803 took precedence of Glarus.) It seems that after Näfels the charter of 1352 came into operation once more, and Glarus appeared at a confederal Diet in 1397 as a member, was allied on equal terms with Zurich in 1408, and became (it seems likely) a full and equal member of the Confederacy as eighth canton in 1473.

The Reformation tore the canton into two. The two parts, Glarus Reformed and Glarus Catholic, had each of them all the apparatus of a state (a separate post, a separate salt monopoly, and of course a different calendar, as well as separate *Landsgemeinden* and governments). Yet the apparatus of the joint state also continued in being, and a rigid geographical separation was never quite attained. It was only by a protestant-liberal *coup d'état* in 1836–37 that the canton was finally united into a single public body (for all purposes except certain church endowments) under a single executive, parliament and *Landsgemeinde*. Today it is, as it always has been, in some ways traditional and in other ways progressive: the two facts which are widely known about Glarus throughout the country are that the last witch[4] in Europe was executed there in 1782, and the first Factory Law on the mainland of the continent was passed there, in 1864.

SCHAFFHAUSEN

Schaffhausen looks peculiar already on the map, for (apart from bridgeheads) it lies wholly north of the Rhine. A small part of the canton, Stein am Rhein, reproduces the main canton in miniature, and is quite separate from it, while little German exclaves lie islanded in the canton, and are now administered as part of it, while a long tongue of German territory, with the big village of Jestetten, separates it from another exclave containing the village of Rüdlingen, also north of the Rhine and adjacent to the Zuricois Rafzerfeld.

The town gained the status of a Free Imperial City in 1415, as part of the same chain of events that caused the Hapsburgs to lose the Aargau, and in 1418 it was visited by Pope Martin V, newly designated at the Council of Constance – an event afterwards commemorated every Friday by the ringing of the great bell. In 1454 Schaffhausen concluded its first treaty with the confederate cantons, and was itself eventually received as a canton in 1501, immediately after Basle. Before this date and during the years of the Reformation the town had acquired titles to approximately the area of the present canton. (Stein am Rhein revolted from Zurich in 1798, hoping to be free, but was allotted to Schaffhausen arbitrarily in 1803, and the canton acquired thereby a catholic village, Ramsen.) There had been some territories south of the Rhine to which Schaffhausen had one sort of claim or another, but these were snapped up by Zurich. To the remaining territories there were all sorts of title, often only the 'lower jurisdiction', the manorial rights, and a full title was often secured only in the course of the seventeenth and eighteenth centuries by purchase, while the present-day border was only finally fixed, by exchanges of jurisdiction, as late as 1839. In 1897 the frontier with Zurich in the stream of the Rhine was settled by recourse to a charter of 1067. The question of which claims ripened into sovereignty and which did not is of general interest; Schaffhausen in very few cases had the high jurisdiction (the right of life and death) that had descended from the Gaugraf, the countships of Hegau and Klettgau, which were often later considered to be the best root of title to sovereignty. The right to hunt in the forest was the securest root of title the town ever possessed, and this came to it from secularization of an abbey. Often the claim was through private ownership of a lordship by a citizen, or a small noble who became a citizen, of Schaffhausen. Here again, the *Mannschaftsrecht*, the right of levying troops, was probably usually decisive, and the turning-point came with the Reformation, for Schaffhausen is a protestant canton and the German territory adjacent is catholic. Any shift of control thus became an issue raising very complex questions for the whole Confederacy. It seems that scarcely any, if any at all, of the area accrued by conquest,[5] though some purchases (such as of the delightful little town of Neunkirch and the village of Hallau, with their vineyards, bought from the bishop of Constance) were concluded only because of the *de facto* occupation by the town.

Schaffhausen, like some other parts of north-west Switzerland, is a country where cultivation is receding and agriculture has been facing difficulties for a long time. In such parts, walking in woods the traveller may come across land which was still in strips when it was abandoned to forest, so that one type or age of tree alternates with another in these strips. (In parts of the border country between Basle Land and Aargau, week-end huts accentuate the pattern of owner-ship for the eye to take in.) Nevertheless, from the aeroplane to Zurich at some seasons one can pick out Schaffhausen territory by its different agricultural pattern to the surrounding catholic Germany, and on the ground the difference is also noticeable. (In the same way, in parts of the Aargau countryside one can distinguish protestant and catholic villages on the ground.) Until a hundred years ago the difference between Switzerland and the adjacent parts of Germany was much less marked: the accentuation of the visual impression of swissness has gone hand in hand with a national self-consciousness – Schaffhausen thought seriously at one distant time, for example, of joining the German *Zollverein*. The visible swissness is to some extent the result of this self-consciousness, of the closing of markets, protec-tionism, and subsidy.

Schaffhausen in the old days had a 'guild' rather than a 'patri-cian' constitution, and its rulers were chosen by these guilds. How-ever, behind this form it developed in the seventeenth and eighteenth centuries into a highly aristocratic city, with some of its leading families descended from the small nobility of the middle ages. As a concession to democratic aspirations, however, the more important governorships were eventually allocated by lot among the citizens, producing in this way some startlingly bad administrators. Serfdom still survived in the countryside, and there was much discontent among the peasantry. After 1790 the countryside was in continual ferment, and the French troops eventually were welcomed.

The economy of the little canton owes much to the Rhine Falls near by, a stupendous spectacle, where the river that has filled the Lake of Constance is here nearly 200 yards wide, and falls 75 feet, carrying a thousand cubic metres of water per second. In the middle ages, Schaffhausen (Ship-houses) was where the freight down the Rhine from Austria and Constance had to be unloaded on to waggons. The salt trade was especially important, because for many centuries salt was almost the only commodity in which early medieval communities were not self-subsistent. In the later part of the eighteenth century and the first half of the nineteenth, when Schaff-hausen decayed, the Falls drew admirers of the picturesque; there-after they became used for great mills, eventually for electricity and a pioneer aluminium-works. Iron is found locally, and from this tradi-tion an important machine manufacture has sprung, the workers in which were famed for their radicalism (being infected from Germany) and later were famed for communism. The exposed position north of the Rhine, however, much softened attitudes during (and after) Hitler's rule in Germany. The industry and the picturesque compete: at one time it was proposed to dynamite the Rhine Falls to make them viable for traffic.

ST GALLEN

The abbey of St Gallen derived its name from an 'Irish' missionary, who came to this place as a hermit in the year 612, one of a large number from Britain who spread Christianity among the heathen Germans in the succeeding centuries. A century and a half after the death of Gallus it went over to the Benedictine rule, and for the three succeeding centuries was one of the most famous places of learning north of the Alps. The town that sprang up at its gates received the same name. In the old Confederacy, abbey and town were, independently of each other, 'permanent allies' of the Thirteen Cantons, and were indeed cantons for most purposes, but not in name. They attended the confederal Diets regularly, and were included in the more important treaties.

The abbot was a prince of the Holy Roman Empire, and did homage as such, until the end of the old regime, but the town, a Free Imperial City, had accepted the Reformation and considered itself as released from the empire after 1648. While the town never succeeded in extending its boundaries in the immediate neighbourhood, the abbot was effective sovereign of a considerable area, of which Wil was the administrative centre, still called the Fürstenland. The abbot was also constitutional monarch (as one might say, anachronistically) of the Toggenburg, in which his power was so limited that the Upper Toggenburg – where Zwingli was born – took the reformed faith. To this nucleus of abbey and town, in 1803 Napoleon added territories that had previously been subject lands of one, two, eight, nine, or all cantons – the Rhine valley Bailiwicks, where the abbot had the manorial (lower) jurisdiction and the right of raising troops, together with Sax, Gams, Werdenberg, the land to the south of the Churfirsten range, and the large and important *Vogtei* of Sargans, including the abbey of Pfäffers and the gorges of the Tamina. The effect is that the new canton completely surrounds Appenzell and includes the north-east corner of Switzerland. Its new constitution of 1803, dictated by Napoleon, was brought back from Paris by a former administrator of the prince-abbot's, Carl Müller von Friedberg, who remained as head of the canton he had fathered until he was displaced by Jakob Baumgartner in 1831. Baumgartner had been the leader of liberal demonstrations in 1830, under the threats of which a new constitution was elaborated, and before that had been the protégé of Müller-Friedberg, as Müller had been of the last prince-abbot, and showed equally little gratitude. He ruled the canton for many years, gradually moving to the right (as his predecessor had done) and retired in 1841 from politics, for a time, to emerge in 1845 as the leader of the catholic-conservative party in the canton, and to dominate the political life of St Gallen in one capacity or another until 1864.

The canton, being composed of so many fragments, is of mixed religious and political allegiance, with two-thirds of the population traditionally catholic. The abbey, dissolved in 1798, was never refounded, but the splendid church is now cathedral of a bishopric. The capital town has a lively university, the only one in east Switzerland. Economically, the canton has for centuries specialized in textiles, but the present trend is towards diversification.

APPENZELL

Appenzell is completely surrounded by Canton St Gallen, and consists of the foothills and the slopes of the isolated Säntis mountain. The people of the canton give the visual impression of belonging to a peculiar race, and one might well have surmised that here was an ancient people, perhaps descended from an older population of pre-Roman days, and the effect is heightened by the place-names ending in -wil, which one might have surmised were Roman. Actually, the district was settled so late in time that the progress of settlement can be more or less followed from documents, spreading from the neighbouring townships in the valley, and from the 'Abbot's Cell' of Appenzell, mentioned in 1071 as standing on newly cleared ground. The inhabitants, at first herdsmen, then cultivators, were often serfs of the abbot of St Gallen and lived under his supreme jurisdiction, or under the rule of knights who were feudal tenants of the abbot. The emperor had claims over the territory in virtue of his advowson over the abbey, but these claims never actually ripened into sovereignty. In the fourteenth century the abbot's claims over Appenzell started to be resisted by its inhabitants, while at the same time the town of St Gallen was acquiring the first stages of its later independence. In 1377 the communities of Appenzell joined the alliance of the south German cities, and in 1402–03 Appenzell entered into an alliance with Schwyz, having fallen out with the League of the Swabian Cities as well as with the abbot.

In 1403 the Appenzellers and their allies won a battle at Vögelinsegg, and two years later one 'at the Stoss': these were their Morgarten or Näfels, and seem to have followed the same tactic. The institution of the *Landsgemeinde* in Appenzell dates from around this period and was apparently a direct importation from Schwyz. It then seemed for two years as if Appenzell were going to be a leader of a south German peasants' federal republic, the *Bund ob dem See*, but a military defeat at Bregenz put an end to this dream. In 1411 Appenzell entered into a permanent union with seven cantons (without Berne) and can be classified as an Ally, *Zugewandter Ort*. In 1513, rather surprisingly and at the last possible moment, Appenzell was admitted as a full canton: the full union took place just too late for the new canton to obtain a share in the Italian bailiwicks in the Ticino. The monies from the agreements with France to supply mercenaries were used to buy out the feudal rights of the abbot, and provided the basis for the take-off of the handwork industry of Outer Rhodes.

The capital village of Appenzell itself was the centre of a district (called a Rhode, the word probably derives from *rotulus*, a roll or list, rather than from *Rod* or *Reute*, a clearing: the *h* comes from a mistaken classical analogy). This district subsequently increased into six portions, all called Rhodes. But it remained a single ecclesiastical mother-parish (*Kirchhöre*), a compact area, the centre of the little state, the source of its name and the beneficiary of its reputation. This district was called 'the inner Rhodes'. The outer Rhodes, on the other hand, were before 1400 within parishes whose mother church was in the low country – the Rhine valley, the shores of Lake Constance, St Gallen town or abbey. They had been settled late and had been almost uninhabited when the parochial structure was first evolved. After the wars of independence, the bigger villages of the outer Rhodes built churches of their own and were raised to the rank of parishes, with the right of presentation of the ecclesiastical living most often left in the hands of the abbot of St Gallen.

In 1522 the reformed doctrines started to be preached by clergy in the outer Rhodes, educated in universities touched by the Reform – Vienna, Basle, Freiburg im Breisgau (as well as Paris and Pavia). They were encouraged by the great Vadianus – who was reformer of the town of St Gallen and belonged to one of its patrician families. In 1525, things in Appenzell had reached so advanced a stage that the *Landsgemeinde* decided that

> a vote shall be taken in each parish which faith shall be followed, and the lesser part shall follow the greater, but nevertheless, belief shall be free and each shall follow his conscience, going to another village's church if he does not like his own, but so that only one type of service is held in any one church.[6]

This is the famous *Kirchhörprinzip*, the parochial principle, and it was this which ultimately led to the division of the canton – for the great parish of Appenzell did not accept the Reformation (except in the outlying village of Gais).

Because of the parochial principle, the Rhodes organization became of secondary importance (it was chiefly a military and electoral unit) as against the parish. In the inner Rhodes the parish was a
larger unit than the Rhode, but, in the outer, parish and Rhode were
usually identical, leading to a divided Rhode when a new church
was built.

To the original religious division, political discords became
added – the custody of the documents and banners, the acceptance
of the Gregorian calendar and holidays by the catholic districts, the
founding of a Franciscan (Capuchin) monastery in Appenzell, the
surviving right of ecclesiastical presentation by the abbot of St
Gallen, the vote in the confederal Diet, and so on:[7] all these were for
a time reasonably settled, and the final breaking-point was an issue
of foreign policy. In 1597 the catholic cantons settled for the Spanish-
Austrian alliance, while the protestant (and Solothurn) preferred the
French: the matter was of internal importance because of the treaty
rights to raise mercenary soldiers. Appenzell found itself unable to
agree which alliance to join, and so on this point the protestant and
catholic parishes went different ways. The canton split into two half-
cantons. The decision to divide was taken peaceably and by agreement.

The details of the division are fascinating to the helvetologist. In
the Oberegg the decision was left to the personal conviction of
individual landowners, so the boundary (until 1637) was moveable,
and thereafter was a sort of religious and cantonal archipelago. Two
nunneries,[8] Wonnenstein and Grimmenstein, were enclaved in protestant territory under catholic sovereignty. There were rights of
alpage, questions of precedence, and every sort of minor complication, but, except for a short time under the Helvetic Republic, the
two half-cantons, Inner and Outer Rhodes, have remained separate
states ever since, usually taking opposite sides in every conflict.

Inner Rhodes (apart from two tiny exclaves) is compact and
homogeneous, with its capital and *Landsgemeinde* in Appenzell
village. But the Outer Rhodes has no natural centre, and its two parts
are only connected by a wasp-waist, which itself is severed by the deep
valley of the river Sitter. The district 'in front of the Sitter' (to the
north) has Trogen as its centre, and here the *Landsgemeinde* is held in
the even years and here is the centre of justice where the gallows used
to stand. But the district 'behind the Sitter' has no unity or centre. In
the odd years the *Landsgemeinde* is held at Hundwil, while the seat of
the administration is permanently at Herisau.

THURGAU

Thurgau, like Aargau and Vaud, bears a great and ancient name, but is a 'new' canton. It is peculiar among the cantons – the opposite case to Geneva and Basle – in that its natural and historic chief town, Constance, is in foreign territory. But the rivalry between Frauenfeld, the capital under the old regime and the administrative centre of today, and Weinfelden, the anti-capital, the centre of radicalism, is entirely typical.

As with Aargau, its former unity was interrupted by centuries of rule by the Confederacy, until in 1798 it reasserted itself. Again in 1830, Thurgau led the regeneration of cantonal and centralist life. Under the old confederal regime it was a maze of different lordships, scarcely to be distinguished from neighbouring parts of the empire except in the prevalence of Swiss-owned manors, and the possession by the Confederacy of the *Gau* countship, ceded by the bishop of Constance after the Swabian War. It is divided into much smaller historic-areas than Aargau, and quite a large number of lordships of manors were nearly sovereign in their independence, like the jurisdictions of the Imperial Knights north of the Rhine. The abbeys and the towns sometimes enjoyed a similar freedom, and Frauenfeld itself had a tiny subject territory of its own.

Thurgau is not a well-known countryside, for it is as undramatic as rural England, and often has the same poetic (but non-epic) quality; an Englishman may find it speaks more to his heart than any other part of Switzerland; indeed in some ways Thurgau is un-Swiss, not sharply divided as to confession, but a land (by and large) of parity and even of tolerance, perpetually moderately *Freisinnig* in politics, receiving immigrants from other cantons and sending emigrants without much heart-searching.

The industry of this countryside is agreeably decentralized, influenced by St Gallen and Zurich, as its agriculture is influenced by Berne.

TICINO

This Italian-speaking, traditionally Roman catholic, canton has already had its fair share of attention in this book (above, pp. 52–7). To these might be added the problem of depopulation of the rural districts and overdevelopment of the towns, and the annually recurring danger of overproduction of tomatoes and fruit when the Ticinese crop in the Magadino plain ripens simultaneously with the Valaisan crop in the Rhône valley – both grow not only the same crops, but usually exactly the same varieties. The serious problems, however, are of course social and cultural ones – the Italian labourers crossing the border daily, and the over-saturation with German-speaking settlers. Ticino, too, belongs to the group of cantons without much native industrialization which have received the benefits and possibilities of modern wealth with excessive enthusiasm, cantons which regard care for the environment as a ploy by the old-rich cantons to keep the late arrivals in their place. In Ticino, in fact, nearly every Swiss problem exists in a heightened form. In its internal politics, its history is one of great factional bitterness between the ideologies and also between the clienteles of the great political parties. These are to some extent the prolongation of regional hostilities, especially between Bellinzona, Lugano, and Locarno.

VALAIS

The Valais is that sword-gash through the highest Alps along which the Rhône flows westward in its upper reaches. At Martigny, it is traversed at right angles by another gash, and the river turns north to the Lake of Geneva, where it resumes its original westward direction. At the beginning of the last century it was said[9] that the whole canton was locked up each night by the porter at the gate of St Maurice (or of Monthey) simply by turning a key, so enclosed is the great valley by its 12,000-foot mountain walls. There is only one considerable valley on the right bank of the Rhône, the Lötschental. But to the south there are long deep furrows of valleys leading up to the great chain of mountains, including Monte Rosa and the Matterhorn, that divide Switzerland from Italy. Each of these valleys, the Mattertal, the Val d'Anniviers, the Val d'Herens, and the branched valley of the Dranse, to name the longest, has a history of its own, for the Valais was once a sort of federal republic in its own right. About half-way along the main valley, opposite Leuk, there is an enormous 'cone of emission' from one of nature's great jests, the Illgraben, a valley entirely composed of gleaming white gypsum. On the spoil heap which the rains bring down from this great half-cone is an ancient, self-sown forest of mountain-pine (*Arven*).

This is the Pfynwald, the boundary between the German-speaking intruders (probably originally settled in the Haslital) and the French-speakers who until the eighth century had been masters of the whole valley. A little farther down, just below Sion, is the rivulet Morge, which was the boundary between the Seven Tithings of the Upper Valais, which until 1798 were sovereign over the Five Tithings (*Zehnden*) of the Lower Valais – so that the usual pattern of German rule over French subjects in the Thirteen Cantons[10] more or less repeated itself.

The Valais had since the year 999 been a prince-bishopric under the bishop of Sion, but Savoy managed to assert a claim over the lands of the abbey of St Maurice, and advanced up to the rivulet Morge (both Morge and Pfyn are boundary names, here as elsewhere in Switzerland). Eventually, in 1475, under the influence of the neighbouring Confederacy and with Bernese help, the communities of the Upper Valais reconquered the Lower Valais (and a bit more), and stepped into the legal position held by the dukes of Savoy, rounding off their territories in 1536. It seemed as if the Reformation would follow, and many of the ruling families in three of the seven sovereign tithings adopted the new faith, but, in the event, the Counter-Reformation got the upper hand with a Valaisan mercilessness, and in 1655 all remaining protestants were expelled: Franciscan friars, pattering barefooted from house to house, saw to it that no ember of heresy survived. Not long after this, in 1677, the power of the Stockalper family was broken – they had opened the Simplon to a great volume of traffic and for some years dominated the canton. The country then relapsed into an era of stagnation, under the double influence of the church and the great local families, which lasted into the 1850s.

The Valais continued to be an independent and sovereign federal republic, allied with the Confederacy (the bishop having been deprived of the name of sovereign by 1613), while keeping a privileged position, until 1798, when the Lower Valais rose a second time in rebellion. In the next year, after a wild resistance in the Pfynwald by the Upper Valais tithings, the republic was invaded by French troops, who displayed a severity of which the memory survives, and it became, first, an administrative district of the Helvetic Republic, then from 1802 until 1810 a vassal state, the Rhodanic Republic, under the protection of France, to which it was formally annexed in the latter year under the name of the Département du Simplon. In 1814 it came finally to Switzerland as a canton, with the usual restoration of the old ruling families but without the former subjection of the lower tithings. From 1830 until 1847 something of the old Valaisan fierceness reappeared in the bloody skirmishes between the liberal lower part of the valley and the conservative upper (German-speaking) valley. Civilization as understood by contemporary Europe came with the railway to Sion in 1860. The valley is dead-flat, so the railway was hardly a notable engineering achievement, and the line only reached Brig in 1878. The Simplon railway tunnel was completed in 1905 (the present tunnel, electrified from the start, dates from 1921), and the Loetschberg tunnel was opened in 1913 – lines which are only now becoming fully used and are even today without the fevered shuttle-work of the Gotthard.

When opened to western Europe, the Valais was a curious and fascinating spectacle. The population was cretinous, poor, dirty, and priest-ridden. The agriculture (which survived into the 1960s) was of an extremely ancient type, in appearance dating from celtic times, or, romantically, from the dark ages of the Saracens and Huns. Each great valley was an economic unit, the villagers migrating as a body up the valley each spring and returning in the autumn. Each family in principle contained all the crafts, so that carpentry, cow-raising, cheese-making, rye-growing, and the cultivation of vineyards – activities with a dozen specialities within them – might be mastered by a single unlettered peasant. Within these main migrations was a complex pattern of subordinate migrations for boys, for women, for men, so a man might several times in the year climb from the searing Spanish heat of the main valley to the glaciers and upland pastures above the tree line. The great valley floor was almost into living memory infertile, the *wadi* of the Rhône, pebbles, boulders, alders, but the side-terraces above the valley, which receive little rain in summer, were artificially watered by leets, some allegedly of vast antiquity and the work of 'the heathen'. The rights to water were the subject of lawsuit and feud, the title to such rights recorded on wooden tallies such as I myself in the 1930s remember seeing hanging outside houses in the Lötschental. This cycle of life was encrusted with ancient usage and church obedience, beautiful and cruel.

The expectations of a really extraordinary antiquity are, as usual, disappointed. The early documents of the thirteenth century show purchases of vineyards by the valley communities being made, and much which is ancient and picturesque may not be older than the seventeenth century: just as there is a take-off stage in development, so there is a run-down stage in anti-development, and ancient forms may be re-created.

Onto a pre-industrial economy, a modern industrial[11] culture has been imposed. The valley was brought into cultivation – the railway dykes were themselves works of canalization of the torrent. The first stage of its reclamation was over by 1900, and the land started to come into real productive use between the wars, and by 1915, the trees were bearing fruit. Irrigated, the valley is marvellously fertile, producing mediterranean fruits or early crops, apricots, and tomatoes. It is a wonder of nature these flourish so, among the mountains, but also a political wonder, for after all, these flourish in Italy more luxuriantly and there is from the cosmic point of view little virtue in these 'grapes in Scotland'.

The gulleys from the snow peaks fall rapidly into the torrid valley. What a chance for electric power, with these torrents regulated by the natural reservoir of the snows, and with artificial reservoirs formed by walls across gorges! Fortunately for the Valais, this idea occurred to prospectors at a time when the art of transmitting electricity for long distances had not been discovered, but when the science of electro-chemistry was making great strides. The result was the implantation of industries within virgin territory. The first great pioneer firm was Lonza A-G, which started in Gampel in 1897 where the Lötschental debouches into the valley plain. At first there was a carbide factory, of which the capital and initiative derived from Basle and Nuremberg. Then Lonza added what was to be its principal works near Visp, powered by a giant turbine using the water of the Saas valley. The next big industry to be introduced was near Monthey, a synthetic indigo works initiated by CIBA of Basle, using the famous salt-works of Bex. This is the part of the Valais south of the Lake of Geneva, at one time a part of Savoy. Then in 1905 the Aluminium-Chippis was founded, a daughter firm of the one started at the falls of the Rhine near Schaffhausen. Here the raw material, bauxite, had to be imported from France and the industry located itself outside Sierre in order to exploit the electric current derived from the Navisence. These three large factories were followed by many smaller ones, producing nitrates and oxygen and other products of electrical-chemical processes, in which typically the management and technical expertness came from outside the canton, while the Valaisans provided the relatively unskilled labour – often as a supplement to some agricultural pursuit on a hopelessly fragmented and subdivided inheritance in a village high up the hillside.

In these years before the first World War, the hotel industry was at the height of the classic period of great-tourism, the tourism of the very rich and leisured. Meanwhile the vineyards were made to produce the best red table-wines of Switzerland. After the war, development was slower and more interrupted, but the new hotel trade for the middle-class visitor proved less sensitive to world events, because the Swiss themselves had started to travel in their own country. This period of consolidation can be seen as a sort of social golden age, where the old and the new achieved a peaceable co-existence.

The next period started in 1950 with an effort by a small group of native Valaisans to develop their own country into a modern industrial canton. As one might expect in a deeply catholic countryside, this movement had an ideological content, a policy of 'industrial decentralization' planned to disturb traditional relationships as little as possible, keeping families together and ascribed to their ancestral land. It needed the co-operation of the church, of the cantonal parliament, of the notables who rule the communes with an iron hand (for in Valais attributes almost approaching sovereignty are in the hands of the larger communes), and it needed an intellectual effort. The group called itself the *Societé Valaisanne de Recherches économiques et sociales*, and, like the British National Economic and Development Council, fathered many subordinate bodies. An industrial hunger has now seized the land, which has had a further stroke of luck in the oil-pipeline under the Great St Bernard with a refinery industry deriving from it. A great building activity has brought in outsiders by the hundred thousand, and destroyed half of the attractiveness of the country which was the one asset inherited from the old regime. The church has had an almost lunatic frenzy of rebuilding (assisted by a timely earthquake and architects prepared to testify that the old church was in structural danger); these rebuildings are often artistically brilliant, startlingly uninhibited, and excitingly original. For my own part, I loved so much the contrast of baroque (or a romanesque tower) with the harsh mountains that I cannot quite reconcile myself to the contrived brutality of these splendid buildings,[12] though they are entirely in the Valaisan tradition, for the country has always lived up to its exaggerated landscape and displayed an un-Swiss ferocity.

GRISONS

While the Valais is a single cleft, fed by long side-valleys to the south and by short steep valleys to the north, the Grisons is a labyrinth, a land of a hundred valleys, whose waters are tributary to the Danube, the Ticino, the Adda, and, principally, to the Rhine. The Rhine and its tributaries flow through deep gorges soon after leaving their upper valleys in the Alps, but the current gathers waters so that Chur (Coire) and the Landquart are nodal points. The broad valley floor that seems today so fertile and to offer such easy access was, like the Valais, until little more than a century ago a wide desolation: the ancient road runs through the town-like villages of Maienfeld and Malans, on the hillside – and the little-used by-road over the Luziensteig was the entry to the valley. The history of the Grisons has a certain symmetry with that of the Valais, an early Christianization and a long enduring influence of Rome, a prince-bishopric undermined by an unruly baronage, and finally a chaotic democratic tyranny itself destined to be undermined by a native gentry. Both Valais and Grisons were pushed into the Confederation by the Napoleonic Wars and the settlement of Vienna, and both long remained socially, politically, and economically eccentric.

Grisons, the Grey Leagues, came under those names to the consciousness of civilized Europe because of the wars of the early fifteenth century (1459, *les trois Ligues grises*; 1525, Grisons). The German name, Graubünden, however, only became an invariable official designation after 1814. For earlier centuries one should (but I shall not) use such terms as Upper Rhaetia, Churraetien, and so on, terms with shifting boundaries.

This area was, it seems, romanized late, but this romanization has left an enduring character upon the country and gives the strange Latin tongues which are spoken in its valleys. By the eighth century,

the bishop of Coire was one of the principal and most powerful
holders of land there, and by the mid-tenth century he held something akin to sovereignty: in the age between these dates, if we are to
credit the documents (and an old anecdote),[13] the bishop had sunk
to an object of contempt. But he recovered his position, in a manner
that is not explained, and in 1170 he was a prince of the empire.
From 1299 he exercised the imperial as well as the episcopal power,
with the right of life and death. But this power as against the emperor
was hollowed away by the encroachments of the feudal aristocracy:
the architectural trace of this encroachment can be witnessed in the
astonishing local abundance of castles in the Domleschg, where
every wild rock seems crowned by a tower or rampart. In the fourteenth and fifteenth centuries this aristocracy itself lost, rather suddenly, both its economic and its military basis, and its downfall was
accelerated by its quarrelsomeness. The story of Inner Switzerland
was repeated. The reality of power passed to the landowning
peasantry organized in jurisdictions (*Gerichtsgemeinden*), which joined
together into three confederacies or leagues, which then themselves
confederated loosely into what we now call Grisons.

The League of God's House appeared in 1367. As its (later) name
suggests, it was formed by the tenants of the bishop, principally in the
town of Coire, in the Engadine, and in the Oberhalbstein district,
which connects the two. They were aggrieved by the ill administration of the episcopal patrimony, but also afraid they might be sold to
the Hapsburgs (who had inherited the Tirol and Vorarlberg in 1363).
The Upper (or Grey) League, which later lent its name to the whole
ramshackle structure, was formed in 1395 and consolidated in 1424.
It included Disentis, a sovereign abbey in the remotest valley of the
Rhine, and Ilanz, a small borough lower down, and at a later date
it stretched to include the Mesocco, on the Italian side of the Alps.

Finally, the small League of the Ten Jurisdictions was added in
1436: this is the district around Davos. The district around Maienfeld, gateway to the whole republic, was subject to the other leagues,
who purchased it, but itself took its turn within the sovereign body,
as having contributed to its own purchase. Some feudal sovereignties
survived within the system, notably Rhäzüns and Tarasp with their
famous castles, and the episcopal enclave itself: these were footholds
of the rulers of Austria.

Four long tongues of this anciently sovereign territory protrude
south of the Alps. First there is the Mesolcina, the valleys of Mesocco
and the Calanca, bought from the family of Sax-Misox by the
Trivulzio family in 1480, who joined the Grey League for protection
against Milan in 1496 and sold their rights to the peasantry in 1549.
This valley is inconspicuous on modern maps, for it flanks Ticino,

but it has a character of its own. Until the 1960s it was cut off from its cantonal capital during the whole winter by snow, so that deputies to the cantonal parliament had to travel by way of Bellinzona and Zurich, passing through seven cantons to reach again their own. Then there is the Val Bregaglia (Bergell), seat of the great local family of von Salis, the valley which leads over the Maloja pass to St Moritz and the Engadine. Though Italian-speaking, it is protestant, and as such its families play an interesting part in the social and economic life of north Italy. Farther east, there is the Poschiavo valley, a back-door to the same destination, and finally there is the Münstertal, partly Romansch-speaking, all that is left to Switzerland of the county of Vintschgau, now Italian South Tirol.

The great sorrow of Grisons history is the loss of the Valtellina, into which the remaining Bregaglia and Poschiavo dovetailed. The whole big territory, a vast cleft not unlike the Valais, was once subject to the Grisons: its wine, *veltliner*, is still felt to be a Swiss wine. The Valtellina had been briefly in the Leagues' hands as conquerors in 1486–87, and in 1512, during the Pavia campaign, they once again seized it together with Chiavenna and Bormio. The French, briefly conquerors of the duchy of Milan, recognized their lawful title in 1516, but the dukes themselves only acknowledged loss of the territory in 1532, and there had been an intermediate time when it had seemed likely to be lost – a small war provoked by the Lord of Musso, a robber baron like The Unnamed in Manzoni's *I Promessi Sposi*. The Valtellina remained uneasily in the hands of Grisons, apart from the vicissitudes of the Thirty Years War, until 1797. The Leagues had never properly established a rule of law in the valley, nor had they found a place for the native Italian aristocracy: attempts to introduce the Reformation there had ended in a massacre. Even in 1797 it could probably have been retained, as was the Ticino, by the Confederation, had the Leagues agreed to take the subject valley into full political citizenship. What might have been the richest agricultural valley of Switzerland has become a poor valley in Italy. For long it closed a stretch of the frontier between Venice and Milan; then it was the meeting-point of Austrian and French zones of interest; then, when Austria annexed Milan, it became a backdoor into Lombardy: the Stelvio pass, which winds just outside the Swiss frontier, was useful to the Austrian strategists. Even in 1814 resolute action might have retained the valley for Switzerland, but the hesitations of democratic practice, and irresolution of personal character, and perhaps protestant urban fear of an extra agricultural catholic canton, lost the sunsoaked valley. The story was to be repeated when Faucigny and Chablais, provinces of Savoy, were offered, and when Vorarlberg became available. The extra votes given to the midget cantons of Inner Switzerland have lost territories vastly greater than Unterwalden and Zug. There is a virtue, of a sort, in not coveting a neighbour's territory, but Grisons would have been glad of the Valtellina.

The polity of the old Grisons contains a hard lesson for posterity: it can be seen as an experiment in total democracy, in continuous revolution, and anarchism. Yet it was cruel, violent, intensely conservative, and dominated by a handful of families, even though elements of peasant democracy were achieved on the threshold of the Reformation. Eventually two-thirds of the republic became protestant, leaving the territories under the influence of the bishop and the abbey of Disentis catholic, and a very few districts *paritätisch* (i.e., with equal rights for both religions). The Reformation had the side-effect of transforming the Romansch tongues into written languages, including a catholic and a protestant idiom.

In this classic stage of Grisons democracy (*c.* 1524–1799), the lawful use of force may be said to have resided in the 48 *Gerichtsgemeinden*, approximately the ancestors of the present *Kreise* or rural districts. These jurisdictions (the number of which increased slightly over the years as a result of subdivision) were in most cases themselves divided into neighbourhoods (*Nachbarschaften*), the ancestors in an imprecise way of the present *Gemeinden* or civil parishes. The jurisdictions grouped themselves into the Three Leagues. The political creature was a confederacy rather than a federal government.

The political-social structure was dominated by the gentry, families which rose from minor nobility or trading wealth at the end of the fifteenth century or a little later. These were the real beneficiaries and motive force of the system; they occupied the ancient castles; they received the bribes; they held the greater offices and prospered from the rule of the subject territory. They were permanently divided into factions, principally distinguished by partisanship of the Austrian–Spanish and of the Venetian-French alliances. These factions drew strength from, but did not coincide with, the confessional split into protestant and catholic (for the Austrian cause was the catholic cause). The great family of Salis dominated one faction, and the Planta family held a leading place in the other. The patrician families found it necessary to be represented in as many jurisdictions as possible, so a Salis house and a Planta house can be found in many villages or miniature townlets, distinguished by the blazon of the willow-tree or the bear's foot respectively. These warring families frequently intermarried. Factionalism limited their power, but also maintained it by providing a cause to rally the citizens to their leadership.

A feature of the league assemblies was the 'referendum', the mandatory instruction of deputies by the electing community, characteristic of confederal government. Bribery, much to be condemned in a sophisticated and mechanical constitutional democracy, circulated some of the fruits of office among the enfranchised and much of it found its ultimate source in Austria, France, and Venice. Mercenary service at the courts of despots kept the local militia more or less in touch with military developments, but it became clear in the seventeenth and eighteenth centuries that these militias were not likely to be a match for professional armies.

During much of the sixteenth century the original communal impulse gave a moral justification to the system, and during most of the eighteenth century the gentry kept turbulence and injustice within the bounds of decency and as a rational alternative to the available systems of government in continental Europe. But the reader of the history of seventeenth-century Grisons, or of the novels written about it, experiences terror and disgust. The torture and judicial murder of Johann von Planta in 1572, the Bloody Assizes of Thusis in 1618, the slaughter of the protestants in the Valtellina, the killing of Pompeius von Salis, are a long, exciting, but ultimately nauseating tale, and perhaps it is the free and immediate resort to torture which finally condemns the revolutionary as well as the regular legal institutions of the old Leagues. As late as 1804 the tariffs for torturing, hacking off various limbs, beheading, and hanging, were unified and revised. To be in a minority, or unpopular, or even poor, in one of the four dozen jurisdictions cannot have been agreeable, however idyllic it may have looked. The uncomprehending traveller saw and heard the simple peasants beneath the spreading tree discussing, uncorrupted, the management of their own affairs with a more than senatorial sagacity. In spite of the evocativeness of the rough voices of the cowherds and the splendour of the eternal snows; the assembly was probably being bribed to burn a widow as a witch.

On the other hand, the evidence of the buildings is clear, the villages among the rocks and mountain grass, crowded with what are almost small palaces of the local gentry families, and the numerous churches, testify to ancient prosperity in terrain that is by nature a wilderness. There is no country to which the wanderer or the exile more longed to return. And the character imprinted on the country during those three centuries has endured till today. The oligarchic democracy of the old regime in Grisons was a great adventure of the human spirit.

LIECHTENSTEIN

Liechtenstein is, of course, not a part of Switzerland in international law, but is a sovereign principality. Yet it is so closely linked with Switzerland, and affords so many parallels with previous Swiss alliances – such as that with Neuchâtel or other allies with the rank of *Zugewandter Ort*, that it is convenient here to consider it as a canton with a special status, not represented in the Federal Assembly nor even fully covered by Swiss neutrality.

The principality is, historically, made up of the sovereign countship of Vaduz and the sovereign barony of Schellenberg, which were purchased by the von Liechtenstein family in 1699 and 1707 in order to attain the dignity of Prince of the Holy Roman Empire. This goal was finally secured in 1718, when the new principality took the name of its owners. The Liechtenstein family were great Austrian noblemen, mesne lords of vast lands principally in Bohemia and Moravia, with sonorous Austrian titles. It was not until 1842 that a prince of Liechtenstein actually had cause to visit the tiny territory named after him. The principality was a member, though not a signatory, of Napoleon's Confederation of the Rhine, but in 1815 it contrived not to be 'mediated' (absorbed) at the Treaty of Vienna, but to continue as a sovereign princedom.

Until 1918 Liechtenstein remained closely linked with Austria and, as regards customs treaties, assimilated to the Vorarlberg. In its internal constitutional structure, too, it followed the same development as the lands of the Austrian crown. In 1919, with economic and political confusion in Austria, entirely new possibilities were opened up, and Liechtenstein and its prince succeeded in disengaging themselves from the Austrian empire's fate. Between then and 1923 the principality entered into its present close relationship with Switzerland.

By virtue of successive agreements, Liechtenstein maintains an embassy in Berne, but otherwise confides its whole diplomatic representation to Switzerland. There is also a postal convention, which leaves to the principality the right of issuing its own stamps – a right that has proved extremely valuable and in past years enabled the country to make its first economic take-off. The convention nevertheless in some ways assimilates the principality's postal administration to that of Switzerland, while leaving to the principality the design and sales of its decorative stamps intended for collectors. Then there is a customs union, by virtue of which Liechtenstein is entirely absorbed within the Swiss customs area, so that Swiss customs officials collect Swiss customs duties at the frontier with Austria, in offices bearing the joint emblems of sovereignty of the Confederation and of the prince. There is no customs barrier on the frontier with Switzerland itself. There is also a police convention, which goes far in the direction of absorbing Liechtenstein within Switzerland for police purposes, and in particular as regards the admission of foreigners. In this complex of agreements can be included the reciprocal rights of Swiss citizens in Liechtenstein, and of Liechtensteiners in Switzerland – nearly absorbing the principality to the status of a Swiss canton. This last arrangement is made easier in that the practice of conferring citizenship as grudgingly as possible is followed equally in the principality and the Confederation.

Liechtenstein, however, is not, strictly speaking, included in the neutrality of Switzerland and therefore is not assimilated to Switzerland for military purposes. Needless to say, it follows the identical practice of neutrality, but can only rely on its own, negligible, military resources and the friendship of Austria, together with the diplomatic protection of Switzerland. During the second World War, Liechtenstein's situation was delicate in the extreme, but the state survived.

The principality's relationship with the Confederation is of interest to the student of federalism, because it displays the limits of cantonal sovereignty. It claims sovereignty in a different sense to the cantons, and is, as it were, in a *Staatenbund* (confederacy) with the Swiss state. The remaining rights of sovereignty are of some economic importance, particularly in the sphere of company law: the principality reserves the right to incorporate limited liability companies, and Liechtenstein company status offers (to put the matter euphemistically) certain taxation advantages in some situations. Evaluation of this feature would bring one into the general topic of small and miniature states and their role in providing a useful, as it were a legitimate, black market to ease the operations of international finance.

In recent years the principality has been sharing the economic prosperity of the Swiss cantons, enjoying the same sort of financial and industrial economy in the same alpine setting.

NOTES

1 Klein-Basel, on the right bank, is an artificial town set out to be a bridgehead, and betrays this origin by its grid plan of streets, and a certain modesty of scale in its houses.

2 A third catholic parish was added after the Treaty of Vienna when a border hamlet was received from France. For the sake of completeness, one may add that Neuchâtel is entirely French-speaking: as with Vaud, a single village on the language frontier has legally a two-language status.

3 I had nearly forgotten the little town of Eglisau, still delightful, although half of it has been submerged by the waters of the Rhine, whose levels have been raised by a great barrage.

4 The witch, Anna Göldi, was actually beheaded for attempted murder of a child by poison. The execution was widely condemned. In the seventeenth century the pursuit of witches in various places in Switzerland – protestant and catholic –

became a mania, and here and there this continued into the eighteenth century: there was a dreadful case in Zug in 1738. The underlying evil was the use of torture to secure confessions in criminal cases, abolished under the Helvetic Republic.

5 Actually, a very large part of the territory of Switzerland was bought for cash, perhaps one-third of it: it is not possible to estimate precisely, because the high jurisdiction might come in one manner and the low in another, with nearly another third by secularizations and the final third by conquest and international cession. Purchases were often preceded by handing over the jurisdiction as pawn for a loan.

6 Rainald Fischer, W. Schläpfer, and others, *Appenzeller Geschichte*, I, Appenzell, etc., 1964. This is an early example of a clear majority principle, but the record of the wording (which is here paraphrased) is from 1588, and therefore not quite contemporary.

7 In spite of its smaller size and population, the political leadership was with the inner and catholic district: in a *Landsgemeinde* canton, the place of assembly is a political factor, and it was even difficult to exercise office from the base of a protestant village. In the last years of the undivided canton, the church council of Appenzell parish insisted that all residents should attend mass and make confession.

8 A parallel, but of course not identical, case is Kloster Fahr near Zurich, which is under the sovereignty of Canton Aargau unless it be dissolved: it owes its survival to this proviso.

9 By Rodolphe Toepffer, in his *Voyages en Zigzag*, a charming souvenir volume among many of the genre in the early nineteenth century.

10 The two French-speaking valleys reckoned in the seven sovereign tithings were themselves subordinate to the two towns, Sierre and Sion, which were reckoned as German-speaking under the old regime. The language frontier in the main valley has shifted a little since then, to the advantage of French.

11 I am indebted to Beat Kauffmann's *Die Entwicklung des Wallis vom Agrar- zum Industriekanton*, Basle Dissertation, Zurich, 1965, for much of this discussion of industrial development.

12 They can be paralleled by the revival of stained glass in the catholic churches of the Bernese Jura, and occasionally by restorations and additions to protestant churches – such as the Chagall windows in the Zurich Fraumünster.

13 The anecdote is that a bishop of Chur was so poor and so unlearned that he refused a beggar alms with the words 'Nihil habeo, nihil gibio'. The documents referred to are of the early ninth century.

Statistics

The source of these figures is the *Annuaire statistique de la Suisse*, 1973, which includes the figures for the Census of 1970.

Population

Resident Population of Switzerland since 1850

Canton	1850	1920	1960	1970	Increase since 1960 %
Zurich	250,698	538,602	952,304	1,107,788	16.3
Berne	458,301	674,394	889,523	983,296	10.5
Lucerne	132,843	177,073	253,446	289,641	14.3
Uri	14,505	23,973	32,021	34,091	6.5
Schwyz	44,168	59,731	78,048	92,072	18.0
Obwalden	13,799	17,567	23,135	24,509	5.9
Nidwalden	11,339	13,956	22,188	25,634	15.5
Glarus	30,213	33,834	40,148	38,155	−5.0
Zug	17,461	31,569	52,489	67,996	29.5
Fribourg	99,891	143,055	159,194	180,309	13.3
Solothurn	69,674	130,617	200,816	224,133	11.6
Basle Town	29,698	140,708	225,588	234,945	4.1
Basle Land	47,885	82,390	148,282	204,889	38.2
Schaffhausen	35,300	50,428	65,981	72,854	10.4
Appenzell Inner Rhodes	11,272	14,614	12,943	13,124	1.4
Appenzell Outer Rhodes	43,621	55,354	48,920	49,023	0.2
St Gallen	169,625	295,543	339,489	384,475	13.3
Grisons	89,895	119,854	147,458	162,086	9.9
Aargau	199,852	240,776	360,940	433,284	20.0
Thurgau	88,908	135,933	166,420	182,835	9.9
Ticino	117,759	152,256	195,566	245,458	25.5
Vaud	199,575	317,498	429,512	511,851	19.2
Valais	81,559	128,246	177,783	206,563	16.2
Neuchâtel	70,753	131,349	147,633	169,173	14.6
Geneva	64,146	171,000	259,234	331,599	27.9
Switzerland	2,392,740	3,880,320	5,429,061	6,269,783	15.5

Religion, Occupation, and Composition of Resident Population (Census of 1970)

	Swiss Citizens	Non-Swiss Citizens	Total
Protestant	2,854,727	136,967	2,991,694
Roman Catholic	2,231,988	864,666	3,096,654
Old Catholic	19,323	945	20,268
Jewish	11,977	8,767	20,744
Others/no religion	71,692	68,731	140,423
Resident Population	5,189,707	1,080,076	6,269,783
Self-employed	287,411	12,455	299,866
Wage-earners	2,060,674	644,599	2,705,273
Primary Sector			
salaried	219,815	9,478	229,293
self employed	103,597	645	104,242
Secondary Sector			
salaried	1,014,244	437,731	1,451,975
self employed	83,344	4,815	88,159
Tertiary Sector			
salaried	1,114,026	209,845	1,323,871
self employed	100,470	6,995	107,465
Total Population gainfully employed	2,348,085	657,054	3,005,139
Total Population not gainfully employed	2,841,622	423,022	3,264,644

Urbanization

Percentage of inhabitants living in towns (i.e. in communes with more than 10,000 inhabitants)

1850	6.4
1920	27.6
1960	41.9
1970	45.3

Local and Cantonal Citizenship

Percentage of Swiss citizens resident in commune and canton of citizenship

	Commune of Citizenship	Canton of Citizenship
1860	58.7	91.0
1920	32.9	75.9
1960	25.2	66.6

(1970 figures not yet available)

Language

Maternal language. Swiss citizens resident in Switzerland (percentages)

Year	German	French	Italian	Romansch	Others
1910	72.7	22.1	3.9	1.2	.1
1970	74.5	20.1	4.0	1.0	.4

A Note on Books

There are not many English books on Switzerland, apart from general introductions, and some older works. There are many more books in French, often, too, rather general in approach. The serious enquirer will almost certainly be driven to the extensive literature in German – even though it is in fact possible to be a serious student of Switzerland while only reading French. The late Jean Meynaud, for example, acquired the position of the leading scholar of contemporary Switzerland, and cites only French sources in his highly original and seminal works.

English Books

Of the books of general impressions of the Swiss civilization, the following is, with justice, the best known:

George Soloveytchick, *Switzerland in Perspective*, London, 1954.

Of the general sketches of Swiss history, it is difficult to recommend one rather than the other, since a note of warning is in each case necessary. Many resemble the Children's Histories of an older generation. Of serious and accessible works there is really only:

H. S. Offler, G. R. Potter, and Edgar Bonjour, *A Short History of Switzerland*, 2nd ed., Oxford, 1954.

Even in this revised edition, the treatment of the nineteenth century is unsatisfactory, but the parts dealing with the earlier periods are useful.

There are, of course, sections on Switzerland in the various Histories of Europe, and Economic Histories (Cambridge, Fontana), and books on Government and on Federalism. There are also books on special aspects of Switzerland.

History Books

The best introduction is probably still Hans Nabholz (with Leonhard von Muralt, Richard Feller, and Edgar Bonjour), *Geschichte der Schweiz*, 2 vols., Zurich, 1938. More 'popular', but also more up to date, is the 3-volume *Illustrierte Geschichte der Schweiz*, Zurich, etc., 1962 (of which there is a shortened, one-volume, version by Sigmund Widmer, designed to be attractive to the young, but entirely usable, published in Zurich, 1965). The authors of the 3-volume version are: Walter Drack, Karl Schib, Sigmund Widmer, and Emil Spiess. There are alternatives to these introductory works, in German and French.

Beyond this, the best guide to history is now the *Handbuch der Schweizer Geschichte* (vol. I, 1972; vol. II was expected in 1974, but the work has been waiting around for many years, presumably on account of dilatory contributors), published in Zurich. The author first named in the book is Hanno Helbing. This is not a work which will afford pleasure to the literary reader, but it is an excellent guide to the books and the journals. The *Historischer Atlas der Schweiz* (by Hektor Ammann and Karl Schib, Aarau, 1951) is a useful companion to such histories, though it is somewhat simplified. The actual historical literature available is, of course, enormous, and the selection from it that is to be found in British libraries is small and arbitrary.

Nearly every canton has its classic history written within the last fifty years: the biggest gap is Valais. It is not always possible, however, to cover the whole history of a canton in a single book by the same author. Many of these histories are excellent, and Richard Feller's histories of Berne are of European rank. Reports of the cantons at the present day are carried in the national newspapers, for example, those written by Otto Frei in the *Neue Zürcher Zeitung* on the cantons of French-speaking Switzerland: some of these, and other writing on current situations in the cantons, are gathered together in the series *NZZ-Schriften zur Zeit*, published by that newspaper from time to time.

For both cantonal and federal history, the person seriously interested is driven to published theses and learned journals: on some periods and places the material is very rich, on others remarkably scanty.

As a guide to the history of Switzerland during the second World War, the later volumes of Edgar Bonjour's *Geschichte der schweizerischen Neutralität*, 2nd ed., 6 vols., Basle etc., 1965–70 (also available in French) are invaluable, replacing an abundant fugitive literature, but now in its turn becoming superseded in this detail and that by new books and articles.

For very modern history, the record in *Année politique suisse* (Peter Gilg and others), published each year since 1965 by the Forschungszentrum für Politik in Berne, for the Swiss Political Science Association, is indispensable.

For Economic History, Albert Hauser's *Schweizerische Wirtschafts- und Sozialgeschichte*, Zurich etc., 1961, is indispensable as a guide and introduction, being the only comprehensive work in this field (at the moment of writing), and it has a bibliography. In detail it is considered to be open to criticism, as any pioneer books of such wide coverage must be. Economic History is a new field in Swiss universities, and one must rely much on biographies and centenary or jubilee works published by firms. Lorenz Stucki's *Das Heimliche Imperium*, Berne, 1968, has made good use of this, sometimes tiresome, material. Textiles and Agriculture are relatively well covered by books, and there is good printed material available on the metal trades, watchmaking, and chemicals.

Law and Politics

For Swiss constitutional law, there are wonderful older works in German, but the English-language reader will probably choose to go to Jean-François Aubert, *Traité de Droit constitutionnel suisse*, Neuchâtel, etc., 1967. For the texts of the various laws and of the constitution itself there is a handy source in the *Recueil systématique des lois et ordonnances*, published by the Federal Chancery of Berne. As regards secondary literature, I cannot forbear to cite my own works: *The Federal Constitution of Switzerland*, Oxford, 1954; *The Parliament of Switzerland*, London, 1962; and, also in English, those of Professor G. A. Codding of the University of Colorado: *The Federal Government of Switzerland*, Boston, 1961; *Politics in Swiss Local Government: Governing the Commune of Veyrier*, Boulder, Colo., 1967. In German, the best introduction to the political structure is now Klaus Schumann, *Das Regierungssystem der Schweiz*, Cologne, etc., 1971. For Political Parties, Erich Gruner's *Die Parteien in der Schweiz*, Berne, 1969, is the necessary guide, and contains a good booklist. For Pressure Groups, Jean Meynaud, *Les Organisations professionnelles en Suisse*, Lausanne, 1963, is the starting-point, but whereas there is an extensive selection of books on parties, there are rather few on the interest-groups. The best, and in a sense the only, introduction to cantonal political life in general is in Fritz René Allemann, *25 mal die Schweiz*, Munich, 1965.

Travel

The traveller to Switzerland is advised to take in his car (for it is heavy) the revised edition of Heinrich Gutersohn, *Geographie der Schweiz* 'in three volumes', but some of the volumes have in fact spread into two volumes. In his handbag he should take the latest Jenny – Hans Jenny, *Kunstführer durch die Schweiz* (I, Wabern/Berne, 1971) and Reklam's *Kunstführer Schweiz und Liechtenstein*, Stuttgart, 1966. In his pocket or rucksack he may prefer an older edition of Jenny. For a map he will need the *Karte der Kulturgüter, Schweiz, Liechtenstein*, Eidg. Landestopographie, Wabern/Berne, 1 : 300,000. This has a wonderful amount of detail, but is printed so faintly that a magnifying glass is needed, nor is it the easiest map to consult in the wind or rain; yet it is invaluable. One needs separate road-maps and footpath-maps: the most convenient of the latter is in the older editions of Fodor's Guides. In general, the large-scale maps and the small-scale maps are excellent, but the intermediate scale that one requires for walking is sometimes unobtainable. This is tolerable if one is fixed with one centre, but it makes expeditions difficult.

To return to guidebooks, there are now, in French, four excellent guides in the series called *La Suisse inconnue* by André Beerli. In German Switzerland, most towns and architectural monuments have excellent booklets written about them: in French Switzerland one can often get only some rather clever photographs from unusual angles, accompanied by a commentary in poetic prose on the beauty of the sunsets. (In Italian Switzerland one is often lucky even to get hold of the door-key.) The best guides are the tool of the historian as well as the tourist.

Maps

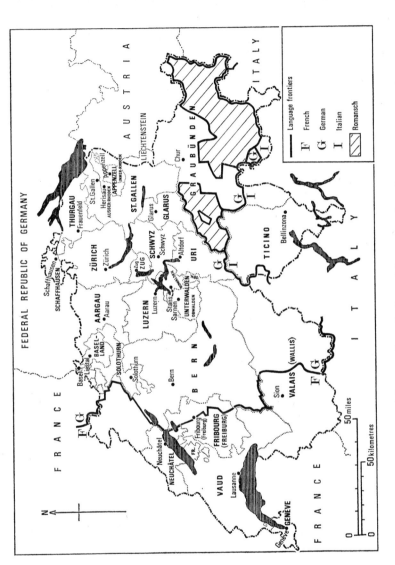

1 Cantonal capitals and language frontiers

2 The geography of Switzerland

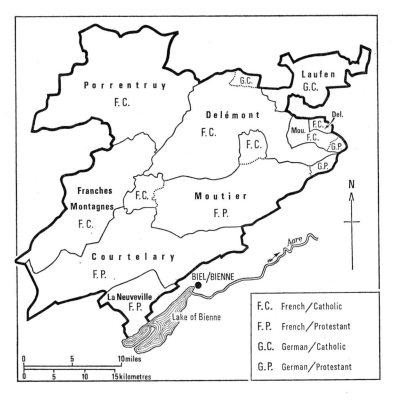

Porrentruy
F. C.

Laufen
G. C.

G.C.

Delémont
F. C.

Del.
F. C.
Mou.
F. C.

G.P.

F. C.

G.P.

Franches
Montagnes
F. C.

F. C.

Moutier
F. P.

N

Aare

Courtelary
F. P.

BIEL/BIENNE

La Neuveville
F. P.

Lake of Bienne

F. C.	French / Catholic
F. P.	French / Protestant
G. C.	German / Catholic
G. P.	German / Protestant

0   5   10 miles
0 5 10   15 kilometres

3 The Bernese Jura

4 *A New Map of Swisserland,* 1798

A B I A

CANTON of HAUSEN
SHAFFHAUSEN
Stein
LAKE of ZELL
CONSTANCE
LAKE of CONSTANCE
Bregenz
Thur R.
Frauenfeld
Winterthur
THURGAU

CANTON ZURIC
ZURIC
Lake of Zuric

St.Gallen
ST GALLEN
Trogen
CANTON of APPENZEL
Herisau
APPENZEL
Sax
RHEINTHAL
Upper Rhine

TOCKENBURG
Thur R.
GASTER
Werdenberg

TON
ZUG
f ZUG

CANTON of SCHWITZ
Schwitz
Glaris
CANTON of GLARIS
Altorf
Reuss R.
SARGANS
Sargans
Mayenfeld
LEAGUE of the TEN JURISDICTIONS

Ilanz
Upper Rhine
GREAT LEAGUE
COIRE
Davos
Tarasp
HE GRISON
Inn R.
County of TYROL

Mt St Gothard
VAL LEVIN
BRENNA
Lower Rhine
LEAGUE of GOD'S HOUSE
Pregalia
Munster
COUNTY of BORMIO
Bormio
Puschiavo

COUNTY of CHIAVENNA
Chiavenna
V.Mesox
VALTELINE
Adda R.

LIAN
BAIT
WICKS
RIVIERA
Bellinzona
Bellinzona
Locarno
Lago Maggiore
Lugano
LUGANO
Lake of Lugano
Lake of Como

STATES of VENICE

Mendrisio
MENDRISIO
COMO

of MILAN

STATES of VENICE

0   10   20   30 miles

✪ Fortified Town
✕ Battle

N

Index

Printed in Great Britain
by W & J Mackay Limited, Chatham